# THE
# TOTAL
# GARDEN

# THE *TOTAL GARDEN*

## A COMPLETE GUIDE TO
## INTEGRATING FLOWERS, HERBS,
## FRUITS AND VEGETABLES

A. M. Clevely

Principal photography by Jerry Harpur
Illustrations by Liz Pepperell

HARMONY BOOKS
NEW YORK

*For my mother, who gave her small boy*
*a handful of radish seeds and so inspired*
*a way of life.*

Published by Harmony Books,
a division of Crown Publishers, Inc.,
225 Park Avenue South,
New York, New York 10003.

HARMONY and colophon are trademarks of Crown
Publishers, Inc.

Manufactured in Spain

Library of Congress Cataloging-in-Publication Data

Clevely, A.M., 1945-
The total garden.
Includes index.
1. Gardening.  I. Title.
SB453.C54  1988  635  88-81387

Designed and produced by
Johnson Editions Ltd,
15 Grafton Square,
London SW4 0DQ

American gardening consultant: Charles O. Cresson

ISBN 0-517-57054-8
10  9  8  7  6  5  4  3  2  1
First Edition

# CONTENTS

# INTRODUCTION

This book is an attempt to marry a gardening tradition that is centuries old with modern techniques and varieties, to produce an alternative and decorative way of raising fruit, vegetables and herbs.

Many years ago, before bulldozers levelled the whole site, I was intrigued by an empty house on the outskirts of Leeds in Yorkshire. Although the garden was semi-derelict and threatened with suffocation by goose-grass and bindweed, its original character was still discernible. Espalier apples, 2.5m (8ft) tall and trained on poles and wires, lined both sides of the brick paths, creating leafy alleys. At their foot grew violets, lavender, bulbs and herbs. Against the house walls other fruit such as pears, gooseberries and red currants had been trained into all the fascinating geometrical shapes I had read about but never seen: triple cordons, arcures, lattices and so on.

There was no separate kitchen garden, but the skeletal remains or seeding survivors of leeks, parsnips, radish and land cress in between the paeonies, foxgloves and montbretia showed that vegetables had been mixed amongst the cottage garden flowers in a cheerful patchwork. It was my first experience of an alternative kind of gardening, quite unlike that recommended by all the manuals. The textbooks I had used as a trainee, for example, all insisted that vegetables, fruit, flowers and herbs had to be kept well apart in strictly defined areas.

Yet few people have either the space or the inclination to divide their gardens into departments, as was once the rule on large country estates. There, the tendency was to concentrate vegetables in walled gardens while fruit bushes were gathered together in huge cages. There were orchards for fruit trees and flowers were confined to ornamental beds and herbaceous borders in the flower garden. A

back garden, whether country half-acre or tiny town patch, is a very different, more relaxed kind of place, less suited to this rigid segregation, and it would be inappropriate to banish food crops from the rest of the garden.

There is something almost puritanical about dividing plants that give pleasure – as though they were merely frivolous – from edible plants, whose cultivation is deemed a serious and virtuous business to be approached with the grim determination of a self-sufficient homesteader. It is not in any case a valid distinction. Vegetables such as chicory, salsify and scorzonera are as attractive as any border plant when in bloom, while the leaves and flower heads of seakale make a dramatic ornamental feature. Set among flowering plants, the foliage of most vegetables adds variety and contrast: the feathery grace of asparagus, for example, or the red stems and bold leaves of swiss chard.

This was the kind of patchwork that could still be seen in that forsaken Leeds garden. Later I learnt it preserved an older tradition – that of the cottage garden – which combined fruit trees, vegetables and herbs with flowers as equal tenants of the same soil. Cottagers grew their gladioli amongst the blackcurrants, and parsley or carrots edged beds of annual flowers. The custom is older still. In medieval monastic gardens plants were tended both for their decorativeness and for use as kitchen crops or medicinal herbs; the unimaginative modern distinction between utility and ornament did not exist. Gardens today, with every centimetre of space counted precious, are ideal for reviving this integrated style of gardening.

People with small gardens have always had to plant more closely than recommended, or squeeze the odd herb and handful of lettuce seedlings into gaps in flowerbeds. The plants grow just as well, if not better, because pests and diseases frequently fail to find them in their more cosmopolitan surroundings.

Yields actually improve when the 'hoe a row' philosophy and wide spacings recommended on seed packets are abandoned. These distances assume that gardeners need to walk comfortably between rows to weed and cultivate them. But recent research has confirmed that highest yields come from beds or squares small enough to be tended without walking on the soil and so closely planted that leaves of mature vegetables touch each other, shading out weeds and retaining moisture which reduces the need to water.

This alternative approach to gardening is explored throughout the book. Some of the ideas question the orthodox rules, laid down as working guidelines when conditions were quite different. The methods usually recommended for growing fruit and vegetables in gardens are not necessarily wrong, but often need modifying in the light of our own experiences and discoveries, and adapting to the area of garden available.

Amateur gardeners everywhere have regularly broken all the rules of established garden practice, and as a result have created gardens that are a joy to live and work in. This philosophy involves experimenting with plant combinations, husbanding the soil at our disposal and growing a little of everything in small spaces. It might ignore the assumptions and concepts of formal garden design, but it is all about enjoying gardening and integrating plants of every kind.

*left: Artist's impression of the garden in Leeds where fruit, flowers, vegetables and herbs co-existed in lively harmony. Immaculate space-saving fruit espaliers and horizontal cordons, a riot of blossom in spring, exploited the vertical dimension of the garden and divided it into a series of intimate beds edged with prostrate herbs. Flowers and vegetables grew together in interesting groups and patches rather than regimented straight rows, so combining ornament with utility, and creating a constantly changing mosaic of colour and crops.*

*Neatly trained fruit trees are usually the most suitable for introducing into established beds without disturbing the growing environment of existing plants. However, half-standard trees on short clear trunks may be more in scale with larger borders, as here where the shapely apple tree does not dwarf adjacent perennials and makes a relaxed contrast with the clipped box hedges.*

decorative shapes often right up to the guttering, their branches carefully tied to frame doorways or windows. Smaller soft fruit and woody-stemmed herbs are useful for training at a lower level, perhaps below the branches of tall fruit fans and espaliers.

Fences are similarly valuable supports, both for fruit and also for tall vegetables such as beans and peas, tomatoes, outdoor cucumbers or courgettes (zucchini).

Plants can be tied directly to wires or nails fixed permanently to the fence or wall, or a section of netting can be suspended from these to support plants that cling or twine. It may be possible to hang netting or vertical strings from the undersides of low roofs (such as those of bungalows or sheds) for runner beans or climbing peas, but make sure the structure will be strong enough to take the weight of a possibly wet mass of foliage.

## TREES AND HEDGES
Few useful crops will grow beneath tall, spreading trees or near mature hedges without some preliminary work to reduce shade and competition from roots. Garden trees will usually stand a little thinning, which often improves their shape as well as transforming

heavy shadow into the kind of dappled shade that suits leafy woodland plants such as angelica, sweet cicely or woodruff. Many similar herbs together with rhubarb and gooseberries can be planted, mixed with bulbs and flowering plants which appreciate shade, to make attractive arrangements in what were previously barren areas.

Hedges not only cast shade but also tend to root beyond the limits of their top growth. Chopping down with a spade along the line of the hedge and forking out the severed roots will check this invasiveness, and allow other plants a chance to establish nearby. Consider reducing both the height and width of large hedges so that they cast less shade and occupy a smaller space. The soil beside a hedge and near trees will probably have been exhausted by the roots, but once revived with heavy dressings of manure or garden compost will provide valuable extra space for fruit and vegetables. Taller fruit trees planted within an established hedge will supply useful crops, and add height and interest to an otherwise plain feature.

## POTS AND CONTAINERS
Most gardens have hard-surfaced areas on which to stand pots and tubs of fruit or vegetables mixed with flowering plants. A collection of herbs and annual bedding flowers can be grown in a group of terracotta pots, arranged in a sunny corner of a patio or yard, or beside garden steps. They may be left there for much of the year if severe frost is not a problem, the arrangement perhaps being changed as plants finish flowering. In districts with cold winters, however, all but the largest pots will need to be moved under cover to prevent their contents from freezing. Larger containers such as half barrels can usually be left in place all the year in mild areas; they are ideal for growing specimen fruit trees, underplanted with dwarf herbs and flowers, or trained fruit against a wall or fence.

# THE NEW GARDEN

Creating a garden where before there was nothing but bare ground or weeds is an exciting challenge. How to begin, however, depends very much on the condition of the soil. If the garden surrounds a new house, the soil may contain all kinds of rubbish, such as bricks, timber and other building materials, and these must first be cleared.

Where topsoil has been spread, dig down 30 centimetres or so to find out how deep it is and to reveal the original earth; if this is heavy clay the ground may need some kind of drainage system, which is best installed before planting anything. Take samples of the soil from several sites around the garden, and have them tested for acidity and nutrient levels, so that any deficiencies can be corrected at an early stage.

If the garden is to be made out of grassland, mow the turf as short as possible, and then skim off the top 2.5-5cm (1-2in) wherever paths and beds are to be made. Do not discard this valuable humus, but either dig it in deeply or stack until decayed (see p.179). On bare ground annual weeds can be turned in as green manure, but any perennial weeds must be removed and either composted or burnt.

## ASPECT

There is usually little one can do to change the site and lie of the garden without major alteration, but there are ways of adapting unfavourable positions. Where the garden is shaded by trees, including those in neighbouring gardens, explore the possibility of removing, thinning or lowering the height of some or all of them to reduce the amount of shadow (this may involve the advice and assistance of a specialist contractor). Although this could be a large job, it is necessary if plants are to have enough light to grow well.

A sloping site can be terraced to prevent erosion by heavy rain. This will create a series of

*As this view of the garden at Barnsley House, Gloucestershire demonstrates, design and layout are most easily undertaken in winter when the essential framework is clearly revealed.*

level gardens or beds, each supported by a steep bank or wall, against which fruit can be trained: if the banks face south or south-west, they may provide sufficient heat to protect comparatively tender varieties, but later-flowering kinds will thrive on walls facing north or north-east. A hedge or fence at the bottom of a slope can trap cold air and create a frost pocket: reduce this danger by creating an opening or by lowering the height.

Note the parts of the garden exposed to sun at various times of the day, and arrange plantings accordingly, bearing in mind that direct early sunlight on a frosty morning can be injurious to slightly tender plants. Frost-sensitive fruit is best planted away from the sun so that flowering is delayed for a few weeks, by which

time the weather may have warmed up; late-maturing fruit, on the other hand, needs maximum autumn sun to finish ripening fully.

## ESTABLISHING A FRAMEWORK

The overall shape of a garden is usually defined already by its boundaries, which cannot be altered. If the boundary is a fence, consider its potential for supporting climbing or trained plants. A low fence can be raised by adding open trellis panels, or by planting tree fruit and training the branches as espaliers above the top. Where a boundary hedge is to be made, decide on its eventual height and width before choosing the plants. Gooseberries and myrobalan plums can be clipped as formal hedges while still producing a crop, and taller fruit trees may be planted at intervals for extra height. Remember, though, that access will be needed for clipping and for clearing trimmings.

Within the garden, fruit can be used to create productive and ornamental fences and divisions, tougher species also acting as wind-breaks in exposed positions. When planning where to grow fruit trees, do not forget that even those on very dwarfing rootstocks need room to grow, and it is important to consider their eventual height and spread with normal pruning. It is usually recommended that rows of fruit should run north-south for uniform ripening; this is not necessarily important, and an alternative axis may be an advantage because delayed ripening on one side can extend the picking season.

Decide where permanent paths are to go and prepare the ground thoroughly, making them as wide as possible. Plants can then be allowed to spread over them, softening their edges without limiting access, and adding interest even to straight concrete paths. Amongst beds and beside rows of fruit, paths can be remade each season as required, using stones raked from adjacent beds, coarse mulching materials such as shredded tree prunings, or from grass purposely sown to grow for a year or so and then lifted for stacking.

Unless a path will be subject to constant heavy traffic, such as from a wheelbarrow, arrange to leave occasional spaces for planting with tough prostrate herbs. Any paved areas such as a patio, terrace or yard should have similar planting areas, together with a perimeter bed that can be filled with edging plants to trail on to the paving and relieve its angular outlines. At the foot of the house walls, leave room for a bed 45-60cm (18-24in) wide which can be planted with fruit to take advantage of the vertical support.

## BUSINESS AREAS
Every garden that is used and tended frequently needs provision for stacking waste materials, and for raising young plants. It is possible to manage without a seed- and nursery-bed by growing seedlings wherever there is a space amongst other plants, but it is often easier to

reserve a small patch exclusively for this purpose. Some gardeners will want to allow room for a compost heap, or perhaps an incinerator for burning waste, and a greenhouse or cold frame for protecting tender crops.

Organic gardeners in particular must allow for one or more compost heaps, together with a stack of leaf mould and perhaps another built of discarded turves. Since there is little point trying to hide these essential features, the best approach is always to keep them tidy and if necessary enclose them with a hedge or fence of trained fruit which will probably benefit from any nutrients leaching out of the heaps.

## BEDS AND BORDERS
Mark out the shape of these with a length of hose or rope, and make them large enough to accommodate any proposed shrubs and trees when full grown. Once the outline is established and the ground cleared of perennial weeds, the whole bed can be dug or rotavated in one go, if possible after spreading a layer of manure or garden compost. Soil that is already in good heart may simply be mulched to prevent its drying out, individual planting sites being prepared as and when required.

Ideally, trees, shrubs and soft fruit bushes should be arranged and planted first, together with any supports and training frameworks. Follow these with perennial flowers, herbs and vegetables, leaving areas free for bedding with edible and flowering annuals. When arranging plants, take into account their winter appearance; patterns of trained fruit branches, for example, can look very decorative after all the leaves have fallen, whereas herbaceous plants that die down for winter may leave unexpected gaps in a bed.

In theory stock bought in containers can be planted at any time when the ground is not frozen or waterlogged, while bare-rooted plants are moved during dormancy – the best time for most is autumn in milder districts or spring

where winters are very cold. However, although unseasonal planting is more likely to succeed with pot-grown specimens, even these benefit from autumn or spring planting, which avoids the risk of frost damage in winter and drought in summer.

*Although relatively new, this compact London garden is already maturing into a colourful and cosmopolitan blend of summer vegetables, herbs and flowering plants.*

# FITTING IT ALL IN

Books and visits to gardens generate a host of ideas, but very often apparent shortage of space deters people from trying them out in their own gardens. Although there is never room for everything we would like to fit in, especially the larger plants, it is usually possible to increase the variety of plants by careful choice of cultivars and, in the case of vegetables, by concentrating on those that mature quickly.

In a small garden it is best to start by integrating a few favourite crops. For instance, it is worth growing lettuces, spinach, small carrots, parsley, beans and peas, because home-grown produce is always superior to the bought version. Where space is short, concentrate on these crops, which are harvested while still young and eaten straight away, and leave cauliflowers, swedes or maincrop potatoes to market growers.

Some crops seldom appear fresh in shops and therefore deserve priority in the garden. Red and white currants, sweet corn (maize), endive and many of the alternative salads, seakale, artichokes and numerous herbs are all attractive plants, much better eaten fresh than canned, frozen or dried.

## GROWING TIME

It is important to know how long a vegetable will take to mature in a normal season, bearing in mind that the time will vary slightly according to soil and locality. Some plants are comparative 'sprinters' and may be cleared after only a few months, whereas others take a whole season or even a year to mature and should therefore be planted where they will not be in the way. Perennial crops, of course, need permanent homes and their siting requires the same consideration as any herbaceous perennial flower or shrub. A few of the more commonly grown vegetables and their growing times are listed in the table.

| SPRINTERS | DAYS | LONG-SEASON CROPS | DAYS |
|---|---|---|---|
| Beans | | Brussels sprouts | 90-100 |
| climbing | 60 | | |
| dwarf | 50-60 | | |
| Beet | 60 | | |
| Broccoli | 55 | Celery | 105-130 |
| Cabbage, summer | 60-70 | | |
| Carrots | 70 | Leeks | 120 |
| Cauliflower | 50-60 | | |
| Endive | 90 | | |
| Kale | 55-65 | Lettuce, heading | 75-90 |
| Kohl Rabi | 45-60 | | |
| Lettuce, leaf | 45-50 | | |
| Onions, salad | 100 | Onions, maincrop | 170-300 |
| Peas | 60-70 | | |
| Potatoes, early | 100 | Parsnips | 105 |
| Radish | 20-30 | | |
| Spinach | 40-50 | | |
| Squash, summer | 50-60 | Squash | 80-120 |

## VARIETIES

The different cultivars of a particular vegetable often vary considerably in height, the space they require and the time taken to maturity. As a rule early varieties are the fastest to grow, and these are the ones to choose when a quick succession of crops is needed or where space is available only for a short while. Although these varieties are nominally 'early', they can be sown throughout the season; a maincrop carrot, for example, will take six to eight months to reach full size, during which time two or three successive sowings of an early variety can be made for pulling while still small and sweet.

Another advantage of sowing only fast, early varieties is that the end product is usually smaller and therefore occupies less space.

Early carrots, beet and potatoes, for example, need only half or two-thirds the room taken by maincrop varieties. Although not specifically early, dwarf or compact varieties of some vegetables are available – cabbages, lettuce or cauliflowers, for example – and these, too, are recommended for restricted areas. Not all dwarf kinds are necessarily the best, however. Dwarf Brussels sprouts or kale are smaller only in height and occupy almost as much ground as tall kinds; they are the ones to choose in exposed, windy gardens.

Fruit trees and bushes, too, have their early, mid-season and late varieties, but they differ in their picking season rather than stature. Choice of season depends more on aspect and average spring or autumn temperatures; space can be saved instead by selecting a dwarfing rootstock to keep trees small, or by pruning to restrict growth. Varieties of herbs differ most in appearance and flavour, although some kinds are distinctly smaller than others. However, their size, too, can be regulated by pruning.

## SPACING

As explained elsewhere, traditional spacings of vegetables were determined by the need to hoe between rows. These distances were not the most appropriate for intensive cultivation, and research has shown that closer spacing often increases yield, which must be first priority in a small garden. Dwarf or early varieties are normally planted closer than maincrop kinds, but if they are tended from an adjacent path or lawn there is no need to leave room for access between the plants, which can be planted at a density where they just touch when fully grown. Arranging plants in blocks or patches in staggered rows helps them to fit closer together than if plants are side by side in regular rows. Crops such as lettuce or spring cabbage can be spaced at half the normal distance; harvest alternate heads while still young and leave the remainder to grow to maturity.

## SUCCESSION

Part of the skill in maintaining a sequence of crops from a small area lies in never leaving ground vacant. Sometimes a catch crop (or one sown to take advantage of a temporary space), can be grown amongst other plants and cleared just when these need room to spread; in this case there is obviously no need for another crop to follow immediately.

Where the ground is not required by neighbouring plants, however, the soil should be broken up and fortified with a little garden compost or other humus, and immediately filled with another batch of young plants. With the exception of roots normally grown in situ, sowing seeds in the vacant space wastes several weeks, because in most cases the seedlings can be raised beforehand to be ready for transplanting when required.

Wherever plants are approaching maturity, plan a successional crop in good time; to have seedlings large enough to transplant, sow about four to six weeks beforehand (times are given where appropriate under individual entries in the book). Sometimes it is possible to plant the following crop before the existing one is cleared; brassica seedlings, for example, can be spaced

*The same bed in spring, summer and early autumn demonstrates the ease with which successive crops can be fitted amongst the more permanent occupants. (top) In the centre the young foliage of a standard gooseberry is just unfolding, while at the edge a 'step-over' apple espalier is in full bloom. Between these are young broad beans and lettuce growing amongst parsley, wallflowers and polyanthus. By the time the gooseberries are ready for thinning (centre) the beans are large enough to pick and the lettuce is ready to cut. Fennel is now growing and other summer plants are basil, chervil, carrots, onions, French beans and petunias. In early September (bottom) the last dessert gooseberries are nearly finished and the apples are almost ripe. Red endive has replaced the lettuce while the broad beans have been succeeded by transplanted Brussels sprouts; parsnips have replaced the carrots and dahlias are blooming.*

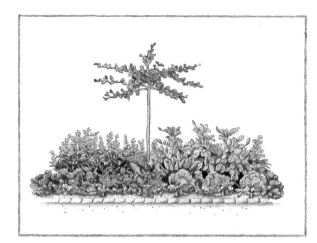

between lettuces, roots or potatoes, provided they are not disturbed when the previous crop is harvested.

## SEED BEDS

If space can be spared, a separate seed bed is a useful aid to raising successional batches of seedlings for transplanting wherever an area becomes vacant in the garden. It is also valuable as a small nursery bed for cuttings, divisions or for temporarily housing plants whose home is yet to be decided. The soil need not be especially fertile, but for quick, even germination it should be thoroughly broken up to a depth of several centimetres; seeds need friable soil, and it is worth riddling (sieving) the topsoil to remove all stones and hard clods that might cause irregular emergence.

Where a seed bed or waiting bed seems a waste of ground, seedlings can be raised in a number of alternative ways. If a greenhouse or cold frame is available, most sowings can be done there, either in containers or directly into the soil of a border. Otherwise, small amounts can be sown thinly in pots of good soil or potting mixture, and the pots then plunged to their rims in the ground (see **Lettuce** p.143); sow larger quantities in seed trays, or cell trays, which eliminate pricking out, and stand these on a path or other hard surface. Seeds may also be sown amongst plants in the garden, either in short rows, or small circles, which occupy very little room (see **Sowing** p.172).

## ROTATION

Many people are confused by recommendations to 'rotate' crops, or grow different vegetables in a certain sequence. This practice arose for several reasons. With one or two exceptions (notably onions and runner beans in healthy soil), growing a crop year after year in the same soil gradually depletes some of the essential nutrients and also eventually creates a reservoir of pests and diseases. Vegetables have different requirements – for example, cabbages need plenty of rich food and also lime, whereas heavy dressings of manure make the roots of carrots divide or 'fork', and freshly limed ground causes scab on the skins of potatoes.

By rotating crops in a three- or four-year sequence, the soil can be dressed with manure or lime at the appropriate time, while specific disorders tend to die out during the interval between successive plantings of the same crop. Where vegetables are integrated with other garden plants the same principles apply (flowers of the same family as adjacent vegetables can contract the same diseases), although frequent small applications of well-rotted manure or garden compost gradually improve the overall productivity of the soil without the sudden increases in fertility that distort root crops. Nevertheless, a basic rotation is a valuable precaution against pests, diseases and exhaustion of nutrients, even in apparently healthy soil.

For practical purposes, vegetables are divided into three groups: brassicas (cabbage family), which includes radishes, swedes/rutabagas and turnips; onions and legumes (peas and beans); and roots. The sequence for a three-year rotation is: 1. manure and lime the ground if necessary, and grow onions and legumes; 2. brassicas; 3. roots. If potatoes are grown, these can be included with roots or may be added as a fourth year after roots, and before onions and legumes (in this case manure the soil before the potatoes and lime afterwards).

Vegetables that do not fit these groups may be included anywhere. The rotation is arranged season by season, which means that several successive crops of roots, for example, can be grown in the same soil during a single season, but the following year should be grown elsewhere. If a three- or four-year rotation is not possible because of space restrictions, avoid growing the same crop in two consecutive years on the same piece of ground.

*Tall peas, such as this purple-podded variety, can be grown in a cross formation to save space.*

**LOCAL VARIATION**
Soils differ considerably even within a small neighbourhood, and this will affect the choice of suitable kinds of fruit and vegetables. Varieties recommended in this book are selected mainly for flavour and reliability, but many others exist that may be better adapted to a local soil type. Neighbouring gardeners or some seed catalogues will usually be able to recommend suitable kinds.

There are also likely to be wide variations in climate within a given region, and these too will modify the choice of plants and time of sowing or maturity. In many districts frost is a particular risk in late spring or early autumn, and this may mean adjusting recommended sowing times or perhaps using cloches to extend the growing season. Severe or prolonged winter frost can cause widespread injury and may threaten the survival of many perennial plants, even those nominally hardy.

Because hardiness is such a vague concept, the United States Department of Agriculture devised a scale of ratings according to typical minimum winter temperatures, to help gardeners assess the chances of a plant's survival over an average winter (see table). Originally designed for North America, where it is widely used, the system has been extended to cover Europe: Britain lies mainly within zone 8, with small areas in zones 7 and 9. Where appropriate, zone numbers are given in the text to indicate the limit of a plant's hardiness, but the system is only an approximate guide. Observation of local conditions such as altitude and aspect (northern versus southern slope for example), even different parts of a garden, must govern choice of variety.

| MINIMUM TEMPERATURE RANGE | | |
|---|---|---|
| Zone | degrees C | degrees F |
| 1 | below −45 | below −50 |
| 2 | −45 to −40 | −50 to −40 |
| 3 | −40 to −34 | −40 to −30 |
| 4 | −34 to −29 | −30 to −20 |
| 5 | −29 to −23 | −20 to −10 |
| 6 | −23 to −17 | −10 to 0 |
| 7 | −17 to −12 | 0 to 10 |
| 8 | −12 to −7 | 10 to 20 |
| 9 | −7 to −1 | 20 to 30 |
| 10 | −1 to 5 | 30 to 40 |

# FRUIT INTRODUCTION

Some gardeners still visualize fruit in terms of impossibly large standard trees that carry few if any apples far out of reach, impenetrable spiny blackberries insinuating their way into choice shrubs, exhausted strawberries with a season of only two or three weeks, and ancient clumps of rhubarb tucked away where nothing else will grow. However, this picture is far from the truth today. The modern development of dwarfing rootstocks, pest and disease resistance, and late-flowering or early-bearing varieties has removed most of the risks and problems and all kinds of fruit can be raised with ease in the smallest garden over a long season.

The improved quality and health of available varieties has encouraged a rediscovery of traditional training methods, by which most fruit can be shaped to fit confined spaces or awkward corners, as well as transform walls and fences into ornamental and profitable parts of the garden. In recent years, for example, the once popular single espalier apple has been revived as the 'step-over tree', ideal for edging paths and borders, while 'festoons' are a modification of the nineteenth-century arcure espalier. With careful summer pruning these combine high productivity with a decorative appearance by bending branches into arcs studded with fruiting spurs.

All the different types of fruit tree and bush can be incorporated into a garden to provide productive yet very attractive features. As large trees, top fruit such as apples, pears or peaches add height to the overall scheme and with a little shaping can make fine specimen trees, which, quite apart from their crop, contribute beautiful spring blossom, summer shade and tinted autumn foliage. Smaller versions may be grown against walls, trained to geometrical shapes around windows and doors or beside paths, and even pruned to crop successfully in large pots.

Bush fruit – such as gooseberries and redcurrants – can be planted as decorative shrubs among flowers; however, they look (and crop) best trained on walls or fences as cordons, or as standards, in this way also economizing on the amount of ground occupied. Cane fruits, such as thornless brambles or raspberries, have practical value as slim hedges, fences or divisions within the garden, or trained up single poles or tripods as upright features within beds and borders. Even such herbaceous fruits as strawberries and rhubarb have handsome foliage which can be shown off to advantage if the plants are used as edging, or unusual ground cover beneath taller fruit, or indeed combined with flowering plants.

Every fence or house wall can carry a crop of fruit, trained flat as cordons, espaliers and fans. By growing varieties that mature in sequence, it is possible to exploit the different aspects to provide a succession of crops of the same fruit, starting with an early variety on a south or south-west wall, and ending with a late kind facing north or north-east. Alternatively fruit may be chosen according to aspect, using the warmer walls for plums, peaches, apricots, figs or grapes, and reserving the others for hardier fruits: cherries, plums, pears and currants will flourish facing east or west, while brambles, gooseberries, early pears and cooking cherries do well on a north wall.

All these wall-trained fruit economize on space, and grown at the back of a border will still leave plenty of room for other plants to grow in front. Similarly, using trained fruit for divisions or to flank paths takes up little more ground than fences or archways, with the valuable bonus of flowers and produce. No elaborate preparation is needed: soil that supports good vegetables or flowering plants is ideal for fruit, and each individual tree or bush can be placed in a relatively small area without disturbing surrounding plants. Finally, in addition to such versatility, growing fruit gives

the gardener the opportunity to collect and preserve classic or favourite varieties no longer to be found for sale in shops.

*Fruit of all kinds will blend readily into an integrated garden to enhance its overall appearance in a number of ways. Depending on their shape and size different varieties can function as edging, divisions or specimen features. Both alpine and large-fruited strawberries (1) make attractive and profitable edging to beds and borders, or ground cover around taller plants and shrubs. Soft fruit such as white currants (2) and blackcurrants (3) can be grown amongst flowers in the same way as conventional flowering shrubs, but many kinds will also submit to decorative shaping – the cruciform cordon gooseberry (4), for example, or a standard red currant (5). Raspberries (6) can be used for wind-breaks or divisions, as can trained top fruit (see Leeds garden, Introduction p. 6), which are equally at home on a garden wall. Walls and fences will in fact support many fruits, from an informally trained grapevine (7) to apples and pears pruned to such traditional patterns as arcures (8), serpentine cordons (9), or lattice espaliers (10). On sunnier walls, fans of fig (11) and golden plum (12) benefit from the extra warmth, and citrus fruits make decorative small standards in portable containers (13). Where there is room, fruiting trees such as mulberries (14) develop into handsome features, and also provide welcome shelter from wind, and shade from hot summer sunshine.*

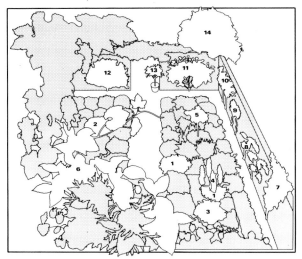

# APPLE

**Season:** July (earliest varieties) until March.

**Life:** 20-30 years on dwarf rootstocks; standards 50 years or more.

**Yield:** depending on rootstock 4.5kg–several hundred kilos (10lb–several hundredweight).

Some self-fertile, but others need pollination by one or more different varieties, or by a crab apple nearby.

This is probably the most popular hardy tree fruit, a staple crop that has been grown since earliest historical times for eating fresh or storing, sometimes until late spring according to type. Many varieties still grown today are very old (Court Pendu Plat, for example, is thought to be Roman in origin), while others are regional specialities. Typical of these are Devonshire Quarrenden and Cornish Aromatic, both adapted to a higher rainfall than most dessert apples.

Although sometimes failing the modern test of commercial profitability, many older varieties are valuable not just for their unique flavours, but also because they often display notable resistance to diseases or frost. Another name for Court Pendu Plat is the Wise Apple because it flowers so late in the season; despite its age it has been used for breeding frost evasion into modern hybrids.

Commercial priorities have restricted shop supplies to a very few dependable kinds and many people have never tasted some of the older russets, pippins or pearmains, but private gardens can provide sanctuary for these classic varieties which, eaten fresh and fully ripe, often have better flavours. On dwarf rootstocks a selection of choice apples can be grown, even in small gardens, to give a varied succession of fine fruit.

## VARIETIES

Any shortlist is inevitably a personal selection. Numerous apple cultivars are available and hundreds more can be grafted to order by specialist nurseries. Some varieties, however, are not very suitable for garden cultivation. Susceptibility to diseases and intolerance of poor soil make Cox's Orange Pippin, for instance, difficult to grow well in some gardens; while even on a dwarf rootstock the cooking apple, Bramley's Seedling, needs a lot of room and is slow to start cropping heavily.

When choosing apples, consider their suitability for the site and locality, and make sure they will pollinate each other, or that compatible pollinators grow nearby. Varieties described in catalogues as 'triploid' – such as Gravenstein or Ribston Pippin – need to be grown with two other trees for efficient pollination. Remember, too, that with a few exceptions early varieties will not keep, but that a selection of several different dwarf or cordon apples can be chosen to give a succession of fruit from a small area. Avoid tip-bearing varieties for pots or formal training.

The following varieties are all suitable for small gardens or restrictive training.

**\*Cortland:** dessert, cooker, cider. Ripens late September and stores well. Red flushed green skin with white flesh. Does not discolour when

*Tall standard apple trees with their exuberant show of blossom and enormous crops are traditional in larger gardens. Apple trees on dwarfing rootstocks occupy less room and are easier to manage if space is limited.*

cut, also good for freezing. Slightly tart. Best in northern regions in zones 4-6.

**Empire:** dessert. Ripens mid-September. Improved McIntosh with redder skin. Grows better in south. Resistant to fire blight and cedar-apple rust. Zones 4-7.

**Gala:** dessert, cooker. Ripens early September. Red to yellow flushed red. Sweet, crisp and juicy. Zones 5-8.

**\*Golden Delicious:** dessert, cooker, cider. Ripens October, stores well. Yellow skin, flesh does not discolour when cut. Moderately sweet, aromatic. Self-pollinating and good pollinator for other varieties. Zones 5-8.

**Liberty:** dessert. Ripens early September. New McIntosh type. Stores well. Immune to scab, cedar rust, resistant to fire blight, mildew. Prolific. Zones 4-6.

**McIntosh:** dessert, cooker, cider. Very popular. Ripens early September. Red to green, firm and tart. Fireblight resistant. Best in northern areas. Zones 4-6.

**Northern Spy:** dessert, cooker, cider. Ripens mid-October, stores well. Red and green skin, tart, juicy, crisp. Fire blight resistant. Zones 5-7.

**Mutsu:** dessert, cooker. Ripens mid-October. Bred in Japan, Golden Delicious type. Very large with slightly tart flavour. Zones 5-8.

**Prima:** dessert, cooker. Ripens late August, stores well. New variety resistant to fire blight, mildew, scab. Zones 5-8.

**Priscilla:** dessert. Ripens mid-September. New variety, resistant to scab, fire blight, cedar rust. Pollinates Prima. Zones 5-8.

**\*Red Delicious:** dessert, cider. Ripens late September. Bright red, sweet, juicy, crisp. Fire blight resistant. Zones 5-8.

\* denotes varieties good for pollinating other varieties

**Crab apples** (zones 4-8)
**Dolgo:** red, tart. Extremely hardy and disease resistant. Good pollinator.

**Golden Hornet:** small upright tree, pale pink flowers, heavy crop of small golden apples in October. Good pollinator.

**John Downie:** upright tree, white flowers and heavy crop of large golden-orange apples in September.

**Malus hupehensis:** handsome vigorous tree, dense white blossom in May, small red fruits in November. Fine pollinator.

## ORNAMENTAL VALUE
Apples are highly decorative both in flower and fruit. They can be grown in a number of forms: bushes, half-standards or pyramids as free-standing trees; or trained as cordons, festoons, fans and espaliers of many kinds. Trained apples make attractive and profitable use of walls and fences without occupying a lot of ground, while also gaining some protection from frost. Grown on wires they can be used to divide a garden into compartments, or as edgings for paths, ranging from horizontal 'step-over' cordons only 30cm (lft) high to tall espaliers which can be trained over a path to make a tunnel. Single-stemmed columnar forms are becoming available, and these can be grown like pillar roses within flowerbeds. Compact varieties on dwarf rootstocks are ideal for tubs and large pots.

## SITES
Although cooking varieties will tolerate light shade, a sunny aspect with some shelter from cold winds and frosts in the first half of May helps apples to give the best crops. In wet districts cooking apples are often more reliable than dessert kinds which prefer dry conditions when ripening. Soils must be well drained to avoid problems with diseases.

*Combined here with violas and trim box hedging, apples are equally decorative in fruit as in bloom.*

## CRAB APPLES
Although always popular as extremely decorative trees, in flower and also in the autumn when laden with brightly coloured fruit, crab apples are valuable, too, for practical reasons. Their small sour apples, often produced in enormous quantities, are traditionally used to make an excellent fruit jelly. Commercially certain varieties are grown to ensure good pollination in apple orchards. The varieties listed are chosen for their combined decorativeness and utility.

## SOIL PREPARATION

On the whole apples are not fussy about soils, provided they are not too shallow and have been thoroughly cultivated before planting (see **Making Fruit Comfortable** pp.60-62). Although very light or heavy soils should be improved by digging and manuring to produce a moisture retentive and workable loam, some varieties are far more tolerant of extreme conditions than others: James Grieve, Lord Derby and Sunset, for example, crop well on heavy clay, while Charles Ross and Gascoynes Scarlet are excellent on alkaline ground.

## PLANTING

Plant as early as possible between late October and late March, when the ground is not too wet or cold. Trees should be set at, or a little below, the soil mark on the stem. Always stake trees securely, especially those on very dwarf rootstocks which will often need permanent support (see panel on **Rootstocks**).

## CULTIVATION

Apples establish much faster where there is no competition from grass or weeds during the first few years; lay a metre square section of carpet around each stem, or mulch with cut grass or bark. Older specimen trees that grow too vigorously can be restrained by underplanting with grass, bulbs and forget-me-nots. The first year after planting, make sure trees never dry out, especially those trained on walls and fences. Water regularly, giving each tree a good bucketful every time and mulch to prevent evaporation. If garden compost or well-rotted manure is used for mulching, additional feeding will be unnecessary; otherwise dress with a balanced fertilizer early each spring.

*Variegated strawberries and parsley provide ground cover beneath young apples in the process of being trained on interlocking arches. Eventually it may be possible to remove the metal supports.*

## HARVEST AND STORAGE

Test each apple for ripeness by lifting it gently with the palm of the hand (never squeeze with the fingers): its stalk should part from the stem without needing to be pulled or twisted. Varieties ripen differently: the first early apples are sometimes better slightly under-ripe and will not hang long, whereas late varieties can often be left on the tree for many weeks. For storage, fruit must be ripe, dry and undamaged, so pick carefully on a fine day and handle the fruit gently. Do not store any without stalks. Apples keep longest in surroundings that are cool, but frost-free and dry, although not so dry that they shrivel. Lay the fruit in single layers, or, with care, two deep on shelves, or in wooden boxes lined with newspaper stacked one above the other. When removing fruit always check carefully through the rest and discard any with signs of decay.

## THINNING AND PRUNING

Most years healthy apple trees will shed a proportion of their tiny young fruit in what is called the 'June drop', but too many may still

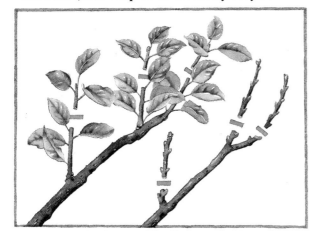

*Summer pruning is essential to limit surplus growth on trained apple trees. Shortening their side shoots to five leaves in summer encourages the formation of fruit buds, while winter pruning back to two buds re-establishes the original outline.*

### ROOTSTOCKS

Apples can be grown from pips and also on their own roots, but for predictable performance it is best to graft choice varieties on to a known rootstock. The most popular and useful of these are:

**M27:** the most dwarfing, growth to about 180cm (6ft). Ideal for trees in pots, and cordons or bushes on very fertile soil only. Makes a small root system and needs permanent staking. Plant cordons 60cm (2ft) apart, bushes 120cm (4ft).

**M9:** very dwarfing, growth to 2.4-2.75m (8-9ft). For cordons, small espaliers and bushes on good soil. Needs permanent support. Plant cordons 60cm (2ft) apart, bushes 180cm (6ft).

**M26:** dwarfing, growth to 3.5m (12ft). The most valuable rootstock for general garden use and for all trained forms, except on poorer soils. Plant cordons 75cm (2½ft) apart, bushes 3m (10ft).

**MM106:** for larger trees 4.5-5.5m (15-18ft) high, and for trained forms on poorer soils. Too vigorous for very small gardens. Plant cordons 90cm (3ft) apart, bushes 3.5m (12ft).

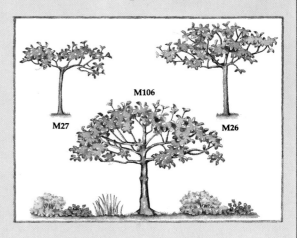

remain after midsummer to ripen comfortably. Where trees are not too large, congested fruit can be thinned. Remove those with holes on the surface (evidence of a maggot inside) and any that are misshapen, and thin clusters of young apples to one or two of the largest. Always summer prune trained apples in late July, by shortening side shoots to five or six leaves; in winter prune these again to one or two buds. Shorten leaders by a third each winter until the stem is the required length, after which it can be cut back to this point each year. With free-standing trees, prune out any dead wood each winter, together with shoots that cross or crowd the centre. Do not shorten new side shoots on tip-bearing varieties, otherwise fruit buds will be removed; fruited shoots can be pruned back in winter.

# APRICOT

**Season:** mid-July to end of August.

**Life:** at least 20 years with careful cultivation.

**Yield:** up to 22kg (50lb) under glass, much less outdoors in Britain, but up to 90kg (200lb) per tree in warmer areas.

Self-fertile. There is some evidence that cross-pollination between two varieties improves yields.

A very hardy and ornamental deciduous tree from China, where it still grows in the wild. It was probably introduced into Britain during the reign of Henry VIII and quickly became popular, but changes in the climate have restricted its modern cultivation to sunny walls and greenhouses where the early blossom is protected. Apricots are widely grown outdoors as specimen trees in gardens in warmer areas of the USA.

## VARIETIES

**Goldcot:** good for canning and drying. Early July. One of the hardiest varieties for northern areas. Zones 5-8.

**Hungarian Rose:** good on both east and west coast of US. Zones 6-8.

**Moor Park:** large round yellow fruit with red markings, juicy with rich flavour. Late August. Usually grown on west coast. Excellent under glass. Zones 6-8.

**Stark Earli-orange:** earliest to ripen, large fruit. Late June. Good on east coast. Zones 5-8.

Apricots are best grafted on apricot seedlings which are nematode resistant, but sometimes plum seedlings are recommended for heavier or cool northern soils.

*Apricots are handsome trees at all times of the year, but especially when the fruits ripen to a warm golden-orange amongst the deep green foliage.*

## ORNAMENTAL VALUE

Indoors as dwarf pyramid trees in 25-30cm (10-12in) pots or as trained fans and espaliers grown in a greenhouse border. Outdoors as fans and espaliers on warm walls, or in warm sheltered gardens as small specimen trees with decorative foliage and blossom – Moor Park has often been successfully grown in this way.

## SITES

To fruit well apricots need sunshine and warmth. In Britain the best sites are west walls for early and mid-season varieties, while later varieties should be trained on south-facing walls, the only reliable position from the Midlands northwards and in cooler regions of the USA. Soils should be well drained, not too light, and high in lime. Although they are a very drought-tolerant stone fruit, apricots need plenty of water at the roots in summer.

## CULTIVATION

Break up heavy soil deeply and add porous materials to aid drainage. On light soils mix in plenty of humus to conserve moisture and prevent fruit from dropping or splitting; avoid using a lot of manure, though, because this can lead to excessive leaf growth and few fruits. Except on alkaline soil, top-dress with 500g/sq m (1lb/sq yd) lime.

Plant trees in autumn, spacing two or more 4.5-5.5m (15-18ft) apart. Firm into place and stake securely, or tie to wall wires. Water well in dry weather the following summer. Late every spring mulch the root area with 5-7cm (2-3in) of lawn clippings, topping up when necessary during the summer.

Protect early blossom from frost on outdoor trees by hanging fine net over them, removing net on mild days to allow pollination. To assist this shake or knock the branches whenever passing, or lightly spray the open flowers with a garden hose. Thin fruits as for peaches (see p.45).

(see p.45).

## APRICOT VILLAGE

In nineteenth-century England it became fashionable for landowners to grow apricots on the walls of their tenants' cottages. In 1839 6,000 fruits were picked in the village of Kidlington, near Oxford. At Aynho in Northamptonshire, once known as Apricot Village, a few elderly trees still survive on house walls. Conditions were ideal: soil beside the walls was free-draining and rich in lime. Ted Humphris, former head gardener at Aynho Park, remembers that the apricots grew best in the days when there was no guttering to prevent the rainwater from running off roofs to the thirsty trees, and before modern gardening techniques so enriched cottage wall borders that trees tended to produce leaf growth instead of fruit.

## HARVEST AND STORAGE

In very bright hot weather shade the fruit with net curtains to promote even ripening. Pick fruit when fully coloured, or just before, allowing them to finish maturing indoors; ripe fruit do not hang for long and soon lose condition. Freeze surplus, or dry as halves.

## PRUNING

Apricots fruit on short spurs that form on the long stems. Train the latter in to fill the available space, and pinch back to 5-7cm (2-3in) any side shoots produced along their length in summer; these will form new spurs to replace any that are obviously ageing and which are cut out after fruiting. Remove any shoots growing outwards from the wall. Fruit is also formed on short slender side shoots. Where space allows tie these in any vacant spaces and leave them to bear; alternatively shorten them to five leaves in midsummer and again to two in early autumn to form fruiting spurs.

*Although apricots fruit on short spurs, these can become exhausted after a few years. By shortening growth in summer, pruning aims to develop side shoots as replacement spurs or as stems to fill vacant spaces.*

# BLACKBERRY

**Season:** late July to first frosts.

**Life:** 20 years or more.

**Yield:** 3.5-9kg (8-20lb) per plant.

Self fertile.

With the exception of Ashton Cross, cultivated blackberries seldom possess the true wild flavour, but give much heavier crops of larger juicy berries from hardy, easily trained plants.

## VARIETIES

**Darrow:** large fruit. Upright habit. Best for northern regions and north-eastern US. Crops early August. Zones 4-6.

**Himalaya:** the most vigorous. Crops from August to October on 4.5m (15ft) canes. Berries produced on both young and older wood, so very suitable for hedges. Widely grown in Canada. Zones 7-8.

**Rosborough:** heavy-cropping upright variety for the south. Late May. Zones 7-9.

**Thornfree:** medium-sized fruit on semi-upright canes. Genetically thornless. Late July. Zones 6-8.

---

**Hybrid berries** – because of their natural promiscuity blackberries, and the closely related raspberry, have produced numerous hybrid berries, most of American origin. Grow in the same way as blackberries, either on their own or as a mixed row 3m (10ft) apart. The best of these are:

**Boysenberry:** large mulberry-coloured fruits in late summer. Very hardy and drought resistant. The thornless form is easiest to handle. Best in mild regions of western US. Zones 7-9.

**Loganberry:** long juicy fruits in late July-August, rich flavour when ripened to a deep crimson. Heavy yields when well fed. Best strain is the thornless LY654 from virus-free stock. For mild areas of west coast. Zones 7-9.

**Tayberry:** a modern prolific hybrid. Large purple fruits like mild loganberries in flavour and cropping a little earlier. Medana stocks are virus-free. Zones 5-8.

## ORNAMENTAL VALUE

Brambles need support. The vigorous Himalaya Giant is best grown as a hedge, but all other varieties, together with hybrid berries, can be trained flat on fences, trellis or wires, against walls and sheds, and make excellent wind-breaks or screens around compost heaps. Oregon Thornless is very decorative trained over arches and arbours or up vertical posts like climbing roses.

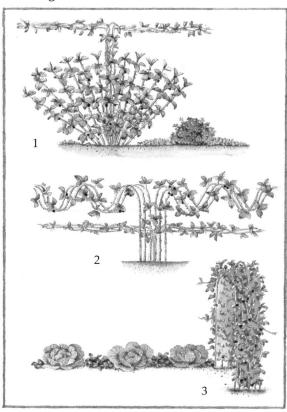

*A trained blackberry or hybrid berry can be arranged as a fan (1) on a wall or fence, or looped onto wires (2). The parsley-leaved Oregon Thornless is particularly decorative when tied to cover an arch (3). As they grow, the new season's stems must be kept out of harm's way, either by tying them temporarily amongst the fruiting canes or by gathering them on a spare wire above or below the trained plant.*

*Blackberries are a little less vigorous in pots and fit more easily into confined spaces, as here where stems will be tied to the wooden trellis. Flowers, herbs and a pot of sage grow nearby.*

## SITES
Plants will thrive in semi-shade and on most soils, but for heaviest crops prefer the same conditions as roses: a sunny position in heavier soils rich in humus. Planting in different parts of the garden will extend the normal season of a particular variety.

## CULTIVATION
Blackberries are greedy and need heavy feeding for best yields. Dig heavy ground deeply and work in bulky organic manure; light soils will need heavier dressings of this to help conserve moisture.

Plant during autumn, or spring where winters are cold, 180cm (6ft) apart for less vigorous varieties, up to about 4.5m (15ft) for Himalaya Giant; the base of the stems should be just below ground level. Cut down to 7-10cm (3-4in) high after planting. Mulch in late spring with nitrogenous manure and thoroughly soak during dry periods, especially when berries are swelling.

New canes left to sprawl over the ground are liable to be damaged; tie them out of the way temporarily as they grow, and then secure in place after old canes have been removed (see **Fig** p.32).

## HARVEST AND STORAGE
Pick fruits before they become too soft, gathering them every two or three days throughout the season, and more frequently during humid weather. Cover surplus fruit with salty water for an hour or two to extract any grubs, wash and then freeze or bottle for future use.

## PRUNING
The best fruit is produced on young canes growing from the base of the plant. Prune fruited stems to the ground and tie young canes in their place, choosing half a dozen of the strongest. Himalaya Giant continues to fruit well on old wood and some of this can be left each year where plants are grown as a hedge.

# BLACKCURRANT

**Season:** end June to early September.

**Life:** twenty years or more. Crops from two years old.

**Yield:** varies according to variety and season. Averages 1-2kg (2-4½lb) per bush.

Self-fertile; crops heavier if two or more varieties are grown together.

The earliest cultivated bushes bore sparse, small currants. In Britain, until about 200 years ago, they were used only to treat ailments such as quinsies (acute sore throats), hence its old name 'quincy berry' – and elsewhere in Europe to flavour wines. Both uses survive today: the syrup (rob) is an effective remedy for coughs and sore throats, while in France the fruits are used to make cassis.

## VARIETIES
Blackcurrants are alternate hosts to the white pine blister rust which destroys the economically important eastern white pine. Consequently, laws against growing blackcurrants exist in many states and they are rarely cultivated in areas where white pine is grown. South of zone 6 they require shade from the hot sun.

**Baldwin:** the yardstick against which other varieties are still measured. Medium-sized fruit, with tough skins and one of the highest vitamin C contents; hangs a long time when ripe. Compact bushes, susceptible to mildew. Best variety for light soils.

**Consort:** developed in Canada. Resistent to white pine blister rust. Self-fertile and consistently heavy bearer.

**Crusader:** another Canadian hybrid resistant to white pine blister rust. Large fruit in loose clusters ripening after Consort. Needs pollination for best crop.

Blackcurrants are exceptionally high in vitamin C; home gardeners can use the fresh fruit for summer desserts, while surpluses can be frozen for jelly and winter pudding. Blackcurrants may also be dried and in this form thin-skinned varieties are often used, like elderberries, as a substitute for ordinary currants in cakes. Since they have a strong taste a little goes a long way and a small quantity may be added to enhance an apple pie or to flavour custard, yoghourt or milk drinks. They also make an excellent rich red, country wine.

## ORNAMENTAL VALUE
Because fruited stems are cut out each year, blackcurrants are usually grown only as bushes. However, these can be spaced closely to form a hedge, although stems must be thinned carefully to prevent overcrowding. Vigorous varieties will grow successfully close to sunny walls and fences to which their young growth is tied as fans to provide a plant which is both productive and decorative.

## SITES
Blackcurrants tolerate light shade but yield best in open sunny positions. Bushes themselves are bone hardy, but early blooms are easily injured by cold weather and shelter from cold winds is advisable; a blackberry hedge is useful for this. Alternatively, choose a late-flowering variety to avoid cold conditions.

## CULTIVATION
Blackcurrants dislike hot soil, preferring a cool, moist root run. They root deeply, so dig the ground thoroughly at least 30cm (1ft) deep, mixing in plenty of rotted manure or other humus, especially on light sandy soils.

Plant one or two-year-old bushes between autumn and spring, spaced 150cm (5ft) apart each way (120cm/4ft for erect varieties; Ben Sarek 90cm/3ft; hedge plants 75cm/30in apart). Set plants 5-7cm (2-3in) lower than the soil mark on the stem, and cut to ground level immediately after planting (wait until early spring in very cold gardens).

Make sure the soil never dries out during the following season. Mulch in late spring with well-rotted manure to conserve moisture and also feed the new growth. This is especially important on light soils, where mulching should become an annual routine.

---

### JOSTABERRY

A Dutch blackcurrant x gooseberry hybrid, with smooth-skinned fruits resembling very large blackcurrants, rich in vitamin C and with a flavour somewhere between both parents. Mature bushes may reach 180cm (6ft) tall and as much across, with spreading thornless branches, and can yield 4.5kg (10lb) or more in July. There is some evidence of resistance to powdery mildew and currant aphis. Grow like a blackcurrant.

---

## HARVEST
Deter birds by draping fine netting or old net curtains over bushes. Some varieties ripen unevenly, and where these do not hang for long pick over several times; fruits that mature together can be cleared wholesale. Pick complete bunches to avoid damaging fruit.

*Blackcurrants can be pruned at the same time as harvesting the fruit. Cut out at least a third of the old stems to leave room for young replacements, and strip the fruit indoors.*

## PRUNING
Although older dark stems will carry some fruit, the best currants are borne on one-year-old branches. Prune at picking time or in October when cuttings can be taken from the pruned wood. Remove up to a third of fruited stems, cutting them back to ground level, or to a young side shoot if insufficient new stems have been produced.

---

### MULTI-CROPS

Some commercial growers harvest three different crops from blackcurrant bushes. The old branches are pruned complete with the ripe fruit which is stripped indoors. Buds are then cut from the branches, each with a tiny sliver of bark, and sent to France where they yield a fragrant oil used in perfume manufacture. Finally the cut and stripped branches are stored in the dry for use the next season as pea-sticks.

---

# BLUEBERRY

**Season:**  mid-July to late August.

**Life:**  50 years or more; can take 3 or 4 years to start cropping.

**Yield:**  up to 9kg (20lb) per bush.

Self-fertile, but two or preferably more varieties needed for good pollination.

Although bilberries and lowbush blueberries have always been harvested from the wild, the highbush blueberry as a crop is a comparatively recent development. The plants have been selected and hybridized only during the twentieth century and since then have been widely cultivated in the United States, New Zealand and parts of northern Europe. In Britain they are rapidly becoming popular for their fruit and decorative appearance.

## VARIETIES
**Bluecrop:**  early August. Vigorous upright bush, hardier than most, fairly drought resistant. Heavy crops, fine flavour.

**Coville:**  mid-August. Upright, moderate vigour. Large sprays of berries, very good flavour.

**Earliblue:**  earliest variety. Tall vigorous growth. Very large berries.

**Goldtraube:**  late August. Fast growth, heavy crops of medium berries with good flavour.

**Herbert:**  mid to end of August. Vigorous bush, often needing hard pruning. Very large thin-skinned fruit with outstanding flavour.

All varieties zones 4-8.

## ORNAMENTAL VALUE
The 150-180cm (5-6ft) tall bushes are only grown as free-standing specimens, although cultivation is possible in large pots and tubs.

*In late spring the dense clusters of pendant flowers set against the fresh green foliage make blueberries a valuable addition to the shrub or flower border.*

Heavy heads of pinkish white flowers like lily of the valley appear in spring, followed by the berries which gradually change from green to red to blue, covered in a light bloom. The attractive leaves assume brilliant autumn tints, and bushes are good additions to a shrubbery.

## SITES
Acid soil is essential, and blueberries only grow where rhododendrons and heathers flourish, preferably in full sun. They need an open, porous soil, consistently moist but with free drainage. Bushes are hardy except in very exposed gardens.

## CULTIVATION
The fine fibrous roots must have an easily penetrated soil. Break up the ground at least a spade's depth, and add plenty of peat or rotten leaves for acid humus; large quantities of peat will make neutral soils suitable for blueberry culture, if additional dressings are given as a mulch each year. Potted bushes must be grown in ericaceous (rhododendron) compost.

 Plant two-year-old container grown bushes 150cm (5ft) apart in autumn. The following spring mulch with damp peat or sawdust, mixed with a little rotted manure, and make sure bushes do not dry out at any time during the season. In the first spring remove any flowers that form. Continue to mulch every spring and keep the bushes moist at all times.

## HARVEST AND STORAGE
Fruits normally ripen unevenly, and a crop needs several pickings. Berries are not fully ripe until 7-10 days after turning blue and the bushes need netting to keep birds away. Surplus berries can be frozen, bottled or dried.

## PRUNING
Do not prune bushes until 3-4 years after planting. In winter cut out all slender, weak growth and any stems that cross within the bush, leaving the sturdier young stems to bear fruit. Remove at ground level a quarter of the older fruited wood each year, or cut them to a strong low side shoot if new growth is sparse. If bushes are producing very small berries, shorten the tips of stems at pruning time to leave 4-5 flower buds.

*Provided they have acid soils and plenty of water, blueberries give heavy and reliable crops.*

# THE EXISTING GARDEN

For the majority of gardeners change occurs through evolution rather than revolution. Although garden designers might argue otherwise, the development and alteration of a garden is a gradual experimental process; and while many people can visualize what an area will look like when it is finished, the actual results are usually modified by trial and error. Fortunately, long-lived plants such as fruit and perennial vegetables will, as a rule, tolerate being moved once or twice to more suitable positions, and annual crops have a lifespan of only a few months, a distinct advantage where schemes and combinations have not worked.

## INTRODUCING FOOD CROPS

There is no clearly defined start to the gardening year, and transforming a conventional segregated layout into a mixed integrated garden can begin at any time without major upheaval. Container-grown fruit, for example, can be introduced amongst other plants whenever the soil is fit to cultivate, as can annual vegetables when a vacant space arises. Only the immediate planting area needs to be prepared, in most cases by forking over and mixing in some kind of humus. This is particularly important in flowerbeds, which are rarely given anything more than a dressing of fertilizer each year. Feeding the soil wherever vegetables are to be planted improves fertility of the whole bed, to the benefit of all its occupants.

Existing beds, borders and lawns do not have to be altered. Standard soft fruit and dwarf trees take up little room at ground level, and have straight stems that raise the fruiting branches above the height of many herbaceous perennials. Even a tripod of runner beans or climbing peas will fit over a group of daffodils, and grow up to hide the fading bulb foliage. Perennials such as rhubarb, sage or artichokes can be fitted between existing plants.

*Poppies of all kinds thrive anywhere in cultivated soil. Annual poppies seed themselves liberally and may be transplanted where required. Brightest of these is* Papaver commutatum *'Lady Bird' – crimson with a black centre – here romping amongst rows of raspberries and potatoes to provide a bright splash of colour.*

Where an area is regularly bedded out for spring or summer display, it is an easy matter to plan an arrangement that includes a proportion of edible plants: for example, geraniums (pelargoniums) mixed with dwarf beans and edged with small lettuces and parsley, or wallflowers combined with dwarf curly kale. Instead of planting standard fuchsias or roses, try standard soft fruit such as gooseberries or red and white currants; as an alternative to a pillar rose or clematis, plant a small apple or plum to train as a festoon, or grow a grape vine up a single pole to trail down and fruit like a weeping tree.

## INTRODUCING FLOWERS

Where a herb or vegetable garden is already established, the opposite procedure can be adopted, reviving the old estate practice of growing flowering plants around the edges of kitchen garden beds. The rows of annuals such as cosmos, stocks or rudbeckias, and perennials like pinks, pyrethrum and Michaelmas daisies were cropped as cut flowers, but also served to attract bees and other pollinating insects on to the fruit and vegetables. Herbs, too, were often grown as edgings or dwarf hedges around vegetable beds, especially woody kinds such as rosemary, lavender, hyssop or germander.

## PATHS

Although primarily functional, any path can be made more attractive by the careful use of edging plants. A formal path can be enhanced by planting on each side neat, parallel rows of compact annual vegetables such as lettuce, endive or dwarf broad beans, or a more permanent arrangement of fruit trained as cordons or low espaliers. Informal paths, especially those of brick or decorative stonework, invite edgings of alpine strawberries, prostrate herbs or patches of carrots and parsley, all of which can be underplanted with bulbs or mixed with small annual flowers; the cracks and spaces within paths can also be planted with mats of low-growing herbs.

## WALLS AND FENCES

In many gardens walls and fences are neglected features, whereas fully exploiting their vertical surfaces will considerably increase the working area, often doubling the size of a small garden. All walls, including those of the house itself, can be used to support plants. Roses, clematis and ornamental vines are commonly grown against house walls, but fruits of all kinds are equally at home. Tree fruits such as apples, pears, plums or cherries can be trained in

# CHERRY

**Season:** June to August.

**Life:** 60 years or more.

**Yield:** very heavy where protected from birds.

A few cherries are self-fertile, but most need pollination by another specific variety (see panel).

Cherries are an ancient fruit crop. There is evidence that they were popular amongst early Mesopotamian cultures, and one of their names at this time still survives in the German word 'Kirsche'. Until recent years cherries have usually been grown on large trees in orchards where they give enormous yields, but good results can be achieved in gardens from carefully pruned trees. Many good varieties such as Governor Wood, Van and Stella were bred in North America reflecting the considerable popularity and commercial importance of the crop there since the last century.

## VARIETIES
**Bada:** red with yellow flesh. Mid-season. Can be eaten raw or used for canning. Resistant to cracking. Zones 5-8.

**Bing:** deep red. Mid-season. Eat raw or freeze or can. Susceptible to cracking. Zones 6-7.

**Compact Lambert:** deep red, large, sweet, juicy. Late. More compact than the standard variety. Zones 5-7.

**Compact Stella:** deep red, good quality. Use raw or can. Resistant to cracking. Genetic dwarf reaching a height of 3-4.5m (10-15ft). Self-fertile. Zones 6-7.

**Napoleon/Royal Ann:** red blush on yellow skin. Mid-season. Use raw or can. Susceptible to cracking. Zones 5-7.

**Stark Gold:** yellow. Tangy flavour. Mid-season. Usually ignored by birds due to colour. Zones 5-7.

**Starkrimson:** deep red. Early. Self-fertile. Possibly the best compact variety. Genetic dwarf reaching 3-4.5m (10-15ft). Zones 5-8.

---

### Acid or pie cherries
**Meteor:** late June, light scarlet, zones 4-8.

**North Star:** early June, wine red, zones 4-8.

Both these are smaller-growing trees reaching 3.5-4.5m (12-15ft) and 180cm-2.75m (6-9ft) respectively and are exceptionally hardy.

## POLLINATORS

| variety | pollinators |
|---|---|
| 1 Bada | 2 3 4 5 6 7 |
| 2 Bing | 1 4 6 7 |
| 3 Compact Lambert | 1 4 6 7 |
| 4 Compact Stella | self-fertile |
| 5 Napoleon/Royal Ann | 1 4 6 7 |
| 6 Stark Gold | 1 2 3 4 5 7 |
| 7 Starkrimson | self-fertile |

One of the main problems in choosing cherry trees is that most sweet varieties need to be pollinated by another cherry if they are to produce a crop (Stella is an exception and will crop on its own). As only certain compatible varieties are any use to a particular tree, cherries are divided into a number of groups. None of the varieties within a group will fertilize each other, and must be pollinated by a cherry from another group.

## ACID OR PIE CHERRIES

These trees are smaller and hardier than sweet cherries and produce sour fruit, usually cooked for pies, preserves and wines; however, if left on the trees until very ripe they have a good, slightly sharp flavour raw. Heaviest yields are borne when two kinds are planted together, but each is self-fertile and may be grown on its own to give good crops of large cherries. Although often said to be unattractive to birds, they should be netted, because once any neighbouring sweet cherries have been cleared blackbirds turn readily to the acid kinds.

Unlike sweet cherries, these varieties fruit best on one-year-old shoots. As soon as the cherries have been picked, prune by cutting each fruited shoot back to a young stem growing from its base; this will bear fruit the following summer.

## ORNAMENTAL VALUE
All cherries are magnificent in flower. The trees themselves are handsome, with large, serrated, dark green leaves, and in many cases bark that is strikingly ringed with rich brown or silvery patches. Trained forms such as fans, espaliers and inclined cordons can be grown against high fences and walls, and are particularly decorative when in flower or fruiting.

## SITES
Any deep, well-drained soil, other than heavy clay. Naturally alkaline soils are best, but lime can be added to those that are deficient. A warm site protected from late frosts will give best yields. All varieties can be trained on south or west walls, while a Morello will flourish on any wall. Acid varieties are more drought resistant than sweet cherries.

## CULTIVATION

Dig the planting site deeply and work in garden compost or old leaves. Do not use manure because cherry trees in gardens need restraint rather than encouragement. Add 25-50g (4-8oz) ground limestone or garden lime per square metre (sq yd) before planting, and repeat every third or fourth winter.

Plant in autumn preferably, or any time while trees are dormant. Spread out the roots horizontally and take care not to damage or cut the bark, and so admit disease over winter. For trees on Colt rootstock (see panel) allow about

*Although not immune to attack, acid cherries such as Morello (below) are less attractive to birds than are sweet varieties. Trained and pruned in the same way as peaches, they are prolific and occupy very little room when grown as fans on fences or walls, especially those with a north-facing aspect.*

3m (10ft) between bushes, 3.5m (12ft) for fans, and 60cm (2ft) for cordons.

An annual mulch of garden compost should satisfy potash requirements, and also protect the shallow roots from damage. Soak trees growing against walls every week when they are carrying fruit. Free-standing trees are best underplanted with grass after three or four years, to protect the roots and restrain growth.

## HARVEST

Tall standard trees cannot be protected against birds, but bushes can be covered with tents of netting, which can also be draped in front of wall-trained specimens; do this before fruits start to colour. Once protected, ripe cherries will usually hang for a long time and can be gathered wholesale. Pick sweet cherries with stalks, taking care not to pull off fruiting spurs; acid varieties should be cut with scissors.

## DWARF ROOTSTOCKS

Until recent years cherry varieties were grafted on to seedlings of wild cherry species, or on to a particular strain of these that had shown consistent performance. These either produce large orchard trees which are expensive to manage, or trained garden specimens that need careful pruning to restrain their vigour. Several new stocks and naturally occurring dwarf forms are under trial. The best new rootstock to emerge so far is Colt, on which most popular cherries are now available. Varieties grafted on Colt yield more heavily, but are not so hardy in northern gardens and the individual fruit is a little smaller than on conventional rootstocks. Although the trees are smaller and come into bearing quickly, Colt is not a true dwarfing stock and if not kept under control trees can still grow to a large size – 6m (20ft) or more (older stocks grow to 9-12m/30-40ft). However, on Colt, cherries in small gardens are much easier to grow in pots or as trained trees and, perhaps most important, are more easily netted against birds.

## PRUNING

Sweet cherries fruit on short spurs carried on mature branches. Train bushes to have an open spreading framework of branches; any that grow too vertically can be bent down using plastic bags filled with soil as weights. Once established, bushes will need little pruning beyond the removal of dead wood and inward growing branches.

Prune trained sweet cherries in summer by shortening side shoots to about 7cm(3in) long, pinching off any for which there is no room. Shorten these again to one or two buds no later than September. Eventually branches may become overcrowded with spurs, in which case a few should be removed as soon as fruit has been picked.

Always protect large cuts with pruning paint, and avoid silver-leaf disease by pruning only in summer when wounds heal quickly.

*Sweet cherries (above) are pruned like apples, by shortening side shoots in early summer and autumn to maintain permanent spurs. Stems of acid cherries (below) are replaced annually after fruiting in the same way as peaches.*

# CITRUS FRUITS

**Season:** all year round under good cultivation.

**Life:** many years, depending on rootstocks. Seedlings have a long period of thorny juvenile growth, and can take 30 years to bear fruit.

**Yield:** very variable. For example, an 8-year-old Meyer's Lemon in a 45cm (18in) pot could bear 15-20 fruits two or three times a year under ideal conditions.

Mostly self-fertile or parthenocarpic (set fruit without pollination).

Given heated accommodation under glass all the many kinds of citrus could be grown in Britain and the northern states of America, even limes, perhaps the most tender of all. Lemons and kumquats are the most cold tolerant, with the latter sometimes grown outdoors in London (zone 9) gardens. Oranges need a little more heat to ripen their fruit where summers are cool, but crops will often ripen on pot-grown trees that stand outdoors in summer and are brought inside before the frosts.

## VARIETIES
### Kumquat
***Fortunella japonica:*** the species, sometimes known as 'Round Kumquat'. Large spiny shrub for conservatories or, in zones 9-10, as an espalier on a warm wall. White flowers, fruits small, round and bright yellow.

**Nagami:** dwarf cultivar, slightly hardy but best grown as a potted tree. Very decorative white flowers, followed by aromatic rectangular golden fruits.

### Lemon
**Imperial:** vigorous tree, best in a greenhouse or conservatory border. Regular crops of large fruits if pruned regularly.

**Meyer's Lemon:** thought to be a hybrid, mostly lemon with a little mandarin orange, hence its near hardiness. Compact enough for pot culture, but useful outdoors in zones 9-10. Medium-sized fruit of good quality. Prolific and decorative.

**Villa Franca:** vigorous bush, almost thornless. Heavy crops of large, high quality fruit.

### Orange
***Poncirus trifoliata* (Japanese Bitter Orange):** citrus relative, hardy in full sun on well-drained soil to zone 5, often used for rootstocks. Spiny, medium-sized deciduous

shrub, good on walls. Large, sweetly-scented white flowers in spring, followed by yellow edible oranges 5cm (2in) across.

**Silver Hill:** a mandarin orange and almost hardy (has survived −6°C/20°F). Small spreading tree, good in pots. Fruits medium sized, deep orange and virtually seedless.

**Washington:** reliable navel cultivar with high quality dessert fruit, very juicy and sweet. Needs heat to finish well.

## ORNAMENTAL VALUE
Plants are evergreen with dark glossy leaves, bearing fragrant white flowers either in spring or periodically throughout the year. Citruses are attractive as miniature productive trees in pots; taller kumquats can be trained as espaliers on warm sheltered walls.

## CULTIVATION
Soils outdoors should be light, fertile and well-drained – stagnant water at the roots leads to decay. Plants need nitrogen, but only little and often to avoid excessive leaf growth; stop feeding at midsummer where plants must withstand cold conditions during winter. Keep the roots consistently moist and spray foliage regularly to deter red spider mite.

## SITES
Citrus fruits need protection from frost, shelter from wind, and exposure to as much sunshine as possible. About −6°C(20°F)is the lowest tolerated, and then only by the hardiest cultivars; the ideal temperature is 12-15°C (55-60°F) with a minimum of 4°C (40°F). Potted trees must have maximum light and are best moved outdoors at the earliest opportunity.

## HARVEST
Ripe citrus fruit will hang for a long time, often preventing further flushes of flower. Cut or gently twist off fruits as they ripen, and immediately shorten the fruited shoots.

Most kinds of citrus fruits are easy to grow provided they are guaranteed frost-free conditions. The most cold-tolerant are lemons which, with careful pruning of surplus growth and regular small applications of nitrogenous fertilizer, can give three crops every year, one set of fruit often overlapping with the next flush of blossom (top). In regions where frosts are common, citrus trees are usually grown as large pot plants, kept in good light indoors over winter and moved to a sunny, sheltered position outside as soon as all danger of frost is past. Lemons in particular make attractive evergreen bushes when grown in decorative terracotta pots or wooden tubs (right), and with annual pruning and repotting will remain productive for many years to come.

## PRUNING

Thin overcrowded branches at any time, and shorten fruited shoots to about a couple of centimetres from their base: citrus trees nearly always fruit on young wood. If large fruit is wanted, be prepared to thin a heavy set to one or two fruits per branch.

### HARDINESS

Rootstocks can make a difference to the hardiness of a variety. Rough Lemon is the most vigorous and can produce large trees in a few years. More restrained is *Poncirus trifoliata*, which imparts greater hardiness to its tender scion and is the stock most often supplied by nurserymen. Experiments suggest that both kumquat and citrange (sweet orange x poncirus hybrid) might prove useful in this respect. There is plenty of scope for amateur experiments.

## FIG

**Season:** August, September. Outdoors in England and the northern United States, only one crop can be expected. Under glass an additional crop in June is common. With heat three crops are possible – in March, July and October.

**Life:** 100 years or more.

**Yield:** up to 9-11kg (20-25lb) from a mature tree.

Figs flower inside the immature fruits. Some Near Eastern varieties must be fertilized by a tiny wasp but the Adriatic or Common fig cultivars do not need pollination to set fruit.

Although Charles II reaffirmed the biblical right of every man to sit at the end of the day beneath his own fig tree and grape vine, figs are sometimes said to be a waste of time in a non-Mediterranean climate. Nevertheless, they have been grown in England since the early sixteenth century, while tradition claims that Thomas à Becket planted fig trees near Worthing, Sussex during the twelfth century. In the United States figs are commonly and easily grown in the south (zones 7-10) and further north with special care.

## VARIETIES
Figs grow in zones 7-10 unprotected, zones 5-6 with protection.

**Brown Turkey:**  early heavy crop of pear-shaped fruit of moderate size, purple-brown with red flesh, very sweet and richly flavoured. Most reliable variety outdoors in the north.

**Celeste:**  small fruit, light brown to bronze with pink flesh. Eye closed. Ripens early at the same time as Brown Turkey. Most common variety in south-eastern states.

**Kodata (Dottato):**  fruit green to yellow in hot climates. Eye open but sealed with honey-like drop which excludes insects. Good in the south-east, Texas and California.

**Magnolia:**  largest fruit, greenish brown and unevenly pear-shaped. Pale flesh, pink at the centre. Excellent flavour. Vigorous leafy growth – in the north needs restriction by root pruning to encourage more rapid fruiting

## ORNAMENTAL VALUE
Wall-trained trees with their handsome palmate leaves provide a dramatic rich green background for other plants during the growing season. In autumn the leaves turn bright yellow before falling. Where it will grow in the open a bush or standard tree can be an exotic feature in the garden.

*Whether formally trained or, as here, allowed to develop a more natural shape, fig trees have lush, handsome foliage that contrasts with their silvery-grey trunks.*

## SITES
Figs need the same conditions of heat and sunlight as late-ripening grapes. When fan-trained on a back wall of a larger greenhouse (USA, zones 5-6) the flavour and yield of all varieties is considerably improved. Bush or standard trees succeed in only the mildest gardens (in the southern states and up the west coast in the USA), but good crops are possible from figs trained on sunny south-facing walls outdoors.

In very severe winters top growth can be killed altogether unless protected, but trees nearly always regenerate from ground level in spring. To protect the trees, first shorten the stems to 90-150cm (3-5ft), tie them together and wrap with newspaper, straw, sacking (burlap), or other insulating material, and finally cover with a waterproof layer of plastic. In areas with very cold, dry winters, loosen the roots on one or two sides, lay the tree down and cover it entirely with soil or mulch topped by a waterproof cover.

Trees can also be grown in tubs or large pots, which both restrains root growth and allows them to be moved under cover in winter. Avoid shading figs in any way.

## SOIL PREPARATION
Soils should be very freely drained, but not too fertile – rich living or an unlimited root run both encourage figs to produce lush foliage at the expense of fruit. Planting in a paved yard is one way to avoid this; container cultivation is another, although yields are inevitably lower. Elsewhere restrict roots by spreading a solid layer of rubble or stone slabs about 60cm (2ft) below the soil surface. Figs appreciate lime: except on alkaline soils, mix in garden lime 100-200g/sq m (4-8oz/sq yd) according to soil acidity before planting.

## PLANTING
Plant in spring unless winters are normally mild in the district. Tread or ram the soil firm after planting. Figs for wall training should be spaced 4.5-5.5m (15-18ft) apart.

## CULTIVATION
Do not add manure or fertilizer to the soil unless there is very little new stem growth each year, but cover the planting area with a mulch before summer drought sets in. As a sudden soak can cause maturing fruit to split, try to keep the soil consistently moist at this time.

## HARVEST
Pick the figs when they are soft, fully coloured and part easily from the stem.

*The long, flexible branches of figs are ideal for arranging against walls and fences where they are easily protected from hard frost; the fruit benefits from the shelter and radiated warmth. Here, young side shoots are starting to grow from the rather severely pruned branches and will be tied in to fruit the following season.*

## PRUNING

Figs are always said to resent the knife. Untrained trees can be left unpruned except to remove dead and crossing stems, and to shorten any that are too vigorous. Wall-trained figs are best pruned by pinching off the tips of any new shoots up until the longest day; thin these out in July. After the leaves have fallen, tie in the new shoots wherever there is room; if the tree's growth eventually becomes congested, cut out enough fruited stems to make way for the new shoots.

## GOOSEBERRY

**Season:** June until August.

**Life:** Although they will live much longer, bushes are best replaced after about 20 years.

**Yield:** 1-1.5kg (2-3lb) from a mature single cordon, up to 7-9kg (15-20lb) from a large bush.

Gooseberries are self-fertile and solitary bushes crop well.

Earliest of the berries to ripen, the large-fruited European gooseberry is cultivated in Britain, where it is thoroughly hardy and dependable for heavy crops in most seasons. In the United States, most varieties are hybrids between several native species and the European gooseberry. The first recorded cultivation in Britain was in 1275 when bushes were imported for planting at the Tower of London by order of Edward I. Since then they have had varied fortunes. At one time 722 varieties were listed in cultivation and there were numerous societies of enthusiasts dedicated to raising and exhibiting the largest berries. Many cultivars have since been lost, while only a few gooseberry clubs now survive. Gooseberries used to be an important commercial source of pectin, and would no doubt still be widely grown in Britain if American mildew had not entered the country in 1905 and rapidly devastated plantations. Another reason for commercial decline and disappearance from shops is a general dislike of picking amongst the thorny bushes ('gorse berry' is one early form of the name). With intelligent pruning, however, bushes can be easy to pick and will also yield larger berries. These are first gathered green for cooking, preferably with a few elder-flowers, leaving the rest to ripen for dessert.

The popularity of gooseberries in North America is also limited because they act as the alternate host for the white pine blister rust as discussed under **Blackcurrant** (p.24). They must be planted no closer than 275m (900ft) from the nearest white pine and some states prohibit their cultivation.

## VARIETIES

Flavour, upright habit and resistance to disease are more important criteria than colour or season when choosing varieties for the garden. The European types, for example, are more troubled by mildew than American varieties. Gooseberries are generally considered a fruit for the northern half of the USA and Canada (zones 3-5). Only Glendale is heat tolerant enough for cultivation as far south as Virginia and Arkansas.

**Chautauqua:** European type. Pale green, larger fruit than American types. Small bush which is very susceptible to mildew.

**Downing:** large pale green fruit good for canning. Mid-season. Makes a large bush. Very productive.

**Fredonia:** European type. Large fruit ripening to dark red. Late season. Vigorous, open, very productive bushes. Very susceptible to mildew. Grown in New York State.

**Glendale:** successfully grown as far south as Virginia, Tennessee and Arkansas.

**Pixwell:** large oval green fruit ripening with a pink blush. Fewer thorns allow easier picking. Very hardy and commonly listed. Recommended for North Dakota.

**Poorman:** large fruit ripens to red. Good for eating fresh. Vigorous bush that yields well. Short thorns.

**Welcome:** medium-sized red fruit with pink flesh and good flavour. Spineless fruit and nearly thornless stems make picking easiest.

## ORNAMENTAL VALUE

Most varieties occupy little ground when trained into neat fans and single or multiple cordons against walls and fences, or on horizontal wires as a fruiting fence in the open garden. As half-standards they can be grown as a second tier above bush gooseberries, or within flower borders in the same way as roses. When planted more closely than usual a row of bushes makes a fruitful and impenetrable hedge, although clipping inevitably reduces the yield. Varieties with arching pendulous habit can be grown over low walls or in large tubs around tall central plants.

*Gooseberries grown as ornamental standards can produce heavy crops of high quality fruit, without occupying a lot of ground.*

## SITES

Because gooseberries crop well in full sun or light shade, they can be planted where other fruit would be less successful. Traditionally they were grown in apple orchards, and they are still the best fruit for planting beneath taller fruit trees. By training several varieties on walls with different aspects the season can be prolonged, with berries ripening in succession from very early kinds on a south wall to late varieties facing north. In southern US gardens, bushes should be planted facing north to delay early growth and reduce damage from severe spring frosts.

*Like red and white currants, gooseberries are readily trained as fans against a fence or wall, or (as here) on wires. Crops such as salads can be planted in between.*

## SOIL PREPARATION

Although good yields can be expected in most gardens, gooseberries prefer a cool moist situation with good drainage, and it is worth improving hot dry soils by digging in any available humus to hold moisture; this is particularly important beside walls. Prepare a large area because the plants root widely, and thoroughly clear perennial weeds at this stage. Trying to fork them out from beneath the prickly bushes can be a painful experience and could also disturb the roots.

## PLANTING

Autumn (spring in the USA) is the best time to plant gooseberries. Plants should have a clear single leg, 10-15cm (4-6in) high, between ground level and the lowest branches to allow easy soil cultivation; bushes for hedging, however, are better planted as stools with several branches arising from below ground. Make sure the planting hole is large enough to spread roots fully to the sides, and tread the soil over them gently to avoid damage. Exposed standards may need to be supported with strong stakes, each surmounted by a wire ring to take the weight of the long branches which otherwise tend to break. Plant bushes 120-150cm (4-5ft) apart, fans 2-2.5m (7-8ft), while the various kinds of cordons are spaced so that the fruiting stems are no closer than 30-37cm (12-15in).

## CULTIVATION

Gooseberries should never want for water. Make sure the soil is consistently moist while berries are swelling, since irregular watering can cause them to split. A mulch is particularly beneficial because in addition to conserving moisture it discourages many weeds. These must be pulled by hand, or lightly hoed or forked out, because the shallow roots are easily injured. Feed plants annually with potash; the lighter the soil the more they will need. Where

*Gooseberries should be chosen to suit the particular site. Some kinds have robust, upright stems, ideal for confined positions, but others produce lax, spreading growth which may need support (above) when laden with fruit.*

bracken is available maintain a thick mulch of cut fronds because these slowly release potash. Otherwise, dress plants at 250g/sq m (8oz/sq yd) with bonfire ash in spring or rock potash in autumn.

## HARVEST

Pick the first fruits when they are large but still immature, and use them for cooking or freezing. Leave the rest of the berries about 7cm (3in) apart to ripen for dessert, but be prepared to net them against birds which can suddenly strip plants at this stage.

## PRUNING

Prune in summer and late winter. With bushes aim for a number of strong branches radiating around an open centre; picking will then be a painless matter of lifting each branch to gather the suspended berries, while improved circulation of air reduces the risk of mildew. About midsummer prune all new side shoots to five or six leaves, shortening them again to two buds in winter. Prune the ends of branches in winter: cut the extension growth on each to half its length, until the required size is reached, then prune back to one or two new buds.

Gooseberry hedges simply need clipping once or twice after fruiting. With neglected bushes selectively prune out a third of the old wood each year until plants have been rejuvenated with a framework of new, well-spaced branches. See **Pruning and Training** (pp. 62-66).

# GRAPE VINE

**Season:**  outdoors early to mid-autumn; under glass early August until November.

**Life:**  200 years and more (starts to fruit from two years after planting).

**Yield:**  very variable outdoors; under glass: one bunch per side shoot.

Most kinds are self-fertile.

Grapes have been cultivated for at least 6,000 years. They still grow wild in the Middle East where they were first tended, and despite the existence now of over 10,000 cultivars, these wild species are still used for breeding hybrids that combine natural pest and disease resistance, early ripening and vigour with the quality of cultivated grapes. Although the Roman Tacitus in the first century BC thought Britain's climate was too wet for grapes, their culture became so extensive that by the time of the Normans the fenland city of Ely, for instance, was also known as the 'Isle of Vines'.

In the nineteenth century grapes were increasingly grown in greenhouses or trained on sunny walls in large gardens to supply dessert fruit. Growing grapes for wine is an expensive and highly skilled undertaking, but all gardens have room for at least one vine which most years will reward a small amount of attention with many bunches of dessert grapes. The handsome leaves are edible, too, as are the immature berries thinned from the bunches on greenhouse vines.

## VARIETIES

This is just a small selection of dessert or table grape varieties All set and ripen their grapes well outdoors where hardy, although all can be grown under glass where crops are often heavier in cool northern areas.

Table grapes generally fall into two important groups:

**American or native fox grapes** are very hardy and adapted to the humid mid-eastern and north-eastern states (zones 5-8). Distinctive 'foxy' flavour and 'slipskins' that separate easily from the flesh.

**Canadice:**  red seedless. Very early. Medium-sized berries in large compact bunches. One of the most highly acclaimed new varieties.

**Concord:**  blue-black. Medium-sized berries. The most popular variety ever developed. Hardy to −9°C (−15°F).

**Fredonia:**  black. Early medium-sized berries. Hardy to −9°C (−15°F).

**Niagara:**  white. Medium to large yellow-green berries in large bunches. Distinctive foxy flavour.

**European grapes** are adapted to the warmer, drier climate of California. Difficult in the east. Thinner skins firmly attached to the flesh.

**Emperor:**  red. Mid-late season. Large berries in large bunches. Very popular table grape.

**Muscat of Alexandria:**  white. Mid-season. Large amber berries. Classic greenhouse grape of Europe. Outstanding muscat flavour when fully ripe.

**Thompson Seedless:**  white seedless. Mid-season. Light green berries in large bunches. Widely planted on the west coast.

**Tokay:**  red. Mid-season. Very large berries. Best in cooler areas of west coast.

## ORNAMENTAL VALUE

Vines are ornamental plants in any form, their foliage lush and exuberant during the growing season, turning to brilliant red and gold tints in autumn. They will cling with tendrils if allowed to ramble over netting or into trees, or they can be trained and tied to cover pergolas, fences, arbours, or even vertical poles in the same way as pillar roses. On walls and in greenhouses where they are to crop intensively vines are best trained as formal espaliers or with vertical branches ('rods') like a series of cordons.

## SITES

Grape vines need sun and warmth to produce the sweetest fruit. In cool climates a sunny wall, southern slope or an unheated greenhouse will help protect grapes from late frosts and wet summers. When grown in the open garden avoid very heavy ground, frost pockets and low-lying mists which can encourage mildew.

## SOIL PREPARATION

Dig the planting site deeply. Grapes prefer light gravelly soils, although they will crop elsewhere provided they have good drainage. Very thin soil is best dressed with a little well-rotted manure or tree-planting compost, but do not make it too rich: very fertile conditions encourage leaf growth at the expense of fruit. It was once customary to bury a dead animal beneath a new vine to provide a slow and constant supply of nitrogen. A more easily handled substitute is bone-meal, added before planting at the rate of 60g per sq m (2oz/sq yd).

## PLANTING

Plant pot-grown vines in spring. The roots are best loosened from the ball of soil and evenly spread out horizontally about 15cm (6in) below the surface (10cm/4in on heavier soil). Plant 120-150cm (4-5ft) apart if growth is to be carefully controlled during the season, although under more relaxed management a single vine

*The branches of greenhouse vines are always arranged evenly on wires and pruned to remove any unnecessary growth, partly to expose the fruit and stems to all available sunshine. Grapes grown outdoors primarily for their fruit are also strictly trained (top), but where vines are used to cover fences or form divisions, as in the vine hedge beyond the rose bed in the picture on the right, more foliage can be left, provided this does not create too much shade. When the leaves have fallen at the end of the season, however, it is best to prune the vines back to their original framework to avoid tangled stems and eventually dwindling fruitfulness. Cut all new shoots back to within two or three buds of their base in the same way as for greenhouse vines.*

can be trained to each side to cover 9m (30ft) or more of garden fence. Cut all vines down to 30cm (1ft) high immediately after planting.

## CULTIVATION

Once the soil has warmed up in spring and while it is still moist, hoe off any weeds and mulch vines with grass clippings or, if under glass, with a thin layer of old manure. Do not dig or fork deeply lest the shallow spreading roots are injured. Tie in growth before tendrils take hold and while shoots are still pliable. Outdoors flowers will be pollinated by insects, but vine rods flowering under glass need to be tapped or lightly sprayed with a hose each day to ensure adequate fertilization. A good set of fruit, especially under glass, will need to be thinned when the grapes are the size of peas. Use long-nosed pointed scissors and a slender stick to avoid handling the berries. First thin the centre of the bunch to reduce overcrowding; snip off any tiny berries and thin the rest to leave remaining berries about a centimetre apart. Larger thinnings can be cooked like gooseberries.

## HARVEST AND STORAGE

Cut ripe bunches (at the point where their stems meet the branches) for immediate use. Grapes will mature and hang over several weeks, but for longer storage cut bunches when fully ripe, each complete with 23-30cm (9-12in) of main stem. Insert the end of the stem in a bottle of water, wedged on a shelf at such an angle that the grapes hang clear. In a cool, dark place bunches should keep in good condition for several months, although they should be regularly checked.

## PRUNING

First establish a permanent framework (see **Pruning and Training** pp. 62-66). Whether on a simple cordon or a complicated lattice of rambling branches, the bunches of grapes will be produced on side shoots that grow from spurs on the branches every spring. Cut these side shoots back each autumn after leaf fall to leave two buds at their base. When shoots start to grow from these buds in spring, keep the stronger one and cut or pinch off the other. Stop the remaining shoot above the two leaves beyond the first bunch of flowers, or if no flowers are formed stop it after five or six leaves. Pinch out any further side shoots after one leaf. Tie in shoots bearing heavy bunches to avoid breakage.

### TRAINING UNUSUAL FORMS

One old form that deserves to be revived is the weeping standard. Using an outdoor variety planted with a strong stake, grow a single main stem vertically to about 2m (7ft) high. Develop a head of five or six permanent spurs by pruning back to this point, removing all other side shoots to leave a clear trunk. Fruiting stems will grow from these spurs each year and trail to the ground. Support the stems at the top of the tree with a metal ring or square timber frame attached to one or more stakes, and prune to this point annually, leaving two buds as is usual.

Years ago grapes were served at table still growing in pots. This was contrived with a shoot from an established vine, training it through the base of a pot filled with compost. At the end of the first year the shoot is pruned to 30cm (1ft) above the top of the pot. From this train two side shoots the following season, trim them as normal fruiting side shoots and support with thin canes. When the grapes are ready, cut the stem below its pot and take to the table. The vine will remain productive for several more seasons if pruned and fed.

*Left unchecked, most vines are vigorous and make a lot of excessive growth. For the best yields of fruit, shoots must be stopped just beyond a bunch of grapes and further growth kept under control.*

# MEDLAR

**Season:** late October – December.

**Life:** variable; a tree planted at Hatfield House, Hertfordshire, in the reign of James I still survives. Grafted trees can start fruiting from about 3 years old.

**Yield:** very variable.

Self-fertile.

The fruits of this close relative of the pear and hawthorn have fascinated people for centuries. The ancient Greeks and Romans grew them, while later writers were intrigued by the curious shape – rather like a small russet apple with a hollow fringed nose – and by the need to leave them until over-ripe or 'bletted' before they are edible.

Medlars have always been a connoisseur's fruit, their grainy texture and flavour like a mellow dry wine, but not appealing to

everyone. They are more widely appreciated in France and Germany, where the fruit can be found for sale during its short season, and in many Mediterranean countries, warm enough to fully ripen the fruit on the trees. In Britain, they are usually grown for ornamental value with fruit as a bonus. In parts of the USA, on the other hand, the medlar is a popular hedging plant; it is tough and hardy, and deserves room in gardens for its handsome appearance alone.

### VARIETIES

There have never been many medlar cultivars, and today only two are generally available.

**Dutch:** forms a small tree, almost weeping in later life. Large leaves and very large fruit 5cm (2in) in diameter, brown when ripe and well flavoured. Flowers comparable to those of a wild rose. Makes an excellent ornamental specimen tree.

**Nottingham/Narrow-leafed Dutch/Common Medlar:** less vigorous than Dutch and smaller in stature. The leaves are more slender and the golden-brown fruits only 2.5cm (1in) across, but these are borne in large quantities and are considered to have a particularly fine rich flavour. The better for bush or pyramid trees.

Medlars are normally grafted on to thorn or quince stocks.

### ORNAMENTAL VALUE

The medlar is a small, spreading tree with slow, graceful growth, very large solitary white flowers in summer, and hairy oval leaves that turn red and russet in autumn. As a specimen shade tree on the lawn or in a hedge it is attractive even in winter when its branched, eventually gnarled and twisted trunk is visible. Depending on the rootstock, medlars can be grown as standards, bushes or pyramids. Scions can be grafted or budded on to stout stems within a hawthorn hedge to make standard trees.

*With the modern preference for sweet flavours, the medlar has fallen out of fashion as a crop. Even if they are not grown for their fruit, medlar trees deserve to be planted for their spreading, graceful habit, and the large, solitary white or pink-tinted flowers that appear in early summer.*

## SITES
A deep moist soil is best, although trees will flourish in most gardens provided they are well drained and lighter soils are improved with plenty of humus. On very light ground, trees budded or grafted on whitethorn will be more thrifty. Frost is not harmful (some consider it actually improves the fruits' flavour), but trees prefer a warm sunny site with shelter from cold winds.

## SOIL PREPARATION
Prepare a generous planting site by digging the soil deeply and working in plenty of rotted manure or garden compost to prevent dry conditions at the roots during summer.

## PLANTING
Autumn is the best season, but any time from November until March is suitable provided the ground is workable. Stake trees securely. Standards will need 4.5-6m (15-20ft) of space, bushes and pyramids 3-3.5m (10-12ft).

## CULTIVATION
Medlars need little attention, especially when grassed down or growing in a lawn. Trees in cultivated soil should be kept weed free and given a mulch of well-rotted manure each spring; if the fruit is left to fall in the autumn, mulch thickly instead with grass clippings.

## HARVEST AND STORAGE
The fruits need to be over-ripe before they are edible raw. Either leave them to fall from the tree when ripe, gathering them up as they become dark and soft, or pick about mid-November while still hard and greenish-brown – at this stage they can be made into jelly. For dessert use carefully store the under-ripe fruit, calyx (the hollow nose) downwards, in a single layer on shelves covered with clean newspaper. Keep cool and free from damp. After about a fortnight they will be mellow and soft enough.

## PRUNING
Once the young tree is shaped (see **Pruning and Training** pp. 62-66) the only pruning necessary will be the removal of dead wood and any branches that cross each other. Medlars naturally fruit both on spurs, like apples, and at the tips of branches, so that pruning should be avoided unless essential lest fruiting wood be cut off.

*Medlar fruits have a typical deep rosette at the end where the flower once grew. The leaves, fresh and green for most of the summer, assume conspicuous red, gold and bronze tints in autumn.*

# MELON

**Season:** from early July under glass, August outdoors.

**Life:** melons are tender annuals and must be sown each year.

**Yield:** 2-4 fruits per plant from larger varieties; up to 20 from smaller fruited kinds.

Self-fertile, but plants under glass need manual pollination.

Melons require a long hot growing season to bear, but in cool areas such as Britain or the northern United States melons can still be grown with a bit of help. Many gardeners still think of melons as a luxury crop grown in large heated greenhouses or imported from warmer climates, but modern varieties are in fact easier to grow in the garden than is often supposed. The Victorians regarded their cultivation as a specialized skill and adept gardeners were often given the title 'melon master'. In the nineteenth century melons and horses were considered inseparable, because enormous quantities of stable manure were needed for the construction of hotbeds on which the plants were grown, but today equally fine greenhouse crops can be raised in growing bags (or pots). In most summers fast-ripening varieties do well outdoors in a cold frame or under cloches which otherwise would be unoccupied.

## VARIETIES
The most worthwhile distinction is between melons that usually need a long southern summer or greenhouse cultivation sometimes with heat, and varieties such as canteloupes which can be relied on most years to crop outdoors with a little protection, even in the north. Listed here are varieties for shorter seasons and small gardens but the choice is much greater in southern climates.

**Gaylia:** an F1 hybrid already popular as a commercial variety for outdoor cultivation under plastic. Greenish-gold fruits with netted skins, usually 10-15cm (4-6in) across, but can be much larger in greenhouses. Sweet, green flesh. Mildew resistant (65 days to ripen).

**Minnesota Midget:** for cool greenhouse, frame or outdoors. A compact variety, growing about 90cm (3ft) high, bearing a large number of small sweet fruit with rich gold flesh. Excellent for short growing seasons (60 days).

**Musketeer:** bushy compact grower. Sweet juicy fruit 14-15cm (5½-6in) across with good flavour. It should be securely netted to prevent splitting (90 days).

**Ogen:** for frame, cloches or warm site outdoors. Where generously fed and watered, the vigorous vines may bear as many as 8-10 small fruits, golden with green stripes. Pale green flesh, well flavoured, sweet and very aromatic (70 days).

**Sweetheart:** for cool greenhouse, frame, cloches or outdoors. A fast-maturing F1 hybrid with outstanding flavour. The strong vines bear 3-4 medium-sized fruit, pale grey-green with orange aromatic flesh (65 days).

*In a warm summer, melons grow well in the open garden. Keep ripening fruits clean by resting them on tiles, slates or pieces of polystyrene (above).*

## ORNAMENTAL VALUE
Melons are annuals rather than permanent tenants in the garden, and their decorative contribution is therefore transient. Given a sufficiently humid atmosphere, they can be grown in conservatories where their long vines clothed with large hairy leaves and bright yellow flowers have a lushly tropical appearance. In a warm sheltered corner outdoors, trailing kinds can be tied to cover wooden trellis-work against walls, or allowed to sprawl over the edges of patio paving where reflected heat will help ripen the fruit.

## SITES
Melons originally came from Africa and even modern hybrids need full sun, rich moist soil and shelter from cold winds outdoors. They can be grown in the shelter of a wall, protected with a sheet of glass leant at an angle against the wall (a cold frame light can be used or even an old window frame or car windscreen/windshield).

## SOIL PREPARATION
Enrich individual planting sites: dig a spade's depth, drop a forkful of rotted manure in the bottom, and replace the topsoil, leaving it slightly mounded.

## SOWING AND PLANTING
Start melons five to six weeks before planting out. Sow seeds on end in pairs in small pots or soil blocks. Germinate in a temperature of 18-21°C (65-70°F). Remove the weaker seedling from each pair, and grow the other in warmth 12-15°C (55-60°F), moving it to a larger pot if planting is delayed. Pinch the growing tips from plants for outdoor cultivation when they have made four true leaves. In hot climates they may be sown directly in the garden on mounds or hills 90-150cm (3-5ft) apart. Sow six to eight seeds per hill; thin to the three or four strongest.

In a greenhouse or conservatory plant in April or as soon as temperatures can be maintained above about 15°C (60°F). Allow two plants per growing bag (38cm/15in pot) or grow singly in 25cm (10in) pots. Melons for outdoors can be planted mid- to end of May on the prepared mounds in the centre of frames and under cloches. After the last frosts, they may also be planted in the open air, but be ready to cover with cloches if the weather turns cold.

## CULTIVATION
Water regularly and consistently. At every other watering feed plants in pots and growing bags from about six weeks after planting. Under glass damp down daily to maintain a humid atmosphere.

## TRAINING
In greenhouses and conservatories grow in the same way as cucumbers (see p.137). Elsewhere train along the ground the side shoots produced after pinching out the main stem. In a frame train four, one to each corner, stopping them when they reach the sides. Under cloches retain two, leading them in opposite directions along the row and stopping them when 45-60cm (18-24in) long. These stems will produce flowering side shoots.

Male and female flowers are formed separately. In the open air insects will take care of pollination provided frames and cloches are opened daily during flowering; otherwise hand fertilization is necessary. Pick a fully opened male flower, carefully strip the petals and leave it pushed face downwards into a female flower.

Allow one melon to form on each flowering shoot, with a maximum of four per plant on large-fruited varieties (two to three in a dull summer). Pinch out fruiting shoots two leaves beyond the set melons, and stop all others at two or three leaves. On plants trained vertically, cradle ripening fruits in squares of netting; protect melons lying on the soil by resting each on a piece of board, slate or glass.

*Melon flowers are either male or female, the latter distinguished by a tiny immature fruit immediately behind the yellow petals. Unlike greenhouse cucumbers, female melon flowers must be fertilized – outdoors this can be left to pollinating insects, but under glass the pollen must be transferred manually.*

## HARVEST
Melons are ripe when they are fully coloured, and a crack appears at the union between fruit and stalk; indoors there will also be an obvious strong perfume. Cut each fruit with a couple of centimetres of stalk.

# MULBERRY

**Season:** August, September (midsummer under glass).

**Life:** trees are known to have lived and cropped for 600 years. Crops from 8-10 years old, much earlier in pots and tubs.

**Yield:** variable.

Self-fertile.

Botanically the mulberry is known as *Morus*, a name derived from the Latin word for delay in reference to its habit of breaking into leaf only when the danger of frost is past. Mulberries were widely cultivated in Egypt and Greece, and by the Romans who valued them as a treatment for oral and digestive ailments. It was the Romans who seem to have introduced the fruit to Britain, although it was not widely planted until James I encouraged its cultivation with the aim of self-sufficiency in silk production. It was introduced to America for the same purpose.

Unfortunately the scheme foundered because most of the trees were black mulberries, *Morus nigra*, whereas silkworms prefer the leaves of the white species, *M.alba*. Although the latter produces fruit, it is comparatively insipid and trees are normally planted solely for ornament. Further attempts were made at silk production, and in the eighteenth century white mulberries were even 'let' at a pound a year for feeding silkworms, but today it is usually the black mulberry that is grown.

## ORNAMENTAL VALUE
The black mulberry is a medium-sized tree, slow-growing to 9m (30ft) tall or more, with a spreading habit and eventually an attractively gnarled trunk. It was traditionally planted in avenues, but with its large heart-shaped leaves it makes a fine specimen shade tree for the lawn. For fruit production trees can be pruned as bushes or pyramids, and are particularly successful trained as fans and espaliers on a warm wall: in the last century outstanding examples grew at Holkham Hall, Norfolk, each covering 30m (100ft) of a 5m (16ft) high garden wall. Mulberries will fruit very young as bushes in tubs or large pots under glass.

## VARIETIES
**New American, Trowbridge** and **Thornburn** all bear well. Heavy crops of large fruits resembling loganberries in shape, very deep red and juicy when fully ripe. Distinctive brisk rich flavour. Zones 5-10.

## SITES
A warm aspect is best, sheltered from cold winds; in exposed gardens mulberries are better grown on south-facing walls. They are excellent town trees, withstanding smoky and polluted air. They are not suitable for courtyards or patios, however, because the fruit falls as soon as it is ripe and will stain concrete or stone paving.

## SOIL PREPARATION
Dig the ground deeply, taking great care to add large amounts of organic matter to dry shallow soils, and to open up heavy clay to improve drainage. Make sure the planting site is thoroughly broken up, otherwise the brittle roots may be injured during planting.

## PLANTING
Plant container-grown trees in autumn or spring. Try not to disturb the root ball as the roots are easily broken and tend to bleed from injuries. Work friable soil around the root ball

*A good crop of mulberries in early autumn just starting to turn colour, as are the large handsome leaves which contrast well with the more delicate trifoliate leaves of the currants growing beneath.*

and tread firm carefully. Trees will need staking. Plant standards 6m (20ft) apart, bushes and pyramids 3m (10ft), fans and espaliers 4.5-6m (15-20ft).

## CULTIVATION
Mulch trained trees and others in cultivated ground with well-rotted manure each spring. During summer months water regularly, especially when grown against walls. Older branches laden with fruit may need support to prevent breakage; provide this in good time, and also remove any suckers that form as these will spring from the rootstock.

## HARVEST
The traditional way to gather from standard trees is to shake them and so dislodge the ripe fruit which is caught on sheets or newspapers spread on the ground below. This often damages the soft fruit, and where possible trees are better trained so that the fruit is easily accessible for picking. Mulberry juice stains the skin, and some gardeners prefer to wear thin plastic gloves while picking.

## PRUNING
Trained forms are pruned to shape the framework of branches (see **Pruning and Training**, pp. 62-66); these bear the fruit on short spurs which are formed by pruning young side shoots to six or seven leaves in summer, shortening them again in winter to four buds. Free-standing trees need little more than the removal of dead, diseased or misplaced branches to maintain fruiting. However, unpruned mulberry trees eventually spread so far to each side, that the combined weight of fruit and foliage may become too heavy for the relatively weak branches. As trees increase in stature, either prune the ends of branches to limit their size, or be prepared to prop up those growing from older trees, using stout timber or metal supports strapped in place.

# NUTS: HAZELNUTS AND FILBERTS

**Season:** mid-autumn.

**Life:** 100 years or more. Bushes take 5-6 years to start cropping heavily.

**Yield:** up to 9kg (20lb) from a large, well-pruned bush.

Mostly self-fertile, although some cultivars produce little pollen; planting two different kinds together often improves yields, or twigs bearing catkins from another bush may be hung amongst the flowering branches.

Hazelnuts (cobnuts) and filberts are ideal plants for anyone who enjoys pruning. Apart from theft by squirrels, the main cause of poor yields from hazels in gardens is lack of pruning, for prolific crops only result from conscientious removal of much of the vigorous growth that, left unchecked, will quickly turn fruitful bushes into spreading multi-stemmed trees. Hazels used to be grown for cutting back (coppicing) every few years to provide the flexible branches and stems widely used in thatching, hurdle-making and many other country crafts. Even now some gardeners deliberately grow small hazel bushes for a regular supply of pea-sticks continuing the old tradition of using the freely-branching twigs to support dwarf varieties.

## VARIETIES
Hazelnuts, or cobnuts, have rounded fruits that are barely covered by their husks; filberts are longer, slimmer and fully enclosed by a tapering fringed husk. In all other respects they are identical.

**European Filbert Nuts** (zones 4-8)

**Barcelona:** large round nuts with good flavour; vigorous and productive. Susceptible to eastern filbert blight but resistant to bud mite.

**Daviana:** medium to large, thin shelled. Pollinates Barcelona. Not very resistant to bud mite.

**Royal:** nuts larger than Barcelona, easy to crack.

## ORNAMENTAL VALUE

Hazels are handsome bushes or small trees with dark green, woolly leaves, conspicuous male catkins in late winter and fringed nut clusters in

*Untrimmed hazelnuts will eventually grow into very large and spreading trees. However, they will stand pruning to crop in relatively small areas, or (as below, left and foreground) they can be grown as compact ornamental shrubs whose strong, twiggy stems can be used as pea-sticks.*

autumn. They are particularly attractive (and fruitful) pruned as symmetrical open-centred 'goblets', and in this form have often been used to form alleys or nut walks. Individual specimens make decorative multi-stemmed trees or short-stemmed standards, while rows of closely spaced bushes will grow into excellent thick garden hedges or screens that also bear a little fruit.

## SITES

Hazels do well in full sun or partial shade on most light to medium soils, even poor stony ground. Drainage must be good, while rich conditions will encourage lush growth at the expense of nuts. Because the flowers appear in

late winter, it is worth avoiding full exposure to seasonal north-east winds. Plants will not flourish in areas with very hot summers.

## SOIL PREPARATION

Thoroughly dig the planting area in autumn, and open up heavier soils by mixing in grit, small stones or sharp sand. There is no need to add manure, but partly decayed leaves will help to stabilize light soil and improve the drainage of damper ground.

## PLANTING

Plant during October or November. For hedging, plant bushes 90cm (3ft) apart; space fruiting trees 3-3.5m (10-12ft) apart or more according to available ground (trees 180cm/6ft high can extend to as much as 5.5-6m across/18-20ft). Only single-stemmed specimens will need staking.

## CULTIVATION

Apart from hoeing or forking out weeds, hazels need little soil cultivation. In very dry ground a spring mulch of grass clippings or decayed leaves will help prevent water loss. Bone-meal is a valuable spring fertilizer, hoed in annually at 60g/sq m (2oz/sq yd). Since hazels are wind pollinated, it is worth shaking branches during still weather to disperse pollen from the catkins on to the tiny red female flowers. Pull up any suckers unless required for propagation.

## PRUNING

Hazels fruit on spurs and twiggy side shoots carried on a set of permanent branches. Develop this framework in a young tree by shortening branches to half their length in winter, cutting to an outward-facing bud until an open-centred arrangement is established, about 180cm (6ft) high with ten to twelve evenly-spaced branches.

Pruning for fruit is done in early spring during flowering, treating each branch as a

cordon. Cut the end shoot of each branch to leave a third or less of the growth made the previous season. Leave unpruned all short spurs and weaker laterals carrying plenty of catkins and female flowers. Prune strong older side shoots back to 7-10cm (3-4in) long, unless they are needed for replacement to fill a vacant space. Remove vertical shoots and any growing into the tree, and thin congested growth. In August break or twist strong new side shoots about 30cm (1 ft) from their origin and leave them to hang until pruned the following spring; this helps to ripen the wood without causing a flush of new growth.

Nut hedges can be pruned similarly, although more branches are left in the centres of bushes; or they may be clipped in the same way as a beech hedge, in which case they will be denser but less fruitful.

## HARVEST AND STORAGE

Gather nuts in autumn when their shells and husks are brown, and the nuts part easily from the husk. For storage, dry in the sun or on a shed floor for a week or two, and then keep in boxes in a dry place, safe from mice; they should last in good condition until the spring.

# NUTS: WALNUTS

**Season:** mid-autumn.

**Life:** very long lived in good soils. Trees will start fruiting when 10-12 years old, and much earlier if grafted.

**Yield:** variable from very prolific to nothing, depending on the season and the quality of the tree.

Self-fertile, although the blooming of male and female flowers may not synchronize on some trees; poor crops will result unless another tree is growing nearby.

Nuts from *Juglans regia*, sometimes known as the English or Persian walnut, have been valued for centuries for both medicinal and culinary use. The ancient Greeks called them 'royal nuts', while they were known as Jupiter's acorns by the Romans for whom they were also a fertility symbol: nuts were thrown like confetti at Roman wedding processions. Together with hazels, walnuts were part of the travelling rations of Roman soldiers.

It is not certain whether they first brought walnuts to Britain, but the trees seem to have been grown since then, for fruit and for the decorative timber. Crops are not dependable, partly because trees are usually raised from seed, but chiefly because the very early flowers and the stem tips on which the nuts are borne are very vulnerable to frost damage. Although attempts have been made at commercial cultivation in Britain, walnuts are probably best regarded as decorative trees with the nuts a frequent and sometimes generous bonus. It has been found that sugar syrup can be made from the sap in the same way as from maples, but this has never been widely exploited.

## VARIETIES

Numerous cultivars exist in France and the USA. Cultivars worth searching for are Payne and Ashly for the west coast. In the north-east the Carpathian strain is the hardiest English type (zones 4-9) while Lake and Champion are also recommended (zones 5-9). The American black walnut too has a fine flavour. Thomas has large nuts that crack more easily. Black walnuts require cross-pollination (wild trees are common in the east) and produce Juglone, a substance toxic to some plants growing under them.

## ORNAMENTAL VALUE

These stately trees, with their handsome winter framework of branches, can eventually reach 18-24m (60-80ft) tall in larger gardens. Even

*While they are developing, walnuts are enclosed in a thick green husk. At this stage they can be harvested for pickling whole, but if wanted for their kernels the husk is removed when dry and brown.*

grafted bushes will occupy many square metres of ground. They are excellent grown as specimens in lawns where the attractive foliage (similar to that of an ash tree), their satin grey trunks and conspicuous late winter catkins can all be seen to advantage.

## SITES

Walnuts prefer a deep, well-drained loamy soil with a little lime. They thrive in towns although they are better not planted where deposits of honeydew from aphids might be a problem. Because of their sensitivity to frost, shelter from cold winds is advisable.

## SOIL PREPARATION

Deeply dig the planting site, breaking the soil thoroughly if it is heavy. Manure is unnecessary but bone-meal is valuable used at 60g/sq m (2oz/sq yd). If planting in a lawn, remove a circle of turf 180cm (6ft) across and keep this area of ground permanently free from any grass.

## PLANTING

Plant in autumn (spring in northern USA), choosing trees about four years old, either in containers, or open ground plants with an undamaged tap root, since injury to this may seriously delay establishment. Plant and back fill the soil carefully to avoid bending or damaging roots, and stake securely.

## CULTIVATION

Little will be needed beyond weeding round the young tree. Dress heavily productive trees each spring with bone-meal and give an occasional thorough soak in particularly dry summers.

## HARVEST AND STORAGE

For pickling gather any nuts shed naturally during June or pick from the tree in July. The main crop will be ready in autumn when the skins turn brown. Either shake them from the branches, or leave to fall if pests are not a problem. Dry by spreading in the sun or on a dry floor until the husks fall off easily. Scrub shells clean of remaining particles of skin that may develop mould, and store in tins, or in boxes of sand.

## PRUNING

In the early stages gradually prune lower side shoots back to a clean trunk, retaining a balanced head of branches. Once established walnut trees need little pruning beyond the occasional removal in autumn of dead or congested growth. Bush varieties can be induced to fruit by pinching off the tips of vigorous stems in summer, taking care to leave intact the weaker shoots which will bear the male catkins. Do not prune between mid-winter and mid-spring when severed stems may bleed heavily. There is no cultural basis for the advice offered in the traditional rhyme:
'A woman, a dog and a walnut tree,
The more they are beaten the better they be.'

# PEACH

**Season:** mid-July to mid-September (all varieties a little earlier under glass).

**Life:** 30 years or more.

**Yield:** up to 20-24 fruits on a small bush. Wall-trained trees: one per 30 sq cm (1 sq ft) outdoors, double that under glass.

Peaches and nectarines are self-fertile, but as they flower when the weather can often be very cold, it may be necessary to hand pollinate them.

There is no comparison between home-grown peaches or nectarines, and those bought from shops. Since commercially-grown peaches for market must withstand long journeys and rough handling, resilience comes before eating quality, whereas the best varieties, freshly picked in the garden when fully ripe, are so juicy and tender that they bruise at the slightest pressure. Although raising them to perfection involves careful siting of the trees, together with vigilance against pests and diseases, there is no reason why with care and cunning the fruit cannot be grown in all but the bleakest of small gardens. It is certainly worth being adventurous with both sites and choice of varieties.

## VARIETIES

Where peaches are hardy in the USA, summers are generally warm and long enough to grow free-standing trees in the garden. Selected varieties should include early, mid-season and late-ripening types. All are generally hardy in zones 5-8, but some show greater hardiness, particularly regarding flower buds.

The slightly less hardy nectarines, a little smaller and with a smoother skin, are distinctive forms of the peach, although very closely related – the nectarine Lord Napier, for example, was grown from a peach stone, while the Peregrine peach arose from a Spenser nectarine stone. Freestone peaches are generally of higher quality, with very soft juicy flesh, whereas the firmer clingstone varieties are the kind normally sold in shops or used for canning.

### Peaches

**Elberta:** yellow, freestone, August to September. A standard old-time favourite variety of peach.

**Madison:** yellow with red blush, freestone, August. One of the hardier varieties – firm flesh and easy peeling make it good for canning.

**Red Haven:** yellow ripening to red, freestone, late July to August. Medium to large, firm flesh, very bud hardy and productive.

**Reliance:** yellow, freestone, August. Medium to large, extremely bud hardy, recommended for the coldest peach areas.

### Nectarines

**Mericrest:** tangy flavour, early August, one of the most cold hardy, developed at the University of New Hampshire.

**Redgold:** yellow-red, freestone, distinctive aromatic flavour, juicy, very productive. Mid-August, very winter hardy and resists spring frosts.

**Stark Delicious:** yellow-red, very large, early August.

**Sunglo:** yellow blushed orange, very large, early August, vigorous.

### Other rootstocks

Siberian C is recommended for northern areas for increasing scion hardiness but breaks dormancy too early in the south. *Prunus tomentosa* (Nanking Cherry) is the best dwarfing rootstock.

*Even ripening is ensured by training branches against a warm wall, painted white to reflect heat and light.*

## ORNAMENTAL VALUE

With the exception perhaps of pears, peaches are the loveliest fruit trees when in blossom. In early March their side shoots are thickly studded with rich pink flowers that appear a fortnight or more before the leaves and often last for a month before fading. In warmer gardens bushes and trees can be grown in the open above spring bulbs and early flowering plants, while short-stemmed or standard fans are very decorative when trained on garden or house walls. Peaches also can be trained as oblique single or multiple cordons; when pruned as bushes in pots, they make remarkable flowering as well as fruiting plants in greenhouses and conservatories.

## SITES

A warm sunny position is essential, especially for later maturing varieties, together with natural or contrived shelter from early frosts and cold winds. In Britain in the south, west and milder parts of East Anglia bushes may be grown outdoors. Elsewhere, grow against house walls or garden walls taller than about 180cm (6ft), since fan-trained trees need height as well as shelter. They are not suitable for very heavy or wet ground.

*Outdoors in cooler climates, peaches grow most reliably when trained against a wall. Fruit has set too heavily here; thinning will improve eventual size and quality.*

## SOIL PREPARATION

Dig the soil deeply, adding plenty of garden compost or decayed leaves, but avoiding manure unless the soil is very poor. Break up heavier soils thoroughly. Mix in bone-meal 60g/sq m (2oz/sq yd), and garden lime up to 250g/sq m (8oz/sq yd) unless the soil is naturally alkaline.

## PLANTING

Plant from autumn onwards, and no later than February. Make the soil very firm, and stake or tie trees securely. Plant bushes 2-2.5m (6-8ft), fans 4.5-5.5m (15-18ft) apart.

## CULTIVATION

Annual mulching helps retain moisture; watering should be generous and regular while fruit is swelling. Dress a wide area around each tree with 60g/sq m (2oz/sq yd) garden lime every autumn. Protect the blossom from frost by draping fine-mesh netting or old net curtains over the trees at night and during frosty days. Gently shake or tap branches to help fertilize the flowers in cold weather.

## PRUNING AND THINNING

Peaches crop on young side shoots which have to be renewed each year by cutting out the fruited shoots to make way for the new growth that will fruit the following season. The technique depends on recognizing the two different types of bud that grow on peaches. As with most tree fruit, leaves and new shoots develop from the long, slender, pointed buds while the fat, round buds produce first flowers and then fruit. The difference between the two types of bud is best seen in February as growth gets under way; at this time flower buds are noticeably large and swollen compared with the thin, sharp leaf buds.

Cutting back to a flower bud often prevents it from opening, and the whole shoot may die back. Pruning to just beyond a leaf bud on the

*Efficient pruning depends upon recognizing the distinction between the fat, rounded flower buds and the sharp, narrow leaf buds.*

other hand will start that bud growing into a shoot in whichever direction the bud is pointing. Leaf buds often appear in pairs or threes. Since each of the buds will break to give a new shoot, prune back to such a group if growth is needed to fill a space on a wall. Unwanted shoots can be pinched out early to leave only the strongest to grow on.

During the summer, each fruit-bearing shoot develops young side shoots from the many leaf buds along its length. Remove all but two: one at the shoot's base, to grow on and fruit the following year, and one at the tip to draw sap along the branch to feed ripening fruit. In autumn cut off the fruited stem just above the basal side shoot left to grow on. If the tree is growing on a wall this newcomer is tied in place and trimmed to length.

It has been calculated that about forty leaves are needed to ripen each peach fully and in practical terms this means reducing the number of fruits until one is left for about every 30cm (1ft) of stem. Start when the tiny peaches are the

size of hazelnuts, picking off any in awkward places and reducing groups to single fruits. When the remainder are as large as walnuts, thin again to the final spacing. Although this seems a great sacrifice, the remaining fruit will be sure of growing to maturity.

From top: *Fruiting shoot with young replacement. The tiny, young fruits are thinned leaving two on the shoot to mature. After harvest remove the fruiting shoot and tie in its replacement.*

### HARVEST
Test for ripeness by cupping fruit in the hand and lifting carefully: if it comes away freely it is ready. Take care not to mark the delicate bloom on the skin and cause bruising. Ripe peaches can be left to drop in their own time, but some method of cushioning their fall is needed. Where wind is no problem, a thick layer of straw, hay or crumpled newspaper beneath the tree will soften their landing. Alternatively, where fruit is protected against birds, the netting can be tucked loosely under the lowest branches to catch the peaches. Check daily for fallen fruit.

## PEAR

**Season:** late July until November.

**Life:** 30-50 years, often much longer, especially where trees are not grafted.

**Yield:** 4.5-27kg (10-60lb) or more according to variety, location and form of tree.

Self-fertile or one to two pollinators.

Dozens of fine classic pears are still available from fruit nurseries, while in France where pears grow to perfection 1,000 cultivars are known. Yet in Britain varieties in shops are usually limited to Conference and Williams Bon Chrétien (in the USA the common varieties are Bartlett, Bosc and Anjou), an even greater poverty of choice than with apples. Good pears do not travel well, nor are they totally dependable; as might be expected from an aristocratic fruit (Homer called them 'one of the fruits of the Gods'), pears are very particular about site and season. Furthermore, many of the choicer kinds seem to be at their best for only a few days, even hours, and carefully timed gathering and subsequent ripening are both often critical.

Gardeners should not be deterred from growing them, however. Gardens are ideal sanctuaries for the wide range of finer varieties, and it is only by growing one's own that the quality and nuances of flavour can be rediscovered and appreciated. Pears flourish in warmer conditions than apples, and are slightly less hardy, but this need not be an obstacle: since the best fruit grows on trained trees they are perfect for fences and walls, especially house walls where they can grow to a great height.

### VARIETIES
As with apples any selection inevitably omits countless others of equal worth. The following varieties, readily available from specialist

nurseries, are all distinguished by their eating quality together with other virtues which merit their inclusion in the integrated garden.

Unfortunately, one of the best flavoured of all, Comice cannot be recommended because of inconsistent cropping and susceptibility to disease.

Most varieties require cross-pollination. Generally any two pears are compatible, except Bartlett and Seckel which will not pollinate each other.

**Anjou:** large greenish yellow with pink blush. Firm texture and mild flavour, very susceptible to fire blight. Zones 5-8.

**Bartlett:** yellow blushed red, juicy tender flesh with sweet mild flavour, late August. The most popular variety, widely adapted throughout the US. Zones 5-7.

**Bosc:** sweet, firm, crisp flesh with russet skin. Stores well. Adapted to the north-east and Pacific north-west. Zones 5-8.

**Kieffer:** exceptionally adaptable to the north and the south. Large yellow fruit mid-October which stores well and is resistant to fire blight. Zones 4-9.

**Moonglow:** large yellow with red blush, similar to Bartlett. Ready for picking in mid-August. Resistant to fire blight, very good pollinator. Zones 5-8.

**Seckel:** small, very sweet spicy flavour, mid-September. Moderately fire blight resistant. Zones 5-8.

**Starking Delicious/Maxine:** large yellow fruit with good flavour. Ripens in early September. Similar to Bartlett. Resistant to fire blight, very good pollinator for other varieties of pear. Zones 5-8.

**Tyson:** small sweet pear similar to Seckel but ripens in early August. Fire blight resistant. Zones 5-8.

**Quinces** *(for details see panel)*
**Champion:** American quince of good quality; large, round and golden. Mild flavour, ripens October.

**Meech:** another American variety, pear shaped and golden with fine flavour. Heavy crops after 3-4 years.

**Orange:** orange-yellow flesh, round, ripens late August.

**Pineapple:** flavour similar to pineapple, white flesh, round.

---

### Rootstocks
Provence and Angers quince rootstock clones are the most popular for dwarfing in the USA. They are ideal for restricted forms, but are not as winter hardy as pear rootstocks in the north. Pear rootstocks produce large trees, slow to start cropping, and although long-lived and eventually prolific bearers they are difficult to manage in smaller gardens.

### QUINCES
The common quince, *Cydonia oblonga*, is a valuable fruit in its own right although seldom grown today; do not confuse with the flowering quince (chaenomeles), whose fruits are rarely worth using. As the flowers are large and very attractive in spring, while the foliage develops brilliant golden autumn tints, it is a particularly suitable tree on a lawn or within a border. Although the round or pyriform fragrant quinces are too acid for eating raw, they are traditionally used in preserves and for flavouring blander fruit – they are very aromatic and should not be stored near other fruits. The self-fertile trees are compact and require little pruning beyond thinning some of the branches.

*The quince variety 'Champion' has fruits like large pears, golden when fully ripe with a strong, characteristic aroma.*

### ORNAMENTAL VALUE
Pears are the ideal medium for artistic pruning, because the growth can be trained into an infinite number of very precise decorative (and quickly productive) shapes, both on walls and as specimens in the open garden. French gardeners were masters of the art, training intricate espaliers, fans, multiple cordons, goblets and even simple topiary outlines from the long flexible branches.

They may be grown as dwarf bushes in pots and containers, while cordons and espaliers in rows can flank a path and join overhead as a

tunnel, a device that often defeats birds, since the fruits are suspended beneath the canopy of foliage. In spring the white blossom is unsurpassed, while the foliage of many varieties assumes brilliant autumn colours, and pears should always be planted where they complement other subjects in the spring or autumn garden.

## SITES

Areas where cool summers, very mild winters or heavy rainfall are common do not suit pears, but otherwise they will grow satisfactorily in most gardens, and flourish on moister or heavier ground than apples. The ideal soil is deep, warm and moisture-retentive, with efficient drainage. Since shelter from cold winds is important for early-flowering varieties, these do best on south- or west-facing fences and walls, which will provide both warmth and protection.

## SOIL PREPARATION

Dig the planting site deeply to ensure drainage is adequate, and reinforce lighter soils with garden compost or rotted leaves. Manure is unnecessary at this stage, but the surface of the prepared site can be dressed with bone-meal at 60g/sq m (2oz/sq yd).

## PLANTING

Plant in autumn, or up to March if the weather is mild. Spread out the horizontal roots carefully; firm well after planting, making sure the graft union is above soil level, and stake or tie in place. Plant cordons so that the fruiting branches are 45-60cm (18-24in) apart; bushes need 2.5-3m (8-10ft), fans and espaliers 3-4.5m (10-15ft) according to the vigour of the variety.

*Apples and pears grow readily together and can be trained in a number of ways to fit confined spaces. Here, for example, they transform a plain garden path into a productive and slightly mysterious tunnel.*

## CULTIVATION

Moisture is important. Water young trees in dry weather, and mulch each spring with grass clippings or very old manure to prevent the shallow roots from drying out. Do not use manure that is too fresh, or lush sappy growth, vulnerable to disease, will result, and do not attempt to feed pears until they have started fruiting regularly.

## THINNING

Trees often set far too many fruits, and these will need thinning to ensure good size and discourage biennial cropping (the alternation between glut and scarcity). Some of the fruitlets in each cluster will drop naturally during June; others that swell precociously after attack by pear midges will also fall about this time (always gather and destroy any immature fallen fruits as these may contain midge larvae). Thin those that remain to leave one from every cluster if the very best dessert fruit is required; otherwise thin to two at each site.

## PRUNING

Fruits are borne on permanent spurs, which are usually produced in great numbers and may therefore need thinning out occasionally; long

*Summer pruning side shoots to five to six leaves, and then to two buds in winter, is essential on trained trees.*

elderly spurs can be cut back to half their length in winter. Routine pruning of trained forms is simple: allow the main branches to extend, cutting off the end 7-10cm (3-4in) each winter, until they reach their required length when their tips are treated in the same way as fruiting spurs. Shoots arising from spurs are cut back to five to six leaves in July, and then in winter shortened to one or two buds. Standard and half-standard trees need little pruning beyond removal of dead or crossing branches and the thinning of overgrown spurs.

## HARVEST AND STORAGE

Pears picked too early will shrivel in store; too late and they will be dry or 'sleepy' (brown near the core). The right time to pick depends on variety and season; the most reliable guide is to lift one or two of the fruits until they are horizontal, when they should part from the stem with minimal pressure. Late-ripening varieties should be left as long as possible on trees. Gather fruit carefully, when dry. Store undamaged fruit only, spread out in single layers on shelves in a cool, dark, airy cupboard or shed that is safe from frost. A crop will not ripen all at once and may take between a few days and several weeks; check them regularly, and as they begin to colour bring a few at a time into the warmth of the home, where they will develop their full flavour.

---

# PLUM

**Season:** mid-July to October.

**Life:** 50 years and more if disease free.

**Yield:** 18-45 kg (40-100lb) or more from a mature tree, less from fans.

Some varieties are self-fertile and give good crops on their own; others need a pollen partner with the same flowering season.

Plums are often neglected in modern gardens because they are reputed to produce large trees, difficult to prune and susceptible to pests and diseases. In Britain gardeners who do plant plums usually choose Victoria, an admirable dual-purpose variety and conveniently self-fertile, but highly vulnerable to silver leaf, which often strikes when its overladen branches break. There are, however, dozens of superior dessert plums which, grafted on a semi-dwarfing rootstock such as Pixy, will occupy much less room and require less skilled management than varieties on more vigorous stocks. In America the most popular plum is Stanley, a European variety, which is grown with good results. On the west coast of the United States Japanese varieties are the best adapted, but many different types can be grown in the east.

## VARIETIES

**European types** are characterized by oval, usually purple fruit with firmer, less juicy flesh. The easiest to grow in northern areas, particularly the north-east. Prune plums have particularly high sugar and low water content for drying. At least partially self-fertile. Zones 5-8. Train free-standing trees to form an upright central trunk.

**Earliblue:** similar to Stanley but ripens a month earlier. Later bloom reduces frost danger. Good flavour with soft flesh, freestone. Self-fertile. Late July.

**Mount Royal:** the best for northern areas such as northern Wisconsin. Prune type with good flavour for dessert or canning. Purple skin, freestone. Extremely hardy to zone 4.

**Stanley:** the best-known variety. Prune type. Excellent for eating fresh, canning or drying. Purple skin with golden flesh, freestone. Recommended for the north-east, mid-west and upper south. Early September.

**Japanese types** are round and juicy with black, red, or yellow fruit. Clingstone. Take southern summer heat better. Some have very low winter chilling requirements. Not self-pollinating. Zones 6-9, warmer parts of zone 5.

**Red Heart:** large, juicy, red oval fruit with red flesh. Use fresh, canned or in preserves. Early August. Pollinate with Shiro or Starking Delicious.

**Shiro:** golden plum for eating fresh or canning. Good flavour variety. Ready late July. Pollinate with Red Heart or Starking Delicious.

**Starking Delicious:** purple-red with red flesh. Juicy, good flavour, clingstone. Disease resistant. Early August. Pollinate with Shiro or Red Heart.

---

**American hybrids** are bred for hardiness from the very hardy American bush plum and Japanese varieties. Developed in Minnesota. Zones 4-8. These plums are trained so that they have an open centre as seen in peach and apple trees.

**Ember Golden:** yellow blushed orange red. Good for eating fresh but even better for canning. Mid-August. Pollinate with Underwood.

**Underwood:** red skin with yellow flesh. Good dessert quality. Ready late July. Pollinate with Ember.

---

### Rootstocks
Myrobalan 29C and Marianna 2624 – most commonly used. Vigorous and in good soil make a large tree unless regularly pruned. Resistant to root knot nematode.

*Prunus besseyi:* dwarfing stock, restricting most varieties to about 2.75m (9ft) tall. Ideal for containers or small gardens, and is very hardy but requires staking for support. Permits closer spacing than St Julien A.

## OTHER PLUMS

Damsons and cherry plums are all worth growing in gardens, often succeeding in districts too cold for large-fruited varieties. Damsons are extremely hardy and make tough wind-breaks or hedge trees, and small specimen trees that blend well amongst herbaceous flowers. The richly flavoured fruit, like long black cherries, is used for cooking or wine. Very attractive in flower and mostly self-fertile, they are excellent pollen sources for larger plum varieties. Best – **Merryweather** with the largest fruit, ripe late September; **Shropshire Damson/Shropshire Prune**, a compact tree with the best flavoured fruit, ready October. Both these damson trees are hardy to zones 5-8 in the USA.

Cherry, or Myrobalan, plum is a species, *Prunus cerasifera*, with small crops of well-flavoured red or yellow fruits like large cherries in August. Highly ornamental in bloom early in the season. Easily propagated from cuttings, it is often used for rootstocks and for tough impenetrable hedges that can be clipped formally. Zones 4-8.

The small-fruited American bush plums and sand cherries do not fruit well in Britain, although in the USA they are particularly useful in difficult climates and are worth including in small gardens. The bush plum (*P. americana*) is hardy in zone 4 but will grow as far south as Florida. The beach plum (*P. maritima*) thrives along the New England coast. The sand cherry (*P. besseyi*) is hardy to zone 3 and thrives in the difficult climate of the great plains. Useful for making syrups and preserves, they are generally rather too acid to be eaten as dessert.

## ORNAMENTAL VALUE
As standards and half-standards on vigorous roots plums make handsome orchard and hedgerow trees. Grafted on Pixy or *Prunus besseyi* they seldom exceed 2-2.5m (6-8ft)high and can be included within flowerbeds as compact bushes or small specimen trees with a graceful, slightly weeping habit and a spectacular display of blossom in early spring. They can be trained against walls as fans, or as espaliers and cordons (both forms too restrictive for the more energetic St Julien A rootstocks).

*A plum fan, heavily mulched with compost and trained on wires, with canes to support the young branches. This form is very productive and ornamental, especially on a wall, but demands careful pruning.*

## SITES
Plums tolerate various soil types, although they resent drought and like other stone fruits must have a good supply of lime. Trees flourish on well-drained clay. They like a light airy position, but the early blossom requires shelter from late frosts. In Britain cooking varieties will grow on east walls or in the open, and usually succeed better in cooler areas than dessert kinds, which in northern gardens are best

*Where there is room, standard plum trees can bear enormous crops without much attention, although pruning and thinning always improves the quality of the fruit.*

grown against south- or west-facing walls. In the USA European plums are hardy further north but south and west walls should be avoided as this would add to the danger of precocious flowering coinciding with late frost; Japanese and hybrid varieties will tolerate summer heat further south in the USA. Avoid sites where frequent cultivation may injure the wide-ranging surface roots, with recurrent suckering as the result.

### SOIL PREPARATION
Break up heavy clay, and enrich light soils – plums are greedy feeders and welcome liberal manuring. Top-dress more acid soils with garden lime up to 500g/sq m (1lb/sq yd) after thoroughly burying any manure.

### PLANTING
Autumn is best, otherwise early spring (best in the USA, except in the south). Spread out

horizontal roots fully, and firmly tread the replaced soil, on light ground even ramming it with a length of stout timber. Stake or tie in place, and mulch with well-rotted manure. On St Julien A rootstock plant bushes 3.5m (12ft), fans and large trees 4.5-5.5m (15-18ft) apart (in the USA plant standard trees on Myrobalan and Marianna rootstocks 4.5-5.5m/15-18ft apart, and fans at a similar distance); space plums on Pixy or *P. besseyi* two-thirds of those distances.

### CULTIVATION
Free-standing trees, especially on Pixy, will need support for five or six years; but those on *P. besseyi* may need it permanently: check stakes and ties annually. Plums competing with weeds suffer up to 50 per cent reduction in growth in the first two years; keep the ground clear by hoeing and mulching until cropping is regular. Remove suckers, clearing soil away and pulling them off at their source. Every third or fourth year lime the soil at 125g/sq m (4oz/sq yd). In dry weather water wall-trained trees freely and regularly, otherwise fruit might drop prematurely or suffer cracking later. Support heavily laden branches to prevent breakage.

### THINNING AND PRUNING
Heavy crops left unthinned produce small plums, many of which may fail to ripen. In June remove misshapen fruits and those at the centre of clusters. Later in the month some immature plums are shed naturally; afterwards thin the remainder to 5-7cm (2-3in) apart, or on free-standing trees simply break off the end third of long side shoots.

Annual pruning of larger trees is simple: in spring remove branches that cross or overcrowd the framework; then in June or July cut out entirely elderly or vigorously upright branches. Pinch shoots of restricted forms such as bushes or pyramids back to five to six new leaves in summer. On wall-trained trees, rub off misplaced buds or shoots at an early stage, and

in summer pinch back long, new side shoots to five to six leaves, shortening them again by half the following spring.

Older trees that seem to have stopped growing can be cut hard back, training resulting growth into a new framework of branches. Reduce the risk of disease by pruning only in spring and up to midsummer.

### HARVEST
Few varieties hang for long once ripe. Check regularly when fruits develop a bloom and begin to feel soft. They will part readily from their stalks when ready; plums to be kept for a few days should be picked or cut with their stalks. Shake cooking varieties from the branches on to a thick mulch of grass clippings. Clear all fruits at the end of the season to prevent a carryover of disease.

## RASPBERRY

| | |
|---|---|
| **Season:** | July until frosts. |
| **Life:** | 10-20 years or more. |
| **Yield:** | 225-340g (8-12oz) per plant, according to variety. |
| Self-fertile. | |

Many classic raspberry varieties have died out or been superseded because of susceptibility to virus diseases, a threat even where modern kinds are grown; with reasonable care, however, stocks can be kept clean and productive for many years. By planting a dozen canes each of two or three varieties, together with a reliable autumn raspberry, small gardens can produce a long succession of fruit.

### VARIETIES
The best up-to-date raspberries combine flavour with robust constitution; older varieties

are still worth planting if they come from virus-free stocks. Golden varieties have a distinctive and delicious taste, as do black raspberries.

## Red and yellow raspberries

**Fallgold:** yellow. Autumn-bearing, sweet golden fruit. Long bearing season. North-eastern states to mid-south. Zones 4-8.

**Heritage:** red. Autumn-bearing – probably one of the best. Large mild-flavoured berries. Strong upright canes. Adapted to north-east, north-west and north central states. Zones 4-8.

**Latham:** red. Summer-bearing. Very large fruit, best for canning and freezing. Vigorous, and nearly thornless. Disease prone. North-eastern states and mid-south. Zones 3-8.

**Southland:** red. Autumn-bearing. Adapted to more southern areas than other raspberries. Medium-size berries with good tart flavour. Disease resistant. Zones 5-8, parts of 9.

## Black and purple raspberries

**Black Hawk:** black. Early, large berries good for freezing. Vigorous and drought-resistant. Resistant to Anthracnose. Zones 5-8.

**Cumberland:** black. Mid-season. Large fruit. Reliable bearer, but susceptible to anthracnose and virus diseases. Pacific north-west and north-eastern states. Zones 5-8.

**Royalty:** purple. Hybrid between red and black raspberries. Resistant to insects and virus. Highly recommended new variety. Zones 4-8.

## ORNAMENTAL VALUE
Neat rows, tied to wires or wooden trellis, make precise divisions within gardens or allotments, and slim hedges beside paths; strawberries, herbs and short annual flowers will flourish at their feet. Elsewhere, groups of canes can be

*Flowering shoots developing on a row of summer-fruiting raspberries* (left), *with next season's replacement canes starting to grow at ground level. Autumn varieties extend the season until the first frosts; these 'Heritage' fruits* (top) *were photographed in October.*

tied up to central stakes or arched outwards to a ring of canes. Fruits of all types are decorative against their contrasting fresh green foliage.

## SITES
A sunny or lightly shaded position on rich soil, moist but freely drained, is essential. Raspberries are a cool climate fruit, very hardy and reliable in northern gardens, and they resent heat and drought. Plants flourish on heavier ground if well prepared, but can be unthrifty on alkaline soils. Shelter black and yellow varieties from cold winds.

## SOIL PREPARATION
Break up heavy ground thoroughly and ensure drainage is efficient; lighter soils need bulky organic material generously worked in. Remove perennial weeds to avoid root disturbance later.

## PLANTING
New canes usually have an L-shaped root, along which new growth will emerge. Plant in November (early spring in the USA) 5-7 cm (2-3in) deep 38-45cm (15-18in) apart, pointing the horizontal root along the row. Cut canes back to 15cm (6in) high after planting.

## CULTIVATION
Future crops depend on vigorous renewal growth. Encourage this by mulching annually with manure, compost or a thick layer of grass mowings. Water generously during prolonged dry weather as fruit ripens. Digging or forking out weeds may disturb the roots: hoe, or mulch and hand weed instead. Pull up unwanted suckers emerging far from the plants. Also pull up and burn any unthrifty plants to reduce risk of virus infection.

## HARVEST

A ripe raspberry parts readily from its core, or 'plug'; pick with great care to avoid crushing less firm varieties. Since wet fruit rapidly decays, gather only when dry – in a wet season, snip off rotting fruit to confine the spread of infection.

## PRUNING

Autumn-fruiting varieties bear on the current year's growth; cut fruited canes to the ground each year in late winter and tie the new canes in place as they grow. Prune other kinds

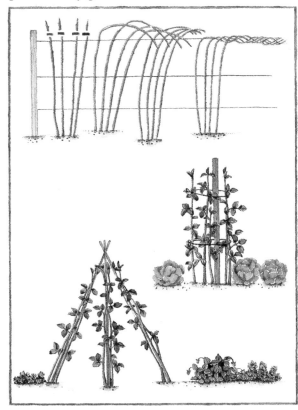

*Examples of some ways to support raspberries. The tops of plants tied to wire (top) are cut to height, bent in arcs or woven along the top wire. Groups can be cut to varying heights and tied to a central stake (centre), or they may be trained up a tripod of canes.*

immediately after harvest, cutting fruited canes to ground level. After leaf fall, tie in their place the strongest of the new canes, thinning them to 10-15cm (4-6in) apart in rows and shortening alternate canes (see **Pruning and Training**, p. 62). Excessively tall canes may be trimmed to height, or their tops arched over and tied to the top of the support. Both summer and autumn crops can be achieved in a small garden from the same autumn-fruiting variety by pruning a proportion of the canes as if they were a summer-bearing type, but this system is demanding and the plants may need extra feeding.

# RED AND WHITE CURRANT

**Season:** July – October.

**Life:** 30 years or more.

**Yield:** cordons, up to 500g (1lb); bushes and fans, 2-3kg (4-6lb).

Self-fertile.

Red and white currants are ideal fruits for home cultivation. In shops they are either scarce or very expensive – white varieties especially – even though most seasons the plants give heavy and consistent crops. Hardy, long-lived and tolerant of most garden positions, they can be trained easily into a number of productive and decorative forms, making maximum use of a small space. Although variants of the same fruit, red and white kinds have distinct flavours, and both are highly valued as refreshing summer fruits.

## VARIETIES

Growth habit is variable, as are seed size and the thickness of skins. They grow best in the northern half of North America where summers are cool, zones 3-5, but can grow as far south as

the mid-Atlantic states. Although less susceptible to white pine blister rust (see p.24), they are still seldom seen and are banned in some areas.

**Red Lake:** light red. Mid-season to late. Most widely offered variety. Large fruit in clusters makes picking easy. Upright plant. North-east, mid-west, northern California.

**White Grape:** large, mild flavour. Good cropper.

**White Imperial:** large berries, almost sweet in flavour. Spreading growth habit.

## ORNAMENTAL VALUE

Currants are some of the most beautiful garden fruits with their handsome palmate leaves and long bunches of glowing scarlet or pearl white berries. In the sixteenth century they were popular for edging herb and vegetable beds. For this purpose bushes grown on clear legs are ideal, perhaps with prostrate herbs beneath; or rows of vertical cordons could be used, grown to 150-180cm (5-6ft) tall from cuttings inserted direct – a 'fence' of these with strawberries along its base might edge a patio or path. Half-standards on 90cm (3ft) stems will stand clear

*A young red currant in its second year of training as a fan, the rapid growth of its main branches encouraged by a thick mulch of spoiled hay.*

above bushy herbs or flowering perennials of intermediate height. The ripe fruit is particularly attractive hanging like miniature bunches of grapes on oblique cordons, fans or espaliers against walls.

## SITES
Except for damp or heavy ground, any ordinary fertile garden soil is suitable in sun or partial shade. As the wood is brittle, some shelter from strong wind is advisable. Crops on walls mature in succession according to aspect, starting with plants which are facing south; fruit ripens last on north walls and hangs there for the longest time in good condition, often for a month or more.

## SOIL PREPARATION
Dig heavy ground to a good tilth. Add plenty of well-rotted manure or decayed leaves to sandy soils, together with a generous dressing of bonfire ashes or 125g/sq m (4oz/sq yd) rock potash, as plants are sensitive to potash deficiency.

## PLANTING
Plant in autumn or spring, 2-2.5m (6-8ft) apart for fans, bushes 120-150cm (4-5ft), cordons 30-45cm (12-18in). Make sure bushes have a clear leg several inches high; shorter stems can be lengthened by cleaning off some of the roots, leaving only the lowest. Plant firmly, and prevent wind damage by securing promptly.

## CULTIVATION
Currants fruit on short spurs carried by a permanent framework of older branches: plants should therefore be fed for fruit, not for new wood. Every third or fourth spring mulch with thoroughly decayed manure, but use bone-meal 90g/sq m (3oz/sq yd) in intervening years and mulch with compost or lawn mowings. Plants particularly dislike drought while maturing their crops.

*Red currants and red gooseberries growing as colourful companions with vegetables and flowers* (above). *Both red and white currants fruit on side shoots which are best kept short by pruning them in both summer and winter* (below).

## PRUNING
For consistent heavy crops prune in summer as well as winter each year. In June or July shorten new side growth to 4-5 leaves; in addition to checking growth this will admit sunlight to the ripening fruit, but on hot walls fruit will keep in condition longer if pruning is deferred until after picking. Leave extension growth on the ends of branches intact. In winter prune both terminal and side shoots back close to their base to keep the spurs compact. Remove dead or exhausted branches in winter, leaving unpruned a suitable replacement.

## HARVEST
Gather fruits while dry and before they become too ripe to handle easily. Pick entire bunches and strip the currants from them later with a table fork.

# RHUBARB

**Season:** April (earlier forced) – September.

**Life:** 10-15 years before division.

**Yield:** up to 2-2.5 kg (4-5lb) from a mature crown, much less forced.

Self-fertile.

With the wide availability of imported fruit all the year round, rhubarb has lost some of its former popularity as the first garden 'fruit' of the season. Nevertheless, it has much to commend its cultivation: plants are permanent and virtually indestructible, and since it is the leaf stems which are gathered, there is no need for pruning or pollination. Rhubarb has a sufficiently dramatic appearance to merit room as an herbaceous ornamental. Its season is long, especially if mature crowns are forced into early production of tender juicy sticks. Later pickings are delicious cooked with elderflowers and sweet cicely (see p. 95).

## VARIETIES

The natural season normally starts between late March and early May, lasting until July, when most varieties become unpalatably acid.

**Cherry Red:** heavy red stalks of sweet flavour. This variety is adapted to regions which have mild winters.

**McDonald:** bright red stalks with tender skin which makes peeling unnecessary. Possibly the sweetest flavoured rhubarb variety.

**Valentine:** heavy deep red stalks of good quality. Sweet flavour.

**Victoria:** an old standard variety with green stalks shaded red. Tart flavour. Also available from seed.

All zones 4-8.

*All too often clumps of rhubarb languish in otherwise unproductive corners. The large, crinkled leaves, however, have a bold, fresh appearance and deserve more prominent siting, beside paths, or a garden pool.*

## ORNAMENTAL VALUE

Rhubarb is outstanding as a lush accent or foliage plant, with thick green or red stems and large, deep green, wavy leaves often a metre across. The stout spikes of creamy white flowers are spectacular, sometimes 2-2.5m (7-8ft) high and long-lasting. Well-fed and watered crowns make handsome specimens 2m (7ft) across in tubs or large containers, or for planting beneath flowering and fruiting trees.

## SITES

Rhubarb needs to grow undisturbed for many years. Any deep fertile ground is suitable, in full sun or partial shade. For early crops, choose a warm corner sheltered from cold winds. In America it grows best in northern areas with cool summers and cold winters.

## SOIL PREPARATION

Dig the soil 60cm (2ft) deep, working in as much rotted manure as possible: the richer the soil, the better the quality of the sticks. Heavy ground must be well drained, while sandy soil liable to dry out quickly needs large quantities of moisture retentive humus.

## SOWING

Varieties raised from seed are sown outdoors in March, very thinly in drills 2.5cm (1in) deep. Thin the seedlings to leave the strongest 23-30cm (9-12in) apart, and grow on until February.

## PLANTING

Plant one-year-old seedlings or bought crowns 90cm (3ft) apart in February, providing each plant with a hole large enough to take the root comfortably and cover the tops with 5cm (2in) of soil. Firm around the plants, taking care not to injure the tops with their dormant buds. Mulch with manure after planting.

## CULTIVATION

Do not pull sticks the first season after planting, with the exception of Glaskin's Perpetual, strong specimens of which may yield one or two sticks when only 6 months old. In the second season a few sticks may be taken, but stop pulling at the end of July; the following year crowns may be cropped freely. Mulch each spring with manure, and water liberally in dry weather. For optimum crops remove flower stems as they appear; otherwise cut them as flowers fade and before seed is produced.

## FORCING

The simplest way to advance crops by 2-4 weeks is to cover each established crown, in January after mulching, with a special forcing pot, a wooden tea-chest or a wigwam of canes enclosed in a sheet of black plastic. For even earlier sticks, dig up three year-old crowns in November and leave exposed to frost for a fortnight. Then pack in moist soil in wooden boxes under greenhouse staging; or lay them on the floor and cover with old potting compost. Exclude all light beneath the staging with curtains of sacking (burlap). After harvesting, the crowns are useless.

## HARVEST
Pull sticks by grasping them near the base and pressing them outwards, at the same time giving a sharp twist to one side. Always leave 3-4 stems on each crown to avoid over-cropping and so weakening them. Cut off the green leaves and spread as a temporary mulch, or use to prepare a fungicide.

# STRAWBERRY

**Season:** maincrop – June and July (May to September with cloches).

perpetual/everbearing/remontant/autumn-fruiting – August until first frosts.

alpines – June to October.

**Life:** individual plants are best cropped for 3-4 years, and then replaced.

**Yield:** average 450kg (1lb) per plant (alpines much less); new varieties 1.8-2.2kg (4-5lb).

Probably the most popular of all garden fruits, strawberries grow readily in almost any situation, and provided care is taken to buy and maintain healthy plants, stocks can last for decades with regular propagation from runners. Health is important: beds in gardens are often allowed to decline through virus infections, which are the commonest cause of trouble and the most likely reason for the disappearance of so many earlier kinds (in 1870 for example

American varieties were listed with the flavours of apricot, pineapple, raspberry, grape and cherry, all of which seem to be lost). Only plants certified free from viruses should be bought.

The largest berries are usually carried on two-year-old plants, which will often bear their heaviest crop the following year, although individual berries will then be smaller. Successive generations are produced from runners to replace plants whose yield falls after three or four years. June-bearing varieties produce their only crop in summer and have high yields. Perpetual (everbearing) varieties have moderate crops in June, then crop again after a short pause, continuing through late summer and autumn. Alternatively, the early flowers can be picked off to reserve energy for a much heavier production of fruit in autumn.

In the United States the newly developed day-neutral varieties bloom and produce runners continuously regardless of day length, although high summer temperatures may reduce flowering; the yields on these varieties are quite high.

Alpine strawberries are less widely grown, although their distinctive flavour is uniquely concentrated and enhanced by a strong perfume. Referring to this kind, William Butler wrote in the sixteenth century: 'Doubtless God could have made a better berry, but doubtless God never did.' Although their soft dry fruits are little larger than wild strawberries, the bushy plants crop heavily over a long season and tend to be less prone to attacks by pests and diseases than large-fruited kinds.

## VARIETIES
With modern strawberry cultivars high yield and disease resistance are usually higher priorities than flavour. In wetter districts choose naturally upright varieties that hold their flower and fruit trusses clear of the ground. Selection of varieties bred for regional conditions is important for success.

**Alpine strawberries**
**Alexandria:** good crops of small fruit, bright red and juicy. Excellent flavour. Compact upright plant. No runners.

**Reugen Improved:** a newer richer variety.

**June-bearing strawberries**
**Cardinal:** mid-season. Medium to large red berries with red flesh and a long neck. Use fresh or frozen. Resistant to disease and spider mites. Warm southern Pacific and Gulf states.

**Catskill:** mid-season. Firm, glossy, dark red berries on vigorous productive plants. Dessert, freezing. Northern central, north-eastern states.

**Earliglow:** very early. Shining red berries with excellent sweet flavour. Eastern central states.

**Fairfax:** early to mid-season. Excellent flavour. Hardy variety for north central, north-east.

**Guardian:** mid-season. Disease resistant variety with large glossy red berries. Eastern states.

**Red Chief:** early. Medium to large deep red berries. Dessert, freezing and canning. Disease resistant. Eastern states.

**Sunrise:** early. Glossy light red berries with pale flesh of good flavour. Disease resistant and drought tolerant. Widely adapted to mid-eastern states, south-western and Gulf states.

**Surecrop:** mid-season. Dependable and disease resistant. Fair quality, good for freezing and canning. Mid-west and central Appalachia.

**Everbearing strawberries**
**Ogallala:** hardy and disease resistant. Medium-size dark red berries with good flavour. Freezes well. Hardy enough for the northern plains and Rocky Mountain states.

**Ozark Beauty:** bright red skin and flesh with good flavour. Vigorous, with many runners. Good in eastern states.

**Day-neutral strawberry:**
**Tristar:** bears fruit continuously, even on runners before they have rooted. Excellent for hanging baskets. Medium-sized berries. Good quality and flavour. Widely adapted.

## ORNAMENTAL VALUE

Most strawberry varieties form neat plants with attractive rich green foliage. Apart from conventional cultivation in rows or beds, they can be grown in pots, strawberry jars and even hanging baskets. They are very productive and decorative planted on banks or terraces, where the fruit receives full sun and can hang clear of the ground.

Alpine varieties have smaller more numerous leaves and make large compact bushes ideal for edging beds, paths or paved areas; or for mixing with shorter flowers such as bushy nasturtiums, phacelia, violets or primroses. Most do not produce runners and therefore remain tidy with low maintenance. As they do not mind partial shade, they can be grown beneath fruit bushes and shrubs.

## SITES

All strawberries prefer soil that is rich in humus and does not dry out in summer; however, wet or heavy land is not suitable without improvement. On chalky ground plants may turn yellow and refuse to thrive. While alpine strawberries enjoy the light shade of woodland conditions, large-fruited kinds prefer full sun: this is essential if early varieties are to crop their best. The early blossom is susceptible to frost damage, and where spring is regularly cold, plants are best sited on the highest part of the garden or close to the shelter of warm walls.

*While strawberries are usually grown in rows, they are equally fruitful when used as a form of carpet bedding, leaving the runners to root amongst the parent plants. Such patches are easy to net when fruiting, and look attractive throughout the growing season.*

*Alpine strawberries make ideal ground cover beneath flowering plants and climbers.*

Where cold, dry winters are common, a winter mulch such as straw or salt hay is essential for survival of the crowns, but there is a danger in wetter climates of the crowns rotting.

## SOIL PREPARATION
More than most other fruits, strawberries prefer organic to chemical cultivation. Plenty of humus is necessary in the form of rotted manure, garden compost or decayed leaves: it is better to enrich the ground for the full life of the plants than to add manure in following seasons. Thoroughly break up heavy ground and make sure drainage is efficient. Since strawberries prefer slightly acid soil, it is worth dressing planting positions with an inch of peat, together with 60g/sq m (2oz/sq yd) bone - meal, lightly forking this into the surface. Do all preparations at least a month before planting, as strawberries will not establish easily in soft ground that has not settled. Never plant where strawberries have been grown recently.

## PLANTING
Plant between July and October, or March to April, using home-grown runners or bought plants (either bare-rooted or best of all pot-grown). Runners or new stock planted from July to September will be sufficiently well rooted to bear crops the following summer. Plants set out in October or early spring should not be allowed to flower the first summer, with the exception of perpetual (everbearing) varieties which crop lightly the first autumn.

In the United States, except in the far south, plant commercially obtained stock (which will generally be supplied bare-root) in March or April. Home-grown plants from runners are planted mid- to late summer.

It is a mistake to crowd strawberries – space single plants 45cm (18in) apart, or, if stocking a larger bed, plant in groups of three, 60cm (2ft) apart, with 30cm (1ft) between individual plants. Alpines need only two-thirds these distances.

Tread the ground firm if it is light or recently prepared. Using a trowel make holes large enough to spread out roots to their fullest extent. Plant very firmly, keeping the neck at surface level: strawberries rot if planted deeply, while shallow planting leaves them vulnerable to drought and frost disturbance. On heavy or wet ground it is sometimes an advantage to mould up the soil like potato ridges and plant on top of these.

## EXTENDING THE SEASON

Crops may be brought forward by 3-4 weeks if plants are covered with cloches in February. Keep them protected until the first flowers appear, when they should be uncovered on warm days to allow pollination; in very hot weather remove the cloches altogether to avoid excessively high temperatures. Ventilating plants as berries develop will encourage air circulation and prevent mildew. Autumn-fruiting varieties can be covered with cloches in September to prolong their season by a month or two. In southern California and Florida, crowns preserved in cold store until needed are often planted in autumn to give winter crops.

*Large-fruited strawberry varieties have always been popular as pot plants, either for forcing out of season under glass, or as here grown in special strawberry pots.*

## CULTIVATION

Immediately after planting, and later as the strawberries grow, hoe around the plants but never closer than 7-10cm (3-4in) from the crowns lest their shallow roots are injured. Tread firm any plants which have been loosened by winter frosts. In very cold districts it is worth covering the plants with straw, drawing it away as the weather improves. Mulch every April with peat.

Strawberries are usually cropped for three or four years, taking runners from the best young plants to replace older stock as its vigour declines. Plants intended to crop in their first summer should have their runners removed until they have finished fruiting; later plantings are best disbudded for their first season but can be allowed to produce runners.

To protect ripening berries on large-fruited varieties from soil splashes, mulch with peat, tuck straw or dry leaves around the plants while still in flower, or use special strawberry mats beneath the trusses of fruit. Where only a few plants are grown, maturing berries can be tucked inside jam jars, laid on the ground and slightly tilted to prevent any water from accumulating inside; these will help to shield the berries from persistent rain and also from birds. Elsewhere, plants must be covered with netting supported clear of the plants by wire hoops or canes to protect them from birds; where these are a real menace, the normally immune alpine varieties may also need protection.

Plants need to be consistently moist while fruiting; water well in dry weather, although if the ground has been prepared with plenty of humus this may not be necessary. After fruiting, remove the older leaves either by clipping with shears or by running a rotary mower, set to cut 7-10cm (3-4in) high, along the rows; clear away these leaves, surplus runners and any straw or other loose mulching material for composting.

*Even when tucked amongst annual flowers, strawberries are easily netted over wire hoops.*

Any plants that develop stunted, persistently crinkled or yellow mottled leaves should be dug up and burnt, as the secret of success lies in maintaining good health and vigour.

## HARVEST

Check daily for ripe fruit, gathering these when fully coloured and dry. Nip them off complete with plug and a piece of stem, taking care that adjacent immature fruits are not accidentally pulled off at the same time. Alpine strawberries are picked without their plugs and will hang for longer without deteriorating. Fruits left to become over-ripe or any decaying after wet weather are best removed to prevent infecting other berries.

## FORCING STRAWBERRIES

By starting with runners rooted in July and grown on in pots, early strawberries can be ready for picking in April in a warm greenhouse or conservatory, a few weeks later in an unheated house. A naturally early variety should be used, although some may tend to develop botrytis under glass unless well ventilated.

Either dig up earliest established plantlets for potting, or root runners direct into small pots plunged to their rims in the ground (at first secure the runners with wire pegs or weight them down with stones). Once the small pots are filled with roots, transfer each plant to a 12 or 15cm (5 or 6in) pot and leave outdoors on a hard surface or, where severe frost may be a problem, buried up to the rim.

Water whenever necessary and pinch off any runners or precocious flower buds that start to form. In early January bring the strawberries indoors after first cleaning the pots and removing any dead leaves, weeds or surface moss. Position them where they receive as much light as possible. For the first month merely keep plants free of frost; the temperature may then be raised to an overnight minimum of 7°C (45°F) to force earliest crops.

The flowers will need to be fertilized: as they open, lightly dust their centres with a ball of cotton wool or a soft paint brush. Feed plants every week as their fruit develops; expose them to full sun and thin to leave the first three or four fruits on each truss. Arrange the ripening trusses to hang over the sides of the pots or support them clear of the potting mixture with thin forked twigs. When they have finished fruiting, plant outdoors for a possible second crop late in the season.

# MAKING FRUIT COMFORTABLE

## SOIL

Good fruit trees and bushes are not cheap to buy, but with care will crop for years and repay the investment many times over. It is important to give them a flying start in life by paying a little attention to preliminary soil preparation. This need not be arduous work, especially since soft fruit and dwarfing rootstocks are relatively shallow-rooted and will grow well wherever vegetables and herbaceous perennials flourish. In most cases it is enough to prepare individual planting holes, as are described in the separate fruit entries.

Drainage must be efficient, for no fruit tolerates waterlogged ground. Where subsoils are heavy, break up the bottom of planting holes with a fork and work in generous quantities of coarse or gritty materials such as sand, crushed brick rubble, cinders or twiggy garden compost. Never discard surplus turf: torn into large pieces, its fibrous texture is ideal for opening heavy soil and encouraging root development. Mix compost, peat or partly decayed leaves into heavy topsoils when planting (replacing the soil with a lighter proprietary tree-planting compost merely creates a soakaway into which water will drain from the surrounding ground).

Although most kinds of fruit need lime in the soil, problems can arise in very alkaline ground or shallow soils above chalk. Here there is a case for replacing the material excavated from planting holes with better quality soil, but where this is not practicable, work in large amounts of peat and decayed leaves, and give an annual top-dressing of these in autumn, gently forking them into the soil around the plants. Most other soils will benefit from liming, especially if stone fruit is to be planted; old mortar rubble is ideal but seldom to be found

*Soft fruit, such as red or white currants and gooseberries (left) are easy to grow as standards, a traditional form that makes a very unusual and graceful addition to any garden. Because the fruiting branches are produced at the top of a clear single stem, the plants cast little shade. Flowers, herbs or vegetables, such as these maincrop onions and ornamental cabbages, can be planted beneath standards without the risk of malformed growth from lack of light. Standard soft fruits usually need permanent support, as here, with a cane or stake, and where wind is a problem it may also be advisable to prevent heavily-laden branches from breaking by resting them on a simple wooden frame or stout wire ring attached to the supporting stake. Prune and feed standards in the same way as for normal bushes, but rub off any side shoots that start to appear on the main stem, especially with gooseberries which are usually grafted at the top of a vigorous Ribes aureum stem.*

these days, and the best alternative is to mix in 250g/sq m (8oz/sq yd) of garden lime before planting (check individual fruit entries for specific requirements).

For general soil conditioning and improvement, see p.171.

## ASPECT

Before choosing kinds and varieties of fruit, consider the character of the proposed site at each season. Most fruits need full sun to ripen crops and the fruiting wood for the following year, although some, such as gooseberries, will tolerate shade and do well even planted beneath fruit trees. Cold winds at flowering time may affect yields of certain fruits: black-berries, for example, withstand considerably more exposed sites than loganberries. Some varieties are more resilient than others and crop more reliably where wind is a problem; alternatively, consider using other fruit and shrubs as wind-breaks.

Shelter may also be needed from spring frosts, which can severely damage blossom. Comparatively frost-resistant varieties of most fruits are available, and it would be sensible to choose these in regularly affected gardens. However, the risk may be reduced or eliminated altogether by avoiding known frost hollows, by siting susceptible fruit near the house or a warm wall, or by growing the tree trained on a wall rather than as a free-standing specimen. Plant near the top of sloping sites, because frost tends to move downhill and may linger there if its path is blocked by a garden wall or hedge.

## PLANTING

Fruit with bare roots is planted while dormant, preferably in late autumn, although it is better to wait until spring if winters are normally very cold. Container-grown fruit can in theory be planted any time of the year, but much more care is needed with watering specimens planted while in active growth. Do not plant any kind of

fruit during hot dry weather, nor when the ground is frozen or waterlogged. If bare-rooted trees cannot be planted straight away, either lay them in a shallow trench and completely cover the roots with soil, or in severe weather keep them in a shed, covering their roots with peat, leaves or a damp sack.

When planting, always dig a hole about one and a half times the width and depth of the root ball. Break up the excavated soil, and also the bottom of the hole if it is solid. Remove the pots from container-grown plants, and spread out some of the larger roots; cleanly trim any that are torn on bare-rooted stock. Holding the plant upright in the centre of the hole, replace the soil, settling it between the roots by gently shaking the plant occasionally. Tread the soil firmly in place. Level the surface, making sure it coincides with the depth at which the plant previously grew, and leave the top few centimetres loose. Watering will not be necessary if trees are dormant; otherwise, give a good soak after planting.

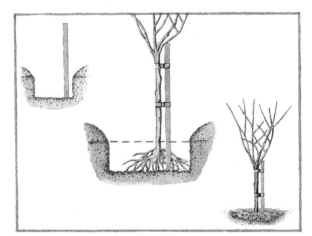

(top) *Always excavate a hole larger than the root ball of the tree or bush, and drive in supporting stakes before planting.* (centre) *Plant the tree at the depth at which it grew previously, and evenly spread out the roots to each side.* (bottom) *After planting, tie the tree to its stake, level the soil and mulch.*

*Three possible methods of support. Proprietary tree ties (left) are adjustable and incorporate a protective buffer between the tree and its stake. Stout twine is acceptable (centre) if abrasion is prevented by two or three thicknesses of hessian sacking (burlap). As a simple alternative (right) old nylon tights are both strong and elastic.*

## SUPPORT

While bushes can be planted without any additional support, trees and trained soft fruit will need staking, permanently for those on very dwarfing rootstocks, and for the first two or three years for others, until well rooted. Always put a stake in place before planting a tree, to avoid injuring the roots. Secure its stem to the top of the stake and again halfway down, using proprietary straps; stout string may be used instead if soft protective material is first wound round the stem and also wedged between tree and stake. Check annually to loosen or re-secure ties as the tree grows.

Fruit grown against walls will need to be tied with weatherproof twine, either to a wooden trellis firmly attached to the wall, or to horizontal wires 30-38cm (12-15in) apart and threaded through vine eyes or wall nails driven into plugs in the mortar joints. When training stems vertically or as a fan, secure them at first to canes tied temporarily to bridge the gaps between wires.

Cane fruits grown in rows in the open garden require a similar arrangement of tightly stretched wires 45cm (18in) apart, or rustic poles nailed to posts. Tie the canes in place with soft string. Raspberry canes need not be tied individually, but can be secured by a continuous length of string looped round each cane in turn along the wire.

### FEEDING, WATERING AND MULCHING

All plants should be given a thorough soaking periodically while the fruit is ripening, especially if growing against a wall which will tend to absorb moisture from the soil as well as sheltering it from rain. On dry ground water larger trees occasionally by leaving a garden hose trickling at their base for a few hours.

Feed fruit annually, either in spring with a dressing of a balanced compound fertilizer, or by mulching in autumn or spring with a layer of well-rotted manure. A mulch will also help prevent evaporation of water from dry soils; as an alternative to manure, materials such as decayed leaves, grass clippings or shredded compost can be used in conjunction with a dressing of fertilizer.

### PROTECTION

The chief pests and diseases likely to attack fruit are listed with their remedies in the First Aid section (pp. 180-182). Birds are often a particular nuisance and can clear a row of ripe gooseberries or redcurrants in a few days. Be prepared to erect temporary tents of plastic netting over vulnerable plants as their fruit turns colour, especially after summer pruning when a whole crop of nearly mature fruit may suddenly be exposed.

Avoid trouble by keeping plants clean. Cut out any dead wood before it starts to rot, and clear all prunings, dead leaves and unpicked or decaying fruit, both on the ground and still hanging, to prevent the incidence or spread of infections. In a garden where productive plants are also to be decorative, these measures should be part of regular maintenance. Aim to keep fruit comfortable rather than merely alive; integrated with the rest of the garden, it will be possible to appreciate the interest and beauty of the various stages of growth, and also recognize signs of distress before they become serious.

*Where there is a great amount of unprotected fruit dispersed around a garden, it is often possible to harvest large crops without significant losses from attacks by birds. Smaller plantings, however, are often quickly stripped by resident birds as they ripen and these will probably need protection, especially fruits such as redcurrants, peaches, raspberries and strawberries, which can be temporarily covered with wire or plastic netting as they ripen. Wall-trained peaches are easily surrounded with a simple framework of timber or canes, over which a sheet of netting is suspended from the wall (top). Raspberries grown in rows can be enclosed with netting (centre), draped over wires or strong twine stretched between permanent timber supports. Cross-pieces attached to vertical poles at each end keep the netting clear of the fruit which would otherwise still be vulnerable. Protect individual fruit bushes within the garden by surrounding them with a pyramid of three or more canes tied together at the top. Evenly arrange a square of netting over this, so that it covers all sides of the bush, and tie it to the foot of the canes to prevent its lifting in the wind (bottom).*

# PRUNING AND TRAINING

### PRUNING

Good crops depend upon intelligent pruning to divert a plant's energies into producing fruit rather than leaves and branches. There is no mystery about the art other than the apparently miraculous response of a tree or bush to a few carefully chosen cuts. Very often it is sufficient merely to bend a branch down to restrain its growth rather than to cut part of it off, for over-enthusiastic pruning is as much a mistake as not pruning at all. Since pruning is a stimulus that prompts new growth, cutting back hard often merely results in a thicket of young shoots. Knowing when and when not to prune is the key to successful fruit growing.

There are several reasons for pruning. In their early years pruning helps to train trees to a balanced and productive shape. Left uncontrolled a fruit tree will achieve its own compromise between new growth and fruit, but crops will be lighter and of poorer quality than from those pruned for maximum yield. The tree will continue growing until it reaches full size, which is usually too large for domestic gardens, particularly where fruit is integrated amongst other plants; pruning therefore regulates size as well as yield.

To set and mature properly, fruit needs sunlight, which is why large, neglected trees with a jungle of unpruned branches often bear their crops out of reach on their topmost branches. A circulation of air is necessary to prevent diseases from taking hold, and an important aspect of pruning is therefore thinning growth at the centre of a tree to admit light and air. Finally, stems and branches die back from a variety of natural causes, and these must be promptly removed from the tree if fungal infection is not to thrive and adversely affect the health of the whole tree.

## PRUNING FOR FRUIT

### Renewal pruning

The most basic kind of pruning is the total removal of stems that have borne fruit, to make way for new growth yet to crop. The raspberry is the most familiar example of this type. Stems are produced one year to flower and fruit the next, after which they die; pruning consists merely of cutting the old canes down to ground level after the fruit is gathered, and tying in the current season's canes as replacements. The same principle applies to autumn-fruiting raspberries, which crop on canes that have grown in spring and summer of the same year.

Blackcurrant stems and some brambles do not die after fruiting and will continue to crop, but

*Espalier apples and pears will crop for many years, but need firm pruning to shape every summer and winter to avoid congestion of the fruiting spurs (below).*

their yield and quality deteriorates. The best fruit is produced on young growth, and pruning concentrates therefore on removing as much old wood as can be replaced with new growth. Age or lack of feeding will depress growth and there may be insufficient young stems to replace those that have fruited, in which case only a proportion of the old stems can be cut out, otherwise yields will suffer. It is often possible to replace all the fruited wood of young plants which are in good condition with new growth.

This cycle of replacing old stems with new also applies to tree fruit such as peaches, grapes, apricots and acid (pie) cherries, where the best crops are carried on young side shoots that grow from a permanent system of main branches. Replacing these annually rejuvenates the trees, prompting the development of new growth while avoiding a gradual accumulation of old and eventually barren stems.

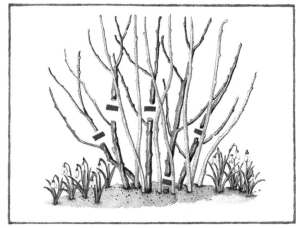

*As blackcurrant branches age their yield declines. Always aim to prune out as many dark, old stems as can be replaced by younger ones growing either from below ground level, or as low side shoots.*

### Spur-pruning soft fruit

Although gooseberries and red currants often develop one or two new stems each year, most of their fruit is borne on short side shoots from branches that live for many years, and clearly the method of renewal pruning practised on blackcurrants would be unsuitable. These main branches are preserved as a permanent framework, and pruning concentrates on maintaining a system of spurs (short, permanent fruiting side shoots) while cutting out all surplus growth unless needed for replacement. This work is done in two stages, in summer and winter.

In late June or July all new shoots growing from the fruiting spurs are shortened back to 10-12cm (4-5in) from their base. In addition to checking growth, removing this large mass of foliage will expose the ripening fruits to sunlight (as it also opens them to attacks from birds and other possible pests, summer pruned fruit should be netted immediately afterwards). At this stage do not shorten new growth at the tips of the branches, nor any stems needed to fill spaces left by the removal of dead wood.

In winter after the leaves have fallen, shorten the side shoots again, this time to just two buds from their base. If the main branches are to continue extending, shorten the new growth at their tips by half; otherwise, cut those that have reached full length back to two buds. Winter pruning will return the plants to their original outline, allowing the fruiting spurs to lengthen by only about 1cm (½in) every year; if these spurs eventually become too long, they may be shortened to 2.5-5cm (1-2in) from their base.

### Pruning top fruit

A few apple varieties carry their fruit at the tips of long slender shoots and therefore need little pruning if these are not to be cut off. These kinds, however, are rarely suitable for growing in gardens and will not tolerate strict training in decorative forms. As a rule, most apples and pears fruit on short stumpy spurs which produce side shoots in summer in much the same way as gooseberries and red currants, and their pruning follows a similar principle.

Side shoots are shortened in summer to five leaves long, and again in winter to one or two buds from their base to keep the fruiting spurs compact. Where the leading shoot from the end of a branch has not yet reached its full length, it is shortened in winter to between a third and a half of the growth made during the summer; when it is full size prune it in the same way as a spur, cutting first to five and then two buds. Fruiting spurs gradually lengthen over the years and will eventually need rejuvenating during winter by cutting back first to half their length, and then the following winter to two or three fruit buds near each base; these can be recognized by their fat rounded appearance compared with the thin, pointed leaf buds.

Sweet cherries are also spur-pruned although it is important to avoid exposing open wounds during autumn and winter when the risk of disease is at its highest. Acid or cooking cherries, on the other hand, together with

grapes, apricots and peaches, depend for productivity on a regular supply of new side shoots and their management follows the renewal pruning method.

The close regulation of growth is critical to success with trained fruit. Large standards and orchard trees, however, cannot be summer pruned with ease and are best dealt with after their leaves have fallen. First remove dead or damaged branches, followed by any that cross each other or that have grown into the middle of the tree; aim always to keep the centre of the tree open to air and sunlight, and to preserve a simple even arrangement of main branches. Do not shorten side shoots in the way described for trained fruit, but leave them to grow naturally, simply thinning them wherever they become congested by cutting a few back to their bases. Very strong, sappy shoots on the upper surface of branches should be cut out entirely.

### Pruning tools

It is a mistake to leave trained fruit untended until major surgery becomes necessary. Much of the regular maintenance pruning of fruit trees and bushes can be done with nothing more than a pair of secateurs (hand pruners), and even their use will be reduced to a minimum if unwanted growth is noticed at an early stage when misplaced buds can be rubbed off and soft young shoots pinched out with finger and thumbnail. However, even the best kept tree will eventually need an overhaul to remove dead material or to rejuvenate old and exhausted wood; with a carefully chosen selection of comfortable and efficient tools, this work need not be arduous. Handle all tools before buying to test their weight and balance, and be prepared to pay a little more to invest in good quality cutting edges.

### Secateurs (hand pruners)

By-pass secateurs (curved blade hand pruners) are the best kind, operating like scissors and

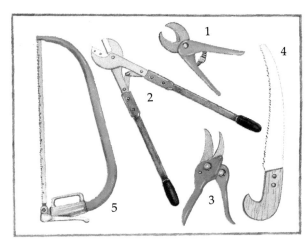

*Secateurs and loppers have by-pass (1,2) or anvil actions (3). Grecian (4) and bow saws (5) are best for pruning.*

leaving a clean, close wound where they cut. For light pruning, parrot-bill models which cut with both blades are suitable, but for thicker stems single-bladed kinds with a guillotine action are the sturdiest and most efficient. Anvil secateurs (pruners), with a cutting blade that closes into a notch on the face of the opposing jaw, are usually less expensive. Although adequate for snipping off slender growth, they tend to crush thicker stems even when sharp, but on some improved models the blade operates with a sliding action which allows a better cut without crushing the stems as much.

### Loppers

These are powerful secateurs (hand pruners) with long handles, used for cutting branches too thick for smaller tools. Models with wooden handles or a rubber cushion stop are the least tiring to use.

### Tree-pruners

Growth otherwise out of reach from the ground may be trimmed with a tree- or long-arm pruner, a cutting blade mounted on the end of a long pole and operated by a wire attached to the handle.

## Saws

Branches too thick to be cut with secateurs (hand pruners) must be sawn off. The teeth on ordinary carpentry saws are too fine and closely set, and soon clog when used on live wood. The most useful kind for pruning is the Grecian saw, whose slim curved blade is easily manipulated in confined spaces; its teeth are set in the opposite direction to normal saws and cut on the return stroke. For dealing with larger branches use a bow saw, which comprises a thin disposable blade held tautly between the ends of a bent tubular frame.

For the maintenance and care of pruning tools, see p.170.

## TRAINING

Training is as important an art as pruning in the production of the decorative fruit tree. Whether the plants are produced at home from cuttings or by grafting, or have been bought in as young stock, they will need to be encouraged in their formative years to establish the framework of their final shape. This process includes pruning, to multiply branches or redirect their growth at an abrupt angle, and tying, both to support the branches and also to guide them into gentler shapes.

## Pruning for shape

The shape of a young fruit tree or bush is first formed by pruning. Whereas pruning for fruit consists of removing or restraining excessive growth to direct energy into productive wood, pruning for shape involves a knowledge of the natural habit of a particular tree and how its growth can be artificially stimulated or diverted. The hormones that control growth are normally to be found around the buds along any shoot, with the greatest concentration at the tip bud. If this is cut off, the bud (or buds) at the end of the severed shoot becomes dominant and will grow on the following season to form an extension to the shoot.

By this means, cutting back to a pair of buds will stimulate them into growth and so produce two branches where formerly there was one. Since a bud will grow in the direction in which it points, it is possible to realign a branch by pruning to an appropriately placed bud. The more a branch is cut back, the more vigorous its response, which is why severe pruning, mistakenly intended to control growth, often merely results in a thicket of young shoots. This is also the reason for hard pruning rooted cuttings of soft fruit after planting: it encourages the formation of strong bushes. Always cut just above the chosen bud – a long section of stem left beyond it may rot and introduce disease.

## How to make a bush

With the exception of blackcurrants which are cut to the ground after planting, soft fruits to be grown as bushes are pruned to encourage a number of branches to radiate evenly from a main stem. Rooted cuttings will have two or three young branches when transplanted; bushes bought from a commercial grower may have more. All can be doubled in number by cutting them back in the first spring after planting, shortening each to 12-15cm (5-6in) from its base. A new shoot will grow from each bud; shorten this in the same way the following spring to double up again. The bush should then have a good head of branches, each starting to form fruiting side shoots, and pruning thereafter will follow the normal annual routine.

Bushes of top fruit varieties are formed in the same way, starting either with maidens (whips, or single-stemmed grafts) which are cut back first of all to 45cm (18in) high to stimulate the growth of side shoots; or with young bought bushes, which have a few, but seldom enough branches. In both cases, double the number of branches by cutting each back to 30-45cm (12-18in) from its base, and repeat this until the final framework is formed.

## How to make a cordon

A single stem soft-fruit cordon is developed from a rooted cutting by allowing the topmost bud to continue its upward growth, removing all other buds or shoots produced lower down. Each winter, shorten this vertical shoot by half its new growth until the final height is reached. Side shoots are then summer and winter pruned as above (see **Spur-pruning soft fruit**), while the terminal shoot is cut back in winter as if it were a spur.

Single stem top-fruit cordons are similarly made, after first cutting back the grafted maiden to about 30cm (1ft) above the graft. In successive years shorten the extension to the leading shoot by half; this stimulates the growth of side shoots which are spur-pruned in summer and winter, as is the leading shoot once it has attained full height.

Multiple cordons are formed by allowing two or more shoots to develop at the top of the cutting or shortened maiden. These horizontal arms are tied in place and then shortened in winter to upward-facing buds, from which the vertical or oblique stems will grow. On a multiple cordon these should be 30-38cm (12-15in) apart.

*Cordons have single or multiple stems, trained vertically, at oblique angles (above), or even horizontally.*

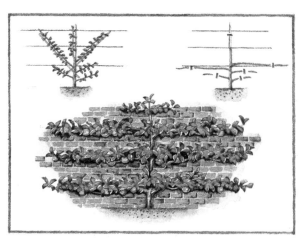

*The horizontal arms of an espalier are trained as cordons and tied in at an angle for their first season, and then lowered to their final position.*

## How to make an espalier

Horizontal wires or wooden trellis will be needed to secure the arms in a horizontal position. After planting, cut the stem of the maiden tree about the level of the first wire just above three good buds. Tie in the shoots that grow from these buds, the topmost one vertically, the others to left and right at an angle of about 45 degrees. The following winter lower these arms to a horizontal position and prune to remove about a third of their growth; cut the vertical shoot at the next wire to repeat the process the following season.

Any side shoots on the main branches are summer pruned to five leaves and shortened again in winter to two buds to form spurs. Where an espalier is trained against a wall or fence, rub off buds of shoots that point in towards it. Continue shaping a tier each year until the final level is reached, where only two stems are allowed to grow for training to each side along the top wire (single-tier espaliers or step-over trees are created in the same way as this top level). Each of the horizontal arms of an espalier is pruned and extended in the same way as a single-stem cordon.

## How to make a festoon

Apples, pears and plums trained on walls often develop tall upright stems at the top. Cutting these off merely stimulates further growth, and gardeners usually prefer to tie these down in an arc which checks growth and instead encourages fruiting side shoots to develop along their length. Whole trees can be trained in this way as decorative festoons.

Allow the tree to grow as an unpruned maiden until it is 2.5-3m (8-10ft) high. Bend the leading shoot over in an arc and secure its tip to the trunk of the tree; treat any other very long side shoots similarly. The following year festoon any further branches that are long enough. Summer prune side shoots growing along existing arcs of apples and pears to start forming fruiting spurs.

Individual arcs are pruned in successive seasons like cordons. Side shoots from plums, however, are left to grow and fruit until long enough to tie down in the same way or cut out for replacement by new shoots. Eventually the main branches will be permanently curved and their ties can be removed.

*As well as creating a very attractive, almost 'weeping' profile, festooning a fruit tree is a profitable technique that diverts the flow of sap through the bent branches into the production of fruiting side shoots.*

*Many kinds of fruit trained as fans will crop prolifically, especially on a warm wall, while occupying very little ground. Tie the branches in an even arrangement against the wall to expose them to maximum sunlight.*

## How to make a fan

Maiden trees and soft fruits for training as fans are first cut back to 30-45cm (12-18in) above the ground, and the resulting branches tied in like the ribs of a fan. Cut away any growing towards or away from the wall and prune those retained to 20-30cm (8-12in) long to encourage the production of enough branches for a fruiting framework. Bought fans usually have about six branches ready for tying in, but as many more are needed, these will need to be shortened in the same way to induce the formation of others.

Train branches while young, arranging them to radiate symmetrically against the wall, and where necessary, tying them to canes secured at appropriate angles to the wires. Do not force lower branches into position as this may result in breakage; tie them first to canes fixed at an oblique angle, and lower these once or twice during the growing season until the branches are in the required position. Aim first to develop the main framework, but once the basic structure is established, side shoots can be allowed to fill spaces, provided they are evenly dispersed and exposed to sunlight.

# PROPAGATION

Many gardeners who propagate their own flowering plants each year by seeds, cuttings or division, do not have the confidence to try increasing or creating their own fruit trees and bushes, even though the same principles are involved. With a few basic skills, and often using surplus plant material usually discarded when pruning, exhausted plants can be replaced for little or no cost. In this way old varieties no longer in general cultivation may be saved from extinction; similarly, new forms or 'sports' that sometimes occur can be reproduced as independent varieties.

Authorities often discourage home propagation on the grounds that it frequently transmits diseases, especially viruses. This is a constant danger, and it is essential always to start with thoroughly healthy plants. Sometimes noticeable lack of vigour is due merely to old age and exhaustion, and propagation may restore vitality, but it is wise to isolate new plants rooted from suspect stock for a season or two until they have demonstrated their sound health. Otherwise, only propagate from the best, most productive plants, avoiding any which display persistently discoloured leaves, sparse fruit, distorted growth or general unthriftiness.

### SEEDS (for methods, see p.172)
Unlike most vegetables and many herbs, few hardy fruits are normally grown from seed although it is an inexpensive alternative way of raising rhubarb, alpine strawberries and seedling rootstocks. Because of the element of chance involved in pollination, plants grown from the same batch of seed usually display differences in appearance and habit. Select only the best for growing on – they can then be perpetuated by cuttings or division – and discard weaker plants unless these have some strongly redeeming quality.

### CUTTINGS
Most fruit cuttings are taken at pruning time, when much of the current season's growth is cut away to restore shape to the plants and concentrate fruiting on the framework of main branches. It is worth striking one or two cuttings annually from the best specimen of each kind as an insurance against possible loss or decline of existing plants, even if these new stocks prove unnecessary. Outstanding or classic varieties deserve to be propagated and will always be in demand by other gardeners.

In autumn select healthy cutting material from the longer straight growths produced during the summer, trimming each cutting ideally to 30-38cm (12-15in) long, although shorter pieces can be used where unavoidable. Cut them immediately below a leaf joint. Rub off all but the top four or five buds from cuttings intended to produce plants with a clean, single stem, but on blackcurrant cuttings and gooseberries for hedging leave all buds intact to make new growth from below ground.

Plant the cuttings 10cm (4in) deep in open, cultivated ground, spacing them 15cm (6in) apart in rows, or alternatively in small circles,

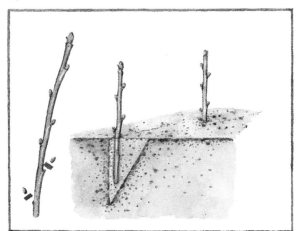

*Most soft fruits are easily propagated from cuttings, which must have good drainage at their base. On clay soils they will root best planted into sharp sand.*

and leave undisturbed until the following autumn when they are moved to their permanent sites. On lighter ground make planting holes with a dibber or simply push the cuttings into place, treading the soil firm around each. On heavy ground make individual planting holes or open a slit with a spade; sprinkling some sharp sand or coarse ashes in the bottom will help the cuttings survive in possibly saturated surroundings.

### LAYERS
Layering means rooting young growths without separating them from the parent plants until they are self-sufficient. Blackberries and hybrid briars produce long flexible canes whose tips will root at the points where they rest on the soil at the end of the season. To encourage the formation of sturdy young plants ready for transplanting the following spring, make a hole 15cm (6in) deep with a dibber in August, and push the growing tip into this, keeping it in place by treading the soil firmly. In spring cut the young plant free from the main stem and move to its new home.

Other fruits such as figs, blueberries and hazelnuts can be similarly layered, by burying suitably placed stems a few centimetres from their tips. Accelerate rooting by peeling back a short strip of bark where each touches the ground, or by cutting at an angle halfway into the stem on the lower side and wedging the wound open with a piece of matchstick. Lay the prepared section in a hole 7-10cm (3-4in) deep, cover with soil and tread firmly; where a layer may be disturbed by wind, peg it in place with a bent piece of stout wire or rest a large stone on top. These layers will often need a full year to root before they can be safely severed from the parent plant.

Most strawberry varieties are propagated by layering the young plants produced at intervals along thin runners. These usually root without any assistance, and can be cut free for transplanting in autumn. The first plantlet on each runner is the strongest and the earliest to root; where sufficient are formed, choose these and discard the rest. However, subsequent smaller plantlets on runners are useful where large numbers of new plants are needed. Even the smallest unrooted plantlets can be cut from their runners and will quickly root if pressed into moist soil in a closed cold frame, or into a box of potting compost in a cool greenhouse. For early forcing, runners may be layered direct into small pots (see **Strawberry,** p.59).

*Strawberries are layered from runners which will root where they lie, although on poor soils they are better pegged down into pots. Young blackberry canes are layered at their ends by pegging down or by inserting each tip in a hole in the ground.*

## SUCKERS

New stems springing from below ground can often be dug up with a few roots for replanting elsewhere. This is the usual way to propagate raspberries which regularly throw suckers from the long shallow roots extending from the rows. Separate these in autumn by chopping down cleanly with a spade to cut the roots joining them to the main plants. Carefully dig up each sucker, making sure it has several fine roots of its own, and replant elsewhere immediately to prevent these roots from drying out. Other fruits, for example nuts and occasionally loganberries, and some plum and seedling rootstocks produce suckers which may be similarly transplanted.

## USING ROOTSTOCKS

Whereas most soft fruits grow on their own roots and are easily propagated by cuttings, layers or suckers, a selected variety of top fruit is usually joined by budding or grafting to a special rootstock of known performance. Before the advent of modern rootstocks, gardeners would often transplant wild seedlings into their gardens and graft them with improved cultivars. Although seedling crab apples, pears, plums or cherries make very successful rootstocks, the size and productivity of resulting trees is unpredictable because plants raised from seed are liable to variation.

Seedlings are still used to provide the roots for such fruits as apricots and peaches, but for most other kinds varieties are grafted on selected strains of rootstock with consistent performance. Named rootstocks can be ordered from good fruit nurseries, and planted for grafting or budding the following season, or they can be used as stock plants to provide an annual supply of rootstocks. They are no harder to propagate than fruit cultivars. Some will grow from cuttings, but others, such as those used for apples and pears, do not root easily by this means and must be grown instead from layers, root cuttings or as suckers which are induced to grow on permanent parent plants, known as 'stools'.

## PROPAGATING ROOTSTOCKS

Fruit rootstocks respond to propagation at different rates and with varying degrees of success according to the method used. The most foolproof is layering because the potential cutting remains part of the parent until actually rooted. However, to layer many kinds efficiently, stocks must be planted deliberately at an angle to lower their naturally upright growth sufficiently to bury or peg it in the soil.

An easier method for garden propagation is stooling. Bought rootstocks, planted upright at the same depth at which they previously grew, are left to establish for a season; they can be spaced as close as 30cm (1ft) apart and will therefore occupy little space. During the winter a year after planting all stems are cut down to ground level. Several new shoots will appear from each stool when growth recommences. These are earthed up to half their height when about 15cm (6in) tall and the soil firmed around the stems; this is repeated as growth continues until the mound of soil is 20-23cm (8-9in) above ground level. The following winter, carefully break open the mound to expose the original stool, and cut off all the stems, most of which will have developed roots from their buried portions; plant out the rooted stems elsewhere for later budding or grafting, and discard any without roots. Leave the stool exposed until growth recommences in spring, when the process is repeated.

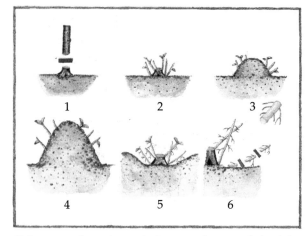

*If the young shoots from a fruit rootstock are partly buried in soil (1-4), most will root and can be cut off (5) for transplanting. Sections of roots (6) can also be taken for growing elsewhere.*

Apple, cherry, pear and plum rootstocks may also be propagated by root cuttings, either by simply cutting off one or two of the stouter roots on bought fruit trees, or by cropping specially planted parent rootstocks. In the latter case the stocks are dug up every second year, and replaced immediately after root cuttings have been taken; if top growth is cut down when replanting, the plants may be treated as stools in alternate years, as described above. Sections about 10-12cm (4-5in) long, taken from younger roots about 50mm-1cm (¼-½in) diameter, are used for cuttings, trimming each so that the end that grew nearer the stem is clearly recognizable. Keeping this end uppermost, cuttings are planted vertically outdoors 7-10cm (3-4in) apart, their tops just covered with soil. Shoots will appear in spring and, where several occur, should be reduced to the strongest on each cutting. The following winter they can be transplanted to wait for budding or grafting.

## BUDDING

By this method a leaf bud with a small portion of bark is united with a suitable rootstock in summer. A section of current season's growth, furnished with several narrow leaf buds, is cut with a very sharp knife from the chosen fruiting variety. Start a centimetre (½in) below the leaf and its bud, making a smooth curving cut behind the bud and emerging the same distance or a little more above the bud. Cut off the leaf so that a short piece of stem remains, and remove the thin slip of wood behind the bark. Low down on the rootstock, make a T-shaped cut in the bark large enough for the bud section to fit behind, and slide the bud into place between the two flaps of bark. Tie these together with raffia over the bud section. A successful bud will produce a shoot the following season; when this reaches 23-30cm (9-12in) long, tie it upright to the rootstock. In autumn cut the rootstock back to the new fruiting stem, and stake the new tree securely.

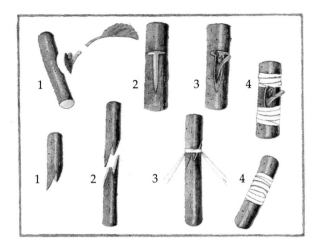

(top) *Budding: a young leaf bud is cut out and trimmed (1). On the rootstock, a T-shaped incision is made with a knife just through the bark (2) and slightly opened for the bud to be inserted (3) and tied in place (4). (bottom) Grafting: a shoot of the chosen variety is cut off obliquely and notched (1). This is then fitted on to a matching surface on the rootstock (2) and securely tied and waxed (3,4).*

## GRAFTING

A little more difficult than budding, this involves joining a short length of fruiting wood (the 'scion') to a rootstock. Scions are prepared from one-year-old shoots, best cut in autumn and planted like cuttings outdoors until needed. In early spring when the stock is once more active but the scion still dormant, the stock is cut through obliquely about 5-7cm (2-3in) from the ground; then a clean notch is cut with a knife across the face of the stump. A matching surface is prepared on the lower end of the scion and on the opposite side to a good bud (the 'stock' bud). The scion is trimmed to three or four buds in length, fitted neatly on to the stock, and tied in place with raffia, taking care not to cover the stock bud. Finally the union is painted with grafting wax or pruning compound. Growth should appear very soon after grafting and can then be supported and trained to form the new tree.

## PROPAGATION OF INDIVIDUAL FRUITS

**Apple:** large-fruited varieties and crab apples are budded in July or grafted in March on the most appropriate rootstock. Species can be raised from seed.

**Apricot:** bud in summer on to plum rootstocks or apricot seedlings.

**Blackberry and Hybrid Berries:** layer the tips of young unfruited canes in late summer.

**Blackcurrant:** cuttings of the current year's growth are taken in October or November – remove the growing tip from each, but leave all the lower buds intact to grow from below ground. Lower shoots of spreading varieties may be layered.

**Blueberry:** propagate by hardwood cuttings; layers; and suckers dug from the sides of bushes in autumn.

**Cherry:** graft in spring or bud in summer on to suitable rootstocks.

**Citrus Fruits:** layering; cuttings in summer; graft in spring or bud in summer where rootstocks are used.

**Fig:** layering; suckers dug up in autumn; cuttings in autumn in a cold frame.

**Gooseberry:** cuttings outdoors in autumn – take more than required, since often only 50-75 per cent root successfully. Unless intended for hedging, remove all lower buds to produce a clean stem. Lax varieties may also be layered. Standards budded in summer on *Ribes aureum*.

**Grapevine:** the easiest method is by cuttings made from the woodier end of shoots removed at pruning time – cut each 23-30cm (9-12in) long and plant the lower three-quarters in the ground in a sheltered part of the garden.

**Hazelnuts and Filberts:** layering is best; suckers can be dug up in autumn, although the suckering habit is often also propagated. Nuts may be sown outdoors and transplanted after two years, but plants seldom come true to type.

**Medlar:** graft in spring or bud in July on to thorn or quince stocks.

**Melon:** seeds.

**Mulberry:** layering; cuttings in autumn. Several years' growth may be gained by cutting a branch 150-180cm (5-6ft) long, known as a 'truncheon', and firmly driving the lower quarter into the ground in autumn; stake securely and it will quickly root, producing fruit within a few years.

**Peach and Nectarine:** bud in late summer on selected rootstocks, or on peach seedlings in warmer regions. Grafting in spring is possible but less reliable. Stones germinate readily and produce useful trees but their quality is a gamble and they may take longer to fruit.

**Pear and Quince:** bud in summer; graft in spring; quince may be layered. (Not all pears are compatible with quince rootstocks – 'double working' is necessary, using an intermediate section of a mutually compatible variety.)

**Plum:** bud in summer. A few culinary varieties grow on their own roots and can be increased by suckers. Small-fruited kinds are propagated by budding, cuttings or seeds.

**Raspberry:** suckers. Also by cuttings 20-30cm (8-12in) long, taken in autumn from the tops of ripened canes and planted outdoors half length.

**Red and White Currant:** cuttings in autumn.

**Rhubarb:** seed; division, by digging up established crowns and cutting them into small sections, each with one or two buds on top.

**Strawberry:** by layering runners; alpine varieties by seed, layers, and division.

**Walnut:** grafting or budding, both with difficulty; sowing nuts, although the quality of trees is unpredictable.

# FRUIT IN POTS

Gardeners with only courtyards or very little cultivated ground can still produce profitable fruit crops by growing trees and bushes in pots or small tubs. This was a very popular method in Victorian times, when success depended mainly on clever pruning and the natural restrictions on growth imposed by root confinement. Modern gardeners have a further ally in the dwarfing rootstock, with the help of which many top fruits can be cropped successfully and easily in pots as small as 30-38cm (12-15in) in diameter.

All fruit in pots of this size will need shelter from severe frosts that might freeze the root ball. Plants are easily portable, however, a particular advantage with early flowering fruits such as peaches and nectarines, apricots and choice varieties of pear, all of which benefit from the shelter of an unheated greenhouse or conservatory while in bloom. Their very attractive blossom makes them a decorative spring asset under glass. Crops are relatively lighter than from trees on the same rootstocks in the open ground – for example, 15-20 peaches from a healthy bush in a 30cm (12in) pot, or 1-2kg (2-5lb) of apples according to variety – but individual fruits are usually larger and of very high quality.

Most top fruits are suitable for pot cultivation. Although young trees can be dug up and transferred to pots after their thicker roots have been trimmed to size, it is easier to start either with container-grown specimens, or with maidens (whips) that still have a small root system and can be trained to shape as they become established. With all top fruits it is best to use the most dwarfing rootstock available, because this will help moderate growth and so reduce the amount of necessary pruning. Soft fruits that crop on a permanent set of branches – gooseberries or red and white currants, for example – also make profitable large pot plants.

Clay or wooden containers are more durable than plastic pots with their tendency to become brittle, and more portable than concrete which is often very heavy. Wooden containers must be treated well with preservative before use according to the manufacturer's instructions. New clay pots, preferably made from frost-resistant material, need preliminary soaking in water. Both kinds should have sufficient drainage holes in the bottom, which are covered before potting with a 2.5cm (1in) layer of pot fragments or large pebbles to prevent saturated compost (potting mixture) from lying stagnant around the roots or blocking the holes. Discourage compost from filtering through the drainage material by covering it with a handful of moist coarse peat.

A loam-based potting mixture such as John Innes No 3 is best (see p.177). The inclusion of a large proportion of soil makes it heavier than peat mixtures, providing stability in wind and an ability to resist the extreme fluctuations of temperature and moisture typical of peat. Fertilizers added to some peat mixtures are often exhausted after a few weeks, whereas the loam in soil-based mixtures provides a slow

*Efficient drainage is critical for healthy growth. A preliminary layer of stones or shards is covered with peat or rotted manure before the potting mixture is added.*

release of nutrients over a longer period. Peat composts can be improved by blending them with an equal proportion of good garden topsoil. All potting mixtures for fruit in pots benefit by the addition of a small amount of crumbled decayed manure, either mixed in or used instead of peat to cover the drainage layer; for figs and apricots, however, substitute bone-meal for manure at 30g (1oz) per 9-litre (2-gal) bucketful of potting mixture.

## POTTING TREES

Spread a good handful of potting mixture in the bottom of the prepared pot and firm it well with the fist. After first removing pot-grown specimens from their containers, hold the tree centrally in the pot and surround its root ball with potting mixture, working it down amongst any loose roots until the pot is half filled. Compress the compost into place with the fingers, occasionally tapping the pot to help it settle, and then compact it with a trowel handle or short length of dowel. Continue to add compost, ramming it thoroughly, to about 5cm (2in) below the pot rim to allow room for water. Level the surface and leave it loose. Do the same with other larger containers.

## REPOTTING

Potted trees are kept in the same size pots all their lives, but every autumn some of the exhausted soil around the roots should be replaced with fresh potting mixture. Make sure the contents of the pot are moist. Holding the tree by its stem so that the base of the pot is suspended just above a level surface, free the root ball by tapping the rim of the pot sharply with a mallet or piece of wood. Clear away any crocks or other drainage material from beneath the root ball and scrape off the top layer of potting mixture.

Using a seed label or short bamboo cane, loosen the outer 2.5-5cm (1-2in) of compost around the root ball and tease it from the roots,

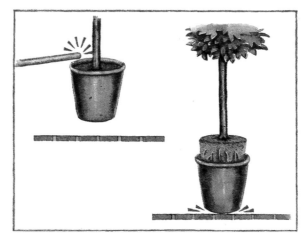

*A tree is easily knocked out of the pot if its root ball is moist. Hold the main stem firmly to prevent any accidental damage to the branches.*

leaving the centre of the ball undisturbed. With the pot scrubbed clean and prepared with a new drainage layer covered with peat or old manure, the tree can be repotted with fresh potting mixture. Trees in tubs or larger pots will not need complete repotting, but the top few centimetres of potting mixture should be replaced every spring.

## CARE AND MAINTENANCE

Fruit trees in pots should spend as much time as possible in a sunny place outdoors to maintain good health and keep growth compact. Either stand pots on level ground where they are sheltered from strong winds, or plunge them to their rims in the ground; this will considerably reduce the need to water them in summer. Never let the pots dry out. Check them every day or two, and whenever trees need water fill their pots to the brim to ensure even and thorough soaking. Feed regularly with a high potash fertilizer or liquid manure from the time the fruit begins to swell until it is picked.

Tree roots are normally tenderer than the above-ground parts. In cold areas (north of zone 8) roots must usually be protected from

severe frost. Pots may be moved into a cold greenhouse, cold frame, garage, buried in the ground or covered with mulch. In early spring potted trees with frost-sensitive blossom are best brought inside or moved into the shelter of a warm wall. Indoors blooms usually need to be fertilized by sharply tapping flowering branches daily. While they are inside, ventilate trees whenever possible and inspect regularly for early signs of houseplant pests and diseases.

The same pruning techniques are used as for plants in the open ground, bearing in mind that growth will naturally be a little depressed by the confined root space. Where applicable, pruning in both summer and winter is advisable. Vigorous growth is best thinned if trees threaten to become congested, and a good set of fruit may also need to be thinned to numbers the tree can expect to mature: reduce any clusters to single fruits and leave these spaced about 7-23cm (3-9in) apart according to the natural size of the fruit.

*With careful management many kinds of fruit can be grown in pots to protect cold-sensitive varieties from spring frosts or to force early crops. Strawberries (front) are easily grown for a season in medium-sized pots and fruit very early. Choice greenhouse varieties of grape (left) fruit well in pots, often the only way in cooler gardens to grow tender citrus fruits (right).*

# FRUIT IN THE GREENHOUSE

Apart from offering periods of shelter for fruit trees in pots, a greenhouse or conservatory is an ideal permanent home for fruit growing in large containers or planted direct into a soil border. Most kinds of fruit appreciate conditions under glass, especially if they are trained flat up the side of the house or against a wall, where they benefit from radiated heat and the uniform exposure to sunlight. In lean-to structures the rear wall is often wasted, but figs, peaches, nectarines and apricots in particular flourish in this position, occupying very little floor space while producing earlier and better quality crops than outdoors.

*Greenhouse grapes are normally grown in a border and trained up beneath the glass roof. In lean-to houses, use the walls for peaches, nectarines or apricots.*

With the minimal protection of an unheated greenhouse a wider range of fruit varieties may be grown, especially those renowned for flavour and quality. Most figs, for example, are improved by being grown indoors and will often produce two or even three crops instead of one as is the rule outdoors in Britain or the northern United States. Given freedom from frost, many kinds of citrus make highly decorative and profitable pot plants, while glasshouse grapes are far more choice than hardy varieties.

Whereas fruit in pots or tubs may be moved outdoors in summer, trees growing in borders are totally dependent on greenhouse facilities for their health and welfare. Very small greenhouses or conservatories, for example, are seldom able to provide sufficient air circulation unless extra ventilators have been fitted. An opening side window is at least as important as roof ventilation if a stagnant atmosphere and excessive heat in summer are to be avoided.

It is also essential that fruit trees are given maximum light, and they will rarely do well if the glass is shaded by trees or buildings outside. The best kind of structure is a greenhouse or conservatory facing south or south-west, with one or more side windows together with a door that can be wedged open in hot weather, and a 2m (7ft) minimum height at the ridge or back wall in the case of lean-to houses.

The border in which a tree is to grow should be at least 60cm (2ft) wide and twice that long; although this ground space needs to be accessible once a year for top-dressing with manure or fertilizer, it can be used for the rest of the time to grow vegetable crops or ornamental plants. Although traditionally grapes are trained up beneath the roof while other fruits are grown against a back wall, all kinds will thrive in both situations and may, for instance, be planted in the often unused soil beneath greenhouse staging for training up the glass above a display of pot plants.

## SOIL PREPARATION

The border should be dug out to a depth of at least 60cm (2ft), keeping the topsoil separate from that below. Although a major task, this is essential if the tree is to thrive and crop well, and will only need to be done once in its

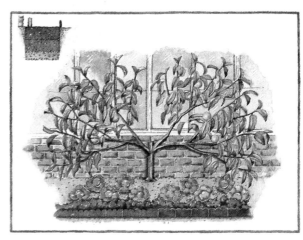

*A greenhouse border needs deep and thorough preparation if a fruit tree is to be long-lived and fruitful. Train the branches so that they, together with other plants grown in the border, receive plenty of light.*

lifetime. Where a fig is to be grown, first line the excavated pit with broken paving slabs or sheets of corrugated iron to restrict its roots and so prevent growth at the expense of fruit.

In the bottom of the pit spread a layer of broken bricks, stones or other drainage material, covered with a layer of old upturned turves or garden compost. Half fill the pit with the excavated soil if it is in good condition; otherwise replace it with garden soil. Add a 9-litre (2 gal) bucketful of garden compost per square metre (yard) and fork this in – peat may be used instead but should be mixed with 60g (2oz) lime per bucketful to counteract its acidity. Complete filling the hole with the excavated topsoil. Tread the soil very firm as it is replaced, level and leave the surface loose.

## PLANTING

Plant during late winter. Remove the pots from container-grown trees, disentangle and spread out any of the larger roots, and plant firmly at the depth at which previously grown, leaving a space of 7-10cm (3-4in) between the stem and the wall of the house. Water in thoroughly. Tie in the top growth to horizontal wires according to the proposed shape. Where a tree is planted in the soil under greenhouse staging, trim off any side shoots up to this level, take the main stem up behind the staging and tie in place. Training and pruning follow the same principles as for trees outdoors.

## MAINTENANCE

Keep the soil just moist until growth begins, after which the border should be given a thorough soaking whenever it appears dry, at the same time wetting the floor overall to raise humidity. Every spring spread a 9-litre (2-gal) bucketful of decayed manure evenly round each tree but do not let this lie against the main stem; alternatively dress the surface of the soil with 250g (8oz) per tree of compound fertilizer containing trace elements. Trees in fruit will benefit from liquid feeding every week.

Lightly spray the foliage with water occasionally on warm sunny mornings to clean the leaves and maintain good health. Apart from the normal houseplant diseases and pests, the greatest threat is usually infestation by red spider mite, a pest encouraged by drought and low humidity. A return to the traditional practice of regularly spraying foliage, floors and staging with water will normally prevent its occurrence as well as providing a more buoyant growing atmosphere for the plants.

Even in cold weather the windows should be opened daily for long enough to change the air. Most fruits prefer winter temperatures to be kept as low as is compatible with their hardiness, otherwise they will not experience the necessary period of dormancy. In summer ventilate whenever possible, never allowing temperatures to soar much above 21°C (70°F); in very hot weather damp down the floor and staging once or twice a day. Where birds are a problem, windows may need to be netted to protect fruit, and care should be taken whenever leaving the door open for ventilation.

To ensure adequate fertilization, tap the branches of flowering fruit trees and repeat daily until the fruit is clearly set. Alternatively, lightly spray the open flowers with water, but only on bright sunny mornings when they have a good chance of drying before nightfall. Do not allow leaves or other debris to collect around the trees, especially under greenhouse staging where it can accumulate and will invite disease as it decays.

## GRAPES UNDER GLASS

Many gardeners tempted to grow a grape vine in their greenhouse or conservatory are deterred by needless fears about pruning or the space a vine is thought to require. Although a single vine may be trained to cover several hundred square metres of glass, simple pruning can confine it to only one or two fruiting stems, or 'rods', to fit a small greenhouse. Heat is unnecessary for outdoor varieties and most glasshouse kinds – in fact they prefer fairly spartan conditions, which makes them unsuitable companions for tender greenhouse plants in winter. However, if heating is available, a long-season grape, such as Muscat of Alexandria, can be ripened to perfection, either by starting it into growth earlier or by raising the temperature to finish the ripening of the crop in autumn.

Prepare the border and plant as for other kinds of fruit (the traditional method of planting outdoors and then leading the main stem inside through a hole in the wall is only used where a greenhouse border does not exist). Cut back after planting to 30cm (1ft) high if trained against a back wall, or to windowsill level where it is to be grown up the side of a greenhouse. During the first year allow the main stem to grow vertically, tying it in to horizontal wires 30-38cm (12-15in) apart; side shoots that form are trained along these, one to each wire, cutting out altogether any that are surplus. In the autumn shorten the main stem to 120cm

(4ft) high, and prune the side shoots to two buds; if more than one vertical rod is required, cut the lowest side shoot on each side to about 90cm (3ft) long; extra rods are trained up from these the following year.

Each of the two buds on the stumps of last season's side shoots will usually produce a shoot. Remove the weaker one, or the barren shoot should only one flower (where neither bloom, leave one and stop it after five leaves). Tie in retained side shoots to their wires and pinch out the tips two leaves beyond the flower trusses; any side growth that forms on the flowering shoot is stopped after one leaf. The main stem is allowed to grow a further 90-120cm (3-4ft) each year until it reaches full height, where it is stopped and its tip pruned as a fruiting spur.

When the flower trusses open, tap the wires each day to disperse the pollen. Berries need thinning (see p. 36); as they swell feed the vine regularly with a balanced liquid fertilizer unless the border has been mulched with manure. Damp down the floor of the greenhouse daily except when the grapes are turning colour.

After harvest, ventilate freely (except during winter frosts) until growth is started once more in early spring.

*A black grape trained beneath a greenhouse roof. The berries have been thinned to allow even, healthy ripening.*

# HERBS INTRODUCTION

Although Vita Sackville-West designed a traditional herb garden at Sissinghurst in Kent, she was also alert to the unexpected results of combining herbs with flowering plants in mixed beds. She wrote, 'I like muddling things up, and if a herb looks nice in a border then why not grow it there?' This precedent is still followed at Sissinghurst, and visitors may discover many herbs dispersed around the borders.

This blending of plants or 'muddling things up', has a long pedigree. The term, herbs, once embraced a much larger range of plants; in addition to culinary and medicinal herbs, of which many more were recognized and used centuries ago than today, a large number of vegetables were included as pot herbs, for they were also known to be beneficial plants.

In practice there is very little to distinguish a vegetable from a herb, especially as some can be classed as either. If a plant also has an attractive flower, as many herbs and vegetables do, distinctions become pointless; flowers were always needed for decorating medieval churches and altars, and therefore had equal status in the monastic garden with edible and medicinal plants.

The formal herb garden, with herbs (as defined today) arranged in a pattern of symmetrical beds, became an attractive ornamental feature of large, grand gardens. Its revival in more recent years has seldom been successful in smaller modern gardens, where the complicated knots and formal patterns often look cramped and out of scale with their diminished surroundings.

A sturdier and more appropriate tradition is that of the cottage garden, in which a little of everything was inevitably 'muddled up', not just as part of a naturally artless gardening style but also because of the limited space available. Charming combinations and effects were achieved by simply fitting in a plant wherever

there was room, and taking a chance on the result. It is this long tradition which is more appropriate to the modern garden and its prevailing informality.

Growing herbs together in a special garden creates problems. While the impact of a herb garden usually depends on neatness and a visible pattern, herbs grow as determinedly as any other plant and the strict outlines of the pattern are soon blurred by a few weeks' exuberant growth. Herb gardens need constant attention to clipping and shaping, whereas planted amongst vegetables and flowering plants, or as a contrast to the immaculate lines of trained fruit, individual herbs can achieve their natural size and form with little disruption to the overall scheme.

A further disadvantage is that exclusive collections of herbs tend to present an unexciting and uniform appearance. Gathered *en masse*, the deep greens, soft greys or brilliant golds lack sufficient vitality or variation to have lasting interest. Dispersed throughout the garden, however, they gain by contrast both with more flamboyant flowering plants and against the green background of many leaf vegetables. If herbs are to be enjoyed for their many varied qualities, they must be worked into the main body of the garden.

It is not difficult to find suitable homes for them: there is a herb for every situation, and conversely some place in the garden that will enhance, or be enlivened by, a particular herb. If the various species and cultivars of herbs are considered as flowering or foliage plants in their own right, herbs will immediately lose their purely dietary or medicinal associations and instead become known as an adaptable and easily managed group of decorative plants.

Although some of the traditional medicinal uses are included in the alphabetical herb list, no specific dosages are given. For these and for advice on any serious medical problem consult a qualified practitioner.

*A chamomile path (flowers 22), studded with paving stones to limit wear on the plants, leads to a stone bench and a boundary hedge of clipped bay (1). Mint (2) is confined in a pot to restrict its spread, while a standard redcurrant (3) and trained blackberry (4) relieve the angular outline of the seat. Box-edged borders each side of the path demonstrate the versatility of herbs as decorative plants. In the left-hand bed fennel (5), normally grown as a tall background plant, grows as an imaginative corner feature. Chives (6), thyme (7) and catmint (8) are all compact herbs for the front of the border, while the soft exuberance of alchemilla/lady's mantle (9) contrasts with the formal hedging. Behind these, angelica (10) makes a lush and dramatic feature. Lemon thyme (11) and rosemary (12), growing beside the hive, are both noted bee plants.*

*The right-hand border has parsley (13), strawberries (14) and rue (15) for dwarf edging, while the more vigorous lemon balm (16) balances the fennel across the path. Feverfew (17), sage (18) and sweet cicely (19) add height and contrast to the centre of the bed. For the back of borders, or for growing against fences and walls, hops (20), dog roses (21) and honeysuckle (23) are all virtually indestructible, and give rapid cover over a large area. Yarrow (24), verbascum (25) and globe artichokes (26) are attractive taller plants, of sound cottage-garden pedigree, as are the old-fashioned roses (27), and poppies, whose laden seed capsules (28) ensure their survival in any cultivated soil.*

# HERBS IN THE GARDEN

As their individual descriptions show, the popular culinary and medicinal herbs are of very varied habit and appearance, making them suitable for a wide range of sites. There are many less common herbs not included in the separate entries, and the adventurous gardener will want to explore further the ornamental as well as practical value of plants such as mugwort (*Artemisia vulgaris*) with its deeply-cut grey foliage; the imposing yellow-flowered elecampane (*Inula helenium*); or the stout, medicinal Russian comfrey (*Symphytum* x *uplandicum*) with its purple blooms and continuous supply of compost material.

With the exception of such large-flowered plants as borage and calendulas, the greatest visual appeal of herbs lies in their attractive leaves. They are foliage plants *par excellence*, from the threadlike tracery of fennel to the lush, broad leaves of lovage. Their range of colour is unique, too. A large number of herbs have silver or green leaves – the various artemisias such as wormwood and southernwood, or the different cultivars of lavender – and planted amongst green foliage, their soft colouring lifts their neighbours into prominence. Many herbs have forms with purple, gold or variegated foliage, which often more than compensates for their relatively insignificant flowers.

## HERBS AS HEDGES

At different periods through the centuries hyssop, rosemary, sage and wall germander (*Teucrium chamaedrys*) have all been used to form dwarf hedges around vegetable beds or within formal knot gardens. They are woody evergreens that respond to regular clipping by producing clean outlines and solid banks of foliage, from about 15cm (6in) high in the case of germander, up to 75-90cm (30-36in) with taller rosemary cultivars. Inevitably the two or three necessary trims each season prevent the

shrubs from flowering, but the clippings can usually be saved and dried for later use. Plants need close spacing, 15-30cm (6-12in) according to species, if they are to develop quickly into a dense hedge. Thoroughly cultivate a strip of ground twice as wide as the proposed hedge, and take care to remove fragments of perennial weeds as they will be difficult to fork out after planting. Set out the young plants in spring, either in a single line or staggered in a double row for a wider hedge. Water when necessary and mulch around the plants to help them to establish quickly. Encourage bushy growth by trimming the plants to shape from an early age.

## EDGES, MATS AND CARPETS

Tall, herbaceous perennial herbs add height and body to the garden, while the smaller creeping kinds provide ground cover. There is no need for hard outlines to paths and beds; those herbs that tend to grow as dense, rounded mats can be allowed to spill over on to paths or grass, softening the defined edges. They all tolerate clipping and can therefore be trimmed back if they encroach too far. Alternatively, a traditional idea is to plant such herbs to make scented paths; often the best way to establish a path is to allow the herbs to spread from either side until they meet.

## SCENTED PATHS

Although garden paths are usually made from hard-wearing materials or perhaps grass, some of the prostrate herbs are equally suitable where traffic is not too heavy. Thyme is an obvious choice since it is evergreen and will last for

*The varied and visually satisfying qualities of herbs can be exploited in the overall context of the garden, using fennel with bergamot (left) and mulleins (right), for example, to provide both height and flowering colour, here emphasized by a neat mound of helichrysum (left, foreground) and the tiny yellow buttons of santolina (right). Herbaceous geraniums, thyme and marjoram fill the spaces in between.*

several years before needing replacement. The low-growing wild thyme (*T. serpyllum*) or golden thyme (*T. vulgaris aureus*) are both particularly useful. Tiny *Mentha requienii* (Corsican mint) hugs the ground in moist places and is surprisingly resilient. Remember, though, most areas of the garden need dry access in winter, which could make a herbal path rather impracticable. It might be better to allow herbs to creep across from the edges, leaving just enough hard surface in the middle.

## CHAMOMILE

The most traditional of all lawn and path herbs is chamomile, and many gardeners hope it might provide an interesting alternative to grass. Although a pleasant scent certainly accompanies anyone walking across it, maintenance can pose some problems, so much so that a good example of a chamomile lawn is

rarely encountered. It will never match the colour or density of well-kept turf, nor can it be mown so closely; trimming has to be done with shears or a rotary mower set high. Without constant care, weeds quickly gain a foothold amongst the matted growth and have to be removed by hand because there are no specific herbicides such as can be used on a grass lawn. When bare patches develop and perennial weeds become invasive, the path or lawn will need reconstruction.

As edging, or for a seldom-used path, chamomile can be much more successful, provided no more is expected from it than from any other herb. The only form worth using is 'Treneague', shorter and more vigorous than the flowering species. Make sure the site is throughly weed-free and reasonably fertile. Space young plants or cuttings 10cm (4in) apart; water, feed and weed them until established.

## CARPETING HERBS

In commercial orchards trees are grown in grass or soil kept bare with weedkillers, according to the type of rootstock; this is a waste of space in a garden. Fruit trees growing in a lawn can be underplanted with a pretty combination of naturalized bulbs such as narcissi, grape hyacinths or crocuses, mixed with forget-me-nots. If fruit is trained against a wall or along the edges of a path, the soil beneath is best used for dwarf and prostrate herbs.

Alpine strawberries flourish in the semi-shade, and those varieties that produce runners eventually knit together to form a fruiting mat of plants. Suitable herbs for these shaded areas are those suggested for paths, together with golden sage, trailing rosemary, wild basil (*Calamintha clinopodium*), and sweet woodruff. If the soil is in full sun, creeping savory, perennial marjorams and dwarf lavenders can be added to the list.

Between and amongst these permanent plants annual herbs such as parsley and chervil

*A mature herb garden in midsummer, planted informally and demonstrating some of the dramatic contrasts of colour and stature possible between species of widely differing appearance, all of them popular with bees when in flower. In the foreground three-coloured sage,* Salvia officinalis 'Tricolor' *provides perennial interest with its grey-green, cream and mauve mottled leaves, emphasized by the grass-like clumps of chives, here in full bloom. Their colour is echoed by the flowers of the hyssop. Orach or mountain spinach (centre left) is usually grown as a vegetable for its succulent deep red leaves but if left to flower makes a tall and spectacular plant that may need supporting with a cane in an exposed position. The rich colour makes it an ideal companion for borage (centre right) with its soft grey-green foliage and bright blue pendulous flowers; this too, will tend to sprawl unless supported. In the background a bold clump of feathery-leaved fennel provides height and a bright patch of yellow flowers.*

will grow happily. Plants normally grown in the flower garden need not be excluded (see pp. 100-102): lady's mantle, sweet violets, lily of the valley, primroses, Welsh poppies, pinks and double daisies all have some herbal importance and harmonize with the more familiar herbs. Finally, underplant this ground cover with bulbs, such as chives and other alliums, or any of the smaller decorative kinds.

## A HERB SEAT

In Tudor times gardens often included a seat sculpted from banks or mounds, and planted with aromatic herbs such as chamomile or thyme. Such a seat would only be useable in dry weather, of course, but the idea can be adapted to provide an attractive and secluded alcove, occupying very little space and offering produce combined with perfume.

Either cut the shape of a seat from a mound or bank of soil, or alternatively position a ready-made bench where it can be enclosed by plants. The seat itself is best made of solid material such as wood or stone, rather than prostrate herbs, but the back and sides of an excavated bench, together with the ground beneath a free-standing seat, can be planted with any of the mat-forming herbs. Larger plants such as rosemary, evening primrose, anise hyssop (*Agastache anethiodora*), or the taller lavenders may be grown nearby to provide extra fragrance when brushed against.

Enclose the sides and rear of the seat with a metal or wooden framework on which to train climbers, such as sweet-scented roses combined with honeysuckle or variegated hops (see photograph on p.86). The enclosure itself can be grown by planting apples or pears on dwarf rootstocks at each end of the seat and also behind. Train the tops to meet overhead, and their side shoots like those of an espalier sideways, until the spaces between the trees are filled by a framework of horizontal branches clothed with fruiting spurs.

*The well-known stone, brick and chamomile seat in the herb garden at Sissinghurst, Kent, constructed for Vita Sackville-West by her chauffeur, and popularly referred to as 'Edward the Confessor's Chair'. This is just one of the many possible ways to incorporate herbs into garden features such as banks and seats, the latter rarely intended for use, especially as most of the species commonly used will not tolerate hard wear.*

## ENCOURAGING BEES

Apart from their decorative contribution when grown with vegetables and fruit, many herbs in flower are valuable sources of pollen and nectar for bees and help to attract them on to neighbouring plants which need pollination. Beans and courgettes, for example, do not crop well without pollination, but planting borage or basil amongst such vegetables will often encourage large numbers of bees to visit them. Most of the strongly aromatic herbs such as thyme, marjoram, hyssop and sage are popular food plants for bees. These will also tend to attract other beneficial insects. Hoverflies are typical: they love to browse on the flowers of thyme and fennel, and will then lay their eggs in the vicinity wherever a plant is affected by aphids, on which the hoverfly larvae feed as soon as they hatch.

## HERBS FOR POTS

Most herbs, with the exception of deep-rooting species that prefer moist soil and a shady position, will adapt to cultivation in pots. A number of pots and containers can be assembled in a sunny corner to provide a basic collection of herbs in courtyards or gardens where space is limited, but even if this is not a problem, most herbs are sufficiently attractive to justify being grown in pots as well as in the open garden.

Frequently-used herbs such as thyme, sage, rosemary and basil can be arranged close to hand, especially if several examples of each are potted as replacements for heavily picked plants. Lemon verbena, bay and other slightly tender plants are easily moved into the sunniest positions, or indoors when frost threatens. As well as portability, pots can be useful in restricting the spread of more invasive plants such as mint and tarragon, and for restraining vigorous, leafy herbs like lovage or fennel which will tend to make bushier growth.

Choose the containers with care. The best herbs for pots in sunny positions are those such as sage, thyme, sweet marjoram and rosemary, all of which have a Mediterranean appearance that complements old majolica pots and ornamented terracotta. Small-leaved and prostrate species are best grown in wide pans, or strawberry pots with several holes from which the plants can spread and tumble. Formal herbs, such as trained bay trees or shrubby species clipped to shape, will look best in stone containers or the classic, square wooden boxes still seen today at Versailles.

Very attractive effects can be achieved by growing several herbs in a single large container, either different varieties of the same species or genus, or a varied selection similar to the combinations planted in hanging baskets. Taller herbs in the centre can be surrounded by bushy, variegated varieties, with creeping thymes or mints, trailing helichrysum or scented pelargoniums arranged at the edges to cascade down over the sides.

## ANGELICA (*Angelica archangelica*)
Biennial, or short-lived perennial; zone 3

With its dramatic growth and sculptural shape, angelica is a herb to be used boldly. It is a tall stately plant, often reaching a height of 2-2.5m (6-8ft), and the large fragrant leaves, deeply cut like a stout fern, are hairy and light green. When angelica is two to five years old enormous heads of pale green flowers appear in summer, but after flowering the plants usually die. Grow angelica beside a pool or group three

*Even if rarely used for its culinary and medicinal properties, angelica deserves prominence in the garden as an impressive foliage plant. The flowers can be left to set and scatter their seeds, often producing plants that live longer before themselves flowering and then dying.*

or four together for height at the back of a border, especially if they can be accentuated against a brick wall or dark clipped hedge. It mixes well with bright flowers such as penstemons, anchusa and coreopsis, or the contrasting foliage of rhubarb, mint or fennel; it also thrives in a semi-wild context amongst foxgloves, verbascums and madonna lilies. Although the top growth disappears in winter, angelica is normally very hardy.

### CULTIVATION
Angelica plants are sometimes found in the wild growing near water or in woodland, and in the garden they prefer similar conditions of partial shade and a rich, moist root run. They normally behave as biennials, growing one year to flower the next, but it can be four or even five years before they bloom; plants from self-sown seed especially tend to behave as short-lived perennials. Although it is possible to propagate angelica by root division, plants are usually raised from seed, which has a very short viability and is best sown as soon as it is ripe. Either buy plants initially and allow them to flower and scatter their own seed, or sow freshly gathered seed in pots in September. Keep the pots in a greenhouse or cold frame and plant out the strongest seedlings 90-120cm (3-4ft) apart the following spring.

### USES
Once a medieval strewing herb thought to protect people against the plague, angelica is now best known for its candied stems used as sweets and cake decorations. Stems for crystallizing should be cut in May before they become too fibrous. Its roots and stems can be used as a sugar substitute, like sweet cicely, when cooking acid fruits; if they are to be dried for storing, gather in May and June. The whole plant, including its roots and seeds, is still used medicinally to relieve digestive ailments and tension.

## BASIL
(*Ocimum* species and cultivars)
Annual

Several kinds of basil are grown, all of them characterized by a strong pungent scent with warm and typically Mediterranean associations. Sweet or common basil (*O. basilicum*) is most widely grown and has the best flavour. It will grow 60-90cm (2-3ft) tall, with quadrangular stems bearing soft, glossy, oval leaves, bright green and up to 7cm (3in) long, and small whorls of white flowers. Bush basil (*O. basilicum minimum*) is much more compact and dwarf, growing about 15cm (6in) tall, with a less powerful flavour. Dark opal basil (*O. basilicum purpureum*) has deep purple foliage and pink flowers, while the leaves of *O. crispum*, or lettuce basil, are large and crinkled. There are other basils with red or yellow flowers, and some unusual lemon and clove-scented kinds.

Since basil is fairly delicate, it is usually grown as an annual, and can be combined with other annual plants such as marigolds and nasturtiums; the dark opal form makes a spectacular contrast with matricaria, sweet alyssum or pink godetia. All kinds of basil are excellent for edging vegetable beds, particularly when they are planted beside carrots, parsley, lettuce or endive.

### CULTIVATION
Although reliably perennial in warmer climates, basils are only half-hardy in Britain and must not be planted outdoors until all risk of frost is past. A warm sheltered position in full sun is essential, preferably on fertile soil, rich in humus and well drained (basils are notoriously sensitive to wet conditions and are sure to fail wherever heavy rainfall does not clear quickly).

Plants are raised from seed, sown in March in a heated greenhouse or April if unheated.

Seedlings emerge after about a fortnight and, unless sown very thinly, need prompt pricking out individually into small pots, for planting out during May or June 30-45cm (12-18in) apart. Water regularly, preferably before midday to allow surplus moisture time to evaporate. For good leaf development, pinch out flowering stems and clip plants to a tidy shape if they become tall and leggy. Where soil conditions are less than ideal, cultivation in pots may be more successful, either in a greenhouse or a sunny patio or courtyard. Bush basil can be lifted from the garden in September for potting up in rich compost; if placed on a sunny windowsill, the potted plants will extend supplies into the winter months.

## USES
Basil is a very important culinary herb in Italian cuisine, and is frequently added as flavouring to cheese, egg, fish and tomato dishes, using the fresh leaves and tips of stems picked during summer and early autumn when required. As the first frost will abruptly finish the crop, cut one or two plants down just before they flower and dry all the foliage very slowly in the dark and then store in airtight containers for use out of season. Medicinally, the leaves are used as a tonic and stimulant, and for the treatment of nervous disorders; they can also be dried to make a powerful snuff.

## BAY (*Laurus nobilis*)
Shrub; zone 8

Sometimes known as sweet bay, bay laurel or poet's laurel, this is an aromatic evergreen tree or multi-stemmed shrub, hardy when established, and slowly growing to an eventual height of about 9m (30ft), although in Britain it rarely exceeds 4.5-6m (15-20ft) in height and 2.5-3m (8-10ft) in width. In warmer gardens a bay tree may be left to develop its typically

*A lightly-trimmed young bay is the focal point amongst the mixed planting in a fully integrated cottage garden.*

conical outline, eventually making a shapely specimen tree on a sunny lawn. The leathery leaves are dark and shiny, oval with pointed tips and a strong spicy scent, especially if crushed; the flowers are cream and inconspicuous, with male and female forms borne on different plants. The density of this rich green foliage and its tolerance of close clipping have always made bay popular for hedges and elementary topiary. Individual plants can be shaped into mop-head standards, an ideal form for growing in tubs; underplant with bulbs and bushy flowers or herbs, such as columbines, nigella or lemon balm. Willow-leaved bay, *L. nobilis angustifolia* (syn. *L. n.* 'Salicifolia'), with long slender leaves, often proves hardier in cold areas.

### CULTIVATION
Bay is a Mediterranean tree and although reasonably frost resistant once established, it is best grown in a warm position sheltered from cold winds, perhaps in the shade of other trees.

In colder areas it is safer for the first few years to grow bay in a good soil-based potting

mixture in tubs so that they can be moved into a conservatory or a less exposed part of the garden: a tub or large pot 45-60cm (18-24in) in diameter will support a clipped tree 180cm (6ft) tall. Encircle young outdoor trees in winter with a cylinder of bubble plastic or wrap them in a jacket of straw held in place with wire netting. Mulch around the stems with garden compost or decayed leaves. Severe winter weather may cause some of the foliage on mature trees to turn brown, but this damage is usually only temporary and will disappear beneath new growth. When left to grow naturally bay needs no pruning, but mop-head trees should be clipped to shape annually in early summer, and again in autumn if a strictly formal outline is needed. Propagate bay from half-ripe cuttings taken with a heel in September, planted in a cold frame, or in a heated propagator where they will root more rapidly.

### USES
Wreathes made from bay laurel foliage were once presented to outstanding public figures, hence the term 'laureate', but these days it is grown chiefly for culinary use, the leaves being an important ingredient of bouquet garni. They can be picked at any time for immediate use or to dry for storage in glass jars. They have a less familiar medicinal role as a hair conditioner and a treatment for rheumatic complaints.

## BERGAMOT (*Monarda didyma*)
Perennial; zones 4-9

An old-fashioned cottage garden plant, bergamot is one of the brightest flowering herbs and a favourite with bees (sometimes called bee balm). It is a hardy perennial, with compact bushy growth 60-90cm (2-3ft) tall. The quadrangular stems bear oval serrated leaves, and conspicuous whorls of intensely coloured flowers in summer. Bergamot gives a good

*Although vivid red bergamot is the most familiar kind, there are valuable species and varieties in other colours, such as pink, shown in the foreground here blending well with lavender in a mixed border.*

account of itself in an herbaceous border and is valuable as a brilliant highlight amongst foliage herbs. It can be planted to edge beds, and beside pools which suits its preference for damp conditions. Two or three plants flowering together in a large pot will provide long-lasting colour on a patio or courtyard. The most vivid variety is 'Cambridge Scarlet' which also has the best scent for herbal use, but mixtures are available combining scarlet with pink, crimson, mauve and white forms. *Monarda citriodora*, lemon bergamot or lemon mint, is shorter, 30-60cm (1-2ft) tall with pink bracts; wild bergamot, *M. fistulosa*, is a lax-growing species, 90cm (3ft) high with pale lavender flowers.

## CULTIVATION
Plants flourish best in light shade, or in full sun provided the soil is consistently moist. Grow from root divisions in spring, cuttings taken in summer, or from seed sown outdoors in late spring or under glass a month or two earlier, covering the seeds very thinly and keeping moist until seedlings emerge two to six weeks later. Plant out 45cm (18in) apart in rich soil that never dries out: a position beside water is not too wet. Every alternate spring dig up and divide plants, keeping the young outer portions to replant, while discarding the old centres.

## USES
Bergamot leaves and dried flowers are the ingredients of a tisane known as Oswego tea, named after the North American Indians with whom it was a popular drink; elsewhere it is called Gold Melissa tea. Bergamot is also used

to flavour Earl Grey tea. The fresh leaves can be picked at any time for immediate use; for winter both leaves and flower heads can be gathered and then dried carefully in order to retain their colour.

## BORAGE (*Borago officinalis*)
Annual

Since strong, bright blues are comparatively rare amongst flowers, borage with its pendant clusters of brilliant cobalt blue star-shaped flowers and soft grey-green foliage is a valuable decorative addition to any garden. A vigorous hardy annual plant that may survive mild winters unscathed, it grows up to 75-90cm (2.5-3ft) high, with long rough leaves sometimes 20-23cm (8-9in) long. Although sturdy and upright at first, and therefore useful as an edging, the plants tend to sprawl when in full bloom and may need cutting back if they spread too casually across paths. They are excellent grown on banks or on top of hollow walls where the drooping flowers are fully visible. They are also ideal for tumbling over the edge of tubs containing standard trees such as mop-head bays. Borage is attractive planted beneath roses or fruit trees, while its colour and form combine well with marigolds, nasturtiums, carnations, astilbes, white flowers such as lavatera 'Mont Blanc', *Chrysanthemum maximum* (Shasta daisy) or tall white campanulas, and copper or purple-leaved shrubs. Borage is very attractive to bees, hence the plant's popular name of 'beebread'.

## CULTIVATION
Grow initially from seed sown outdoors in spring and again at midsummer for succession; plants normally seed themselves thereafter and the strongest seedlings can be transplanted wherever needed. Sow in rows for transplanting 30-45cm (12-18in) apart, or drop

two or three seeds into shallow holes where they are to grow. Ordinary garden soil is suitable, provided it drains freely, and sunny or very lightly shaded positions are best. To encourage bushiness, occasionally pinch off the ends of spreading branches.

## USES

Because of their vivid colour, borage flowers are often used as an edible garnish for salads, and to decorate summer drinks; the flowers should be picked when fully opened and used straight away. The leaves too, if young and fresh, are edible with a flavour similar to cucumber, and may be added to salads or cooked in the same way as spinach. Rich in minerals, borage has an invigorating effect on the system and is often prescribed as a tonic or remedy for depression.

*Respected since classical Roman times as a potent antidote for low spirits, borage with its blue flowers is particularly effective massed in bold drifts.*

# CALENDULA or POT MARIGOLD
## (*Calendula officinalis*)
Annual

Pot or English marigolds are an easily grown source of colour throughout the season. These hardy annual flowering plants have large, oval, pale green leaves and bold flowers like large daisies, single or double according to type. The typical colour is a rich glowing orange, but varieties and seed mixtures are available in a range from pale yellow to light red. Plants grow to about 45cm (18in) tall, tending to sprawl sideways before reaching full height. The normal flowering period is May to October, although in a mild season plants may stay in bloom almost all year. In areas with hot summers, calendulas bloom and grow best during the cooler seasons. They make a vivid contrast with plants of more sober colour, such as purple shrubs and grey plants like lavender, curry plant (*Helichrysum angustifolium*) and cotton lavender (*Santolina chamaecyparissus*). Grow calendulas as a brilliant carpet beneath all types of trained fruit trees or around the base of delphiniums and verbascums, and as highlights amongst other herbs such as hyssop, borage, sage or chervil.

## CULTIVATION

Almost anywhere is suitable, including poor soils, provided the plants have full sun for most of the day. Choose a good strain of seed – there are many worth growing, although single-flowered kinds have an authentic old-fashioned charm – and sow outdoors in spring, or in warm gardens in the autumn for earlier flowers the following year. Thin seedlings or transplant 23-30cm (9-12in) apart. Pick off dead flowers and occasionally pinch back stems to encourage more compact plants and a longer flowering season, but leave a few seedheads to mature and scatter seed from them to grow during the following season.

## USES

Pick the fresh petals or whole flowers as required. The brilliant and delicately flavoured petals are used in potpourri, as an edible garnish in salads, and to colour butter and rice. Tea made from marigold petals is a tonic and a circulatory stimulant; the flowers are also used in cosmetics and to aid the healing of small wounds. Both petals and whole flowers can be gathered and dried slowly at a low temperature for store.

# CHAMOMILE, Roman/Lawn
## (*Anthemis nobilis/ Chamaemelum nobile*)
Perennial; zone 4

# CHAMOMILE, True/German
## (*Matricaria recutita*)
Annual

Roman chamomile is a hardy perennial, growing about 30cm (1ft) tall. Its fine, ferny leaves smell of apples when crushed (the name chamomile comes from the Greek for 'apple on the ground') and they often keep their bright green colour longer than turf in hot summers. Small white daisies, single or semi-double according to type, are produced from June until August. The non-flowering clone 'Treneague', only 5-7cm (2-3in) tall, is usually considered best for lawns. True chamomile, on the other hand, is a hardy annual with a similar appearance but grows up to 60cm (2ft) tall; its flowers, which resemble small Shasta daisies, appear continuously from May until the frosts. Anthemis stands moderate wear and can be planted densely as a lawn on dry soils, in smaller groups as mats beside paths, and between paving slabs or rockery stones. The taller matricaria is a valuable contrast to bright, stouter flowering plants, such as pot marigolds, dwarf rudbeckias, godetia or bedding dahlias.

## CULTIVATION

Both lawn chamomile and matricaria prefer sunny positions on rich light soils with very good drainage, although lawn chamomile will tolerate a little shade. Sow matricaria sparingly in spring or autumn where it is to grow and leave unthinned; although an annual, it usually seeds itself freely around the garden and may be transplanted to where needed in future seasons. Lawn chamomile can be sown in March under glass for pricking out into pots or trays; keep these young plants in a cold frame over their first winter and plant out the following spring 10-15cm (4-6in) apart. Alternatively, divide established plants or take cuttings in spring (named clones must be propagated in this way). For chamomile lawns, see p. 77.

## USES

Pick the flowers of both kinds, without stalks, when they are fully opened, either for immediate use or to dry rapidly for storage in airtight containers. Roman chamomile is sometimes made into a herbal shampoo and hair rinse. Matricaria is the medicinal chamomile used to treat gastric and digestive ailments, and also has a reputation for doctoring sick plants, especially roses, if grown beside them.

# CHERVIL (*Anthriscus cerefolium*)
Annual

Chervil resembles parsley in habit, with more delicate lacy foliage – pale bright green and 30-45cm (12-18in) tall. Inconspicuous white flowers appear during late summer. Although plants usually behave as annuals, they are very hardy and may survive over winter if picking prevents their flowering the first year. The dainty foliage of chervil makes it excellent in a flower border or sown in drills for edging beds,

especially in partially shaded positions, and it contrasts well with pinks, pansies and purple-leaved forms of sage, basil or *Begonia semperflorens*. Like parsley and dill, it may be sown between slower growing vegetables or beneath fruit trees and bushes, whose shade will protect plants from midsummer heat and so prevent their bolting to seed.

## CULTIVATION

Chervil flourishes on most lighter garden soils in full sun, except during midsummer. Sow fresh seed sparingly in drills or patches in spring and again in late summer for a continuous supply (in hot regions where plants bolt rapidly, sow at fortnightly intervals). Thin plants to 10-15cm (4-6in) apart, keep well weeded and water frequently in hot weather to prevent sudden bolting; if the odd plant is left to seed itself, however, future sowings may not be necessary. Chervil is not easily dried, but winter supplies can be ensured by cloching outdoor plants or by sowing a pinch of seed in pots in late summer.

## USES

The sweet and aromatic leaves are an important ingredient of fines herbes, and can be picked as required once plants are about two months old. They are used for decorative garnishes (often as an out-of-season substitute for parsley) and to flavour soups and sauces. One of the traditional Lent herbs, chervil is used medicinally to cleanse the blood and aid digestion, and as a lotion for skin disorders.

# CHIVES (*Allium schoenoprasum*)
Perennial; zone 3

Chives are traditional edging plants for kitchen garden beds, the rows quickly developing into a decorative and useful dwarf flowering hedge. A hardy perennial bulbous plant, chives grow

*The vigorous chives bulbs are not seriously weakened by flowering and remain fully productive until the autumn frosts.*

in clumps, with blue-green, slender, pointed foliage, about 23cm (9in) high, which dies down in winter. Around midsummer the bulbs produce flowering stems up to 30cm (1ft) tall, each with a small feathery sphere of densely clustered mauve flowers. Chives look well grown with parsley, chervil, tansy and other delicate broad-leaved herbs, variegated thymes, marjorams or sage, and smaller flowering plants such as ageratum, violas, linaria or nigella. Garlic chives, *A. tuberosum*, are larger in all respects, their leaves flat and 30cm (1ft) or more tall, and the 5cm (2in) diameter balls of fragrant white flowers are carried on 45cm (18in) stems; the flavour, however, is less pronounced than that of common chives.

## CULTIVATION

Almost any fertile soil in full sun or light shade is suitable for these easily grown plants. They prefer moist conditions and should be watered well in dry weather, especially after flowering. Either sow small pinches of seed where they are to grow, each group 30cm (1ft) apart, or plant four to six bulbs at this distance in soil enriched with garden compost or a little rotted manure. Cut down exhausted flower stems before they set seed, and in autumn clear frosted foliage. Every three to four years divide mature clumps, while dormant, into small groups and replant.

## USES

A very important culinary herb, chives are used to season all kinds of dishes and impart a mild onion flavour. Bunches of leaves or complete clumps can be cut down to 2.5-5cm (1-2in) from the ground whenever required; healthy plants will quickly grow again to give several such cuts in a season. After flowering cut down a few as yet untouched clumps to provide tender young growth for cutting late in the season. Chives are difficult to store well, and for winter supplies it is best to divide one or two large clumps cut down after flowering and pot up the divisions for growing in a greenhouse or conservatory, or on a windowsill indoors. Chives are a notable antiseptic, tonic and blood cleanser. Some gardeners consider chives a valuable companion plant to deter blackfly and prevent the fungus black spot on roses.

## DILL (*Anethum graveolens*)
Annual

The tall, soft, ferny dill plant blends well into any informal semi-wild garden. A bushy hardy annual, it grows 60-90cm (2-3ft) tall, with dark green and strongly pungent feathery leaves. Flattened clusters of lime-green flowers appear in July and August, followed by large oval and sweetly aromatic seeds. Grow dill amongst plants of stouter, more flamboyant habit, such as bergamot and the scarlet *Lychnis chalcedonica*, or purple sage, rodgersia and other plants with dark foliage. It may also be grown decoratively between lettuces, onions,

spinach or french beans. Indian dill (*A. sowa*) is similar in appearance but grows only 45cm (18in) tall, with a more powerful flavour.

## CULTIVATION

Dill must have full sun and moist, very well broken soil that drains freely. The delicate leaves have little wind resistance and plants should be given shelter without being too shaded. Do not grow near fennel, because the two herbs are compatible and seedlings are likely to develop as useless hybrids. Sow in drills or groups in very fine soil outdoors and thin seedlings until plants just touch; or sow in small pots or cell trays indoors so that seedlings can be transplanted with the least disturbance. For seed production, sow in April to give plants a long season. Where the leaves are required, be prepared to sow at regular intervals from spring to midsummer, since hot or dry weather may cause sudden flowering even while still small, after which plants are useless except to seed themselves for succession. Liberal watering and light mulches of grass cuttings in dry seasons may help to prevent or at least delay flowering.

## USES

Dill leaves, gathered before the plants flower, are a popular flavouring for fish and vegetable dishes, those of Indian dill being especially good for seasoning curries. Unopened flower heads can be added to pickles. The seeds, gathered as they turn reddish-brown and dried in paper bags, are used both in cooking and also to make dill water, a well-known and effective remedy for digestive problems.

## FENNEL/GARDEN FENNEL
(*Foeniculum vulgare*)
Perennial; zone 6

Fennel is a tall foliage plant, useful where height and elegance are needed. It is a sturdy

hardy perennial with stiff upright growth 150-180cm (5-6ft) tall. Thick tough stems carry fine lacy foliage, usually rich deep green, although there are darker forms whose young growth is purple or rusty bronze. Flat umbels of small yellow flowers appear in late summer, followed by heads of long oily seeds, sweetly scented and, like the foliage, reminiscent of aniseed. It makes an attractive contrast with more substantial plants such as angelica, rosemary, foxgloves and silver thistles.

## CULTIVATION

Fennel likes rich, well-drained soil in a sunny position. Sow seeds outdoors in spring, thinning or transplanting them to about 45cm (18in) apart; once established, plants usually seed themselves freely. Alternatively, existing plants can be divided in autumn or, where winters are severe, in spring; in cold regions,

*A luxuriant and established clump of green garden fennel (centre background)* in full bloom demonstrates its decorative merits amongst mints and flowering plants. The plants are surrounded by gravel mulch.

fennel may not be long-lived, and it is worth overwintering seedlings in a cold frame as an insurance against loss. Plant fennel where it is sheltered from the strongest winds, or be prepared to stake the plants, and do not grow near dill with which it will cross-fertilize to produce useless seedlings. Occasionally prune stems back to induce soft new growth. In autumn, cut plants down to 7-10cm (3-4in) and cover with decayed leaves or peat against frost.

## USES
Fresh young fennel leaves can be mixed in salads and used to flavour fish, egg or cheese dishes. The seeds should be gathered while still light green and dried very slowly indoors. They can then be used to season pickle and to make gripe water to relieve digestive problems.

## FLORENCE FENNEL/FINOCCHIO
(*Foeniculum dulce/Foeniculum vulgare* var. *azoricum*)
Annual

Florence fennel is a shorter, stockier plant than garden fennel, growing only 60-90cm (2-3ft) tall. Though often listed by seedsmen as a herb, it is grown as an annual vegetable. Instead of being dispersed up the main stem, the leaf joints remain clustered together near ground level, overlapping to form a thick swollen base to the stem. The leaves are similar in shape but a paler green than those of garden fennel, although their flavour is comparable. Plants combine decoratively with lettuces, carrots, beetroot or spinach.

## CULTIVATION
Florence fennel likes a rich fertile soil, moisture retentive but free draining, in a sunny part of the garden. Clay soils are unsuitable unless very well broken; all need to be enriched with garden compost. Sow where plants are to grow, thinning seedlings to about 20cm (8in) apart; or sow under glass in cell trays to minimize root disturbance when transplanting. Water freely to encourage rapid growth and reduce any tendency to bolt to seed. Some varieties have slightly different sowing times, for example:

Perfection: very large, broad bulbs. Slow to bolt and may be sown from June onwards.

Sirio: good flavour, fast growth and best sown after midsummer for autumn production.

Zeva Fino: large, good quality bulbs. Very resistant to bolting and can be sown in April.

Zeva Tardo: heavier bulbs than Zeva Fino, but less bolt-resistant. Sow in mid-June.

## USES
Finocchio is grown chiefly for the firm, juicy bulbous base of its stem, which is used as a vegetable, raw in salads or braised, when it resembles celery combined with a sweet aniseed flavour. To prepare the bulb, allow it to swell to the size of an orange, draw up soil to cover half its depth, and leave for about ten days when it will be sufficiently blanched to cut. When the bulb is harvested, its leaves can be used for the same purposes as garden fennel. Plants are not normally allowed to flower or set seed.

## HOPS (*Humulus lupulus*)
Perennial vine; zone 3

A vigorous hardy perennial, hops make excellent screening plants as they rapidly twine up any available support to a height of 4.5-6m (15-20ft) or more. The deciduous leaves are large and vine-shaped, light green or gold according to variety. Male and female flowers are borne in summer on separate plants, the

*Both common green* (above) *and variegated kinds of hop are outstanding screening plants, reaching a great height if supported, but where space is more limited the stems can be thinned while young and later pruned.*

females as pale green cones that mature into the familiar brown, papery hops used for brewing. The vines can be planted to scramble over trelliswork, arbours and pergolas, and in the past were often grown with climbing roses up vertical poles and then trained along ropes or chains slung between the tops of the uprights. In the absence of support their exuberant growth will hang in graceful festoons, and so two or three plants will soon envelop a tripod of canes 2-2.5m (6-8ft) high and make a luxuriant garden feature like a weeping tree, especially if combined with sweet peas, rambling roses or morning glory (ipomaea).

## CULTIVATION

A sunny position is best, on soils that have been deeply worked and enriched with garden compost or rotted manure. Although regular watering is necessary during the growing season, free drainage is equally important for the health of plants. Start in spring with bought plants, root divisions or cuttings of young shoots about 15-20cm (6-8in) long; or sow fresh seed outdoors in the autumn to expose it to frost. Plant in groups of two or three at the base of a support, which must be strong enough to sustain the weight of foliage. Completely clear top growth in autumn. Each spring thin the young shoots when about 15cm (6in) high, leaving the three or four strongest to grow on.

## USES

The young spring shoots can be gathered and eaten raw in salads or cooked like asparagus. Hop cones are left to ripen on the vines in a dry season; otherwise, gather in early autumn for drying indoors. In addition to being used to flavour beer, the slightly sedative female fruits are often made into a tisane or blended with lavender for filling pillows to help induce sleep; they are also used in poultices to reduce external inflammation.

## HORSERADISH (*Armoracia rusticana/Cochlearia armoracia*)
Perennial; zone 5

Horseradish is not a decorative plant, and tends to be difficult to eradicate once established, as even very small remnants of the deep roots can survive to regrow. The first leaves of the season of this hardy perennial are deeply cut and resemble combs, but later foliage is long and coarse, up to 60cm (2ft) long, rough and wavy edged. Long loose heads of tiny white flowers are produced in summer. The roots are stout and tenacious, penetrating deep into the soil

and spreading to colonize neighbouring ground. Some of the best plants are to be seen growing wild on railway embankments and wayside places, and it can be planted in a similar way to naturalize itself in a wild garden, provided there is no danger to other plants when the occasional root is dug up for use. The long stout leaves can provide a solid background to delicate flowering plants such as annual gypsophila or linaria, which will be cleared before much of the horseradish is harvested.

## CULTIVATION

Light soil, deeply dug and well manured, in full sun or partial shade is best. Start plants from root cuttings 15cm (6in) long, planted at an angle 30cm (1ft) apart in early spring and covered with no more than 5cm (2in) of soil. Either leave them to grow as semi-wild plants or, for the thickest and juiciest roots, plant as an annual vegetable crop in rich soil: keep them free from weeds and dig up the whole crop in the autumn, storing the best roots in boxes of damp sand, and temporarily burying thinner pieces for replanting the following spring.

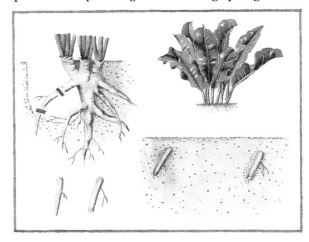

*Any fragment of horseradish root left in the ground will grow. This ability is exploited to start new beds from cuttings of the thinner roots.*

## USES

The root of horseradish is dug up when needed and grated to make a pungent sauce to accompany meat dishes. With its penetrating heat it stimulates the appetite, and is also a valuable ingredient of poultices and a natural antibiotic. Fresh young leaves are sometimes used sparingly in salads.

## HYSSOP (*Hyssopus officinalis*)
Perennial; zones 4-5

Hyssop is a perennial shrub uncommon in small herb collections today, and yet it was once widely planted as dwarf hedging in medieval knot gardens and parterres. Left to themselves the shapely semi-evergreen bushes grow to about 45cm (18in) tall – up to 120cm (4ft) in warmer climates – but with two or three trims during the season a neat dense hedge 30cm (1ft) high can be formed from the slender bright green foliage. However, clipping inevitably reduces the summer crop of flowers, usually blue but sometimes white, pink or purple, clustered in whorls up tall slim spikes. In addition to being a useful hedging plant, hyssop can be surrounded with mats of variegated thymes and marjoram for edging paths or beds, while its upright slender growth will be emphasized if bushes are grown amongst short, broader-leaved plants such as sorrel, heuchera or pulmonaria.

## CULTIVATION

Plants are raised from seed in pots during March, or open ground in April, transplanting seedlings 30-38cm (12-15in) apart in the summer. Alternatively, divide existing clumps in spring, or root cuttings of young shoots in pots of gritty compost. Plant out in light, well-drained soils containing a little lime, in a warm sunny position (where exposed to cold winds, hyssop may lose some or all of its leaves in winter). Trim specimen bushes to shape after flowering, and every three to four years lift and divide mature plants to keep them vigorous.

## USES

While the flowers are very popular with bees and butterflies, an effective moth repellent can be made from the pungent, edible leaves, which are also used to add a pleasantly bitter flavour to salads or vegetable dishes, and to treat coughs or catarrh. The young leaves and tips of shoots should be picked as required, although for drying they are best picked just before bushes flower.

*Hyssop, here in full bloom and combined with variegated sage, should be clipped to shape after flowering.*

## LEMON BALM (*Melissa officinalis*)
Perennial; zones 4-5

Gardeners have always appreciated balm's sweet lemon fragrance and its immaculate sculpted appearance in spring and early summer. Until they flower, plants form tight clumps of bright green, gold or variegated leaves, shaped like ragged hearts and so deeply veined as to seem wrinkled. In moist fertile soil and a warm position, balm grows quickly to about 90cm (3ft) high, developing into broad rounded shrubs that look very decorative in pots, tubs or small spaces amongst paving stones. They are often grown beside paths and doorways to release their strong scent whenever brushed against. Elsewhere in the garden, balm can be used as a prominent foliage plant, combined with ferns, groups of lady's mantle (alchemilla) and hardy geraniums, or for contrast with the tall, pointed leaves of montbretia or striped iris (*I. pallida* 'Variegata').

## CULTIVATION

Balm is very easy to grow, and often seeds itself once established. Green forms may be raised from seed sown in spring, the young bushes then transplanted in autumn (the following spring in cold regions) 38-45cm (15-18in) apart in full sun, or light shade if summers are usually hot. Mature plants are divided while dormant, or young spring shoots can be pulled off as cuttings for rooting in pots. These vegetative methods are essential for variegated kinds, which produce their richest colours if planted in full sun and cut back to 7-10cm (3-4in) high at midsummer to encourage bright new growth. Later in the summer, spikes of small cream flowers develop. These attract bees (*melissa* is Greek for honey bee), but from this time onwards bushes may look thin and dishevelled, and begin to sprawl sideways. To avoid this, remove flowering stems as they

form, and trim the sides of bushes to shape, or prune as for variegated kinds. In autumn cut down frosted foliage to ground level; if winters are normally severe, dig up a plant or two at this time and overwinter in a cold frame for division and replanting the following spring.

## USES

Gather the tips of stems as required, and use to add lemon flavouring to fish, poultry, stuffings and drinks, or to make a pleasant, mildly sedative tea valuable for treating nervous disorders, headaches and insomnia. Leaves may be dried for winter use.

## LOVAGE (*Levisticum officinale*)
Perennial; zone 3

With its lush appearance and tolerance of shade, lovage blends well amongst informal, semi-wild or woodland settings. A stout, handsome herbaceous perennial, it has strong upright growth 120cm-2.5m (4-8ft) high, and its shiny, dark green leaves are large and deeply cut like celery, borne on thick hollow stems; large umbels of yellow flowers in summer are followed by heads of ribbed aromatic seeds. It is a valuable and traditional cottage garden plant, giving height to the back of a border, and providing a cool background to tall flowering plants such as hollyhocks, lilies, delphiniums and foxgloves, or bright geums, cornflowers and scabious. Its stature complements fennel, sweet cicely, angelica and other tall herbs, while the rich colour of its large leaves contrasts with the prickly foliage of globe artichokes and ornamental thistles. Scots lovage, (*Ligusticum scoticum*), is similar but smaller, growing only 90cm (3ft) tall and bearing pink flowers.

## CULTIVATION

Lovage is an easy-going herb, thriving on all deep moist soils except heavy clay. It appreciates plenty of humus, and will grow equally well in sun or part shade. Sow fresh seed in the autumn or bought seeds in spring outdoors, or divide existing clumps in spring, finally planting 90cm (3ft) apart. For full height, water plants whenever dry, especially where they are growing in full sun, and stake if they are exposed to wind. If plants become too tall, stems may be pruned to height. Clear away all top growth after it has died down in autumn.

## USES

Lovage leaves have a yeasty flavour, while the stems and roots taste of celery; all parts are used in soups, stews, casseroles and raw in salads. Young leaves, picked when needed throughout the summer, can be cooked like spinach, or gathered before flowering time and slowly dried for storage. The seeds are often sprinkled on bread and biscuits. It was once common practice to earth up plants to blanch the stems in the same way as trench celery. Medicinally, lovage is used to treat circulatory disorders, and as a deodorant.

---

# MARJORAM (*Origanum* species)
Perennial, annual

Marjorams are excellent edging plants, especially pot marjoram which will quickly flow over the edges of paths or fill joints between crazy paving. With its neat spreading habit, it makes an ideal scented plant for pots indoors as well as hanging baskets in a sunny porch or conservatory. Wild marjoram, too, will grow in hanging baskets, the golden form making a pretty contrast with ivy-leafed geraniums.

*Marjorams need full sun, but will grow happily in close proximity with other dwarf shrubs. Variegated kinds (right foreground)* combine particularly well with the contrasting colours of box hedging and purple sage.

All the marjorams are visibly related to each other, although there are distinct differences in appearance. Pot marjoram (*Origanum onites*) – zone 7 – is a dwarf, shrubby, hardy perennial, forming circular mounds of foliage 15-23cm (6-9in) high, which steadily spread as the prostrate stems creep sideways and root where they touch the ground. The mildly flavoured leaves are rich green and heart-shaped; mauve flowers are produced in late summer on wiry stems 45cm (18in) or more tall. Although sweet marjoram (*O. majorana*) – zone 9 – is a perennial plant in warmer regions, in Britain it is normally grown from seed each year as a half-hardy annual, forming neat bushes of round greyish leaves 25-30cm (10-12in) tall. From midsummer onward tight spikes of white or pale mauve flowers appear on tough thin stems. Wild marjoram or oregano (*O. vulgare*) – zone 5 – is a shrubby perennial (annual in cold climates), similar in most respects to pot marjoram but growing up to 45cm (18in) tall, with downy leaves and pink or white flowers in terminal clusters. The flavour is more pungent than that of other marjorams, especially in a hot summer. There is a strain known as Greek oregano which is particularly fiery, and also an attractive golden variegated form. All marjorams blend well with the silver leaves of cinerarea, artemisia, helichrysums etc, together with thrift, chives and other plants with pointed, upright foliage.

## CULTIVATION
All marjorams prefer positions in full sun, and light dry soils. They will often refuse to grow in heavy ground or soil that lies cold and wet in spring. Wild marjoram grows naturally on alkaline sites and should therefore be given a little garden lime where the ground is known to be acid. Sow sweet marjoram in warmth under glass during early spring, either in pots for pricking out into trays, or in cell trays, two or three seeds to each module. Seedlings grow

slowly and are vulnerable to cold at first; grow on in warmth until the end of May, when they may be planted out 20-23cm (8-9in) apart. Pot marjoram and oregano can be propagated from seed sown outdoors in spring, from cuttings of basal shoots, by layers, or by division in spring (in cold areas do this in autumn and over-winter in a cold frame). Both are planted 30-38cm (12-15in) apart. Trim perennial kinds to shape in autumn, and lift one or two plants at this time, potting them up in a soil-based mixture for supplies out of season. Where winters are cold, either cover plants with leaves held in place with wire netting, or dig up a few specimens to replant in a cold frame.

## USES
The tips of all marjorams can be picked fresh for use in salads, tomato dishes and Mediterranean food. For storing, sweet marjoram plants are cut down to 7-10cm (3-4in) just as they start to flower, and the clippings dried very slowly in the dark. Wild and pot marjorams are more spicy than sweet marjoram, which has a distinctive flavour associated with sauces or stuffings; they are also used in the preparation of disinfectants. Wild marjoram is medicinally valuable for treating sore throats, coughs and digestive ailments.

---

# MINT (*Mentha* species)
Perennial

The mints are a confusing group of herbs, especially as they are usually known only by their common names. The most popular are:

Apple mint (*M. suaveolens*): robust plants, with round, woolly leaves, light green, pale edge. Pineapple mint is slightly more variegated. Pale mauve flowers. 60-90cm (2-3ft); zone 7

Corsican mint (*M. requienii*): creeping mint with minute round leaves, spreading like a green film

in moist soil and between stones. Tiny prostrate purple flowers in summer. 1cm (½in); zone 7

Eau-de-cologne or lemon mint (*Mentha citrata*): oval, dull green leaves, edged with purple. Likes very damp places. 45cm (18in); zone 4

Ginger mint (*M.* x *gentilis*): a vigorous, invasive mint with pale pointed leaves, tinged red, and pink flowers. Its green and gold variegated form, 'Aureo-Variegata' is a brightly-coloured plant when grown in full sun. 45-60cm (18-24in); zone 6

Pennyroyal (*M. pulegium*): prostrate herb with small, dark green, woolly leaves and pale

*In good soil most mints, including variegated ginger mint (above), will quickly spread by underground runners. Either confine plants, or grow in a semi-wild context.*

mauve flowers. It roots as it spreads. 2.5-5cm (1-2in), but flowering stems up to 30cm (1ft); zone 6

Peppermint (M. x *piperita*): white peppermint has narrow, serrated rich green leaves and pink-blue flowers. Black peppermint has dark purple stems and deep bronze-coloured leaves with a slightly stronger flavour. 60cm (2ft); zone 3

Spearmint (M. *spicata*): the most common mint, with long, serrated, bright green leaves, and dense cones of pink or white flowers. 60-90cm (2-3ft); zone 3

The diminutive Corsican mint, which smells of peppermint when trodden on, is invaluable for planting in rock gardens and between paving stones. Pennyroyal has the same uses on a larger scale, but it can be invasive, like the taller mints. These are best grown in their own containers or compartments in the garden, in pots surrounded by impatiens or varieties of *Begonia sempervirens*, or in the wild garden where they can be allowed to spread un-checked and mingle with sweet rocket, honesty, marigolds, larkspur and musk (mimulus).

## CULTIVATION
Most kinds of mint are greedy feeders, quickly exhausting the nutrients in the ground. Pennyroyal and Corsican mint will thrive on all kinds of soil without any additional feeding, but before planting the larger mints it is advisable to work a heavy dressing of garden compost or decayed leaves into the soil; top dress beds with these materials each autumn after cutting down frosted stems. For the heaviest leaf production mint requires very moist conditions in part shade, although colours of variegated forms are more pronounced in full sun, and all mints tend to be sturdier and more compact in the open. Confine

wandering roots by surrounding plants with slates or tiles inserted vertically into the soil, or by planting in an old, bottomless bucket or other container buried to its full depth.

Mints of all kinds can be propagated by cuttings of young shoots taken in spring, by dividing mature plants into small rooted pieces, or most simply by cutting off rooted runners in spring, planting them 5cm (2in) deep and 30cm (1ft) apart. Plants that are in constant use should be prevented from flowering by clipping them to half their height once or twice during the season; cut a few plants right down at midsummer for a fresh supply of young shoots until late in the season. With the exception of plants naturalized in a wild garden, mint beds are best remade completely every two to three years, preferably on a new site, to keep plants youthful and avoid depletion of soil nutrients.

## USES
Several kinds are widely grown for flavouring meat and vegetables, salads, summer drinks and teas. Pick as required, using the ends of shoots which will help delay flowering and encourage side shoots. In late summer runners may be boxed or potted up for indoor supplies in winter. Mint is medicinally valuable for aiding digestion and relieving tension and headaches. Pennyroyal is a renowned insect repellant, particularly where ants are a pest.

---

# PARSLEY (*Petroselinum crispum*)
Biennial; zones 7-8

Parsley is an extremely adaptable and attractive foliage herb for edgings or for filling between broader leaved plants. The kind most commonly grown is curled parsley, a hardy biennial normally treated as an annual. This produces rosettes of stiff, bright green leaves 20-30cm (8-12in) high, each divided into two or

three tightly curled leaflets; tiny, pale green flowers, clustered in flat open heads, appear from midsummer onwards. Recommended varieties of curled parsley: Bravour (long-stemmed, heavy yielding and very hardy); Curlina (dwarf for small gardens or pots indoors); Moss Curled (for general purpose use).

French, sheep's or plain-leaved parsley is a more vigorous strongly flavoured plant, with smooth flat leaves 45cm (18in) tall, while Italian or giant parsley, which also bears large flat, intensely aromatic leaves, often reaches 60cm (2ft) or more. (For **Hamburg Parsley,** see p.169.) Parsley combines well with marigolds, pansies or alpine strawberries, and will remain productive and decorative around the year if grown in pots or specially designed containers.

## CULTIVATION
Parsley is grown from seed, which is notoriously slow to germinate, often taking four to eight weeks. Sow outdoors in rich soil in May and again in August for succession over winter, or sow earlier in pots in warmth; for outdoor sowings, mix with radish seeds which will emerge quickly to mark the site until the parsley appears. Keep the soil consistently moist during first one or two months: most failures are caused by drought during germination. Occasional watering in dry weather will encourage lush growth and a position in full sun, except during summer, is best. By removing flower stems as they appear, plants can be encouraged to crop through a second season, and sometimes even longer. For winter use in cold areas, cloche outdoor plants, sow in September as an edging to a greenhouse border, or grow in pots.

## USES
Parsley is one of the most popular herbs for sauces, garnishes, and as a flavouring for all kinds of dishes. Pick whole leaves as required,

and any surplus may be frozen in bags or cubes. Leaves often become bitter or fibrous on plants that have been allowed to flower. Rich in vitamins and minerals, parsley acts as a tonic, and is sometimes used medicinally to treat kidney and bladder complaints.

# ROSEMARY
## (*Rosmarinus officinalis*)
Woody shrub; zone 8

Rosemary is excellent in prominent positions, such as beside doorways and entrances, where it is brushed in passing to release its lingering, resinous fragrance. A woody, evergreen shrub, growing 120-180cm (4-6ft) tall, it will provide height and colour in winter, although dwarf and prostrate forms are also available. Shrubs develop very hard branching stems covered with small succulent leaves, long and shiny like conifer needles, dark green on their top surface and silvery grey beneath. In early summer small scented flowers, normally blue but sometimes pink or white according to variety, are freely produced in clusters at the base of the leaves; shrubs that are not picked frequently may sometimes flower again lightly during the autumn.

Bushes tolerate close clipping, to enclose garden seats for example, or to form decorative hedges – rosemary was once widely used in knot gardens, either on its own or mixed with lavender for a mixed hedge of green and silver foliage. Smaller specimens combine well with artemisias and santolina, and feathery-leaved herbs such as chervil or feverfew; larger kinds will thrive in a border with fennel, foxgloves and verbascum. Arching and prostrate forms can be grown as ground cover, or to cascade over banks and the top of retaining walls. Apart from the species, the following rosemary cultivars are outstanding for special sites in the garden:

Benenden Blue: smaller stature with narrow dark leaves and bright blue flowers. Ideal for compact clipped bushes.

Miss Jessop's Variety (syn. *R.o.* 'Fastigiatus'): sturdy erect growth, producing a narrow upright bush. Pale blue flowers. Very hardy.

Severn Sea: Dwarf bush with graceful arching growth and rich blue flowers. Slightly less hardy than the type.

## CULTIVATION
With its Mediterranean origins rosemary is very drought tolerant. Sandy, dry soils are ideal, but any light and well-drained situation is suitable, provided plants are exposed to full sun for most of the day and have shelter from the coldest winds. Where winters tend to be cold, grow rosemary against a south-facing wall, as specimen bushes in tubs which can be moved in winter, or as pot plants in a conservatory, standing them in a sunny position outdoors in summer. Seeds may be sown in spring outdoors or in pots for transplanting to a nursery bed in the garden. Growth is often slow, however, and a more efficient method is to take cuttings either in early spring or immediately after flowering. Varieties with arching stems can also be layered. Plant finally in spring, 45cm (18in) apart for hedges. Trim after flowering to encourage bushy growth; hedges will need clipping two or three times during the growing season. In cold areas, mulch plants in autumn with peat, leaves or pine needles (salt hay if available), or cover with sacking (burlap) and take a few cuttings to overwinter indoors, as even mature bushes can suddenly die in long severe winters.

## USES
Rosemary is a popular and powerful culinary herb, used in moderation to season most kinds of food, especially Mediterranean dishes, and also to flavour wine, brandy and other drinks. The sprigs of foliage can be picked at any time of the year for use fresh, but for preserving, gather the trimmings when tidying bushes after flowering and dry carefully. Medicinally it makes a potent tonic for heart and circulatory conditions; it is also a traditional hair rinse and restorer. Rosemary flowers are highly attractive to bees.

*One of the best blue-leaved herbs, rue needs full sun to produce the richest colour. The bright yellow contrasting flowers need to be trimmed off in autumn to preserve the plant's rounded shape.*

## RUE (*Ruta graveolens*)
Perennial; zones 3-9

With its intense and unusual colour, rue is an important decorative herb. It is a rounded perennial shrub, 60cm (2ft) or more tall, with woody branching stems and blue-grey finely divided leaves, evergreen in mild gardens; in cold districts stems may lose some foliage or even die back to ground level. The form 'Jackman's Blue' has the richest colour, while the leaves of the cultivar 'Variegata' have attractive cream markings. From midsummer to early autumn bushes produce conspicuous heads of bright yellow flowers; both these and the leaves have a powerful fragrance and bitter flavour. The bright steely blue of the leaves makes a dramatic contrast with variegated thymes and sages, the light-coloured foliage of lady's mantle (alchemilla) or tansy, and grey plants such as helichrysum and cotton lavender. Both blue and variegated forms can be planted with fritillarias, either behind shorter flowering species or in front of crown imperials (*F. imperialis*). Specimen bushes, perhaps underplanted with Corsican mint, grow well in 25cm (10in) pots on patios or beside gateways where they are certain to be brushed against.

### CULTIVATION
Full sun is essential for the best colour. Rich conditions are not necessary, however, and light soils of poor to moderate fertility are usually adequate, provided they are free-draining. Sow seeds in spring, either in pots indoors or outside once the soil is warm, or take cuttings in late summer, rooting them in a cold frame or in pots; plant out 38-45cm (15-18in) apart. Established bushes will need little attention, although cutting them down to 7-10cm (3-4in) high every two to three years often rejuvenates the plants and helps to keep them bushy.

### USES
Although the leaves and flowers are used fresh in some parts of the world to make an iron-rich infusion and for flavouring wine, rue is a mainly medicinal herb, renowned as a potent antidote to hysteria and nervous disorders, and as a treatment to improve eyesight.

---

## SAGE (*Salvia* species)
Perennial; zones 3-9

The large, rounded, evergreen sage bushes with their softly textured foliage and penetrating scent provide restful colour and form all the year round in a herb or flower border. There are many strains and varieties in cultivation, most of them decorative assets in the garden. Some of the best are:

Garden sage (*S. officinalis*): the species most widely grown for culinary use. A spreading shrub up to 60cm (2ft) tall, with narrow grey-green woolly leaves and spikes of mauve flowers in whorls in summer; broad-leaf sage, an improved kind with larger leaves, seldom flowers. Several variegated forms are worth growing, including *S.o.* 'Icterian' or golden sage, 30cm (1ft) tall with bright yellow leaves.

Mexican sage (*S. azurea grandiflora*): an impressive but tender shrub, reaching 180cm (6ft) or more and bearing bright blue scented flowers. For warm regions only, or pots indoors.

Red sage (*S.o. purpurea/S.o.* 'Purpurascens'): with dull, deep red leaves and stems, and slightly taller than the type; *S.o.* 'Tricolor', whose leaves are irregularly marked with pink, white and green.

*Subtle leaf colours make all sage varieties worth growing among other plants, in particular red sage, used here to fill a box-edged section of a herb border.*

Pineapple sage (*S. rutilans*): a strong-growing, tender species, 90cm (3ft) tall with pale green leaves, small red flowers in summer, and a pronounced pineapple scent.

Dwarf kinds are excellent for permanent edging to beds, while the variegated cultivars make a highly effective foil for plain-leaved plants, especially in winter. Grow green sages with variegated grasses, dwarf chrysanth-emums or lobelias, amongst golden thyme, borage and bergamot, and with vegetables such as coloured leaf beets, peppers or red cabbage. Variegated sages can be grown with lily of the valley, dianthus, poppies or meconopsis, and make striking companions for old-fashioned roses or trained top fruit. The foliage of all kinds blends naturally with brick and weathered stone.

## CULTIVATION

All sages prefer sunny positions, especially the variegated kinds if they are to develop their full colour. Well-drained soil is essential, as bushes with wet feet tend to rot over winter. Otherwise they are undemanding plants, thriving in soils with poor to moderate fertility; they also make easily maintained and attractive pot plants.

Green species may be grown from seed sown outdoors in spring, or propagate by layering or from cuttings taken with a heel in late summer, and rooted in pots or outside in a cold frame (vegetative propagation is essential for variegated sages and cultivated forms such as broad-leaf sage). Overwinter cuttings in a cold frame or indoors, and plant out in spring 45-60cm (18-24in) apart, or 30-38cm (12-15in) apart for dwarf kinds. Trim to shape after flowering and pinch off the tips of long leggy shoots to keep bushes compact. After three to four years bushes begin to look a little threadbare, and they should be propagated and replaced with young plants. Where winters are normally severe, mound leaves or peat up

around the stems. Old bushes can be propagated in this way, earthing them up with soil into which the branches will root; each can then be cut off and planted elsewhere after shortening the stems to encourage branching.

## USES

Sage is a major culinary herb, widely used in stuffings, for seasoning rich meats and flavouring cheese and vegetables. Gather the tips of stems whenever required for fresh use; for storage, clip bushes to shape just before flowering (midsummer with non-flowering kinds such as broad-leaf sage), and dry the prunings very slowly to preserve their colour. Sage is also a versatile medicinal plant for treating coughs, colds and nervous ailments; sage tea is a popular and invigorating drink in some parts of the world, while a powerful antiseptic and insect repellant can be infused from the leaves.

---

# SALAD BURNET
## (*Poterium sanguisorba/ Sanguisorba minor*)
Perennial; zone 3

Salad burnet grows as a rosette of bright green leaves, which are arranged in pairs along gently arching stems. Perennial and almost evergreen, although severe frost can sometimes kill the top growth, the plants are neat and compact, about 30-38cm (12-15in) tall, and in summer produce spherical heads of tiny flowers – at first green but turning red as they open – on thin stems up to 60cm (2ft) high. Provided flower stems are nipped off, plants will remain compact all season and can be sown in a row as a miniature hedge, although separately they are sufficiently attractive to be planted as specimens in front of darker-leaved shrubs or as pot plants arranged with deeper colours such as the blue of rue and plum-coloured red sage.

## CULTIVATION

Salad burnet likes a well-drained soil that includes a little lime and plenty of humus such as old manure or decayed leaves. Plants thrive in full sun, except in very hot regions, or in partial shade. Sow outdoors in spring, thinning seedlings to 30cm (1ft) apart, or start seeds in pots. If plants are allowed to flower, large numbers of self-set seedlings usually result, the strongest of which may be saved and transplanted. However, flower stems should be pinched off at an early stage if a steady supply of fresh growth is needed, or where seedlings may be a nuisance. Pot up for winter use if growth outdoors is normally killed by frost. Cut undamaged plants outdoors back to 5-7cm (2-3in) in spring.

## USES

As the name implies, tender, young burnet leaves, picked whole as required, are often mixed in salads, to which they impart a refreshing cucumber flavour. They may also be cooked in soups, added to drinks, or used as the basis of a mild tonic. Where plants remain evergreen, their leaves are a valuable winter garnish when little else is available.

---

# SAVORY (*Satureja* species)
Perennial, annual

Three kinds of savory are commonly available, each of them attractive to bees. Summer savory (*S. hortensis*) is a slender annual with bushy erect growth 15-30cm (6-12in) tall. Its soft narrow leaves are dark green and aromatic, carried on wiry stems; in summer, short spikes of mauve or purple flowers appear in the leaf axils. Winter savory (*S. montana*) is hardy and in mild areas evergreen (zone 6). A neat woody shrub, it grows 30-38cm (12-15in) tall, its rather weak stems bearing pale shiny leaves similar in shape to those of summer savory. Purple or

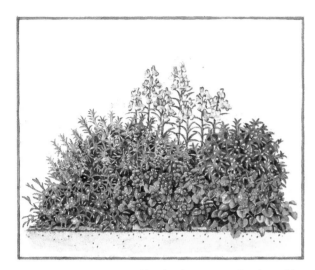

*Both annual and perennial kinds of savory can be planted in close association with dwarf and prostrate flowers for edging and also to attract bees into the garden.*

white flowers are produced over a long season. Creeping savory (*S. repandra*) is a prostrate perennial with white flowers and typical foliage (zone 6).

Savories are often grown amongst beans of all kinds, which they are said to protect from aphids. Summer savory is also an attractive companion for the various basils and other broader-leaved bushy herbs or summer-flowering annuals. Grow creeping savory in rock gardens or amongst the stones of a path, tuck it between rocks and slabs, or group a number of plants to form a dense, although not hardwearing, mat of foliage. Winter savory is useful for edging beds, and in the past was a popular plant for dwarf hedges in knot gardens. With its naturally neat habit, it blends well with alpine plants in a rock garden.

## CULTIVATION
All kinds require very good drainage and prefer dry sandy soils. Winter savory will tolerate partial shade, but the others must have full sun. Sow summer savory in late spring outdoors, or

earlier in pots under glass, eventually planting out 15cm (6in) apart. Perennial savories may be grown from seed, but are usually propagated by division of mature plants in spring or from cuttings taken in summer; plant about 30cm (1ft) apart, a little closer for hedging. Trim perennials to shape each spring.

## USES
The delicate flavour of summer savory is traditionally combined with vegetables, especially beans, while the others, with their more powerful taste, are used sparingly to season egg, cheese and meat dishes. Pick the ends of young stems as required; for storage, cut stems as the first flowers open and hang up to dry. All savories aid digestion, and winter savory is also a useful disinfectant.

## SWEET CICELY (*Myrrhis odorata*)
Perennial; zones 4-6

A handsome long-lived perennial, sweet cicely grows 90-150cm (3-5ft) tall; it has stout hollow stems and large scented leaves like the fronds of a pale green, downy fern. Clusters of small white flowers in flattened heads appear in early summer, followed by long, ribbed, aromatic seeds with very brief viability. Graceful and statuesque, sweet cicely grows well with angelica, lovage and mulleins at the back of a border. With its love of shade and moisture, it will flourish beneath garden trees, beside pools or as one of the taller elements in a wild garden. It can provide an elegant background to Solomon's seal, hellebores, acanthus or hostas, and combines well with rhubarb and artichokes.

## CULTIVATION
Moist (but not waterlogged), fertile soil in partial shade is best. Plants will withstand full sun, provided they are never short of water. Seeds sown as soon as they are ripe will usually

germinate the following spring; otherwise they often take a year to appear, or may not grow at all. Sweet cicely sows itself readily, and the strongest seedlings may be transplanted while still young, spacing them 45-60cm (18-24in) apart. Alternatively, divide mature plants in autumn or spring. Established plants need little attention unless they become too big, in which case the deep rooted crowns must be dug up and divided into small pieces for replanting.

## USES
With its delicate aniseed flavour, sweet cicely is a popular addition to omelettes, salads and drinks, and is one of the ingredients of the liqueur, chartreuse. The naturally sweet leaves are often cooked with acid fruit. Young leaves and stems can be gathered as required, and because plants emerge early in spring and often survive until late in the year, there is a long picking season. For storage, it is best to collect and dry the seeds, which have the same flavour as the rest of the plant. Medicinally, the herb is a valuable tonic and appetizer.

*Sweet cicely, growing here amongst lilies and foxgloves, has a long season – dying down late and reappearing early*

## TANSY (*Tanacetum vulgare*)
Perennial; zone 3

As a once common cottage garden plant, tansy blends most appropriately into the ordered muddle of a mixed border, growing happily with lovage and borage or with most herbaceous perennial flowers of medium height. It is a hardy bushy perennial, with annual stems growing up to 60-120cm (2-4ft) high and dying down again in late autumn. Mature plants form broad-spreading clumps of rich green foliage, deeply cut with a peppery fragrance. Numerous flower stems appear in summer, each bearing flat clusters of highly decorative bright yellow flowers which earn the herb its nickname of 'golden buttons'. The flowers may be dried for winter decoration or as a fragrant yellow food colour. The form *T.v.* var. *crispum* has more delicate, feathery leaves than the type.

### CULTIVATION
Any soil of poor to moderate fertility is suitable, providing it does not lie wet. Although tansy will tolerate partial shade, plants tend to become less compact or brightly coloured and it is better to grow them in full sun. Tansy will spread if not kept in check by cutting off the shallow runners around each plant. Sow in spring outdoors, or divide established plants: this should be done every two or three years to prevent clumps from becoming too congested. Plant 30cm (1ft) apart. If a longer continuous supply of leaves is needed, pinch off flower heads as they appear.

### USES
Tansy is a hot, pungent herb, rich in minerals and valuable as a tonic. It was popularly used as an internal cleanser, and was often a traditional ingredient in some regional British puddings. A powerful insect repellant can be made from the leaves, which are also used sparingly as a flavouring and fresh garnish.

## TARRAGON
(*Artemisia dracunculus*)
Perennial; zone 4

A classic but invasive perennial herb, tarragon has tall, leafy stems that die down in most winters. Two kinds, French tarragon (cv. 'Sativa', zone 5) and Russian, are generally recognized. The former is considered to have the best flavour, although it is less robust, growing about 90cm (3ft) tall and in many gardens succumbing to winter frosts. Russian tarragon, on the other hand, will reach a height of 150cm (5ft) and is more reliable in cold areas, but its flavour is milder and less distinguished. Both kinds have branching stems, produced from underground runners, bearing long, slender, pointed leaves, dark green and smooth in the case of French tarragon, while those of the Russian type are lighter green with a rough texture. The pale flowers are insignificant, and usually sterile on French tarragon.

*Both kinds of tarragon can be invasive if the underground runners are not controlled; but clearly-defined clumps, here underplanted with thyme and backed by a trained fig tree, add freshness to a border.*

Tarragon is quite difficult to place in the garden, and is best treated in the same way as mint, although it prefers open sunny ground and is less happy in a woodland situation. Plants need to be regularly moved to prevent deterioration in quality, and they should be placed where they can ramble harmlessly for a few years. Alternatively, confine the wandering roots in a large tub; in this way tarragon can be a decorative asset, particularly if combined with lemon balm, sage or tansy, and edged with trailing ornamentals such as lobelia, helichrysum, chlorophytums or ivy-leaved pelargoniums.

### CULTIVATION
Plants prefer light soil in full sun or light shade, with a little lime and good drainage. Do not feed with nitrogenous manures, and keep fertility low to restrain growth. Although Russian tarragon may be started from seed sown outdoors in spring, both kinds are usually grown from division of the creeping root-stocks, or from cuttings of basal shoots in early summer. Plant 45cm (18in) apart. Cut down and dry all top growth in early autumn, digging up and dividing the roots for replanting outdoors or overwintering in a cold frame. Alternatively, leave for three to four years before dividing, in the intervening years merely cutting down the blackened foliage in autumn and covering the roots with a generous mulch of leaves or dry peat in cold areas.

### USES
Tarragon has a great reputation as a culinary herb. It is a popular flavouring for chicken, fish and potato dishes, salads and vinegars, the leaves being picked as required. Soon after flowering starts, cut down foliage to freeze or dry slowly for storage. Tarragon has little medicinal use, although legend has always claimed that it has an ability to treat poisonous bites and stings.

# THYME
## (*Thymus* species and cultivars)
Perennial; zones 4-6

Because of its resilience, versatility and the diversity of colours and habits, thyme has always been an outstanding decorative herb. There are many forms of thyme, the majority growing no more than 30cm (1ft) tall, with small pointed, aromatic leaves and tiny flowers in whorls during May and June. The more compact or prostrate forms make excellent fragrant lawns, and can be grown as mats or cushions beside paths and between slabs, or to underplant other edging subjects such as lavender or hyssop. Taller varieties stand clipping as very dwarf hedges, and blend with marjorams, pennyroyal, sorrel or sages, alyssum and ageratum. Several kinds can be combined in a strawberry pot, planting each hole with a different variety, to stand on a patio or step. Gold and white variegated cultivars of most species are available, often more attractive than the green form.

The following is a short selection of reliable species, all of them evergreen:

Caraway thyme (*T. herba-barona*): sprawling habit, deep green leaves and mauve flowers; zone 5

Common thyme (*T. vulgaris*): wiry, bushy growth up to 30cm (1ft); greyish leaves and lilac pink flowers; zone 4

Lemon thyme (*T. x citriodora*): bright green and lemon scented, with pink flowers; zone 6

*T. coccineus*: grey-green leaves and rich pink flowers; zone 4

Wild thyme (*T. pulegioides*): prostrate, mat-forming species with pink flowers; ideal for lawns; zone 5

Wild creeping thyme (*T. serpyllum*): short, neat and fast growing; for mats or paths; zone 4

*Thymes are excellent companions for brick and stone, as here, where a weathered urn raises the plants to a position of prominence amongst larger adjacent herbs.*

## CULTIVATION
Thymes like well-drained soils of poor or medium fertility with a little lime, together with a position in full sun, sheltered from cold winds. In cold gardens, lift and pot one or two plants for cropping indoors. Some species may be started from seeds sown in spring, but plants are more usually layered in autumn, divided in spring, or grown from soft cuttings taken in late spring. Plant out 30cm (1ft) apart, a little closer for hedges, and every 10-15cm (4-6in) for creeping kinds. Clip plants into neat bushes after flowering; thyme lawns may be mown once or twice a year with a rotary mower set fairly high. Divide or replace thyme every four to five years to avoid bare, straggly growth.

## USES
Thyme is an important ingredient of bouquet garni and very widely used for flavouring soups, omelettes and stuffings; stem tips can be gathered at any time. Cut stems for drying just before plants flower. It is often included in potpourri, and used medicinally as an antiseptic, an aid to digestion and to treat colds. A valuable plant for bees.

# VERBENA, LEMON
## (*Lippia citriodora/Aloysia triphylla*)
Shrub; zones 9-10

A deciduous perennial shrub, lemon verbena is vulnerable to frost and therefore is not hardy in most regions, or at least will be cut to the ground in winter. In Britain it is best grown as a container shrub, so that the plants can be brought into the greenhouse in winter. In milder regions or with the protection of a warm wall it will reach 3-4.5m (10-15ft) or more.

It branches freely to produce slim, flexible stems with bright green, lemon-scented leaves arranged in groups of three, narrow and pointed like willow leaves but slightly crinkled and rough on the undersides. In late summer tiny, pale lilac flowers are produced on delicate spikes at the ends of stems; these have the same sweet citrus fragrance as the foliage. If pot grown, careful training and regular pinching back will make bushes compact and dense, or they may be developed to make informal

*Lemon verbena is a tender shrub, not hardy below about −7°C (20°F). However, it is attractive and long-lasting as a pot plant, and grown in this way can be moved under cover in cold weather.*

half-standards with foliage concentrated in a loose mop-head above a clear single stem 120-180cm (4-6ft) high. Around the edge of the container, annual bedding and trailing plants can be arranged to emphasize the shape of the verbena.

## CULTIVATION

Tubs and large pots of soil-based potting mixture provide suitable sites. Outdoor shrubs must have full sun and shelter from cold winds; with a south or south-west aspect and general freedom from hard frost, bushes may be expected to thrive trained on a garden wall, but elsewhere they will need some basic winter protection. The soil should be well-drained and not too fertile, to avoid any risk of injury from producing soft vulnerable stems. Lemon verbena may be propagated in spring by taking soft cuttings of young side shoots, with a heel, and rooting them in pots of potting mixture kept moist and warm indoors. Prune to shape in March and then pinch stems regularly throughout the growing season. Every autumn top-dress trees, both potted and in the open garden, with compost or leaf mould to help feed and protect the roots.

## USES

Gather the flowers in late summer, the leaves and the young tips of shoots at any time in the growing season, and either use straightaway or dry slowly for winter storage in airtight containers. The strongly flavoured leaves are often added to summer drinks and puddings, and are used in potpourri and to make lemon verbena tea. The herb is a gentle sedative and anodyne, valuable for treating such complaints as toothache.

*Best grown in light shade to enhance the colour of its leaves and early summer flowers, sweet woodruff will grow happily at the foot of a wall, as here, underplanted with fritillarias and backed by gooseberry cordons.*

## WOODRUFF (*Galium odoratum/ Asperula odorata*)
Perennial; zone 3

For all its delicate appearance, woodruff is a hardy perennial and makes a tough and durable ground cover plant beneath trees or hedges. The weak stems grow about 30cm (1ft) tall but often become prostrate or nearly so. At regular intervals up their length are flat rosettes of slender pointed leaves, dark green and polished. The flowers are tiny white stars, delicate and sweetly scented, and produced at the ends of the stems in May and June. Woodruff is sufficiently attractive to merit inclusion amongst beds of cultivated plants and should be more widely used to underplant decorative shrubs, or fruit bushes and trees, where it never becomes an invasive nuisance; grown beneath trained fruit flanking a path it makes a restrained and informal carpet of foliage. Woodruff can in turn be underplanted with bulbs such as crocus (both spring and autumn), narcissus, fritillarias and scillas, mixed with primroses and other woodland plants.

## CULTIVATION

In a wild corner of the garden, woodruff will seed itself with moderation. It is a native of woods and shady places, and given a site on moist light soil, with a high level of humus such as might be found beneath trees, plants will flourish and multiply. Although woodruff can be grown from seed, germination is slow and erratic, sometimes taking more than a year. Division of existing plants in spring is more reliable, planting out the rooted segments 10-15cm (4-6in) apart. In very cold gardens, plants may be protected with a covering of autumn leaves, but elsewhere it is enough merely to clear stems blackened by frost and then leave the plants to regenerate.

## USES

Gather whole stems as they start to flower, and hang up to dry so that the edible leaves and flowers release their fresh perfume of old-fashioned meadow-hay. The dried stems can then be used to flavour wine, tea and soft drinks. Bunches of dried foliage are sometimes kept in a linen cupboard to add their sweet fragrance to clothing. Medicinally, the herb has the effect of an invigorating tonic, while at the same time relaxing nervous tension.

## WORMWOOD
(*Artemisia absinthium*)
Perennial; zone 4

This is a large handsome herb which favours dry sunny places. A semi-shrubby hardy perennial it will grow 90-150cm (3-5ft) tall but will die down in winter in exposed gardens. The stout, roughly-textured, branching stems bear numerous deeply fringed leaves, grey with silky down, especially on their undersides. Small yellow-green flowers appear in clusters in August. The silver-grey foliage of wormwood combines well with delphiniums and hollyhocks, penstemons and pyrethrums, or with taller herbs and vegetables such as globe artichokes, flowering chicory and salsify, comfrey or lovage.

## CULTIVATION

Wormwood grows naturally in waste places on alkaline soil. Although it will survive in woodland conditions, it needs full sun for the most intense colour. It is sensitive to excessive cold and wet and therefore prefers light, free-draining soils, with shelter from cold winds in exposed gardens. Although seeds may be sown in spring in pots under glass, their germination is both irregular and uncertain. A more reliable method of propagation is to take cuttings of young shoots in spring and insert them in the open ground or a cold frame. Plant out 45-60cm (18-24in) apart. Wormwood needs little cultural attention, apart from an annual pruning in autumn or early spring when all stems should be cut down to about 15cm (6in) high to encourage new growth to begin at the base of the plant.

## USES

The whole plant has a strong, camphorated fragrance and a bitter flavour, and only small quantities are needed at any one time. It is a mainly medicinal herb of great antiquity, and one of the noted 'bitters'. Best known as an important ingredient of the drink absinthe, it is also a potent antiseptic and insecticide, and can be used internally to treat a number of ailments, especially gastric disorders and fevers. For winter use, cut leaves and stems at midsummer and dry slowly.

*A tantalising glimpse of an informal garden of herbs and flowering plants such as calendulas, bergamot and verbascum seen through this unusual 'moon' gateway in a wall of weathered brick. Rounded mounds of lavender flow over the edges of the path which, beyond the iron gate, winds between sweet bay and clipped box hedges.*

# GARDEN PLANTS AS HERBS

Removing the artificial distinction between groups of plants not only allows herbs to be integrated within the rest of the garden, but also invites the planting of flowers amongst edible crops. The possibilities are infinite, and most garden flowers will harmonize or contrast brilliantly with the subtle tones of popular herbs or the lush greens of many vegetables. Try, for example, growing cream or yellow lupins, underplanted with perennial blue flax, around standard redcurrants, or simply allow the poached egg plant (*Limnanthes douglasii*) to seed itself where it chooses beneath red sage or amongst clumps of chives.

Ironically, many flowers now normally confined to flower borders might equally well be classified as herbs because of their additional curative or culinary uses, recognized by preceding generations more keenly aware of plant virtues, but ignored or unfamiliar today. A few of the more common dual-purpose plants are described here (consult a reliable herbalist before attempting to use them medicinally).

## TALL FOCAL PLANTS
### (90-120cm/3-4ft upwards)

**Broom** (*Cytisus scoparius*): a hardy perennial shrub, tolerant of poor soils in full sun, with yellow, or yellow and red, pea flowers late spring to early summer. Grow with tall herbs and vegetables, with sage and other bushy plants to conceal bare stems. Stems are used for brushes and basketwork, leaves for urinary ailments.

**Elderberry** (*Sambucus canadensis*): a graceful hardy shrub or tree with flat umbels of scented white flowers, followed by edible white, red or deep purple berries. Improved fruiting cultivars, and decorative dwarf, golden,

cut-leaved and double-flowered forms of some species are available. Provides light summer shade for leafy vegetables and herbs. All parts are useful, berries and leaves in particular for wine, soothing ointments, cough syrup.

**Foxglove** (*Digitalis purpurea*): has soft grey-green leaves, and tall spires of cap-shaped speckled flowers, rose-pink or white. The variety 'Apricot' is unusual and attractive. *D. ferruginea* has woolly grey leaves and rusty orange flowers. For moist shade and semi-wild schemes. A potent sedative: use with care.

**Hollyhock** (*Althaea rosea*): classic cottage garden perennial, with tall spires of flowers in shades of yellow, red and purple, single varieties more elegant than doubles. For backs of borders and against sunny walls, with angelica, artichokes and other tall plants. A soothing, cooling plant medicinally.

**Mullein** (*Verbascum*): the species and cultivars form hardy perennial or biennial rosettes of long oval leaves, some grey-felted, and tall spires of summer flowers like hollyhocks, in shades of white, yellow or red. Grow with artichokes, fennel or sweet cicely for contrast, and use to treat chest complaints.

## PLANTS OF MEDIUM HEIGHT
### (45-90cm/18-36in)

**Cornflower** (*Centaurea cyanus*): popular annual flower in shades of blue, red and white. Grow as a cut flower between vegetables (especially brassicas), and bushy herbs for colour all summer. Treats eye troubles and nervous disorders; the flowers are used in salads.

**Cowslip** (*Primula veris*): has neat rosettes of long oval leaves and heads of drooping yellow or red flowers in spring. Prefers sunny well-drained soil.

**Common English Daisy** (*Bellis perennis*): makes perennial rosettes of oval leaves, with flowers in

white and red shades: single, semi-double or double like fat, padded buttons. For edges and bedding with bulbs around fruit or bushy perennial herbs. Where hot summers occur, treat as a hardy annual, sowing in autumn or early spring, as plants may die in the heat. Leaves eaten in salads and used to treat wounds and bruises.

**Greater Celandine** (*Chelidonium majus*): with its delicate golden foliage, and bright yellow flowers like small poppies is a less familiar plant in modern gardens: double and finer-leaved forms available. For damp shade amongst tall herbs, or around fruit trees. Traditional cure for warts (the bright orange sap is slightly poisonous).

**Heartsease** (*Viola tricolor*): this dainty plant has rounded leaves on leggy stems, and purple and yellow miniature pansies all summer. Grows on light soil in sun or light shade. Best allowed to seed and naturalize itself anywhere amongst other plants. A noted tonic and treatment for heart disorders.

**Heather** (*Erica carnea*): produces evergreen wiry stems with small, sweet-scented red, pink or white bells in winter. Numerous cultivars, including many with variegated foliage. Tolerates chalky soils; prefers light, peaty, well-drained soil in full sun. Plant in mats or drifts together with prostrate herbs, and as edging or ground cover. A bee and honey plant, used also to treat coughs and nervous complaints.

**Hydrangea** (*Hydrangea*): hardy deciduous shrub with large flamboyant flower heads in white, pink or blue has numerous varieties. Most prefer partial shade. Eventually large bushes, they can be kept pruned to blend with shrubby herbs, especially variegated kinds. Used to treat rheumatism and disorders of the joints.

**Lady's Mantle** (*Alchemilla mollis*): this hardy plant has rounded, softly pleated leaves and

*Orange calendulas and blue cornflowers are both hardy, easily grown annuals for a long-lasting display of colour.*

delicate yellow-green flowers in midsummer. It tolerates shade, makes an attractive edging or ground cover, and thrives beneath taller herbs and fruit bushes. A tonic and remedy for many female ailments.

**Lavender** (*Lavandula*): is an indispensable aromatic medicinal herb, with slim grey leavès, and spikes of mauve, purple or white fragrant flowers in midsummer. The numerous varieties all prefer full sun and dry soils. Use for hedges and edges; to make a gentle tonic for nervous complaints; and for perfume or to scent clothes.

**Lily of the Valley** (*Convallaria majalis*): is a widely grown perennial with large, oval leaves and spikes of white, occasionally pink, bells. The spreading mats of roots can be invasive in damp shade: chop runners with a spade to contain the plants. Excellent summer ground cover beneath permanent trees and bushes. A potent heart tonic, not for amateur use.

**Mignonette** (*Reseda odorata*): this old-fashioned sweetly scented perennial is best grown as an annual in colder gardens. Greyish leaves and dense spikes of golden brown flowers. Grow in sun amongst mats, short leafy herbs and alpine strawberries, especially on chalky soils. Used to make a calming tea.

**Pimpernel** (*Anagallis arvensis* or *A. linifolia*): is perennial in warm gardens. A bushy plant with brilliant red or blue flowers which open in sun. Combine with mats and cushions of prostrate herbs, or plant as an edging with parsley. Used to treat stings, swellings and rashes.

**Primrose** (*P. vulgaris*) produces oval, crinkly leaves and pale yellow short-stemmed flowers in spring. Many coloured forms available. Likes moist soil in shade or sun. Both are hardy perennials, and ideal for planting with dwarf bulbs anywhere around herbs and fruit and at the foot of low hedges. Used medicinally to treat nervous disorders.

**Sea Holly** (*Eryngium maritimum*): this perennial has unmistakeable prickly silver-green leaves and rich blue flower heads in late summer. Needs light soil in full sun; grow with shrubby herbs and beneath standard soft fruit. Young shoots cooked as a vegetable, or used as a tonic and for chest complaints.

**Soapwort/Bouncing Bett** (*Saponaria officinalis*): an old cottage favourite, tall or sprawling, with fragrant pale pink flowers, sometimes double, in late summer. Revels in light soil in sun or shade. For wild plantings and beneath fruit trees. Used as a soap substitute, and to treat inflammation.

## SHORT PLANTS FOR EDGES, MATS AND GROUND COVER
(under 45cm/18in)

**Candytuft** (*Iberis*): the numerous annual species and cultivars provide flat tufts of pink or white flowers all summer with successive sowings. Plant in full sun to fill gaps between vegetables and herbs, and to contrast with chives or thrift. Used for muscular complaints.

**Houseleek** (*Sempervivum*): has hardy, succulent rosettes of green or grey-green leaves each

*Lavender is one of the most popular cottage garden plants, but particularly valuable for dwarf hedging, as here where it flanks a stone path. The aromatic flowers can be cut before they fade and then dried for pot-pourri or for perfuming clothes. When the plants have finished flowering, they need clipping to shape to keep them tidy and prevent the lower stems from becoming bare. Lavender usually resents being pruned right back into old wood; where mature plants have been allowed to develop bare stems, these should be encouraged to root by pegging them down to the ground as layers, or by mounding soil over the base of the bare branches. Alternatively, dig up the bushes and replant them in the same place but more deeply, to cover the lower stems which will root into the soil by the following year. They are then cut off as separate plants, or the shrub may be left to grow at its new depth; it should be clipped to promote plenty of young bushy growth.*

*A robust and distinctive perennial, sea holly makes excellent edging and complements blue flowers such as delphiniums* (background).

producing spikes of star-shaped flowers, pink, white or yellow. For sunny positions with a little lime; plant in paths, walls and amongst stones. Used for skin disorders.

**Thrift** (*Armeria maritima*): several fine species and cultivars exist, forming mats of short grassy leaves and round heads of tiny flowers, pink, white or red. Mass them in the sun as edging or between chervil and alpine strawberries. Flowers popular with bees and used as a tonic.

**Sweet Violet** (*Viola odorata*): is a small, bushy perennial, with purple or white scented flowers in spring. Prefers rich soil in shade, and thrives at the foot of soft fruit, hedges and beside paths. Used to make a soothing tea, and often crystallized for decorations.

# MAKING HERBS COMFORTABLE

Most common herbs are so undemanding that it is sometimes suggested they need little more than a sun-baked position on the poorest soil. Obviously the preferences of individual herbs vary and some of the more resilient kinds will undoubtedly tolerate these conditions. But there is a significant difference between mere survival and positive good health, and even easily grown plants will repay a little basic care and forethought with dramatically improved appearance and vitality.

## SOIL
Ordinary garden soil in which flowering plants thrive will also suit the majority of herbs. Some of the more pungent species of Mediterranean origin – thyme or oregano, for example – have the best flavour when grown in hot, light soils similar to their native environment. Soft leafy kinds, such as chervil, lovage or angelica, on the other hand, need richer, moist soil if they are to produce their normally luxuriant foliage, while parsley and other heavily cropped herbs revel in very fertile kitchen garden conditions.

Most herbs prefer a little lime, together with some additional humus such as partly decayed leaves or garden compost; unless very well rotted and used sparingly, manure is too rich and will encourage soft sappy growth. Good drainage is essential for all except naturally aquatic or riparian species, and ground that tends to lie wet, especially in winter or early spring, will need to be improved, as will very heavy or sandy soils (see p.171).

## ASPECT
Those herbs which like warm, dry sites usually need long hours of sunshine to concentrate the aromatic oils on which their flavour depends, and they should be planted in very open positions or those facing south. Where full exposure is not possible, choose a site that receives direct sunlight for at least half the day. Many species tolerate or even prefer longer intervals without sun, but they cannot be expected to grow well in gloom, in dark corners or beneath dense conifers, and the best place for them is in the dappled shade cast by deciduous trees, nearby shrubs or north-facing walls. Latitude and typical midsummer temperatures are important influences: in northern gardens plants normally grown in partial shade will tolerate more sunlight; in regions with hot summers many more will welcome light shade.

*The native habitat of herbs should always be borne in mind when choosing a site for them. Mediterranean species prefer full sun and well-drained conditions.*

## SHELTER
Cold winds in spring can injure the stoutest perennial herb, defoliating evergreen kinds and severely checking growth; tender herbs in particular are more liable to be damaged by wind than low temperatures, while bees and other beneficial insects are unable to work flowers in windswept sites. Tall plants may need staking if they are to survive unscathed.

Where possible, protect herbs in exposed gardens by planting them where they are shielded by shrubs or hardy soft fruit, or by a wind-break of trained brambles or hedging plants. A south- or west-facing garden fence or house wall will provide valuable shelter from cold north and east winds without obstructing sunlight. Avoid cold, still corners of the garden, where the soil warms up slowly in spring and lingering frost may injure dormant plants.

## ROUTINE MAINTENANCE
If the ground is already in good condition no additional fertilizers will be necessary during the growing season, and most perennial herbs (see individual entries) need only an autumn top-dressing of leaves, peat or garden compost. This will also protect the dormant roots from frost. On the whole, evergreen kinds tolerate drought, but leafy or shallow-rooted herbs (and young plants of all species) will benefit from occasional watering in prolonged dry weather.

A close watch should be kept on prostrate herbs planted to grow into mats and ground cover. Here, stray seedlings or re-growth from root fragments of cleared perennial weeds may easily escape notice until they are established; remove them if possible while still small enough to avoid disturbing the developing herbs. Support tall species by tying the stems to a single bamboo cane discreetly placed in the centre of each plant.

When gathering herbs for use, pick sprigs from the ends of shoots, because this will improve the shape of the plants by encouraging them to bush out. Most herbs benefit from occasional pruning, especially young shrubby species and those grown solely for their ornamental value. Clipping the plants once or twice during the season will restrain any straggly stems and induce fresh supplies of tender new growth, which in the case of variegated cultivars usually have the brightest colours. Larger pieces can be dried.

## WINTER CARE

Where frosts are a problem, all tender herbs need to be moved under cover. Potted specimens can be brought into a greenhouse, or indoors to as light a position as possible; plants growing in the open garden may be potted up in autumn, or replanted in a cold frame until spring. Herbs of borderline hardiness can be protected in situ with cloches, or by mounding leaves or peat around the base of perennial stems. Cut down the frosted stems of herbaceous perennials and cover the crowns of susceptible varieties with straw, ashes or a mulch of garden compost which can be removed when all danger from frost is past.

As most herbs need to be replaced after a few years, it is sensible to combine their propagation with insurance against winter loss. Always take

*It is a mistake to assume all herbs need poor soils and plenty of sunshine. Although few will thrive in dense shadow, woodland species such as lovage, woodruff and sweet cicely, revel in the moist, leafy soil and dappled shade beneath fruit trees. Since they will be competing for nutrients with the tree roots, it is worth occasionally enriching the soil with decayed leaves and well-rotted manure.*

a few late cuttings from doubtfully hardy plants and overwinter them in pots indoors. Alternatively, lift one or two crowns and replant them in a cold frame or box of soil in a greenhouse, for dividing and replanting in spring. Earth up old bushes of sage, lavender and other similar woody plants, covering the base of their branches with soil; these will root by the following winter, when they can be separated for planting out.

## HERBS IN POTS

Pots and other containers in which herbs are to be grown should be large enough to contain the roots without cramping them – for annuals and smaller plants 12-15cm (5-6in) diameter is adequate; larger herbs will need pots 20cm (8in) upwards, while a 30-45cm (12-18in) container will hold a young bay tree or a collection of small plants. All pots must have drainage holes in the base, covered with a layer of stones or broken pots to help surplus water drain away and to prevent the contents from trickling out. Over this material spread a thin layer of coarse, moist peat.

Use a porous, soil-based potting mixture for filling the pots. This will give them stability, and provide the efficient drainage and slow, steady release of nutrients that herbs require. A homemade potting mix can be prepared using good garden soil blended with an equal volume of leaf mould, garden compost or peat, together with a little sharp sand to produce a crumbly, fibrous mixture. While mixing, add a general organic or chemical fertilizer at the recommended rate.

Pot the plants firmly and keep them out of full sun until they are established and growing steadily. Take care never to over-water since this can be fatal to many herbs; just keep the roots consistently moist. From about midsummer onwards, as incorporated fertilizers become exhausted, add a balanced liquid feed when watering.

# GATHERING AND PRESERVING HERBS

Whenever picking a few herbs for immediate use, consider the overall shape of the plants. Pinch off the tips from the longer stems of shrubby kinds to encourage bushiness, and use the outer leaves of those which grow as clumps or rosettes, such as parsley and lemon balm. Chives and short leafy annuals such as chervil can be trimmed back to half their height with scissors; growth will rapidly regenerate afterwards. The stems of angelica and lovage can be cut while still young, selectively pruning them back to a pair of leaves. Gather flowers that have just opened fully, and ripe seeds.

## GATHERING FOR STORAGE

Herbs have a season in much the same way as fruit and vegetables. If they are cropped late in the year, many of the valuable flavours and medicinal properties will be reduced or subtly changed, and winter may overtake plants before they have recovered from what amounts to severe pruning. Cutting very young plants hard will often check their growth or permanently retard them. The best time to harvest large amounts of foliage is when plants are still growing vigorously and before they flower; then they are in peak condition and will quickly revive to produce a further crop.

Gather the leaves in the morning, preferably during a dry, sunny spell of weather. Leaves wet from rain or dew may become mouldy before they have been fully dried, and will take longer to dry if they are full of sap from recent rainfall. Only pick clean, bright leaves, rejecting those that are damaged or discoloured with age – younger leaves are tender and usually have the best flavour. Handle all foliage carefully as it will easily bruise, and do not gather too much from each plant; while some herbs such as chervil, parsley or chives may be cut hard and will almost certainly recover, perennial kinds should not have more than half their foliage removed unless they are being pruned deliberately to promote new growth.

Remember that herbs which have been integrated with the rest of the garden have an important decorative function. A specimen heavily pruned in midsummer will leave a conspicuous gap amongst the other plants, and where appearance is important it may be better to take two or three smaller crops over the season, thinning some of the stems and trimming back others so that the harvest is less noticeable. Alternatively, space such annual herbs as basil or dill close together, and pull up every other plant for drying, leaving the remainder to close the gaps and supply fresh leaves or, in the case of dill, continue growing for its crop of seeds.

## DRYING
Instructions for drying herbs need not be as dauntingly complicated as some authorities suggest. Although modern commercial methods of preservation are sophisticated and give a high-quality product, most gardeners manage by much simpler means to produce dried herbs that retain much of their flavour.

The traditional method is to tie cut stems in bunches and suspend them in darkness in a warm, airy room or shed until dry. Freely circulating air is important to remove as quickly as possible moisture evaporating from the leaves and to prevent moulds from forming. Gentle warmth helps to dry the herbs rapidly without damaging or discolouring them: too much, as in direct sunlight, and both fragrance and colour will be diminished. But if it is not warm enough, leaves develop a musty, stale flavour and to prevent this, additional heat must be provided, ideally with a fan heater that will also maintain a steady movement of air.

Instead of hanging up the herbs, the stems or individual leaves can be spread loosely on trays

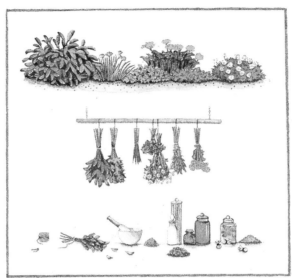

*Successful preservation depends on drying herbs efficiently in circulating air, and then storing the product in airtight containers.*

or shelves covered with a layer of newspaper; this is the best way to dry flowers. If the herbs are not papery dry after a week or two, they will probably need artificial heat to accelerate the process. Drying can be finished in an airing cupboard or cool oven, in either case with the door slightly open to allow air to circulate, or near a central heating boiler. With care, herbs can be dried in a very few seconds in a microwave oven. Leaves and flowers are fully dried if they rustle crisply when moved.

## STORING
Herbs that have been thoroughly dried will quickly reabsorb moisture and start to decay unless stored in airtight containers. For very short-term storage small quantities may be kept in paper bags, provided there is no risk of the contents being crushed, or even hung up in the kitchen. Most of the crop, however, should be stored away from light and air, and metal, plastic, dark glass or glazed crockery containers are all suitable for this. Keep the containers in a

cool, consistent temperature, and label them clearly with both variety and date; even under ideal conditions dried herbs will deteriorate, and stocks are best replaced annually.

## DRYING SEEDS
The seeds of some herbs are as valuable as their foliage, concentrating both flavour and medicinal virtues into an easily stored form. Since new stocks of most herbs can be raised cheaply and readily from seed (in some cases, such as sweet cicely, from fresh seed only) it is important to know how to dry and preserve seeds efficiently.

Leave the seedheads to mature on the plants for as long as possible, but cut them off carefully before the seeds are so ripe that they fall from the pods or cases. Seeds to be saved for re-sowing should be selected from the strongest, healthiest plants, and preferably from the earliest or central flowers or flower heads where several have set seed. Finish ripening the seedheads on newspaper in a dry, airy place, not necessarily in the dark; they will be ready for storing when the seeds rattle loosely or fall from the heads. Shake or rub the seeds free, and store them in packets inside airtight jars in a cool place. Where there is a risk of dampness, include a sachet of silica gel crystals in the jar to absorb any moisture.

## OTHER METHODS OF STORAGE
There are several sophisticated ways to preserve the flavours and active principles of herbs by infusing leaves, flowers or seeds in oil, alcohol, vinegar or sugar syrups, all of them beyond the scope of this book. Freezing, however, is a simple alternative to drying for many herbs, although opinions differ about its effectiveness. Herbs such as parsley, basil, chives or tarragon, which are difficult to dry well, may be frozen without preliminary blanching, either intact as bunches in small plastic bags, or chopped finely and frozen with a little water in ice-cube trays.

# VEGETABLES INTRODUCTION

## FIRST CONSIDERATIONS

These days there is rarely any need to promote the benefits of harvesting fresh vegetables from the garden. Most of us are aware that good health depends on a regular supply of fibre, vitamins and minerals, while flavour, quality and freedom from chemicals have all become important criteria in choosing vegetables.

Having room in the garden to grow them is another matter, though. Many people who would find space for a few pansies or salvias might perhaps refuse the offer of a dozen spare purple sprouting plants or a handful of lettuce seedlings because they are conditioned to think of vegetables as long rows in a separate patch or on a local allotment. Yet the majority of vegetables occupy no more room than pansies or summer bedding, and if grown fast and harvested young while still at their best, many kinds will be cleared in a matter of weeks, to make room for another crop.

Old gardening books always assumed we had room for long rows of vegetables, and the time or inclination to spend hours weeding or hoeing them. This is unrealistic for the average small family. The standard measure when estimating yields and quantities of seed has for a long time been the 9m (30ft) row, the width of a typical allotment or suburban garden. But such a row can produce 40-60 lettuces, 50-100kg (1-2cwt) of runner beans or 18kg (40lb) of beet, very often maturing in a short space of time.

Unless able to store the surplus, few people can use so much, and frequently large amounts of produce go to waste, with disheartening consequences. By sowing frequent small quantities of seed, perhaps beside a path or amongst flowers before they spread to fill the space, the problems of glut and lack of space will be avoided. It is also important to decide which vegetables to grow. There is no point producing a barrowload of turnips if the household uses only one per week, whereas if carrots are popular, a continuous supply of juicy roots can be ensured by making several successive sowings of a fast early variety, each occupying a small amount of ground for only ten to twelve weeks.

For much of that time the soft delicate foliage will be a decorative bonus. When grown well, nearly all vegetables are good looking, often more so than many shrubs given garden room merely because of rarity or fashion. Unfortunately we still tend to think of vegetables in terms of their eventual yield, rather than as plants in their own right. Most of us need to look at vegetables again, to take the time to watch them grow and develop their characters – from the first crooked bean seedlings or neat tufts of salsify, to the prim elegance of mature leeks or the top-heavy eccentricity of kohl rabi. Very often gardeners are surprised to find that crops such as seakale, chard, broad beans or savoy cabbage are extremely handsome plants when seen as part of the whole garden community. They all have individuality and a place within the garden.

## WAITING BEDS

With a little imagination (and willingness to experiment) a place can be found for most kinds of vegetable, but a few may still be difficult to site, especially if they need a long season or are to be grown by traditional methods. Brussels sprouts, for instance, need a position that both suits their height and broad foliage throughout their season, and also allows easy access for picking. Trench celery, too, is difficult. It grows successfully on the flat at high density amongst other plants, but for blanching in a trench it must have a strip to itself. One obvious answer is to grow a substitute, in this case self–blanching celery; alternatively, tuck them out of sight behind taller plants.

*Even a small suburban front garden can be used to grow vegetables without diminishing its decorative impact. Fences are valuable for supporting or protecting many crops, as here where tomatoes (1) and trailing cucumbers (2) are trained at the sides; a block of sweet corn (3) beside the gate and a bushy angelica plant (4) in the corner are sheltered from high winds. In the beds flanking the main path French beans (5), white sprouting broccoli (6) and parsley (7) nestle amongst flowering plants, while globe artichokes (8) and swiss chard (9) provide height and contrasting colour. Beneath the fruit tree, strawberries and summer spinach (10) thrive in the partial shade, as will onions (11) provided they receive full sun for part of the day; lettuce (12) and chives (13) fit neatly amongst the other edging plants.*

*In the centre bed an open pyramid of runner beans (14) straddles low mats of lavender, with cauliflowers (15), courgettes (16) and red cabbage (17) worked amongst the adjacent flowers. Carrots (18) and curly kale (19) add attractive foliage at the edges. Across the path from the red cabbage and Chinese cabbage (20), dwarf peas (21) grow at the foot of the fence.*

*In the nearest bed cabbages (22) make dramatic foliage plants, surrounded by radishes (23), corn salad (24) and carrots (25); lettuces, both green (26) and bronze (27) are used for edging. In the foreground there are tall peas (28) and Brussels sprouts (29) growing against the house wall.*

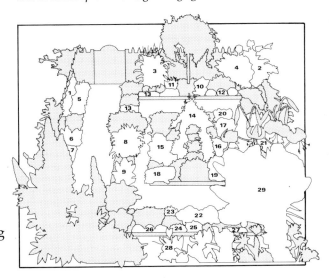

Another solution is to raise them as permanent occupants of a waiting bed. Commercial growers use waiting beds for young plants in need of temporary accommodation; gardeners, too, keep transplanted seedlings and spring bedding plants such as wallflowers in a nursery or waiting bed until the right time for moving them.

While some crops are best sown in situ (in most cases root vegetables can only be grown in this way), others tolerate or even benefit from being transplanted. Grow them on in a waiting bed until they are moved to their final positions when a few weeks old; this will also make it easier to arrange for crops to follow in succession and to avoid any obvious vacancies in beds and borders. Although primarily a reservoir of young stock for later planting out, a waiting bed (or beds, for they need be only small patches of ground here and there) can also be used as a nursery for cuttings, runners or perhaps unbudded rootstocks.

## MUCK AND MYSTERY

It is often mistakenly assumed that ground for vegetables needs special and lavish preparation (see pp.171 and 174). In fact it usually needs no heavier feeding than a flowerbed, but sadly many gardeners return little or nothing each year to the soil in which their flowers and shrubs grow. While most vegetable crops require only moderate fertility, where the soil has been neglected some kind of organic material should be worked in before planting. Flowers growing next to groups of vegetables will soon show a significant improvement in vigour and, as vegetables are rotated amongst the other plants, whole beds will be revitalized.

## CLOSE SPACING

As well as long rows, many books used to advise wide spacings between plants. On a large scale it is often easier and quicker to cultivate widely spaced plants, but this does not

necessarily produce the highest yields; by growing some vegetables at higher densities, gardeners can harvest heavier crops and also fit the plants into a smaller area of ground. Vegetables can of course be too close together, and it is no use packing too many plants into a small area, because eventual yields are often very disappointing. This is a familiar problem with carrots sown too thickly – a proportion mature into useable roots, but many never develop. If thinned to at least 15cm (6in) apart, very large maincrop carrots can be produced; by thinning early sowings to 10cm (4in) apart, roots mature fast with the reduced competition. However maincrops grown later in warmer soil give the highest yields of medium-sized roots at only 3cm (1½in) apart; any closer and competition will tend to depress yields.

A lot of experiments have been carried out on close and precise spacings, and some of the

*Typical summer harvest from the integrated garden. Early potatoes are large enough to dig, together with the first peas and beets. Red shallots (top left) and garlic (top right) are both ready for drying.*

results are particularly interesting for amateur gardeners. Cauliflowers, for example, can make large plants and are often spaced 60-75cm (24-30in) apart each way; however, suitable varieties grown only 10cm (4in) apart in rows 23cm (9in) apart (or about 15cm/6in apart each way) will produce a similar total weight of small heads ideal for individual servings. Adjusting the distances between many vegetables modifies the size of the end product, but there are optimum spacings which give the best yields. Distances recommended in this book are based on that data; do not forget, however, that wider spacing may be necessary to allow access for cultivating or gathering crops.

## VARIETIES

Hundreds of varieties of vegetables have been bred over the centuries, all selected for some outstanding characteristic: good flavour, perhaps, or early maturity, outstanding hardiness or tolerance of dry soils. Not all of them are suitable for garden cultivation, however, especially some of the modern F1 hybrids. Most of these have been developed for a specific purpose, such as simultaneous ripening for mass harvest, or an ability to withstand handling and transport, considerations which sometimes take precedence over flavour and quality.

Some of these characteristics are valuable. Non-bolting varieties of fennel, spinach or Chinese cabbage have made it easier to grow these crops outside the short traditional season, while one of the most reliable ways to control pests and diseases is to grow resistant hybrids. Strains bred to mature all together, such as hybrid peas or Brussels sprouts, are useful if a crop is to be cleared in a single picking for freezing. Most hybrids are remarkably uniform in habit and growth compared with older kinds, and this may be an asset where appearance is particularly important.

Hybrid vigour is a further virtue. Compared with some older strains that no longer perform so well after many years of seed selection, F1 hybrids are notable for their consistent germination and vigorous growth. Because their production is closely controlled, the seeds are more expensive than open-pollinated varieties, but germination rates are high and as a rule every seedling is worth using.

Older varieties should not be despised, though. Some veteran peas, for example, still have the best flavour and resistance to mildew in the autumn. Many non-hybrid Brussels sprouts mature steadily over a long season, ideal for extended picking, and a single sowing of this kind can remain productive for several months. When choosing seeds, all the virtues of a variety should be examined, particularly flavour, small compact growth, disease resistance and an ability to stand for a long time without deterioration, which in a garden context are usually the most important.

Concentrate on early-maturing varieties that sprint to maturity, rather than large maincrop kinds which take many more weeks to crop; in this way a quick turnover of high quality vegetables is possible from a small space. Always grow at least two varieties: the current choice, and another for comparison; retain the better variety to grow the following year along with another new one. This gives an opportunity to discover improvements, although very often an old favourite consistently surpasses any rivals.

## ENDANGERED VARIETIES

It is always worth saving seed from outstanding plants. Gardeners have done this for generations, often gradually selecting a strain adapted to a particular garden with its own unique soil and climate. With an older variety, saving one's own seed may be the only way to keep it alive. The seed trade is highly competitive and ruthless towards any unprofitable variety; since it costs a lot of money to maintain a variety as a pure and vigorous strain, numerous old vegetables have already been deleted from official lists, which means they cannot legally be sold.

In Britain asparagus kale, for example, has been deleted, while Czar runner bean and Avonearly beet are in danger of following suit. The only way to obtain deleted varieties is as a loan or gift of seed from one of the societies dedicated to preserving them. In the USA these vegetables are appropriately known as heritage varieties; since most were valued at one time or another for their flavour or other characteristics, and all are important as a genetic reservoir for breeding new kinds, they are indeed part of our garden heritage.

In an integrated garden it is a simple matter to grow a few plants of a particular variety separate from others of the same kind so as to keep the seeds from cross-fertilization. In this way gardeners can raise an isolated crop of a choice variety – runner beans on a tripod of canes, for example, or a few kale plants at the back of a border – and also save a little seed for following years (for how to store seeds, see **Sowing and Planting** p. 173).

*Tall peas are nutritious and occupy little room grown on fruit cage netting or up tripods. Whole plants can be pulled up and hung until dry, when they are podded and stored for winter use.*

# ARTICHOKES:

## CHINESE *(Stachys tuberifera)*

**Height:** 30-38cm (12-15in)

**Space:** 23cm (9in); rows 30cm (1ft) apart

**Plant:** early spring

**Harvest:** October onwards

**Yield:** 225g (8oz) per plant

Annual crop

A bushy herbaceous plant with fresh green hairy leaves and small pink flowers in summer. At its root tips edible white tubers develop in autumn, each about 5-7cm (2-3in) long and shaped like a conical shell or spring. Plant small tubers 7-10cm (3-4in) deep in rich, well-drained soil, in a warm sunny position. Water regularly during summer. In light ground tubers may be left for digging as required; elsewhere lift in October and pack in dry peat in a box.

## GLOBE *(Cynara scolymus)*

**Seeds:** 25/g; 600/oz

**Germination:** 2-4 weeks

**Height:** 90-150cm (3-5ft)

**Space:** 60-90cm (2-3ft); rows 120cm (4ft) apart

**Sow:** February under glass, spring outdoors

**Harvest:** June to August (September to October first year from seed)

**Yield:** 8-12 heads per plant

Perennial; zones 8-9 (with heavy mulch)

For most of their long history of cultivation globe artichokes were regarded as aristocratic delicacies, reputed to have numerous, rather

*The large swollen flower buds of globe artichokes (background right) are a well known delicacy; the less widely grown cardoon (above) is usually earthed up to produce tender, blanched leaf stems. Both, however, make highly ornamental plants which are a decorative asset in a flower border or within the vegetable garden.*

fanciful medicinal properties. While artichoke root is rarely used these days as a deodorant, the plants are becoming more popular in gardens both as vegetables, for their edible immature flower heads sometimes as much as 15cm (6in) across, and also as strikingly handsome ornamental shrubs.

They look like giant thistles, with long silver-grey leaves and, if allowed to bloom, enormous blue-purple thistle flowers in late summer (in warm regions early summer and sometimes again in autumn). These heads may be dried for winter decoration. Single specimens in small tubs make spectacular pot plants, especially if grown with such slender annuals as cosmos, ursinia or lisianthus (prairie gentian). This combination is equally effective in the open garden, where artichokes deserve a position of prominence within or at the back of flower borders.

### VARIETIES
**Green Globe (Improved):** the most widely available from seed. A reliable old commercial variety. Its purple form, although very decorative, has poor flavour.

**Vert de Laon:** usually supplied as offsets by specialist growers. A classic artichoke of exceptional quality.

### CULTIVATION
Artichokes can be raised from seed to avoid disease problems. Suckers (offsets) may also be taken from mature plants. For a light crop in autumn of the same year, start seeds in February, sowing two to a small pot and thinning to leave the stronger seedling. Plant out 60-90cm (2-3ft) apart in early May in ground that has been well broken and manured. Seeds may also be sown outdoors in April or May,

## CARDOON *(Cynara cardunculus)* zone 9

This is a close relative of the globe artichoke, very similar in appearance but grown for its stems and leaf ribs, which resemble celery when blanched. Plants require similar conditions to globe artichokes, and are raised from seeds sown outdoors in late spring. Thin or transplant seedlings to 45cm (18in) apart, and grow on with frequent watering if the season is dry. Provide each plant with a short stake when it is 30-45cm (12-18in) high, and loosely secure the leaves to this as they grow. In late summer, tie all the stems together at the top and blanch in the same way as for chards. Blanching takes about eight weeks, after which plants are dug up for use.

and the best transplanted in autumn to bear a first crop the following summer.

Alternatively, plant offsets in spring, either bought already growing or prepared from suckers growing at the edges of mature plants. By scraping soil away from their bases, the young offsets can be severed with a knife, each complete with a fragment of the old root. Plant immediately where they are to grow or temporarily in a nursery bed. If kept well watered in dry weather, the strongest should fruit in the autumn.

Established plants in warm gardens need little attention beyond an annual mulch of good compost or rotted manure, either after cutting down the foliage in autumn, or during spring in cold gardens. Artichokes like a rich diet, and with annual feeding plants often crop for 20 years or more, but otherwise they are best renewed every three to four years by offsets planted in freshly prepared soil. In cold areas crowns are sometimes overwintered outdoors

with a deep mulch of salt hay, pine needles, leaves or ashes to exclude frost, although rot is a problem. Overwintering in a cold frame or growing in a large tub to be wheeled inside are more reliable methods. Crowns may even be dug and stored in a cold, frost-free cellar for the winter.

### HARVEST
Cut the fleshy flower heads, each with a short section of stem, before their scales begin to open. The large central 'king' head matures first, followed by several smaller globes on surrounding side shoots; the size of the lesser globes can be increased by removing the king bud while still very small.

### CHARDS

Although globe artichokes are normally grown for their flower heads, the young leaves or 'fronds' are also edible, especially if blanched as chards when about 60cm (2ft) tall. This crisp juicy delicacy is produced from side shoots allowed to grow around established crowns until they are the right height for blanching. Chards can also be prepared from older plants about to be replaced by fresh stock: when the last crop of artichokes has been gathered, cut the whole plant down to 7-10cm (3-4in) high. Fresh growth will soon appear, and can be blanched when 60cm (2ft) high. Tie a cylinder of thick paper or straw around the fronds, and then either mound up soil around the outside or cover with a large pot. After six to eight weeks' growth it will be sufficiently blanched for cutting. Older plants are exhausted by this blanching and will not be worth retaining.

## JERUSALEM *(Helianthus tuberosus)*

**Height:**  3-3.5m (10-12ft), lower if pruned

**Space:**  30cm (1ft) apart

**Plant:**  early spring

**Harvest:**  autumn onwards

**Yield:**  1.8-2.2kg (4-5lb) per plant

Annual crop

Although often recommended as a starch-free substitute for potatoes, the bone-hardy Jerusalem artichoke is a versatile vegetable in its own right, thriving on the poorest soils and providing heavy crops of sweet nutritious tubers that can be left buried until required. In very hungry ground, crops will be small and knobbly, but given a well-dug and moderately fertile site choice varieties yield large smooth tubers with good flavour.

Close relatives of the sunflower, plants produce tall stout stems with large sage green leaves. In warm climates yellow daisy-like flowers appear in late summer, although these are usually removed to increase the crop of tubers; the comparatively dwarf Sunray, however, is an excellent dual-purpose variety for growing at the back of a flower border.

A row makes an effective tall summer screen – which may need support if used as a wind-break – providing beneficial shelter for tender plants such as tomatoes, cucumbers or French beans, and shielding summer lettuces and radishes from hot sunshine. A few plants grown in a sunny or lightly shaded corner will support tall sweet pea plants and still yield a crop at the end of the year.

### VARIETIES
**Dwarf Sunray:**  free-flowering, 180cm-2m (6-7ft) tall. Good yields of crisp thin-skinned tubers.

**Fuseau:** best flavour. Large tubers, white and smooth skinned. Compact growth to 2.5m (8ft).

**Silver Skinned:** the commonest variety, with good flavour and heavy crops. Very tall.

**Stampede:** large, white tubers mature a month before other varieties and give high yields. Very hardy and good in the north.

## CULTIVATION
Tubers too small for culinary use are planted in spring 30cm (1ft) apart and 10-15cm (4-6in) deep, in fertile well-drained soil. A little decayed manure or leaves will improve yields. In windy areas tie the tall growth to canes or horizontal strings for support, and trim to height if necessary.

## HARVEST
Lift from early autumn onwards, digging up a whole plant at a time and making sure no tubers remain behind. Clear dead foliage after frost and in cold gardens mulch the buried tubers, which may be left in the ground until needed.

---

# ASPARAGUS (*Asparagus officinalis*)

| | |
|---|---|
| **Seeds:** | 50/g, 1,250/oz |
| **Germination:** | 3-4 weeks; 70% |
| **Height:** | 90-150cm (3-5ft) |
| **Space:** | 45cm (18in) apart, with 120-150cm (4-5ft) between pairs of rows |
| **Sow:** | February under glass, April outdoors |
| **Plant:** | spring |
| **Harvest:** | late spring until midsummer |
| **Yield:** | 10-20 spears per plant |
| Perennial; zone 3 | |

*Although traditionally cropped in special beds, young asparagus spears may still be harvested when plants are grown as decorative ferns amongst contrasting broadleaf and evergreen shrubs.*

Asparagus is one of the most underrated garden vegetables. Widely assumed to be a luxury crop, with only eight weeks' productivity a year in return for occupying a large amount of ground, it is seldom used to its full potential. There is no need to grow plants in traditional wide beds, nor to wait three to four years before starting to harvest spears: a light cut can be taken from modern F1 hybrids when just one year old. Asparagus is extremely hardy and will grow in almost any region.

Grown on the flat, plants crop as heavily as in raised moulded beds, especially if mulched with decayed manure every autumn. If large quantities are regularly needed, it may be best to grow asparagus in rows, but plants prefer to be treated as individuals, and when content will each bear 20-25 spears annually, often for 20-30 years. Plants may be earthed up, or left to produce green spears.

Where existing plants seed themselves in odd corners and crevices, the decorative potential of asparagus becomes obvious. Its soft feathery foliage, bright green in growth but turning gold in autumn, is frequently cut for vases. The ferny plants are an ideal foil or background for bright flowers in the herbaceous border, and make attractive summer hedges beside paths.

## VARIETIES
**Connovers Colossal:** reliable commercial strain, available as seed or crowns. Heavy early crops.

**Jersey Giant/Greenwich:** F1 hybrids, producing all male plants (female plants waste energy on flower and seed development). Vigorous, with extremely heavy crops. Developed in New Jersey at Rutgers University. Seed or crowns.

**Martha Washington/Mary Washington:** standard American varieties, resistant to rust and generally productive, but somewhat variable long thick spears.

## SOIL PREPARATION
Although not fussy about the type of soil, asparagus must have free drainage. Stiff clay and wet ground must be dug two spades deep and made more porous by the addition of sand, grit or coarse leaf litter. Mix a good dressing of decayed manure or compost into all soils, since plants like rich conditions. This is a permanent crop which resents deep cultivation around the crowns, and special attention should be paid to removing perennial weeds before planting.

## GOOD KING HENRY/MERCURY
(*Chenopodium bonus-henricus*)

One of the first edible crops to appear each year, this native British plant has been cultivated in cottage gardens for centuries. In some districts Good King Henry is a common wild plant, related to fat hen and the various kinds of goosefoot, producing tall spikes of tiny green flowers. It is a hardy perennial, producing in very early spring juicy young shoots which are gathered and cooked like asparagus, followed by arrow-shaped leaves on long stems 45-60cm (18-24in) tall; these thick succulent leaves are used like spinach.

Grow plants in a warm, sheltered part of the garden to encourage early growth, grouping them around trained fruit trees or roses where they can share the annual feeding, making in return an attractive and useful ground cover.

Sow seeds thinly in a seed bed in spring, transplanting them in autumn; or sow where the plants are to grow, two to three seeds at stations 45cm (18in) apart. Each autumn, cover the crowns with mounds of soil 15cm (6in) deep to blanch the shoots and keep them tender; cut them when the tips emerge through the mound. Only a few can be used the first season, but many more appear in succeeding years. Stop cutting in June, expose the crowns again and mulch with compost or decayed leaves. The plant's leaves can be picked thereafter whenever required, although after August they become rather coarse. Do not let plants flower, otherwise seedlings may become a nuisance. Every three to four years divide the crowns and replant in fresh soil.

### SOWING
Soak the large seeds in water for 48 hours. Under glass in early spring, sow two seeds to each small pot or division of a cell tray, and germinate in a minimum temperature of 15°C (60°F). Harden off seedlings, and in late spring plant 7cm (3in) apart in a nursery bed, where they are left until the following spring. Outdoors sow in April or May, spacing seeds 7cm (3in) apart in rows.

### PLANTING
One-year-old plants or 'crowns', either bought or the strongest of those sown the previous year, are planted in spring in individual holes or in a trench. The standard depth is 20cm (8in), but a few crowns planted 15cm (6in) deep will produce spears a little earlier. Spread out the roots of each crown and support its centre on a low mound of soil – take care not to damage the roots or let them dry out before planting. Replace the excavated soil and leave level.

### CULTIVATION
While in growth plants need little attention apart from occasional watering in dry weather. Remove weeds by hand while still young, and cut down any female fronds that form berries, to prevent self-sown seedlings choking the original plants. In autumn cut the dead foliage to the ground, weed thoroughly and mulch with a thin layer of rotted manure.

### HARVEST
Cut with a knife about 7cm (3in) below soil level when spears are 15-20cm (6-8in) tall. One or two may be gathered from F1 hybrids the first spring after planting; leave other varieties to build up strength for a year, before taking a light cut. A little more can be harvested in following years until plants are four to five years old, when they may be cut freely. Stop gathering at midsummer to let plants develop reserves for the next year.

## AUBERGINE/EGGPLANT
(*Solanum melongena*)

| | |
|---|---|
| **Seeds:** | 200/g, 5,000/oz |
| **Germination:** | 2-3 weeks; 75% |
| **Height:** | 90cm (3ft) |
| **Space:** | 60-90cm (2-3ft) apart |
| **Sow:** | February for planting in April in a greenhouse; indoors 2 months before the last frost date for planting outdoors |
| **Harvest:** | 10-15 weeks after sowing |
| **Yield:** | 5-6 fruits per plant |
| Annual crop | |

Gardeners often think of the aubergine, also called eggplant or brinjal, as a modern introduction associated with Mediterranean food. An important and highly productive tropical vegetable for more than 2,500 years in India and southern China, it has in fact been grown fairly widely in Europe since the seventeenth century. In northern latitudes, however, its sensitivity to frost confined its cultivation for a long time to heated greenhouses.

Although aubergines grow as perennial shrubs in their native climate, in colder regions they are usually treated in the same way as tomatoes, as a tender crop raised annually from seed. They thrive in hot regions either in pots and tubs or planted out in the garden. Take care to plant out only after all danger of frost is past and the soil has warmed. In many parts of Britain they are a gamble, unless grown in a very warm sunny position sheltered from cold winds. They are most likely to succeed in a cool greenhouse or conservatory, either planted in a border or in pots.

If grown well, aubergines make spectacular pot plants. The strong, slightly spiny shrubs are

*With their purple flowers and shiny fruits, aubergines (eggplants) add a tropical element to a greenhouse or garden. The fruits should be gathered before they lose their lustre.*

attractive at all stages, their large leaves covered with soft grey velvet, while the gracefully arching flowers, sometimes 5cm (2in) in diameter, are rich purple with yellow centres. The true eggplant has white oval fruits, very decorative but not as well-flavoured as the more common but equally ornamental purple or violet varieties with longer fruits. Surrounded by green basil and blue lobelia, two or three potted specimens would make a flamboyant tropical group in a sunny corner of a courtyard.

## VARIETIES

**Black Beauty:** 80 days. Large deep purple fruits, oval with wide, blunt blossom end.

**Dourga:** 65 days. Cylindrical white fruit, 15cm (6in) long, only 5cm (2in) wide. Sweet flavour.

**Dusky Hybrid:** 60 days. Medium-sized oval purple fruit. Recommended for northern areas with short growing season.

**Tycoon:** 60 days. Slender black fruit up to 20cm (8in) long. One of the earliest for northern regions. Resistant to tobacco mosaic.

## CULTIVATION

For very early crops seeds can be sown in a warm greenhouse from December onwards, but it is more economical to wait until February or March when a germination temperature of 15-21°C (60-70°F) is easier to maintain.

Sow seeds individually in small peat pots, or thinly in shallow pans, using a peat-based compost. Cover with a sheet of glass and newspaper until seedlings emerge. When those in pans are about 5cm (2in) high, transplant first to small pots and then, as these fill with roots, into 12cm (5in) pots.

Plant out 60-90cm (2-3ft) apart, during April for cultivation in a heated greenhouse border, or early May in a cold house. Plants for growing outdoors should be hardened off before planting out after the last frosts, in soil that has been well warmed; cloches may be used to warm the soil for a week or two. Where the aubergines are to stay in containers, they will need potting on, into 20cm (8in) pots if they are grown on their own, or 30-38cm (12-15in) pots where part of a combination with other plants such as ageratum or trailing lobelia.

Keep in full sunshine, and ventilate plants under glass whenever possible. When they are about 15cm (6in) high, pinch off the growing tips to encourage bushiness, and provide each plant with a stake, 90-120cm (3-4ft) long, to support branches as they develop.

Give plenty of water as required, and occasionally spray the whole plant with water to maintain good health and deter red spider mite, the aubergine's main insect pest. Spraying plants when in bloom will help the fruit to set; otherwise, lightly tap or shake flowering branches daily to distribute the pollen. As fruits swell, feed regularly with a liquid fertilizer.

## HARVEST

Aubergines are best picked while still young, after they reach one third of their mature size but while the skin is still shiny. Dull skin and seeds visible in the flesh indicate over-maturity and usually unpleasant flavour. In cooler regions, fruits set later in the season may fail to ripen. Encourage earlier fruits by pinching off the tips of branches after five to six aubergines have formed (12-15 on smaller varieties), and remove any further blossoms.

---

# BROAD BEAN/FAVA BEAN (*Vicia faba* var. *major*)

| | |
|---|---|
| **Seeds:** | 200/pint, 800/kilo |
| **Germination:** | 14 days; 80% |
| **Height:** | dwarf 30-38cm (12-15in); tall 90-120cm (3-4ft) |
| **Space:** | dwarf 23cm (9in ); tall 10x45cm (4x18in) |
| **Sow:** | November to January under glass, February to July outdoors |
| **Harvest:** | June to October |
| **Yield:** | 225-450g (8-16oz) per plant |
| Annual crop | |

The broad bean is a very ancient food plant, once especially popular with the Romans who considered it sacred to Apollo, god of the sun. They used the beans both fresh in religious feasts and dried as tokens when voting. Although in later times the beans, described as 'windy meat' by one cynic, were regarded as peasant fare, they are once more regaining popularity now that the frozen product has shown how delicious they are when eaten young. The decorative black and/or white flowers are sweetly fragrant; it was once thought anyone drowsing in a bean field would never wake up again, so heady is the perfume.

Broad beans are a cool climate crop, enjoying the same conditions as peas and taking about

100 days to mature from a spring sowing, or five months over winter. Since they dislike dry summer heat, site later sowings where they will receive light shade for some of the day, and keep the soil cool with a mulch. The beans themselves are usually either green or white, the former generally best for flavour, while white ones are favoured for freezing. The flavour of young beans, whether shelled or cooked in their pods, is more delicate than large older beans, which many people find too strong for their taste.

## VARIETIES
There are several different kinds of broad/fava beans, although their classification tends to vary. For practical purposes they can be divided into four groups.

**Dwarf:** a bushy kind. Ideal for successional sowing until July, in regions with cool summers. Best: The Sutton, Bonnie Lad.

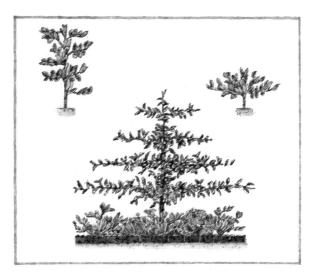

*While the heaviest yields are gathered from conventional tall broad beans* (top left), *dwarf varieties* (top right) *crop faster and repeatedly and make a fruitful edging to the beds in which other plants such as trained fruit trees* (below) *grow.*

**Longpod:** heaviest yielding, with up to 11 seeds to a pod. Tall, needing most room. Best: Masterpiece Green Longpod, Broad Improved Longpod.

**Seville:** hardiest and therefore ideal for autumn sowing in zones 8-9. Best: Aquadulce Claudia.

**Windsor:** largest beans, four or five per pod. The best flavour, but for spring sowing only. Best: Broad Windsor Longpod.

## SOIL PREPARATION
Trials have shown that digging two spades deep has increased yields by up to 95 per cent. Where this is not practicable fork the ground over thoroughly, mixing in plenty of compost or other humus, together with 250g per sq m (8oz per sq yd) of bonfire ash, because the plants need potash. Confine autumn sowings to light, well-drained soils, since plants may rot over winter on cold, waterlogged ground.

## SOWING OUTDOORS
**Autumn:** sow in late October or early November, if the soil is not too wet or cold. Space seeds 10cm (4in) apart, 5cm (2in) deep, in single rows or groups 30cm (1ft) or so away from a protective fence or wall. In open ground in zone 8 or south, sow 10cm (4in) apart in groups, or in two, three or four parallel rows 45cm (18in) apart. Plants usually survive all but the most savage winters to crop from May onwards and sometimes miss black aphid migrations. In very bad weather cover young plants with cloches.

**Maincrops:** sow as soon as the soil is workable, from February until mid-April; dwarf kinds can be sown at monthly intervals in cool climates from March to July to give a succession of beans until the autumn. If the soil is dry, water thoroughly before sowing, and keep it moist until plants appear about a fortnight later.

## UNUSUAL VARIETIES

Many classic broad beans have disappeared over the decades as plant breeders work to increase reliability, seeds per pod, and the number of pods on each plant. Some veteran varieties have survived, however, and it is still possible to find Bunyard's Exhibition, a fine old show bean with very long pods and white seeds, or Johnson's Wonderful, an early variety noted for heavy yields and good flavour. Red Epicure has a prolific crop of long pods containing deep red seeds, which when cooked lose some of their unique colour but none of the outstanding flavour.

## SOWING IN BOXES
Should bad weather prevent autumn sowing, start seeds in boxes of compost in a cold frame or greenhouse, and transplant the seedlings outdoors when conditions allow. Space seeds 5cm (2in) apart each way, 2.5cm (1in) deep. There is no need to use fresh compost – any saved from repotting or pricking out other seedlings will be adequate.

In gardens too cold for autumn sowing, start the beans in boxes under glass about mid-January, using a normal spring variety. After hardening off, plant out in March and they will crop around the same time as an autumn sowing.

## CULTIVATION
Lightly stir around young plants with a fork or hoe to aerate the soil and deter weeds. There is no need to water plants while they are growing unless the season is very dry; too much water at this stage causes excessive leafy growth. However, when plants are in flower, and also while pods are swelling, a canful of water per

## FURTHER IDEAS

Before they get too large intercrop tall varieties with salads such as lettuce, spring onions, radishes, fast carrots or any of the quick-maturing oriental leaves.

Dwarf bush varieties of broad beans make a useful edging to beds and will flourish under trained fruit trees. They can be pruned by cutting back individual branches as they finish cropping, to leave a 5cm (2in) stump. Fresh shoots will appear to prolong the crop, but only if plants are given a top-dressing of compost or fertilizer, and kept well watered.

If despite regular picking old pods remain at the end of the year, dry the large tough beans they contain for winter use or for seed. Buy good fresh seed for next season's crop, but use the home-saved seed to grow green manure in any empty piece of ground – as the plants are legumes they will enrich the soil with nitrogen as well as humus. Sow either in autumn to keep the soil covered during winter, or in early spring, digging the plants in when they have reached a few centimetres tall. Compost old leaves and stems at the end of the season.

square metre twice a week will encourage plenty of blooms and increase the numbers of both pods and beans within.

In windy areas grow dwarf varieties or support tall plants with sticks. When beans are grown in rows support them with string tied to canes on either side of the row and also amongst the plants, or grow them through bird netting; a small group can be tied to a central cane. A mulch of compost or similar material helps stabilize plants and reduces the evaporation of moisture from the soil; alternatively, partially earth up stems with soil.

## HARVESTING

Many gardeners grow for size and so leave picking until the pods are too large. Gather first pods while they are still slim and flexible, about 10cm (4in) long and free from fibre. These are excellent cooked whole or sliced like runner beans. If they are to be shelled for fresh consumption or for freezing, pick pods when the seeds are no larger than hazelnuts. Small young beans make much better eating than older ones with tough skins. Should they reach this stage, either use them to make Brown Windsor soup, or leave on the plants until pods are dry. The beans can then be stored as seed for next season or for cooking as dried beans during the winter. Generally, though, frequent picking while still young produces the heaviest and most prolonged crop of pods.

## FRENCH/SNAP/POLE BEAN
### (Phaseolus vulgaris)

**Seeds:** 2-3/g, 50-70/oz

**Germination:** 10-14 days; 75%

**Height:** 45-60cm (18-24in)

**Space:** 30cm (1ft) apart each way; or 10cm (4in) in rows 45cm (18in) apart

**Sow:** 3-4 weeks before last frost indoors, after frost outdoors until late summer

**Harvest:** late June to autumn

**Yield:** 112-225g (4-8oz) per plant – higher yields for climbing varieties

Annual crop

Gardeners have always disagreed about the respective merits of scarlet runner and French beans. If sown early, French beans crop a few weeks before runners, and many people only grow them to fill in this short period. Others, however, consider the flavour and quality of French beans superior and plan their sowings for continuous supplies until the first frosts (or beyond with the help of cloches).

Known also as haricot, navy, kidney or green snap beans, French beans have a place of their own in the garden. They have been cultivated for several thousand years in central and southern America, but reached their peak of popularity only a century ago when numerous coloured and variegated kinds were grown in Europe and the USA. Today the available selection is much smaller, often limited to green 'pencil pod' varieties used commercially for canning and freezing, but many older kinds still exist, preserved in specialist collections or by amateur gardeners who carefully save seed.

Dwarf or bush types are the quickest to crop, sometimes only 50 days from sowing, and although very sensitive to low temperatures outdoors they can be grown in pots under glass for earlier or later picking. Varieties with flat pods are usually sliced for cooking, while the slim pencil-podded kinds are used whole if picked when young. Most varieties can be shelled for use as green (flageolet) or dried haricot beans, although yields vary considerably according to seed size.

All French beans are versatile decorative plants, with small white, pink or red flowers, and handsome fresh green leaves, each divided into three broad leaflets. Pods may be green, yellow or purple, some with attractive speckling. Provided they have full sun and room to develop, dwarf varieties can be planted in flowerbeds, amongst petunias, nasturtiums, blue salvias or French marigolds for example, and combine well with annual flowers in containers. They fit neatly between the widely spaced poles of runner beans or climbing French varieties, and around the base of tall tomato plants, sweet corn and climbing cucumbers. Tansy is sometimes planted with dwarf beans as a natural insect pest-repellant.

*Rows of runner beans and the slightly less robust climbing French kinds are excellent wind-breaks, especially for sheltering shade-loving crops such as celery.*

## VARIETIES

**Blue Lake/Climbing Blue Lake:** 56 days. Dwarf and climbing forms of the same variety, excellent outdoors or under glass. Slim pods with white seeds that can be dried.

**Burpee Golden:** 60 days. Pole variety but also bears early on short, bushy plants before runners develop. Butter yellow pods.

**Cheverbel:** 55 days. Bushy plants with oval pods for use whole, or shelled as either fresh green haricots or dried beans.

**Goldcrop:** 54 days. AAS winner. Lustrous straight golden-yellow waxy pods on disease-resistant plants.

**Greensleeves:** 56 days. Bush variety, dark green pods. Resistant to common and NY 15 bean mosaic.

**Jumbo:** 55 days. Large flat pods up to 30cm (1ft) long on bushy plants have exceptionally rich flavour. Early bearing.

**Kentucky Wonder:** 65 days. Pole variety. 23cm (9in) green pods. Use as snap or shell bean.

**Purple-podded Climbing:** 55 days. Tall. Deep violet pods, fleshy, excellent flavour.

**Romano/Italian Pole:** 60 days. Pole variety. Flat green pods, snap or shell bean.

**Royal Burgundy/Royalty:** 51 days. Very similar dwarf varieties with purple flowers, dark foliage and clusters of purple pencil pods.

**Tender Pod:** 50 days. AAS winner. Slender round green pods 10-12cm (4-5in) long. Noted for tender fibreless texture and flavour.

**Tendergreen Improved:** 56 days. Popular green pencil-podded variety. Heavy crops and good flavour. Mosaic resistant.

## SOIL PREPARATION

French beans prefer warm soil containing a little lime, and broken up at least a spade deep. A little garden compost or decayed manure forked well in will increase and extend cropping. Good drainage is essential.

## SOWING

Do not sow outdoors until the ground temperature is above about 10°C (50°F); in colder soil the seeds soon rot. For earliest outdoor crops, sow three to four weeks before the last frost date either 5cm (2in) deep under cloches, or indoors in pots or boxes. Plant out or uncover seedlings when the threat of frost is past. In exposed gardens sow or plant earliest crops between lettuces or cabbages for shelter. Sow maincrops outdoors after frost is past. Repeat sowings until late June, July or later in warm regions for continued harvest. Where the

### FRENCH BEANS UNDER GLASS

All varieties are very easily grown indoors, given a minimum temperature of about 12°C (55°F). Plants sown in January start cropping from early April. Sow a compact dwarf variety, such as Deuil Fin Précoce or The Prince (USA: Greensleeves or Goldcrop Wax), 5cm (2in) deep in pots of good soil-based potting mixture enriched with a little decayed manure. Allow four plants to a 20cm (8in) pot or six to a 30cm (12in) pot. Grow in full light and ventilate whenever possible, although draughts should be avoided. Support plants as they grow with a few thin twigs. Lightly mist with water regularly to deter red spider mite, and gently shake plants in bloom to help the flowers to set. Gather pods while young, and give an occasional liquid feed to keep plants productive.

Climbing Blue Lake is excellent for forcing in the same way at the back of a warm greenhouse border, spacing plants 25-30cm (10-12in) apart and training them up bamboo canes 150-180cm (5-6ft) high. Mulch them with decayed manure and then follow with aubergines or tomatoes in the same ground after cutting off the exhausted bean vines at ground level, leaving the nitrogen-rich roots behind.

beans are grown in rows, sow or plant 10cm (4in) apart in lines 45cm (18in) apart; or plant in rows 38-45cm (15-18in) wide, spacing seeds 7-10cm (3-4in) apart. Climbing varieties are sown and planted as for runner beans (p.118).

## CULTIVATION

Slugs love young French beans, and it is a wise precaution to protect the plants with slug pellets or rings of soot. Either hoe carefully

## DRIED HARICOT BEANS

The dried seeds of all French bean varieties can be used as haricot beans, but the best for flavour and yield is Dutch Brown, a traditional home-grown variety for making Boston Baked Beans. Grow the plants in rows as above, or broadcast in wide beds, sowing them in May and thinning seedlings to 15-20 (6-8in) apart each way. Although the green pods can be picked for fresh use, the whole crop is best left until early autumn when all the pods should be brown and dry. In a wet season, pull up plants and suspend them upside down in bundles under cover to finish drying. When the pods are crisp the ripe seeds are shelled out and spread on trays to make sure they are completely dry. Large numbers of plants are quickly hulled by packing them into a sack and then beating this with a stick. Store the dried beans in tins.

around plants or mulch with grass clippings, both to keep down weeds and also to prevent soil compaction which checks growth. In windy positions earth up stems and firm in any plants that topple over; vigorous varieties will also benefit from the support of short twiggy sticks. Unless the season is very dry, plants will not need watering until they are in flower, after which they should be given a good soak every few days to encourage a heavy prolonged crop.

### HARVEST

If for use whole, gather pods when about 10cm (4in) long, nipping or cutting them off carefully at the stem and taking care not to pull off smaller pods in the same cluster. On varieties such as The Prince (USA: Goldcrop Wax), pods remain crisp and stringless until nearly 30cm

(1ft) long; test by bending one of them, when it should snap cleanly. Search for pods that might have been overlooked, because any left to ripen their seeds will reduce the yield by preventing further pods from forming.

## RUNNER BEAN (*Phaseolus coccineus*)

| | |
|---|---|
| **Seeds:** | 1/g, 25-30/oz |
| **Germination:** | 7-10 days; 80% |
| **Height:** | 2.5-3.5m (8-12ft) |
| **Space:** | 23-60cm (9-24in) apart, in double rows 60cm (2ft) apart |
| **Sow:** | 3-4 weeks before the last frost under glass; after danger of frost in the open |
| **Harvest:** | from early July (protected sowings); maincrops, August to October |
| **Yield:** | 1-1.3kg (2-3lb) per plant |
| Annual crop | |

For many gardeners the first handful of runner ('stick' or 'string') beans signals the arrival of high summer. Although regularly voted Britain's favourite garden crop, runner beans are not so popular elsewhere. In Europe French beans reign supreme, as in parts of North America, while in southern USA gardeners prefer the lima or 'butter' bean, but runner beans are best suited to cooler summers.

The plants are perennial by nature. Although normally treated as annuals, sown afresh each year, crowns can be lifted for storage in the same way as dahlias, and if planted again the following May often crop three to four weeks before first sowings. In very mild gardens crowns can be covered with ashes or leaves, and left in the ground all winter, but the young growth may be hit by severe spring frost.

*Ground at the base of climbing beans is often wasted, but can provide midsummer shade for leafy crops such as cabbages, cauliflowers, spinach and chard (above).*

By heavily thinning crops, pods well over 60cm (2ft) long are attainable, but for highest yields large numbers of shorter pods are preferable. Cultivated varieties resemble the wild runner bean in vigour, and with support can climb 3.5-4.5m (12-15ft) high. This, combined with their brilliant scarlet flowers, makes them ideal for decorative screens, especially if a mixture of red, white and bi-coloured varieties is combined with thunbergias or morning glory (ipomaea).

Although traditionally trained up rows of poles or strings, they are equally productive and more easily accommodated if grown on poles arranged as tripods or tents, in containers where necessary. If space is short they can be trained against a house wall, climbing up strings attached to the eaves, or left to scramble into trees, over pergolas or even up sweetcorn plants. Lettuces, dwarf beans, spinach and chicory all grow well at the foot of the poles.

## VARIETIES

**Enorma:** 65 days. Very long handsome pods of outstanding flavour.

**Hammond's Dwarf:** 60 days. A natural dwarf runner, growing to 45cm (18in) in height. It is available in both red and white flowered forms.

**Kelvedon Marvel/Kelvedon Wonder:** 65 days. One of the earliest to crop, even in cool seasons. Can be pinched out as a dwarf.

**Painted Lady:** 68 days. An old variety with attractive red and white flowers. Very decorative, but lower yields of shorter than average pods.

**Red Knight:** 70 days. Stringless pods with a smoother texture. Scarlet flowers.

*Compared with the usual utilitarian straight rows, climbing beans grown up tripods or pyramids of canes economize on space and make handsome decorative features similar to topiary.*

**Streamline:** 75 days. A dependable old variety with very heavy crops of long, finely flavoured beans. May be grown as a dwarf plant with pinching out.

**White Knight:** 73 days. Stringless pods with good flavour. White flowers.

## SOIL PREPARATION
For heaviest yields runner beans need well-drained soil, which is also richer than for other beans. Mix in plenty of good compost or decayed manure while breaking up the ground; if possible first excavate a hole or trench in late winter and bury organic waste such as crushed Brussels sprout stems. Add a little lime if the soil is acid.

## CULTIVATION
Sow and plant in the same way as outdoor French beans. There is little point sowing before the second half of May. Although the scarlet flowers are decorative all summer, they will not set pods in hot weather when temperatures regularly exceed 29°C (85°F). Midday and afternoon shade may improve cropping in midsummer. For heaviest crops space 2.5m (8ft) poles or vertical strings 30cm (1ft) apart and grow a single plant up each. Groups of poles are tied at the top like a tepee, while for rows the poles are arranged in pairs 60cm (2ft) apart and crossed at the top. Loosely tie each bean to its support, after which it will twine naturally. Mulch and water as for French beans, and pinch out the growing tips when vines reach the top.

For early beans pinch off the growing tips when plants are 60cm (2ft) tall and again at 120cm (4ft). Alternatively, plant Kelvedon Marvel or Streamline 60cm (2ft) apart and pinch out their tips when 30-45cm (12-18in) tall. Support in the same way as dwarf French beans, and pinch side shoots every week to keep plants bushy. Hammond's Dwarf is

naturally compact and may be grown like a French bean. Although crops appear earlier on dwarf runner beans, overall yields are lower and pods are often curled or blemished by contact with the soil.

## HARVEST
Pick frequently when the pods are 20-23cm (8-9in) long and still crisp. If left until the seeds swell, pods are liable to be tough and stringy, and production will decline. Surplus pods are easily preserved by freezing or salting, while the seeds may be dried as haricots.

## BEET *(Beta vulgaris)*

| | |
|---|---|
| **Seeds:** | 75/g, 200/oz |
| **Germination:** | 2-3 weeks; 50-70% |
| **Height:** | 30-45cm (12-18in) |
| **Space:** | 10cm (4in) apart |
| **Sow:** | February under glass, one month before last frost outdoors until midsummer |
| **Harvest:** | June to November |
| **Yield:** | 1 per plant |
| Annual crop | |

Already well-known in Europe at the time of the Romans, who grew it as a leaf and root vegetable as well as a fodder crop for animals, beet was not introduced to the USA until 1800. A few decades earlier in Germany, recognition of the roots' naturally high sugar content started the development of modern sugar beet varieties and the sophisticated extraction industry now established in many countries.

Gardeners have always appreciated the sweet flavour of young roots, and also the decorative value of the foliage, bright green or red with a distinct pattern of darker veins. Fast globe

*Although an ideal crop for fitting amongst other plants, beetroot needs full sun and moist conditions for the roots to reach full size. If thinned to avoid congestion, plants make an attractive colour contrast with cabbages and box hedging* (right), *and the soft ferny leaves of carrots* (above), *here shown as an edging to a circular bed of beetroot.*

varieties can mature in just over two months, and crops may be grown amongst white-flowered or grey bedding plants which will spread to cover the spaces left when roots are lifted. Rows make an attractive edging to beds and paths, especially if grown with carrots and parsley, but an open position must be chosen because too much shade discourages roots from swelling.

## VARIETIES
Beet 'seeds' are in fact corky capsules containing several seeds, although 'monogerm' varieties produce a single plant from each capsule. White, yellow and red cultivars are available, while the leaves of many resemble spinach when cooked. Round or globe varieties mature faster than long or cylindrical kinds.

**Albina Vereduna** (formerly **Snow-white**): 55 days. Sweet, pure white flesh, leaves high in vitamins A and C and excellent as 'greens'.

**Boltardy:** 58 days. Red, bolt resistant and widely used for first sowings in early spring.

**Burpee's Golden:** 55 days. Orange skin and yellow flesh. Both roots and leaves have outstanding flavour.

**Cylindrica:** 60 days. Slender, dark red. 20cm (8in) long, 4cm (1¾in) wide. Tender. Cylindrical roots provide uniform slices.

**Detroit Dark Red:** 60 days. Medium-sized, red. Tender, fine grained, sweet. 6-7cm (2½-3in) diameter. Good on sandy soils.

**Early Wonder:** 55 days. Dark red smooth skin, red flesh with lighter rings.

**Lutz Green Leaf/Winter Keeper:** 80 days. Popular variety for summer use and keeping for winter. Dark red flesh. Flavourful greens.

**Red Ace:** 53 days. Dark red, up to 7cm (3in) in diameter, sweet, vigorous. Cooked greens keep good colour. Resists bolting, and leaf spot.

## SOIL PREPARATION
Beet needs well-broken soil, free from clods. Heavy ground must be thoroughly cultivated and opened up, preferably with ashes which also provide the extra potash beet loves. Add garden compost, rotted leaves or well decayed manure, together with a little lime if the soil is acid. Rake level to leave a fine seed bed.

## SOWING
Seed capsules contain a chemical inhibitor and should be soaked in water overnight prior to sowing. For earliest crops, sow under glass in peat blocks or cell trays, sowing four to five monogerm seeds or two capsules of ordinary varieties to each station. Thin to leave groups of four to five seedlings, harden off and plant out 30cm (1ft) apart in March, leaving seedlings in clusters.

Outdoors sow an early variety about 2.5cm (1in) deep three to four weeks before the last frost date, and repeat every three to four weeks for succession. Sow two capsules at stations 10cm (4in) apart each way; if plants are to grow in narrow rows, space these 30cm (1ft) apart and sow 5-7cm (2-3in) apart in each row. Thin clusters of emerging seedlings to one at each station – in cold areas, remove larger seedlings which are more liable to bolt. Sow maincrops in May or June for lifting in October, and make a last sowing of an early variety in July for immediate use in autumn. Beet dislikes high temperatures, so on hot soils sow in early spring and autumn.

## CULTIVATION

Birds are very fond of the tiny seedlings which may need temporary protection with netting. Keep the soil evenly moist at all times, preferably with a mulch of grass clippings.

## HARVEST

Most globe varieties are best used when 5cm (2in) in diameter, although cylindrical and long-rooted varieties will grow much larger. In mild areas late crops can be left in the ground, with a little soil mounded over the roots for protection. Lift maincrops for storage in October, using a fork to loosen the roots from the ground. Cutting off the tops may cause roots to bleed – always twist off foliage to leave a cluster of short stems. Pack sound clean roots in damp sand or peat in boxes, or loose in plastic bags, and store in a frost-proof shed.

## BROCCOLI (*Brassica oleracea* var. *italica*)

| | |
|---|---|
| **Seeds:** | 250/g, 6-7,000/oz |
| **Germination:** | 1-2 weeks; 70% |
| **Height:** | 45-90cm (18-36in) |
| **Space:** | spring heading varieties 45-90cm (18-36in) apart, hybrid calabrese 23-30cm (9-12in) apart each way |
| **Sow:** | calabrese from 6-8 weeks before last spring frost until midsummer; others late April |
| **Harvest:** | calabrese July to October, others January to May |
| **Yield:** | 450g-1kg (1-2lb) per plant |
| Annual crop | |

A lot of confusion surrounds the use of the term 'broccoli'. Large-headed broccoli, for example, is more commonly referred to as winter cauliflower (and is described as such on p. 131), while varieties that mature in spring with slender heads of white or purple buds are loosely known as purple or white 'sprouting'. Green sprouting broccoli, on the other hand, is generally called calabrese, especially those annual varieties that produce large single heads like green cauliflowers.

Sprouting broccoli is one crop that should always be grown in home gardens, for it needs to be used soon after gathering to be fully appreciated. Although the Italian word 'broccoli' originally meant any tender young brassica shoots, its eighteenth-century translation as 'Italian asparagus' is a more accurate reference to the quality and flavour of freshly harvested spears. Late-heading strains of purple and white sprouting are especially welcome because they crop when little else is available from the garden.

*One of the best maincrop calabrese varieties, 'Corvet' (above) is a high-yielding crop in gardens. This F1 hybrid often produces secondary spears alongside the large central head.*

Plants are handsome as well as extraordinarily productive. The hardy blue-green foliage is deeply cut and curled, with prominent veins, while the bushes are stout and widely branching, retaining their decorative shape all winter until growth resumes in spring with the appearance of soft leafy shoots and tight clusters of coloured buds. The plants will thrive beneath fruit trees and amongst evergreen shrubs and herbs, and make a contrasting background for wallflowers and spring bulbs, especially large-flowered daffodils.

## VARIETIES

(see panel for the cultivation of hybrid calabrese varieties)

In recent years hybrid calabrese has largely overtaken sprouting broccoli in popularity; numerous F1 hybrids are available to suit particular localities and seasons. By making successive sowings of different varieties, a long continuous harvest is possible, but as plants of a hybrid variety tend to mature simultaneously there is always the risk of a sudden glut.

**Corvet:** 55 days. F1 calabrese. Height 60cm (2ft). Large round heads, followed by numerous side shoots.

**Emperor Hybrid:** 64 days. Deep green heads, 18-20cm (7-8in) in diameter. Disease resistant. Succession of side shoots for continued cropping.

**Green Comet Hybrid:** 55 days. AAS winner. Highly acclaimed early variety with large heads. Adaptable to various growing conditions.

**Green Duke:** 60 days. F1 hybrid. Height 38-45cm (15-18in). Large heads slightly smaller than Green Comet, rapidly followed by numerous side shoots.

**Green Sprouting:** 85 days. The prototype calabrese, sometimes known as Italian Sprouting. Closer to other sprouting broccolis than to calabrese hybrids, growing 90cm (3ft) tall and producing a medium-sized central head in September. A long succession of side shoots follows, often continuing throughout a mild winter.

**Premium Crop Hybrid:** 58 days. AAS winner. Single headed variety 20-23cm (8-9in) across, without production of significant side shoots. Holds well in the garden until harvest.

**Romanesco:** 85 days. A broccoli with lime-green heads like small cauliflowers in late autumn and early winter. Good flavour and very attractive appearance.

## SOIL PREPARATION

In gardens where sprouting broccoli can be overwintered, it must be grown with little nitrogen if it is to survive cold weather, and plants should be fed only in spring as they commence cropping; green sprouting, however, may be given richer conditions since it is not normally overwintered. Dig in garden compost or decayed leaves well before planting to give the ground time to settle, and add lime to acid soils. Broccoli grows well on clay, which only needs to be made workable; other lighter soils must be thoroughly firmed before planting.

## SOWING

Broccoli is a cool season crop and can take some frost. All varieties of sprouting broccoli can be sown in late spring, 1cm (½in) deep in a prepared seed bed outdoors. Sow very sparingly and thin the seedlings to 5-7cm (2-3in) apart. Transplant them to their cropping positions six to eight weeks later when about 7-10cm (3-4in) tall, watering them thoroughly several hours before lifting with a fork. Plant very firmly with the lowest leaves at ground level, spacing early varieties approximately 60cm (2ft) apart and later ones up to about 90cm (3ft) apart.

### PERENNIAL BROCCOLI (zones 6-7)

For an unusual vegetable well worth growing in a sunny corner or against a section of fence or garden wall, try Nine Star Perennial broccoli, a large variety, which in fertile soil will reach 120-125cm (4-5ft) tall and 90cm (3ft) across, and resembles a cross between broccoli and cauliflower. It will produce eight or nine small pale green cauliflowers during April and May for several years if watered and mulched with decayed manure during the growing season, or given a dressing of general fertilizer each spring. Sow and transplant seedlings in the same way as white or purple sprouting, spacing the plants 90cm (3ft) apart. The first heads will appear the following year. Do not let the heads flower. When plants begin to decline with age, young shoots 10-15cm (4-6in) long can be pulled off as cuttings and rooted in a cold frame or shaded corner of the garden.

For spring crops in very cold regions, sow indoors six to eight weeks before the last frost date, and transplant outdoors four weeks before the last frost and protect on cold nights whenever necessary. These plants must be grown very fast, watering and feeding them regularly to ensure tender heads.

## CULTIVATION

Water plants whenever necessary during the month following planting, after which little watering will be required. Guard against birds and insect pests, and mulch with grass clippings to control weeds. Tall plants may need staking or earthing up in exposed gardens, and after high winds or severe frost the soil around the stems should be trodden firmly. In early spring feed overwintered plants with a dressing of general fertilizer or a mulch of decayed manure to spur them into growth. Water liberally in a dry spring to sustain the production of new shoots.

## HARVEST

Cut the young flower shoots when they are a few centimetres long and the heads are still tightly in bud; do not wait until buds open as this may reduce the yield. If spears cannot be used fresh, freeze them for later use. Each plant will crop for about two months before it is exhausted.

### CALABRESE

Calabrese hybrids with their smaller stature and rapid development take only three to four months to mature from sowing, and may be fitted between slower growing crops or amongst summer flowers provided they are not heavily shaded. They are normally sown from March until early June for cutting between July and October. (In the UK Toro is sown in autumn and overwintered in a sheltered part of the garden). While hybrid seedlings are often transplanted at six weeks old and will go on to give good crops, all these varieties perform best when sown where they are to mature. If grown in rows, space these 30cm (1ft) apart and sow two or three seeds every 15cm (6in) along them, thinning seedlings to leave the strongest; elsewhere, sow at stations 23cm (9in) apart each way and single the seedlings. Cut the large terminal head while still tight, and either discard the plants or leave where appropriate for side shoots to follow in the same way as with sprouting broccoli.

# BRUSSELS SPROUTS *(Brassica oleracea* var. *gemmifera)*

**Seeds:**  250/g, 6-7,000/oz

**Germination:**  1-2 weeks; 75%

**Height:**  45-90cm (18-36in)

**Space:**  60-90cm (2-3ft) apart each way

**Sow:**  February under glass; March to April outdoors (USA: 3-4 months before first autumn frost)

**Harvest:**  August to March

**Yield:**  1-1.3kg (2-3lb) per plant

Annual crop

Although today Brussels sprouts are one of the most popular winter vegetables, they first appeared just over 200 years ago in Belgium as a sport or natural variation of a cabbage. For a long time only one or two varieties were grown in gardens, but once they became a commercial crop numerous strains were developed, culminating in the large and bewildering array of modern F1 hybrids.

Initially wary of these hybrids with strange names, gardeners are beginning to appreciate their particular virtues because, more than any other vegetable, Brussels sprouts have been improved almost beyond all recognition by plant breeders. Since plants need a long season of growth before yielding their individual crops of 1kg (2lb) or more of sprouts, it is important to be able to guarantee results. Hybrid varieties have been designed deliberately for uniformity, predictable maturity and high productivity, qualities that are particularly valuable in the small garden. Contrary to popular opinion, most hybrids will hold their crops in peak condition for several weeks.

They may, however, be harvested wholesale, with all the sprouts cleared at a single picking

*Red varieties of Brussels sprouts, with similar habit and quality to the more familiar green kinds, are outstanding for winter colour and often escape damage from pigeons.*

for freezing. This is an advantage where they are grown amongst other plants, for Brussels sprouts are not the easiest vegetable to integrate into the garden. Although the tall plants with their blue-green or red foliage are handsome, once harvesting starts older varieties can look gaunt and untidy. Plant them amongst cabbages, sage or dwarf shrubs which will conceal the bare stems. Hybrids may be grown wherever height and background foliage is required, perhaps with gladioli and hellebores, removing whole sprout stems for harvest when mature.

## VARIETIES

**Bedford Fillbasket:**  95 days. October to December. An old, tall variety with the heaviest yield of large sprouts.

**Citadel:**  160 days. F1, December to March. Dark green sprouts, firm and medium-sized over a long season.

**Jade Cross E Hybrid:**  85 days. Improved Jade Cross. Taller plants produce large easy to harvest blue-green sprouts.

**Long Island Improved:**  108 days. Improved old standard variety which has a good, distinctive flavour.

**Peer Gynt:**  140 days. F1, October to December. A popular early hybrid, shorter than many others, which bears tight, medium-sized sprouts.

**Prince Marvel:**  90 days. Tight sprouts with cream centres are sweet without bitterness. Easy to pick on tall stalks.

**Rubine:**  105 days. December to January. A very decorative red variety, noted for flavour and high quality.

**Valiant:**  110 days. Sweet, well-flavoured sprouts, tightly packed on tall stalks.

## SOIL PREPARATION

It is a mistake to make the ground too rich or soft. Loose soil results in instability and open, leafy sprouts, while very fertile conditions produce sappy plants easily damaged by frost. Well before planting time fork the ground over, working in plenty of compost or decayed leaves and then leave to settle firmly. Add a good dressing of lime unless the soil is naturally alkaline.

## SOWING

For most crops seeds may be sown 1cm (½in) deep in a seed bed outdoors between mid-March and mid-April, thinning the seedlings to 7cm (3in) apart or transplanting to this distance in a nursery bed. If sprouts are required from August onwards, sow an early variety very thinly in boxes or pots in February, keeping the seedlings in a cool house or cold frame before hardening off for planting out in a nursery bed in late March. (Alternatively, a non-hybrid early variety can be sown in early August and transplanted in October where they are to crop the following year). In the USA, sow seeds three to four months before the first expected autumn frost. In the north, only one crop, harvested through the autumn, is possible. In the south, avoid the summer heat by sowing in early autumn for autumn and winter crops and again in early spring with a rapidly maturing variety for harvest before hot weather arrives.

When seedlings are about 15cm (6in) high (six to eight weeks after sowing), transplant to their permanent quarters. Water them the day before, and where possible choose a still, dull day for moving to avoid too much aftercare. Plant very firmly with the base of the lowest leaves at soil level, 60cm (2ft) apart each way for hybrids or 90cm (3ft) for tall older varieties. In dry weather 'puddle in' the plants (see p. 173).

## CULTIVATION

Do not allow plants to dry out during the first three to four weeks after planting; thereafter there should be no need for watering unless the season is exceptionally dry. Tall varieties may need staking individually in windy gardens, or soil can be mounded up and firmed around the base of the stems. Inspect regularly for signs of insect pests.

## HARVEST

Begin picking as soon as the lowest sprouts are useable, snapping them off cleanly without damaging the stem. Hybrids may be harvested all at once, pulling up plants and stripping the sprouts and tops indoors for immediate use or freezing. Non-hybrids are picked over a long season, gathering the lower larger sprouts as required and removing leaves up to that level, together with any that turn yellow. Either cut off the head and use as 'greens' when the crop

is finished, or remove it when the lowest sprouts are ready; this will encourage the others to mature more quickly. Sprouts are damaged at around −5°C (22°F) unless protected with straw. Where frosts are severe plants can be dug late in the season and placed in a cold cellar to keep until required. When plants are exhausted, pull up the stems; either burn them or, if disease-free, crush with the back of a spade, and bury them where runner beans are to be grown or at the bottom of compost heaps.

---

## CABBAGE *(Brassica oleracea* var. *capitata)*

| | |
|---|---|
| **Seeds:** | 250/g, 6-7,000/oz |
| **Germination:** | 1-2 weeks; 75% |
| **Height:** | 30-38cm (12-15in) |
| **Space:** | for small heads 30cm (1ft ), large heads 45cm (18in), spring cabbage 10x30cm (4x12in) |
| **Sow:** | February under glass, March to September outdoors |
| **Harvest:** | all the year round |
| **Yield:** | 450g-1.5kg (1-4lb) per plant |
| Annual crop | |

The cabbage is the parent of most other cultivated brassicas, although in the wild plants are very loose and unproductive. The first hearted cabbages seem to have been developed in medieval Germany, while the attractively crimped and puckered savoy cabbage appeared in Italy about the same time.

Although always a popular garden crop, especially in winter, most modern varieties have been bred for commercial use and are not always suitable for amateur cultivation. Many F1 hybrids, for example, are designed to mature

simultaneously so that whole fields can be cleared at once. In the garden, however, older strains with their comparative lack of uniformity are often useful for providing a steady succession of mature heads. Winter cabbage hybrids are more valuable, since most have been bred for enhanced hardiness, while the majority of Chinese cabbage hybrids are less prone to bolting during warm weather.

There is considerable variation amongst cabbage types, with a choice of pointed, spherical or flat drumhead shapes, and smooth or crinkled leaves in colours that range from pale green to rich purple. They can be planted

*Brassicas of all kinds blend well with flowering plants, as here where young Brussels sprouts provide a leafy background for a row of everlasting flowers.*

amongst flowers, fruit and herbs wherever background foliage is needed, and when combined with coloured ornamental cabbages and kale make an attractive group on their own in the garden or in tubs.

## VARIETIES

Like their close relatives, broccoli and Brussels sprouts, cabbages are best as cool season crops. They will not do well in hot southern summers but can be grown through the mild winters. In the north, spring, summer and autumn crops are grown, depending on the length of the season. Cabbages can take considerable frost in spring, autumn and mild winters. Days to harvest are given from the transplant date.

### Early cabbage

**Durham Early:** 62 days. Pointed, dark green compact hearts, ready mid-February but stands well. Very hardy, ideal for northern gardens. Usually grown at close spacing for 'greens'.

**Early Jersey Wakefield:** 62 days. Cone shaped heads of mild flavour that stand well until used. 12-15cm (5-6in) diameter. Yellows resistant.

**Emerald Cross Hybrid:** 63 days. AAS winner. Round smooth heads. 15-20cm (6-8in) diameter with good flavour. Vigorous.

**Stonehead Hybrid:** 67 days. AAS winner. Firm, solid round heads. Yellows tolerant.

### Mid-season cabbage

**Copenhagen Market:** 72 days. Solid round heads. 15-18cm (6-7in) diameter. Early sauerkraut variety.

**Greyhound:** 64 days. Old favourite, for use from June onwards; can be sown up to late July for autumn use. Tight pointed heads, juicy with outstanding flavour.

**Gourmet:** 70 days. Round blue-green heads. Yellows tolerant.

*For rotation purposes, dwarf beans and cabbages belong to different groups. Nevertheless, they make ideal neighbours with their contrasting appearance and a shared preference for limed soil.*

**Minicole:** 65 days. F1 hybrid. Very small compact ball head for cooking or coleslaw. Sow February onwards for succession and plant 25cm (10in) apart each way. Mature heads will stand well without deterioration.

### Late and cold storage cabbage

**Christmas Drumhead:** 110 days. Medium-sized flattened heads, very hard and compact with rich blue-green foliage. October to January.

**Danish Roundhead:** 105 days. Round heads 18-20cm(7-8in) wide. Good winter storage and sauerkraut.

**January King:** 115 days. Popular drumhead like a plain savoy with red tinted leaves. Very hardy, useable from November until late February.

**Lariat:** 125 days. Late maturing variety with high frost tolerance for long-term storage. Resists pepper spot and holds colour well. Plant early.

**Wisconsin All-Season:** 100 days. Thick, solid, slightly flattened heads 18-20cm (7-8in) across. Good for winter storage.

### Savoy cabbage

**Chieftain Savoy:** 83 days. Olive green heads, 20cm (8in) across, hold well. Good productive summer crop.

**Savoy Ace Hybrid:** 78 days. AAS winner. Compact heads hold well for extended harvest. Heat and frost resistant.

**Savoy King Hybrid:** 90 days. Dark green, vigorous cabbage for use fresh or cooked.

**Spivoy:** 50 days. F1 hybrid. A fast miniature savoy that can be sown as an early or mid-season cabbage, or a conventional late variety. Plant 25-30cm (10-12in) each way.

### Red cabbage

**Preko:** 70 days. Very early heading red. Holds well.

**Ruby Ball:** 65 days. AAS winner. F1 hybrid. Deep red heads with short cores, 12-15cm (5-6in) across. Keeps well.

**Ruby Perfection:** 85 days. Mid-season variety that is slow to split with good red colour both inside and out. Stores well. Not yellows tolerant.

## Ornamental cabbage

Sown and planted in the same way as conventional mid-season and late varieties. Most kinds need about three months to reach maturity and develop their best colouring from late summer onwards. Puckered leaves like a savoy cabbage, green with white, pink, red or purple centres. Usually sold in mixtures as Decorative, Flowering or Ornamental Cabbage, although single colours are sometimes available, for example Cherry Sundae, an F1 hybrid selection in red and cream.

## Chinese cabbage

**Jade Pagoda:**  68 days. Early Michihili type, bolt resistant, tall, medium-green heads, yellow inside, resistant to speckling.

**Kasumi:**  64 days. F1 hybrid. Bolt resistant. Sow in blocks in April or outdoors in summer. Tall, dark green with broad white midribs.

**Lei Choi:**  45 days. Pak Choi type with habit like Swiss chard. Yields thick, white edible stalks. Does not bolt in hot weather.

**Mei Qing Choi:**  50 days. Pak Choi type, short, broad-based with green petioles. Sweet and mildly flavoured. Slow to bolt.

**Two Seasons:**  62 days, Napa type, equally good for early or late crop. Resistant to bolting.

## SOIL PREPARATION

Although tolerant of most soil types, cabbages are greedy feeders, especially summer and autumn varieties, and need plenty of rich organic matter mixed into the soil, together with a high lime content. Firm thoroughly after preparation, since unconsolidated soil often results in loose open heads with little or no heart. Spring cabbage, too, needs firm ground

*Ornamental or flowering cabbage, edible while still young, can be grown in the same way as an annual flower mixture, the variously coloured plants bedded out wherever there is room amongst more permanent subjects.*

*Individual named strains of flowering cabbages and kale have outstanding leaf or flower colour, such as the ornamental cabbage 'Violet Queen'.*

but is best grown hard in less fertile conditions to avoid winter losses; plants are fed in spring when growth resumes and the danger of severe frost is past. On thin soils savoy cabbages will succeed better than most other kinds.

## SOWING AND PLANTING

**Spring cabbage:** sow thinly 1cm (½in) deep in zones 7-9 in a seed bed outdoors during late July, or in early August where the plants are to mature. Where mild autumns and winters regularly cause early bolting, delay sowing for a week or two. Thin seedlings sown direct, or transplant from the seed bed in September, spacing plants 10cm (4in) apart each way (or the same distance in rows 30cm/1ft apart), and treading them in firmly. In spring some of the plants are gathered young as 'greens', leaving the remainder at 30cm (1ft) spacings to develop hearts. Save a few seedlings for planting in a cold frame as an insurance against winter losses.

## CHINESE CABBAGES

With the current fashion for Chinese vegetables, it is tempting to try Chinese cabbages in the garden. Though sometimes more difficult to grow than normal western cabbages, breeders are creating better varieties less sensitive to day length and temperature. Most do better as an autumn crop, sown in summer.

Commonly grown Chinese cabbages are divided into two groups: Pe-tsai *(Brassica rapa* Pekinensis Group) form heads. Of these, the Napa types have short rounded heads while heads of Michihili types are tall and narrow. They are best as cool season crops. Pak Choi (*B. rapa* Chinensis Group) on the other hand is a leafy non-heading type with thickened succulent petioles or leaf stems. The outside stems can be gradually harvested as needed through the summer.

Few kinds will stand frost, and in most cases temperatures below about 10°C (50°F) induce plants to start forming flower buds, which is why early summer sowings rarely succeed unless a bolt-resistant hybrid is used. For most kinds to mature without bolting plants need shortening days and high temperatures. These requirements are met by sowing outdoors where they are to grow, from midsummer until August (later sowings need protection to finish growth). Seedlings are thinned to stand 25-30cm (10-12in) apart, and once established can be treated as conventional cabbages. They may also be sown earlier, from May onwards, in soil blocks or cell trays in a greenhouse heated to above 10°C (50°F), for planting out after midsummer.

**Early summer cabbage:** sow in pots or cell trays six to eight weeks before the last spring frost date in a cool greenhouse or cold frame, and plant out 25-30cm (10-12in) apart four weeks before the last frost.

**Summer cabbage:** sow in pots or in a seed bed outdoors four weeks before the last frost, and transplant to final locations when frosts are past. The need for firm ground to produce good hearts can be exploited to give a succession of mature heads. Tread firmly around a third of the plants a week after planting, giving remaining plants a gentle tug to loosen their roots slightly. A fortnight afterwards, firm another third, loosening those that are left. Finally, consolidate the rest of the plants a fortnight later. Plants will heart up in three distinct batches.

**Autumn cabbage:** sow outdoors in late spring, and transplant 30-45cm (12-18in) apart six to eight weeks later. First heads will be ready about September and stand for two months.

**Winter cabbage:** sow in May, and plant out 30-45cm (12-18in) apart according to variety at the end of June, for cutting from November onwards, in zones 7-8.

## CULTIVATION

All types of cabbage need plenty of water while in active growth if they are to develop dense juicy hearts. Water regularly and generously, and if possible mulch with decayed manure those plants to be cropped before late winter. Cabbages planted for the following spring should be less succulent to survive frosts, and are best mulched with grass clippings simply to conserve moisture. In late winter stimulate growth by feeding them with a quick-acting nitrogenous fertilizer. Guard all cabbages against birds (red varieties are less prone to attack) and inspect regularly for insect pests. Firm overwintered crops disturbed by high

## JERSEY CABBAGE

This traditional variety, a type of kale, can reach 4.5m (15ft) or more, although 180cm-3m (6-10ft) is more common. The head is edible, like the top of a Brussels sprout plant, but the cabbages are usually grown for their sturdy, straight stems which can be dried and varnished as walking sticks. Plants make an interesting feature amongst hollyhocks, angelica and other tall plants. Sow in March and plant out 90cm (3ft) apart as soon as the seedlings can be handled. Support with stakes and steadily remove lower leaves as growth progresses; these have stout midribs which can be cooked like seakale. In the autumn pull up the stems, trim off the tops and roots, and stand upright in a shed to dry. If left for a second year the stems will be taller.

winds or frost, and in a severe winter mound soil up around the stems. Clear any yellow or discarded leaves promptly, and burn or compost them.

## HARVEST

Cut heads with a knife as required. Start to crop spring cabbage early, pulling up plants here and there for use as 'greens' and leaving the remainder evenly spaced to continue hearting up. Either pull up the stumps, of gathered heads straight away or cut a deep cross on the top of the stump with a knife: a few weeks later a small loose cabbage will develop from each quarter. White and red cabbages can be cut as required, but any still in the ground by late autumn are best dug up and suspended upside down by their roots in a cool airy shed, or cut, trimmed of their outer leaves and then packed in boxes amongst loosely crumpled newspaper for storage in a cold but frost-free place.

## CARROT *(Daucus carota)*

| | |
|---|---|
| **Seeds:** | 1,000/g, 25,000/oz |
| **Germination:** | 15 days; 65% |
| **Height:** | 23-38cm (9-15in) |
| **Space:** | rows 10-15cm (4-6in) apart, or broadcast seed to give 15-20 plants per 30cm (1ft sq) |
| **Sow:** | 3-4 weeks before the last frost date. Repeat at 3-week intervals until 3 months before first frost |
| **Harvest:** | June to December (longer if protected) |
| **Yield:** | 450g (1lb) per 30cm (1ft) row |
| Annual crop | |

The earliest cultivated carrots were not the familiar orange, but purple, in shades ranging from pale violet to nearly black. The dark roots,

*The ideal vegetable garden is always packed with produce, but this need not be to the exclusion of flowering plants. (above) Carrots, beet and lettuce jostle for room, the overall green mosaic relieved by bright marigold flowers and a dual-purpose edging of ornamental cabbages. Carrots grow in more conventional rows (right) in a box-edged bed. Neighbouring beds contain Brussels sprouts, red lettuce, sweet corn and peas combined with roses and perennial herbs.*

originally from Afghanistan, are still popular in eastern countries, but their tendency to go an unappetizing brown when cooked led to their disappearance from European gardens. In Holland during the sixteenth century yellow and orange types were selected and refined into the carrot we now prefer. Even today this search for improved colour continues as breeders try to eliminate the yellow core from some varieties. Sometimes a yellow or white specimen may still appear in a row of modern carrots, a reminder of the vegetable's early ancestry.

During the Second World War, in an attempt to minimize night blindness amongst airmen,

varieties were developed that were high in carotene, the pigment responsible for the orange colour and converted by our bodies into vitamin A. In the nineteenth century carrots were widely used in cakes and desserts because of their high sugar content, but today emphasis is placed more on their importance as a dietary source of fibre, vitamins and minerals, particularly when eaten raw.

Many gardeners tend to take carrots for granted, but to grow them well is not quite as easy as some suppose. However, with a little care together with precautions against the constant threat of carrot root fly, successional crops of juicy young carrots can be pulled over a long season and even stored in the ground for out of season use. The foliage is delicate and finely cut, a valuable decorative asset anywhere amongst other vegetables and flowering plants, provided it is remembered that as roots are harvested gaps may eventually appear unless adjacent plants spread to cover the spaces.

## VARIETIES
Hybridizing has made great advances in flavour and colour in recent years. Often these new varieties are not strictly new varieties but improved selections of established kinds.

**Short-rooted kinds for shallow or stony soils**
**Kundulus:**  68 days. Round, orange. Also suitable for forcing in pots or frames.

**Parmex:**  50 days. Very early round carrot 2.5-3cm (1-1½in) across. Also suitable for pots.

**Red Cored Chantenay:**  70 days. Short and stocky 12-15cm (5-6in) long. Adaptable to most soils.

**Royal Chantenay:**  70 days. Stocky roots to 15cm (6in) long. Tender with good colour.

**Short'n Sweet:**  68 days. Sweet bright orange 7-10cm (3-4in) roots mature well in shallow or heavy soil.

**Intermediate and long-rooted varieties**
**A-Plus:**  74 days. Exceptionally high vitamin A content and sweet flavour. 20cm (8in) long.

**Gold Pak:**  76 days. Deep orange, smooth skinned, 20-23cm (8-9in) long.

**Imperator:**  75 days. Slender, sweet and tender roots. 20-23 (8- 9in) long. Orange-red.

**Nantes Half-Long:**  70 days. 15-18cm (6-7in).

**Scarlet Nantes:**  68 days. Very sweet.

## SOIL PREPARATION
The secret in growing juicy carrots full of flavour is to keep the soil consistently moist, and to remove any obstacle to rapid root development. Light, sandy soils are the best – deep enough to allow growth to drive downwards without encountering a stony or impenetrable clay layer that will cause misshapen roots, and sufficiently rich in humus to avoid drying out in wind or hot sun.

Few gardeners have this ideal soil, but there are ways to improve inadequate ground. Where possible the carrots should follow a crop such as potatoes, peas or beans to benefit from the thoroughly cultivated ground in which these vegetables were grown; the soil will also contain a residue of nutrients sufficient to sustain a sowing or two of carrots. Thoroughly break up clay soils; on heavy ground it is always a good idea to empty surplus or used potting mixture before growing carrots. Improve the moisture retentiveness of very light soil with garden compost or peat. Cultivate to a depth of at least 15cm (6in); on shallower ground grow the very short round-rooted varieties.

## SOWING
The easiest way to handle the small seed is to empty a quantity into one hand and then to take a pinch at a time with finger and thumb of the other hand, dropping a few seeds at precise

### CARROTS IN COLD FRAMES

The carrot season can be extended at both ends with the help of a cold frame, especially if it is in a warm part of the garden. For earliest sowings in late January follow traditional French practice and very thinly scatter the seed broadcast, followed by an equal amount of radish seed. Cover with 1cm (½in) depth of fine soil previously taken from the frame, or use spent potting mixture. Then, using a compact variety such as Little Gem sown earlier under glass or October in the frame, transplant young lettuces into the bed, spaced about 20cm (8in) each way. Keep the frame closed except in mild weather. The radishes will be ready first, followed by the lettuce, which can be replaced by young cauliflower plants to grow on while the carrots are being harvested from April onwards.

At the beginning of August, using an early variety once more, sow a frame with carrots either broadcast or in rows 10cm (4in) apart. The first roots will be ready in late autumn; pull the largest and leave the rest to grow on. They will survive in good condition throughout the winter if covered against severe weather. Once the remaining carrots reach their ideal size, keep the frame closed so that the soil gradually dries out and stores the roots until required.

stations or gently rubbing a light continuous sprinkle into the seed drill (tapping seeds direct from the packet usually results in overcrowding). Seed should always be sown sparsely, because uncrowded carrots produce more shapely roots. Reducing the need for thinning lessens the risk of attracting pests with the scent released as plants are disturbed.

With the exception of round varieties such as Rondo (USA: Kundulus), which can be grown in pots or cell trays, carrots are always sown direct into the ground. They cannot be raised in boxes for transplanting outdoors, because moving the seedlings distorts the shape of the eventual roots. The timing of early sowing therefore depends on the condition of the open ground. For efficient and rapid germination carrots need warmth and moisture; begin sowing three to four weeks before the last frost date and repeat at three week intervals for continuous harvest. Sow earlier by first drying and warming the soil surface by covering for a couple of weeks with glass or polythene cloches. Alternatively, a cold frame or light greenhouse border can be used for these first sowings.

For small scale sowings sow 1cm (½in) deep in rows 10cm (4in) apart for the shortest varieties, 15cm (6in) apart for intermediates. Where long rows are being grown greater distance between the drills may be necessary to allow access for hoeing. Before sowing in dry weather, water the open drill by gently flooding it from a watering can without a spray. When the water has drained away, sow and cover the seed either with moist peat, or with dry soil lightly firmed into place with the rake head. This early supply of moisture makes the difference between success and failure in summer drought.

## CULTIVATION
It is always best to sow sparingly to avoid the need to thin. Where this is necessary, simply drag a rake gently across the seedlings once or twice while they are still small; do this in the evening, clear away the thinnings, and water the remaining seedlings to settle the soil. Keep the plants uniformly moist, and mulch with grass clippings to reduce evaporation. Hoe or hand weed until the foliage is dense enough to suppress weeds.

## HARVEST
Pull roots as soon as they are ready for use, choosing the largest, and firming or watering the disturbed soil around remaining plants. If the ground is dry, first loosen the roots gently with a fork to avoid breaking off the foliage at ground level. In mild areas, carrots can be left in the ground over winter, the plants covered with straw held in place by mounding up the surrounding soil. Elsewhere, dig up the carrots, cut off the foliage to leave about 2.5cm (1in) of stem, and carefully pack sound roots on their sides between layers of dry sand or peat in boxes which are then stored in a cool dry shed until needed.

# CAULIFLOWER (Brassica oleracea var. botrytis)

| | |
|---|---|
| **Seeds:** | 250/g, 6-7,000/oz |
| **Germination:** | 1-2 weeks; 70% |
| **Height:** | 30-45cm (12-18in) |
| **Space:** | from 15cm (6in) to 75cm (30in) |
| **Sow:** | indoors 6-8 weeks before last frost date; outdoors March to May (USA: 10-12 weeks before first autumn frost) |
| **Harvest:** | February to November (all year round in very mild districts) |
| **Yield:** | 450g-1kg (1-2lb) per plant |
| Annual crop | |

Cauliflowers are greedy plants, thriving on the richest soil with plenty of water. In return for lavish treatment they will produce dense succulent curds, white or delicate cream and even deep purple according to variety. They are very sensitive to extremes of heat and cold and are a challenge to grow well in many regions. Few varieties can tolerate high summer temperatures, and crops rarely succeed on hot,

*Summer cauliflowers develop best with protection from birds and bright sunlight; they are therefore ideal for tucking at the base of tall plants such as artichokes.*

dry soils. At the other extreme, most are vulnerable to frost once the curd has started to form.

Unless there is plenty of room in the garden, it is most economical to grow mini-cauliflowers (see panel), or just a few larger heads well, especially as plants from a single sowing tend to mature together, and will not stand for long in good condition. Autumn and winter varieties make large plants that need a long season and wide spacing. Summer cauliflowers, however, occupy much less room and may be more successful tucked beside tall peas, beans, artichokes or other large plants to shade the developing heads from summer heat and sun.

## VARIETIES
**Alert:** 54 days. Early, maturing about a week after Snow Crown. Curds well protected by leaves for good quality.

**Andes:** 65 days. Good self-blanching variety with well protected curds. Excellent-quality deep heads. Good as both early and late crop and is very resistant to both high and low temperatures.

**Early Snowball:** 60 days. Early self-blanching variety.

**Snowball:** 70 days. Self-blanching leaves recurve over curds.

**Snow Crown:** 53 days. AAS winner. F1 hybrid. Widely adapted, vigorous and early. Large heads of excellent quality.

**Snow King:** 50 days. Very early hybrid producing nice round white heads.

**Violet Queen/Purple Cape:** 80-85 days. These purple head cauliflowers are easier to grow and are more cold hardy. They resemble a broccoli with purple buds but develop a cauliflower-like flavour after cold weather sets in. Secondary spears develop after the first harvest. Purple head cauliflowers take longer to mature and can be grown later in the autumn.

## SOIL PREPARATION
Break up the soil well before planting, and thoroughly mix in plenty of decayed manure or rich garden compost. Lime the ground if necessary, and leave to settle for several weeks.

## SOWING AND PLANTING
For earliest summer crops sow in pots or cell trays under glass in January for planting out in March. Alternatively, in mild gardens sow in September, pricking out seedlings 5-7cm (2-3in) apart in a cold frame for transplanting in spring. Follow this with a further sowing in March for transplanting in May in areas with cool summers. Sow autumn cauliflowers outdoors in late April, winter varieties in late May, and move them to their final quarters no more than five or six weeks later – the younger cauliflowers are transplanted, the better. In the USA, for an autumn crop (which is often more successful in many areas) sow a rapidly maturing variety in summer, allowing sufficient time to mature during cool weather but before the first frost date.

---

### MINI-CAULIFLOWERS

Experiments have shown that early summer varieties grown at high density will produce miniature heads of high quality 5-7cm (2-3in) across, enough for individual servings or for freezing whole. By this method a number of plants can be fitted in between other vegetables, shrubs or flowering plants, provided these are sturdy enough to compete with them (less robust plants may be overwhelmed by adjacent cauliflowers, which will try to reach their full size where possible).

Use a variety such as Snow Crown, sowing in the same way as for conventional cauliflowers, but spacing the plants 15cm (6in) apart in blocks. Cultivate as normal. Heads from a single sowing will mature almost simultaneously and can be cleared together, but for succession several consecutive sowings will be needed. The time taken by plants to mature varies from two to three months as the season advances; during warm weather less time will be required while cool temperatures slow maturation.

---

Prick out or thin seedlings to about 7cm (3in) apart. They will have four to six true leaves when ready for planting out. Water the young cauliflowers thoroughly, before and after planting at a depth no lower than that at which they previously grew. Move them with intact root balls and plant very firmly, spacing summer, autumn and winter varieties 45, 60 and 75cm (18, 24, and 30in) square respectively. On dry soils, choose the next wider spacing and set each plant in a depression that can be flooded with water whenever necessary. In very bright hot weather, puddle plants in, and cover them during the day with pots for the first week (see p.173).

## CULTIVATION
Never let cauliflowers dry out. Water copiously in dry weather and mulch the plants with grass clippings, leaves or well-broken decayed manure. Once heads start to form, break a few of the surrounding leaves so that they lie across the curd and protect it from bright sun or frost, depending on the time of year.

## HARVEST
Since sowings tend to mature together, start cutting heads while still tight and before they reach full size. In thundery weather be prepared to gather in the whole crop, as mature heads can quickly break open and bolt. For short-term storage plants can be dug up and replanted close together in a cool sheltered corner, or they will keep for two to three weeks suspended (with their roots intact) upside down in a well-ventilated shed.

---

# CELERY (*Apium graveolens* var. *dulce*)

| | |
|---|---|
| **Seeds:** | 2,000/g, 50,000/oz |
| **Germination:** | 3 weeks; 70% |
| **Height:** | 45-90cm (18-36in) |
| **Space:** | 23cm (9in) |
| **Sow:** | 10-12 weeks before last frost date indoors or when soil temperature reaches 15°C (60°F) |
| **Harvest:** | self-blanching July to October; trench varieties and celeriac October to March |
| **Yield:** | 450g (1lb) per plant |
| Annual crop | |

Raising good celery has always been a test of a gardener's skill, especially when crops were only grown in deeply prepared trenches and blanched by progressively earthing up the

to white with a well developed heart. Stores well in winter.

**Golden Self-Blanching:** 115 days. Tender, stringless stems blanch to waxen yellow. Compact, growing to 60cm (2ft). Nutty flavour.

**Utah 52-70R Improved:** 105 days. Tall vigorous variety with resistance to black heart, boron deficiency and western celery mosaic.

**Ventura:** 100 days. A tall upright Utah type with dark green shiny stalks. Matures early.

---

**Celeriac** (see panel)

**Alabaster:** 120 days. Stores very successfully.

**Globus:** 120 days. Very large stems for later use.

**Jose:** 110 days. Large with round, smooth roots.

## SOIL PREPARATION

Plants need very moist fertile conditions. Add plenty of garden compost, decayed manure or old leaves to the soil, working it in evenly to a full spade's depth. Since celery and celeriac prefer a slightly acid soil, peat can be added either when preparing the ground, or as a mulch. Allow the ground to settle for a few weeks before planting.

## SOWING AND PLANTING

Since celery needs a long growing season it is almost essential to start plants under glass in the north, sowing thinly on the surface of pots or trays during March and April in a temperature of 10-18°C (50-65°F). Do not be tempted to provide too much heat, as seedlings may become weak and spindly, running the risk of bolting after planting out. Sow eight to ten weeks before planting, early crops under

stems. It is hard work, but the tall pure white or pink heads of crisp succulent celery are well worth the effort (see panel). Self-blanching celery is much easier to raise, although even this needs plenty of water and very fertile soil for satisfactory growth and resents hot weather. Varieties of all kinds can be grown on the surface without earthing up; their quality is not as high as that of blanched trench celery, and the stems or sticks remain pink, pale yellow or light green according to type, but they have more food value than traditional white celery.

For the palest stems plants are grown at close spacing, and groups of them can be packed between shrubs and annual flowers, their soft bright foliage adding a delicate shade of light green or gold as contrast to the brilliant colours

*Self-blanching celery will develop paler stems if grown at high density in blocks, especially when enclosed by other plants such as these dwarf bedding dahlias.*

of summer flowers. Self-blanching varieties make good use of cold frames unoccupied after midsummer – frames with solid sides are particularly effective for blanching the crowded plants and will protect them to extend the season into winter. These varieties are not very hardy, whereas trench celery, even when grown on the surface, resists considerable frost.

## VARIETIES
### Self-blanching and green celery
**Fordhook:** 130 days. Short, compact, 38-45cm (15-18in) tall, crisp stems that blanch

glass and maincrops outdoors after the last frosts. Prick out seedlings 5cm (2in) apart in trays as soon as they can be handled, choosing the largest seedlings first, and leaving the rest to grow on for a week or two – plant out the resulting batches in the same order to provide a certain amount of succession.

Grow the seedlings on, in full light and fairly cool conditions to prevent tall, soft growth, and keep them consistently moist. Feed if the foliage shows signs of yellowing: a check to growth at this stage can lead to bolting later. Set plants out a week before the last frost date and cover them in the event of frost, rather than hold them back in expectation of warmer

*The edible leaves of celery are deeply cut and fresh green, a decorative asset when planted next to a contrasting red cabbage, beet and variegated strawberries.*

### CELERIAC

More popular on the continent than in Britain, celeriac or turnip-rooted celery has all the flavour of its better known cousin, together with a few cultural advantages. Plants tend to be hardier and less susceptible to pests and diseases; they are more likely to succeed in dry or less fertile soils, and no blanching or earthing up is required. Generous watering and feeding will produce large tender 'roots' – swollen stem bases – that can be left in the ground under a covering of leaves over winter, or dug up and stored like beet.

Plants are raised as for celery and planted out in similarly prepared soil, 30cm (1ft) apart each way. Cultivate like celery, mulching the plants to conserve moisture, and removing some of the lower ageing leaves during July and August until by October only a crown of foliage is left. 'Roots' are lifted with a fork and used cooked or raw; the leaves, too, may be used for flavouring.

weather. However, make sure they are thoroughly hardened off before planting out. Do not hurry to harden off advanced seedlings in the hope of slowing down growth. This can lead to early bolting, and tests have shown it is better to clip plants back to 7cm (3in) high and keep growing until the weather is warmer.

For a greenhouse crop celery may be planted when seedlings are tall enough and the temperature can be maintained at 10-12°C (50-55°F). Space plants 20-23cm (8-9in) each way (trench varieties 30cm/1ft square), arranging them in groups or blocks so that the crowded plants will tend to blanch each other. Water plants thoroughly a few hours before setting them out, and again immediately afterwards.

### CULTIVATION
Water frequently and generously in dry weather, adding a liquid fertilizer high in potash at every watering on soils that have not been well prepared. Mulch with grass clippings or peat. Celery growing in frames or amongst other plants will tend to blanch as it grows, but in the open garden it is a good idea to surround blocks with boards or a strip of black plastic 30cm (1ft) high to help blanch plants exposed at the sides. Alternatively, tuck straw between the outer plants when they are fully grown, or enclose each in a cylinder of brown paper tied in place at top and bottom. Ventilate celery in a greenhouse or frame whenever the temperature rises much above 15°C (60°F). Snap off any side

## TRENCH CELERY

Blanched celery is unequalled for flavour, and it is worth blanching a few plants by the traditional methods of papering or trenching. Plants of a trench variety grown on the surface can be wrapped in broad strips of brown paper, added as the stems grow and tied with string. This is best on heavy clay soils, but elsewhere trenching can be used as an alternative.

In late winter dig out a trench 30cm (1ft) deep and 45cm (18in) wide for a single row of plants, 60cm (2ft) for double rows; bank the excavated soil in a firm neat ridge on each side of the trench. Loosen the bottom with a fork, work in plenty of manure or garden compost, and leave to settle. As earthing up will not start before August, ridges can be planted with quick crops of salad plants or early dwarf peas.

Raise celery plants as described, and set them out when about 15cm (6in) tall, spacing them every 23cm (9in) down the centre of the trench, or at the same distances in double rows 15cm (6in) apart. Plant firmly and soak the trench afterwards. Cultivate like self-blanching celery until the plants are 23-30cm (9-12in) high, when the trench is filled with soil from the sides to leave just the tops exposed. Draw the stems together when working the soil around plants, and on heavy ground wrap them in paper first.

Repeat as plants grow, until they are buried in a steep ridge, the sides patted firm to shed water. Earthed up plants will survive frost, provided the tops are protected from severe weather. Heads can be dug out as required, replacing soil to keep remaining plants blanched.

growths at the base to concentrate energy in the central head; these shoots can be rooted and grown on in pots or a greenhouse for a late supply of leaves.

### HARVEST

Self-blanching kinds will be ready for use 20-25 weeks after sowing, and should be cleared outdoors before the first severe frosts; hardy trench varieties, on the other hand, are used from October onwards. Lift heads progressively from one end or side of a row or block, using a garden fork to loosen the roots. Shake off as much soil as possible before cutting off the roots by trimming the base to a clean point. Plants which have not produced good stems can still be used in stews, or their leaves chopped raw in salads.

---

# CHICORY *(Cichorium intybus)* and ENDIVE *(C. endivia)*

| | |
|---|---|
| **Seeds:** | 700/g, 18,000/oz |
| **Germination:** | 1-2 weeks; 65% |
| **Height:** | 15-30cm (6-12in) |
| **Space:** | chicory – 15x30cm (6x12in) rows, 15cm (6in) sq; seedling crops broadcast or rows 10cm (4in) apart. Endive – curled 20-23cm (8-9in) sq, broad-leaved 30-38cm (12-15in) sq |
| **Sow:** | early spring to late summer |
| **Harvest:** | late summer and autumn (until spring with protection) |
| **Yield:** | 4 heads per 30cm (1ft) sq |
| Annual crop | |

Both chicory and endive are experiencing something of a revival after years of neglect. The leaves of all kinds are characterized by varying degrees of bitterness, often reduced by

*Thinned seedlings or unused roots of Witloof chicory may be transplanted to the back of flower or herb borders to produce their attractive blue flowers in masses.*

blanching and cool weather at harvest. For a long time the most popular kind of chicory was the forcing or Witloof type (sometimes called French or Belgian endive), whose production is a major industry in some European countries. This crop is easy to raise and force in the garden (see panel), and will be at home in a flower border where unused plants produce 120-150cm (4-5ft) tall stems with beautiful flowers in summer like clear blue dandelions.

In recent years, other types have become more popular. Heading chicory and the red leaved radicchio are like a large, solid cos lettuce, the heart packed with pale crisp leaves with only a hint of bitterness. It is normally raised as a late crop to prevent premature bolting, and in a dry winter will survive until the following year although in most gardens it needs protection from frost. The fashion for seedling or 'cut and come again' salads has led to the re-introduction of numerous Italian varieties with both green and red variegated leaves. These are often sown at close spacing and cut several times for their leaves, or can be left to develop like small bitter lettuces; some may be forced like Witloof chicory.

Two kinds of endive are grown – both of them dislike summer heat but are less sensitive to heat than lettuce. The tender curly-leaved varieties (chicorée frisée) are sown to mature from summer until the frosts, and produce lettuce-like heads of finely curled and crimped leaves, bitter in flavour unless blanched. Broad-leaved or Batavian endive (escarole), on the other hand, is hardier and with protection will survive a mild winter to crop until early spring. Its wide leaves resemble those of a crisp-head lettuce, sometimes waved and toothed at the edges. With their paler centres and sculpted leaves endives are attractive combined with other plants in the same way as lettuces; chicories, too, combine well although the outer leaves of some red varieties can look rather dingy in a wet or windy season.

## VARIETIES
### Chicory/Radicchio and Belgian Endive/Witloof

**Alto:** 67 days. Heat resistant. Similar to Augusto but larger heads. Deep reddish colour.

**Augusto:** 70 days. Large burgundy red heads. Sow mid- to late summer for autumn crop.

**Cesare:** 98 days Early deep burgundy heads. Crisp and tender with mildly bitter flavour.

**Guilio:** 60 days. Compact bolt-resistant variety specifically bred for spring planting. Ruby red heads.

**Marina:** 110 days. Deep red heads. Sow for autumn harvest just before frost.

**Rossa di Treviso/Treviso Red:** 85 days. Long slender leaves, turning red at their tips and margins in cold weather. For heading in autumn, forcing and seedling crops.

**Rossa di Verona/Verona Red:** 86 days. Ball head variety, otherwise similar to Treviso Red.

---

## FORCING CHICORY

The dormant roots of Witloof and some other varieties are traditionally dug up as required from autumn onwards, and forced in darkness for the fat buds or 'chicons' of early growth, crisp and clear white (pink in the case of red chicories). Several methods of blanching are used, both indoors and out.

For winter supplies, dig up a few roots and select the fattest straight ones, cutting off all but 2.5cm (1in) of any leaf stalks, and trimming roots to 12-15cm (5-6in) long. Pack them upright in moist peat or old potting soil in a pot or box, and cover with another to exclude all light. In a temperature of 10°C (50°F) or more the chicons will be ready in a few weeks. Discard roots after harvest.

The variety Witloof forms the tightest chicons with the best flavour if forced outdoors, but this can only be done in late winter or early spring. Cut down any leaves and heap soil over the roots to a depth of 15-20cm (6-8in), smoothing and compacting the sides of the mounds; growth can be hastened by covering the mounds with cloches. Expose and cut the chicons as soon as their tips emerge. Plants can be flowered and then forced, or the roots left in to flower after blanching.

---

**Snowflake/Winter Fare:** 75 days. Heading chicory. Large dense heads, slightly hardy.

**Sugar Loaf/Pain de Sucre/Pan di Zucchero:** 86 days. The commonest green-heading chicory, less hardy than modern varieties.

**Toner:** 130 days. Easier for home production. Force October to March.

**W(h)itloof:** 110 days. The traditional forcing

variety, best buried for full blanch. F1 hybrid is uniform; does not need covering with soil.

---

### Broadleaf/Escarole and Curly/Frisée Endive
**Batavian Full Hearted:** 85 days. Compact and broad-leaved, for autumn and winter use.

**Elodie:** 70 days. Curly green outer leaves surround tight blanched hearts.

**Green Curled:** 95 days. Popular summer endive with pale wavy leaves.

**Moss Curled:** 95 days. Another standard variety, with more finely frizzled leaves.

**Sinco:** 83 days. Broad dark green slightly crinkled leaves with a blanched white heart.

## SOIL PREPARATION
Neither chicory nor endive requires special conditions, although free-draining soils, light and high in humus, are best (Witloof chicory will thrive in organically poor soils). Thoroughly break up clay soils, and enrich all kinds with compost or leaves.

## SOWING AND PLANTING
All kinds are normally sown outdoors, 1cm (½in) deep either in a seed bed for transplanting, or in situ.

Sow Witloof chicory in May where it is to grow, in drills 30cm (1ft) apart, thinning the seedlings to 15cm (6in), or at stations 15cm (6in) apart each way. Heading chicory is sown in the same way in June and July. For seedling crops, sow broadcast or thinly in drills 10cm (4in) apart, from spring to midsummer. Endive is sown from spring until summer (autumn for overwintered hardy types), transplanting or thinning curled varieties to 23cm (9in) apart, broad-leaved to 30cm (1ft).

## CULTIVATION
Regular watering is very important for summer varieties to prevent bolting. Otherwise, cultivate like lettuces.

## HARVEST

Cut seedling crops when they are about 7cm (3in) high; repeat until late summer, when patches can be thinned to leave individual plants 15cm (6in) square to mature. Harvest heading chicory as soon as the heads are large enough; cover late supplies with cloches in cold weather but ventilate whenever possible. For blanched chicory, see panel.

Blanch endive 10-12 weeks after sowing, covering a few dry plants at a time in succession. Loosely loop string or a rubber band around the tops of the outer leaves to enclose the heart – this will partly blanch the centres, which will be sufficient for some tastes. Otherwise, finish blanching by covering the plants with straw, boxes or large pots, their drainage holes blocked to exclude all light. Blanching may need only a fortnight in summer, a month or more in winter.

---

# CUCUMBER (*Cucumis sativus*)

**Seeds:** 30/g, 750/oz

**Germination:** 1 week; 80%

**Height/spread:** bush 60-90cm (2-3ft); trailing up to 180cm (6ft)

**Space:** greenhouse 90cm (3ft) apart; ridge 180cm (6ft) each way; bush 45cm (18in)

**Sow:** greenhouse 3-4 weeks before last frost, outdoors when all frost is past

**Harvest:** greenhouse midsummer to autumn; ridge late summer

**Yield:** 10-20 per plant

Annual crop

---

Domesticated for thousands of years, cucumbers as gardeners know them are never now found in the wild. They are natives of India, and need warmth and high humidity – cucumbers are greedy plants, requiring plenty of feeding and watering. For this reason outdoor kinds are grown traditionally on hills or mounds of soil over pockets of manure or garden compost. This is still the easiest and best way. The trailing stems can be trained upright, fanned out against trellis or netting, or tied up tripods of bamboo canes; or they can be allowed to sprawl amongst courgettes, sweet corn, and taller flowers and herbs.

Plants have large, rough leaves, almost tropical in appearance, with bright yellow, cup-shaped flowers; male and female blooms are produced, the male ones outdoors being left to pollinate the females. Traditional kinds are usually shorter and fatter than European greenhouse cucumbers and their outdoor hybrids, although oriental varieties with long slim fruits are popular and more cold tolerant.

## VARIETIES

Modern varieties are often 'burpless' with thinner skins which aid digestion. Hybridization has also reduced bitterness, increased disease resistance and created space-saving, compact, non-vining bush varieties.

**Armenian:** 70 days. Long-ribbed light green cucumbers originating from southern Asia and India. Good eating quality. Burpless with thin skins and not bitter. May grow to 90cm (3ft) but best picked at 45cm (18in).

**County Fair:** 48 days. Short 7cm (3in) cucumbers excellent for pickling or sliced fresh with tender skins, crisp texture. Seedless if planted alone. Very disease resistant. Resistant to cucumber beetles.

**Lemon:** 65 days. Round, yellow when ripe like a lemon. Unique sweet flavour. Good for pickling.

**Marketmore 80:** 67 days. Improved over Marketmore 76 without bitter flavour and increased disease resistance. Also resistant to cucumber beetle. Excellent for slicing.

**Poinsett 76:** 65 days. Popular for salads. Very disease resistant. Especially good in south.

**Salad Bush:** 57 days. AAS winner. New compact high yielding bush cucumber, 20cm (8in) long with smooth, dark green skin. Downy and powdery mildew tolerant and resistant to cucumber mosaic virus and scab.

**Saladin:** 55 days. AAS winner. Small 10-12cm (4-5in) cucumbers are perfect for pickling with crisp, fine flavour. Very productive. Resistant to powdery mildew, scab and bacterial wilt and mosaic tolerant.

**Spacemaster:** 60 days. Short compact bush variety, with dark green slender fruit to 20cm (8in) long. Disease resistant.

**Straight Eight:** 58 days. AAS winner. Long straight cucumber 20cm (8in) long, deep green.

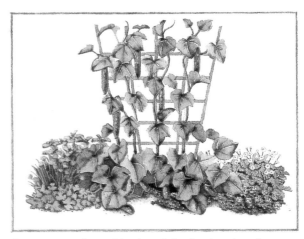

*In a warm, moist position in soil that has been heavily manured, both bush and climbing cucumbers can be grown together. Long cucumbers are easily trained up a wooden trellis, while below bushy ridge varieties will thrive and produce large crops of gherkins at ground level, their foliage providing ground cover and helping to keep the root run cool and moist.*

**Sweet Slice:** 62 days. Sweet flavourful, burpless cucumbers up to 30cm (1ft) long with tender skins that need not be peeled. Dark green. Resists most diseases.

**Sweet Success:** 58 days. AAS winner. Seedless burpless cucumbers, sweet flavour and tender. Up to 36cm (14in) long. Resistant to cucumber mosaic virus, scab and target leaf spot.

## SOIL PREPARATION
Choose a sunny site sheltered from cold winds. Bush varieties need at least 45cm (18in) each way; trailing kinds are planted about 180cm (6ft) apart. Excavate a hole 30-45cm (12-18in) deep and wide, and fill this with a mixture of equal parts decayed manure and garden soil (or old potting mixture). Cover with the excavated soil and leave to settle for a few weeks.

## SOWING AND PLANTING
In cold areas sow indoors four to five weeks before the last frosts, sowing two seeds 1cm (½in) deep on edge in a 7cm (3in) peat pot and removing the weaker one when the true leaves appear. Germinate and grow on in a minimum temperature of 15°C (60°F). Harden off and plant in the centre of the mound of soil, disturbing the plants as little as possible and covering with a cloche in cold weather.

In milder areas, sow three to four seeds slightly spaced out on the top of the mound when the threat of frost is past, and cover with a cloche or jam jar until safely growing. Either leave all the seedlings to grow or thin when a few centimetres tall. Alternatively, seed may be planted in rows along a fence or support.

## CULTIVATION
Pinch out growing tips when the plants have made five to six leaves. Keep the mounds moist, especially when flowering and fruiting starts, but avoid watering directly over the foliage. Train trailing kinds up supports, fanning out

### CUCUMBERS UNDER GLASS
For crops of long straight cucumbers in cooler regions, plants are best grown under protection, using a greenhouse variety. Male flowers must be removed as they appear, otherwise the fruits will be seedy and bitter, but choosing an all-female variety will dispense with this chore. Cucumbers under glass need vigilance against pests and diseases, and consistent heat and humidity; if grown with plants that prefer drier conditions, separate with a screen of plastic sheeting.

Sow in late spring for unheated houses or cold frames, or as early as February if 15°C (60°F) can be maintained (all-female varieties need 5-10° higher). Sow in peat pots as for outdoor kinds, and transplant when about 15cm (6in) tall into growing bags (two per bag) or into individual 25- 30cm (10-12in) pots (bush kinds, 20cm/8in) filled with a bought compost mixed with a little decayed manure. Keep the roots evenly moist and water the floor daily to maintain humidity.

Bushy kinds are pinched out once after transplanting. Trailing varieties are trained up vertical canes or wires, and then stopped; side shoots are tied to the supports and stopped one to two leaves beyond a female flower (this will have a miniature prickly cucumber behind the petals). Any barren side shoots are pinched back to 30cm (1ft) long. Remove any male flowers. In a cold frame, plant in the centre on a hill, pinch out the tip and train four stems to the corners; stop them there and prune. Feed regularly from about six weeks after transplanting, and cut the fruits while still young.

the stems and tying them loosely with string, or spread the stems evenly over the soil and leave to grow. Do not remove male flowers as these are needed for pollination. Mulch with grass clippings or peat to retain moisture.

## HARVEST
Use a knife to cut fruits before they reach maximum size. Ridge cucumbers for cooking can be left until large and yellow (but this shortens the life of the plants); most varieties may also be picked while small as gherkins. For heaviest crops cut pickling varieties about 10cm (4in) long, maincrops 15-25cm (6-10in), and oriental types 30-45cm (12-18in). Whenever a fruit is harvested from a trailing variety, pinch out the tip of that shoot to encourage further branching. Cool damp weather can cause mildew; it is not worth treating it late in the season, and plants should be pulled up.

# EGGPLANT see AUBERGINE

# FAVA BEAN see BROAD BEAN

# ENDIVE see CHICORY

# KALE (Brassica oleracea; B. napus)

| | |
|---|---|
| **Seeds:** | 300/g, 7-8,000/oz |
| **Germination:** | 1-2 weeks; 75% |
| **Height:** | 30-120cm (1-4ft) |
| **Space:** | 30-45cm (12-18in)sq |
| **Sow:** | April to July |
| **Harvest:** | September to April |
| **Yield:** | 1-1.3kg (2-3lb) per plant |
| Annual crop | |

*Plain-leaved kale* (centre) *is welcome for its tender young shoots in spring. At the edge of the picture the contrasting foliage of curly kale is visible.*

Two kinds of very hardy and closely related leaf vegetables are normally grouped together under this name: many of the plain-leaved varieties such as Ragged Jack are in fact forms of forage rape or rape kale *(B. napus)*, while the popular curly, or Scotch, kales are properly known as borecole. Both types are cool season crops, grown for a dependable supply of young tender shoots used as 'greens' in late spring and early summer, although younger leaves may also be gathered from autumn onwards. They seem to have more resistance than other brassicas to club root and cabbage root fly.

With its reputation for hardiness, kale is often planted merely as an insurance against severe winter weather, but if the leaves and shoots are used while still young, and preferably after a little frost, they are succulent and sweetly

flavoured. Plants are very ornamental, too, and have a long tradition of decorative use; the leaves of densely frilled kales have often been substituted for parsley as garnishes, and a century ago the same varieties were recommended for formal arrangements in winter flower beds. Today, tightly curled kales such as Dwarf Green Curled or Westland Autumn (USA: Dwarf Blue Curled Vates) can be combined with the coloured, so-called flowering kales in bedding arrangements, but most kinds will blend anywhere into normal garden surroundings and provide pretty foliage effects from autumn to spring.

## VARIETIES

**Dwarf Blue Curled Vates:** 55 days. Tightly curled blue-green leaves on low 30cm (1ft) plants. Hardy through most average winters to zone 6.

**Dwarf Siberian:** 65 days. Short spreading variety 30-38cm (12-15in) tall with slightly frilled grey-green leaves. Also quite hardy.

**Verdura:** 60 days. A Dutch variety with dark blue-green leaves and sweet flavour.

**Flowering/Ornamental/Variegated kale:** usually sold in mixtures. A wide variety of heights and appearance, the foliage of many plants fringed, crested or deeply cut, and all with silver, yellow, red or purple variegations which are enhanced by frost. Edible, and colourful if used raw in salads (cooked leaves turn green).

## SOIL PREPARATION

Kale is less fussy than most brassicas about soil fertility, although it is best to add compost or leaves when preparing the soil. Provided the ground is free draining, do not work it too deeply: kale is hardiest on very firm soil, and in cold districts it is safer to plant into clean but undisturbed soil after a crop such as peas or broad beans.

## SOWING AND PLANTING

In most areas with hot summers, only autumn crops are grown but seed may be sown very thinly outdoors in a seed bed 1cm (½in) deep during April for early crops, and May for late spring 'greens'. Thin or transplant seedlings 7-10cm (3-4in) apart when large enough to handle, and grow on until late June when earliest varieties are transplanted to their final quarters. Water the plants thoroughly before moving them, and plant them out 45cm (18in) apart each way (tallest varieties 60cm/2ft apart, 30-38cm/12-15in for very dwarf ones). Set them as deep as the base of the lowest leaves, burying any bare length of stem. Plant out later batches in sequence until early August.

Very late kinds of kale, especially forage rape varieties, prefer to be sown in situ from

*Flowering or ornamental kale is a form of curly kale and has edible, crimped leaves splashed with various colours – particularly brilliant in the autumn.*

mid-June to early July, sowing a pinch of seed at stations 45cm (18in) apart each way, and thinning the seedlings to the strongest one. Flowering kale and other varieties intended for decorative bedding should be transplanted to a nursery bed and grown on until required. When planted out, set taller kinds deeply so that the variegated crown is almost at ground level.

## CULTIVATION
Keep plants well watered while in growth, and check that the stems are still firm in the ground after high winds: in exposed gardens it is best to grow dwarf kales or stake taller kinds. Remove any yellow or damaged leaves, and in spring give plants a liquid feed to boost young growth. Towards the end of January cut off the tips of plants to encourage young side shoots.

## HARVEST
Do not gather too much foliage from individual plants at one time, and only pick young leaves or shoots because older ones may have a bitter flavour. Cut shoots when a few centimetres long. The flavour of kale is usually improved after light frost.

---

## KOHL RABI *(Brassica oleracea* var. *gongylodes)*

| | |
|---|---|
| **Seeds:** | 300/g, 7-8,000/oz |
| **Germination:** | 1-2 weeks; 75% |
| **Height:** | 30-45cm (12-18in) |
| **Space:** | 15x30cm (6x12in), or 23cm (9in) sq |
| **Sow:** | in succession March to August, earlier in very warm regions |
| **Harvest:** | June to December |
| **Yield:** | 168-225g (6-8oz) per plant |

Annual crop

When ready for harvest, kohl rabi is an odd-looking plant. At soil level the stem swells to the size of a tennis ball or an orange; this 'bulb' can be cooked like a turnip or eaten raw, when it has a distinctly nutty, fresh flavour. From all round this bulb kale-like leaves, bright green or red according to variety, grow on separate stems, with a tuft of smaller leaves at the top. These, too, can be cooked as 'greens'. The bulbs can reach great size, but usually split and become fibrous when more than a few centimetres across, and kohl rabi is best grown as a fast catch crop amongst other plants.

*Easily grown for its juicy, swollen stems like turnips, kohl rabi is a quick-maturing crop occupying little room and excellent as edging to a path.*

Kohl rabi is an easy-going brassica, moderately hardy and tolerating drought and infertile soils better than most. Its foliage is sufficiently attractive to merit a place, albeit short-term, amongst annual flowers, but for the crispest bulbs the plants are best grown in more fertile conditions between other slower vegetables or as a temporary edging to beds.

## VARIETIES
**Grand Duke:** 45 days. AAS winner. Very early variety with round, white-fleshed, green-skinned bulbs. Tolerant of black rot.

**Green Vienna/White Vienna:** 55 days. Almost identical varieties. Pale green skins and crisp white flesh. Early maturing, they are grown for summer use.

**Purple Vienna:** 60 days. Flesh and flavour similar to Green Vienna. Rich purple skins, and red tinge to leaf veins and stems. Hardier and valuable for later crops, sown in August.

## SOIL PREPARATION
Kohl rabi is a comparatively shallow-rooted vegetable and will tolerate poorer, drier soils than turnips, but the best bulbs are those grown fast without check on moist ground. Lime as for the more common brassicas, and add some form of humus when forking over the soil to a depth of about 30cm (1ft).

## SOWING AND PLANTING
Sow a small amount of seed monthly, using a white or green variety in March, April and May, followed by Purple Vienna in July and August for the latest crops. In most gardens these sowings can be made in situ, 1cm (½in) deep in rows 30cm (1ft) apart, or using a small pinch of seeds at stations 20-23cm (8-9in) apart each way. In cold gardens, or where the ground is temporarily occupied, sowings can be made on a seed bed, in a cold frame, or in peat or soil blocks in a greenhouse. Plant out hardened-off seedlings in blocks when they have made two

or three true leaves; seedlings in the ground should be thinned to 7cm (3in) apart, and transplanted at the same stage. Do not plant deeply, and water before and after moving. Seedlings in rows sown in situ should be thinned to 7cm (3in) and later to 15cm (6in).

## CULTIVATION
Water the plants when needed and mulch them with grass or decayed manure to conserve moisture and accelerate growth. Do not pack the mulch too closely round the stems.

## HARVEST
Pull the first bulbs as soon as they reach about 5cm (2in) across, using alternate plants and leaving the remainder to grow on. The bulbs should be used before they exceed 7cm (3in) across; all varieties are best harvested small – about ten to twelve weeks after sowing, or from six weeks after transplanting.

## LEEKS (*Allium ampeloprasum* var. *porrum*)

| | |
|---|---|
| **Seeds:** | 400/g, 10,000/oz |
| **Germination:** | 2-3 weeks; 65% |
| **Height:** | 30-38cm (12-15in) |
| **Space:** | 30x15cm (12x6in) for large stems, down to 20x5cm (8x2in) |
| **Sow:** | February under glass, March to April outdoors |
| **Harvest:** | September to April/May |
| **Yield:** | 450g (1lb) per 30cm (1ft) row |
| Annual crop | |

Widely praised for their hardiness and ease of cultivation, leeks rarely receive credit for their decorative value. Many gardeners find them a

*Young leeks cast little shade, and many compact vegetables will flourish amongst them provided their harvest does not disturb the growing leeks. These lettuces will be cleared before the leeks become too large.*

milder flavoured and trouble-free alternative to onions, but usually grow them in widely spaced, straight drills in the vegetable patch, whereas an equivalent total yield can be achieved from plants packed closely together in blocks or, better still, in groups amongst more obviously ornamental plants such as bushy herbs or winter-flowering shrubs.

There, the broad, strap-like leaves, usually bright or dark green but sometimes with a strong blue or purple tinge, resemble those of some exotic bulb. Leaving surplus leeks to flower will confirm this impression – each will produce a thick stem 90-120cm (3-4ft) tall the following summer, bearing a large dense sphere of white or pink flowers. Plants are extremely hardy and decorative throughout their long season, and also very adaptable: for example, the same variety can be used to raise

large blanched leeks, sometimes 7cm (3in) across and 38-40cm (15-16in) long, or slim stems like spring onions, which some people consider to have a sweeter, more delicate flavour.

## VARIETIES
**Broad London/American Flag:** 130 days. Thick stems. Recommended for overwintering.

**Catalina:** 130 days. Large vigorous variety from Holland for autumn harvest or overwintering.

**De Carentian:** 90 days. A French variety with mild flavour for late summer and autumn harvest.

**(The) Lyon/Prizetaker:** 135 days. Early and mild flavoured, long thick stems with handsome rich green foliage.

**Titan:** 110 days. A heftier, earlier variety than Broad London.

## SOIL PREPARATION
Although leeks will thrive better than onions on soils with low fertility, for the best crops the ground should be forked over to a depth of 30cm (1ft), mixing in a good quantity of garden compost or decayed manure.

## SOWING AND PLANTING
The normal season for leeks runs from November to April. For an earlier crop, often ready from the beginning of September, sow seeds during February in a cool greenhouse or cold frame. Either sow a pinch of seed thinly in a 10cm (4in) pot and leave unthinned until planted outside in late April, or sow in drills in a soil-based cold frame, thinning the seedlings to 2.5cm (1in) apart. Maincrops are sown outdoors in a seed bed during late March/early April and thinned where necessary before planting out in late May or June.

Leeks are ready for planting out when they are 15-20cm (6-8in) tall. Water them the day before transplanting, and lift outdoor seedlings with a fork to avoid injuring the roots. Sort the seedlings by size; large ones produce bigger leeks earlier, and a single batch, graded from large to small and planted accordingly, will therefore mature progressively.

To save a lot of watering and hand weeding later, mulch the ground with decayed leaves or grass clippings before planting. Using a thick dibber or a broken spade handle sharpened to a point, make vertical holes 15-20cm (6-8in) deep and drop a single untrimmed plant into each, making sure it has fallen right to the bottom. For the largest roots space transplants every 15cm (6in) in rows 30cm (1ft) apart, or 20-23cm (8-9in) apart each way in blocks. Mature stems are proportionately slimmer at closer spacings, down to a practical limit of rows 20cm (8in) apart with seedlings every 5cm (2in), or about 10cm (4in) square if planted in blocks. Water the ground after planting, or carefully fill each hole with water if the weather is dry.

## CULTIVATION

Hand weed or mulch the ground to control weeds; hoeing tends to fill the holes with soil and so restrict the stems from swelling easily. Once the plants have filled the holes, the blanched stems can be increased in length by drawing some of the surrounding soil up to and around the exposed necks to a depth of 7-10cm (3-4in). This is useful on shallow soils.

## HARVEST

Start to lift leeks as soon as they have reached a useable size. Dig them up with a spade to avoid breaking the shank, or loosen them in the soil with a fork and then pull them up very carefully if they are likely to disturb their neighbours. Plants may be left in the ground until needed, but if the space is required in spring, remaining leeks can be dug up and replanted elsewhere in the garden, packing the stems together at the same depth as before to preserve the blanch.

*Lettuces are a versatile crop tolerating most soils and positions, and making productive use of a temporarily vacant strip or patch of ground. Because the great majority of varieties grow rapidly to maturity, they are a valuable 'catch' crop amongst other slower-growing vegetables, which on hot soils may provide them with shade from the summer sun. They are sufficiently decorative, however, to be planted en masse as bedding, especially if two or more varieties with different colours or leaf shapes are arranged in a simple design; the contrast between red and green lettuces (above) is especially effective. In the box-edged bed (left) young leeks are interplanted with red lettuce nearing maturity, while seedlings of a green variety have been set out for succession.*

# LETTUCE (*Lactuca sativa*)

**Seeds:** 800/g, 20,000/oz

**Germination:** 1-2 weeks; 75%

**Height:** 15-30cm (6-12in)

**Space:** dwarf 15cm (6in) sq, early 23cm (9in) sq, maincrop 30cm (1ft) sq, leaf lettuce 12x2.5cm (5x1in)

**Sow:** February under glass, March to August outdoors, October under cloches

**Harvest:** April to December (all year round in mild districts)

**Yield:** 4 per 45cm (18in) sq

Annual crop

Lettuce is not a demanding crop, although it succeeds best in cooler regions, as many gardeners discover in a hot or dry summer when their plants mature all together or suddenly produce tall flowering stems.

Several kinds of lettuce are grown. The cos type, with tall upright growth and crisp well-flavoured leaves, is the most adaptable but difficult to grow well. Although valued for their hardiness, they can also be sown for successive crops throughout the summer, and their seeds germinate well at high temperatures. However, they tend to be slower growing, require plenty of water, and the hearts of some older varieties are best blanched by loosely tying the outer foliage near the top.

Cabbage lettuces are round, larger than a typical cos, and more tolerant of dry soils. Some of them have soft limp leaves, and make loose hearts – these are known as looseheads, bibbs or butterheads, and grow best in cooler conditions (their seeds will often become dormant above 24°C/75°F). Crispheads, on the other hand, usually produce large dense hearts of paler crunchy leaves, surrounded by darker foliage, curled or crimped; the very large, juicy, white-hearted crisp lettuces are often sold as 'iceberg' lettuce. These are the most challenging type to grow and in warm regions are easiest as an autumn crop.

Finally, there is a group of leaf lettuces, sometimes called cut-and-come-again, which produce loose foliage over a long season; many of these are very decorative. Their leaves are picked, a few at a time here and there, or entire plants can be cut down, after which they will grow again to give a second and sometimes a third cut.

## VARIETIES
### Cabbage (Butterhead) type
**Augusta:** 68 days. Large heads of buttery flavoured leaves of good substance. Disease resistant and heat tolerant.

**Burpee Bibb:** 75 days. Superior to standard Bibb. Lacks bitterness, slow to bolt. Delicious small heads.

**Buttercrunch:** 75 days. Long-standing variety that tolerates summer heat. Soft outside leaves, and crisp dense heart like a cos lettuce.

**Tom Thumb:** 65 days. Small fast lettuce, hearting very early but standing well. Good flavour. Sow in spring and grow 15cm (6in) apart.

### Cabbage (Crisphead) type
**Great Lakes:** 90 days. Large heads of excellent quality, crisp and well flavoured. Outer leaves fringed. Holds well in warm weather.

**Iceberg:** 85 days. Crisp medium-sized heads with blanched centres on compact plants. Leaves light green with darker savoyed edges.

**Mission:** 74 days. Particularly heat resistant variety with dense tight heads of good quality.

**Vanguard:** 90 days. Best hot weather type. Developed by USDA. Cream coloured heart with dark green outer leaves. Resistant to tip burn and sun scald.

### Cos (Romaine) type
**Little Gem:** 80 days. One of the best-flavoured cos lettuces, sweet and nutty. Very fast and compact (space 15cm/6in apart), crops spring to late summer, and over winter under glass.

**Paris White:** 83 days. Heavy, self-folding heads, deep green outer leaves but very pale hearts, more so if tied. Crisp with excellent flavour.

**Parris Island:** 75 days. Dark green outer leaves with pale heart. Mosaic resistant.

**Valmaine:** 70 days. Large heads, very crisp

with good colour and flavour. Fairly mildew-resistant, ideal for late crops.

**Wollop:** 80 days. Large heavy (560g/1¼lb) heads similar to crisphead type. Tender, sweet.

**Leaf lettuce** (for cultural details, see panel)
**Green Ice:** 45 days. Very heat-resistant green leaf variety that is late to bolt. Good flavour with only slight bitterness.

**Lollo/Red Lollo/Selma Lollo:** 50 days. Italian varieties with curly leaves, green or red. May heart up, but primarily for cutting all season.

**Ruby:** 45 days. AAS winner. Frilled, bright green leaves shaded with deep ruby red.

**Red Sails:** 45 days. AAS winner. Early and decorative reddish-bronze foliage.

**Salad Bowl/Red Salad Bowl:** 45-50 days. AAS winner. Frilly lettuce that does not heart, bright green and bronze red respectively. Large plants, cuts all summer.

**Valmaine:** see above.

## SOIL PREPARATION
Lettuces have a small, shallow root system; all the necessary nutrients must be available in the top few centimetres of soil, which should stay evenly moist throughout growth. Work in plenty of compost, rotted leaves or peat, together with lime if the soil is acid (more lime will be needed if peat is used for humus). Break up clay soil thoroughly and make sure drainage is free.

## SOWING AND PLANTING
For earliest supplies, sow a fast variety such as Little Gem or Tom Thumb under glass about four to six weeks before planting out: in most seasons this will be February to March for planting March to April. Sow groups of three to four seeds in small pots or cell trays so that there is little root disturbance on planting out.

*Most lettuce varieties make excellent catch crops, especially if gathered while still small and young. Transplant seedlings amongst slower-growing vegetables such as cabbages (above).*

Sow maincrops in situ as soon as soil can be worked, 1cm (½in) deep in rows or as clusters, thinning seedlings to one per station. Small varieties and early sowings can be thinned or planted 23cm (9in) apart, but larger types will need 30cm (1ft) each way. Intermediate thinnings can be transplanted carefully to new sites, after first watering the seedlings thoroughly. Alternatively, sow in a seed bed, thin the seedlings to 5-7cm (2-3in) apart and then move them to their final quarters when 3-7cm (1.5-3in) tall. Smaller seedlings transplant more easily than large ones. (See panel for successional sowing.)

In late summer, sow a quick-maturing variety, preferably resistant to mildew, to mature about ten days before first frost date; these plants will need covering with cloches after weather becomes frosty. In mild areas a hardy variety can be sown broadcast under a cloche in autumn, thinning the seedlings to 5-7cm (2-3in) apart before winter; in early spring plant out successive batches of seedlings, under cloches if necessary, 23cm (9in) apart to crop about the same time as early greenhouse sowings.

Choose a sunny position for sowing and planting in spring and autumn, a slightly shaded site for summer crops. Do not sow too many at one time.

## CULTIVATION
Never let plants go short of water, and beware of pests and diseases – lettuces are prone to more than their fair share. On hot dry soils a mulch of grass clippings or moist peat will help delay bolting to flower.

## HARVEST
If a large number of heads seem to be maturing together, start cutting them before they are fully hearted. Pull up the whole plant, cut off the root and discard – never leave the roots in the ground as hosts for soil pests. Once they start to bolt (when the centre suddenly breaks open and grows upwards) lettuces usually become very bitter, and are best dug up, but leaf varieties grown in flowerbeds can look very attractive in flower.

## LEAF LETTUCE

Although the individual plants of certain varieties never heart up, but provide a succession of loose leaves for cutting, they are not the only kind that can be used in this way. Many cos and crisphead lettuce varieties, if grown at high density, will not develop hearts and instead can be cut nearly to ground level for a supply of leaves, after which they will regenerate. Sow the seeds thinly in rows 12-15cm (5-6in) apart, in patches between other plants, or broadcast in wide bands. Thin the seedlings to 2.5-5cm (1-2in) apart and leave them to grow crowded together. About six weeks after sowing they will be ready for their first cut: gather as required, working steadily across the block of plants, and cutting off entire plants to leave stumps at ground level. These will sprout to give a second crop six weeks later, after which they are cleared. By sowing every one to two weeks from early April to the end of May, cutting can continue from mid-May to the end of August.

## ASPARAGUS LETTUCE/CELTUCE
(*Lactuca sativa* var. *angustana*)

This oriental variety of lettuce has never been very popular in Britain, but is seen more frequently in the USA. It has a high nutritional value, and a flavour resembling that of a mild lettuce. Its leaves are long, slender and pointed, and can be used in the same way as cos lettuce, but it quickly runs to flower, producing a fat crisp central stem. This is cut when 30-45cm (12-18in) high and, together with the heart, is used like celery. Grow plants as for cos lettuce, sowing at two to three week intervals for succession from April to July.

## CORN SALAD/LAMB'S LETTUCE/MACHE (*Valerianella* species)

A hardy green salad crop available from midsummer until the following spring. Various large-leaved, and smaller French or Italian, varieties are available, but all are very similar, making small hardy annual clumps 10-15cm (4-6in) tall with long, rounded leaves, dark green and slightly bitter. Italian strains usually have longer, paler leaves, sometimes variegated, but these plants tend to be less hardy and are therefore not so reliable when grown for use as a winter salad.

The normal season for lamb's lettuce is mid-autumn until spring, although some gardeners sow in spring for summer crops (these often bolt quickly, however). Most soils and situations are suitable, especially in or beside paths, and amongst soft fruit and taller herbs (the name 'corn salad' refers to the tradition of broadcasting seed amongst growing corn).

Sow in late summer, and again in early autumn to provide younger plants more likely to overwinter safely. Either broadcast in patches, later thinning plants to 10cm (4in) apart, or sow in a seed bed in rows 10-15cm (4-6in) apart for transplanting later. Keep the soil evenly moist until seedlings emerge. A few plants can be transferred to a cool greenhouse or cold frame in gardens where severe frosts are common.

Plants may be variable from seed; reject loose weedy specimens and retain more compact shapely plants, which if allowed to flower will usually seed themselves for future crops. A few leaves may be picked from each plant whenever large enough, and plants soon regenerate, but eating quality usually deteriorates when flowering starts. For a less bitter flavour, blanch plants under earthenware flower pots.

## LAND/AMERICAN CRESS
(*Barbarea verna/B. praecox*)

Although it is possible to grow watercress in ordinary garden soil, plants merely survive rather than thrive in the absence of running water. Land cress is an easily grown substitute, with a comparable warm spicy flavour and similar appearance. Incorporate plenty of compost and other organic material into the soil to retain moisture, and choose a lightly shaded site, beneath soft fruit or brassicas, or a dull north-facing corner.

Sow broadcast in patches, or in a seed bed for transplanting on a dull day, finally spacing plants 15-20cm (6-8in) apart each way. For maincrop use, sow between spring and midsummer, and again in late summer for overwintered crops. Water in dry weather. In cold areas cover winter crops with cloches or transplant to a cold frame. Gather young tender leaves, a few from each plant, as soon as they are large enough. Leave one or two plants to flower and self-seed for future batches of seedlings.

## CHOPSUEY GREENS/SHUNGIKU/ GARLAND CHRYSANTHEMUM
(*Chrysanthemum coronarium*)

A decorative green vegetable, equally at home in a border as a hardy annual flowering plant, 60-90cm (2-3ft) tall, with yellow flowers. The leaves are a soft matt green and deeply cut.

Grow in light shade as edging or amongst perennial herbs and dwarf vegetables, leaving a few to flower and set seed. Sow from spring to late summer, thinning plants to 7-10cm (3-4in) apart. Keep well watered. After a couple of months, leaves will be about 15cm (6in) high and ready for gathering; cut them down and leave 2.5-5cm (1-2in) of stem for regrowth.

# MAIZE see SWEET CORN

## THE MARROW/SQUASH FAMILY
(*Cucurbita pepo, C. maxima, mixta* and *moschata*)

| | |
|---|---|
| **Seeds:** | F1 hybrids 5/g, 120/oz; others 10/g, 200-250/oz |
| **Germination:** | 6-10 days; 75% |
| **Height/spread:** | 60-180cm (2-6ft) or more |
| **Space:** | trailing 180cm-3m (6-10ft), bush 120cm (4ft), standard courgettes 60cm (2ft) apart |
| **Sow:** | 2-3 weeks before last frosts indoors for transplanting; outdoors after last frosts |
| **Harvest:** | mid-June to autumn frosts |
| **Yield:** | marrow 3-4 per plant, courgettes 16-20 per plant |

Annual crop

*Trailing marrows (squash) make exotic climbers, as here where they are trained on a simple tunnel framework (left and above) to mingle with sweet peas and sunflowers.*

Botanically, the marrow or squash family (strictly speaking, the gourd section of the cucumber family) is difficult to define because there has been so much interbreeding between species, giving a wide variety of shapes and sizes. They are all tropical, warm season crops that dislike cold weather.

Squash is a term more commonly used in the USA than in Britain. Summer squashes, which include marrows and courgettes/zucchini, come in various shapes and colours, with soft skins and pale, rather insipid flesh. They are eaten fresh and never stored for long, unlike winter squashes (of which pumpkins are the best known in Britain) which have sweetly flavoured yellow or orange flesh, more solid than that of marrows, and hard skins when ripe that allow them to be stored over winter. Very large pumpkins are sometimes grown for show, but although they look impressive they are not the best for eating; their flesh is watery and bland compared with most of the superior, smaller kinds listed below.

Both bush and trailing varieties are grown. The former economize on space, and are not much less productive than traditional prostrate varieties. Although trailing varieties will cover a large area, they tolerate light shade and can be grown amongst taller plants such as soft fruit or sweet corn. Alternatively, train them up fences, trellis and canes, or let them tumble down banks and over walls. Courgette/zucchini plants can be tied to stakes as short standards to keep the fruits off the ground. All varieties have handsome broad leaves up to approximately 60cm (2ft) across, and large edible yellow flowers that give them an astonishing semi-tropical appearance which adds an exotic note to the integrated garden.

## VARIETIES
(Where the growing season is short, choose bush varieties as these start cropping 2-3 weeks earlier than trailing kinds.)

*Bush marrows (squash) grown for courgette production make a rich green foil for dwarf sweet peas, their lush vigour enhanced by the formal box hedge.*

**Ambassador:** 48 days. F1 hybrid, bush zucchini. Very early, heavy crops of deep green fruits. Compact plants, ideal for cloches.

**Autumn Gold:** 90 days. AAS winner. Trailing pumpkin. Yields seven to ten fruits; good decorative value and cooking.

**Blue Hubbard:** 120 days. Trailing winter squash. Large blue-grey fruit up to 7kg (15lb) with tough skin and orange-yellow sweet flesh. Stores well.

**Early Prolific Straightneck:** 50 days. AAS winner. Bush summer squash. Light yellow. Bears over a long season if picked while young at 10-15cm (4-6in).

**Gold Rush:** 45 days. F1 hybrid. AAS winner. Yellow bush zucchini. Early heavy crops on compact bushes with ornamental leaves.

**Jersey Golden Acorn:** 55-60 days for summer fruit or 80 days to mature winter fruit. AAS winner. Semi-bush yellow acorn type.

**Peter Pan Hybrid:** 50 days. AAS winner. Bush patty pan summer squash. Flat round light green fruits with meatier flesh and scalloped edges. Mild flavour; prolific.

**Sunburst Hybrid:** 53 days. F1 hybrid bush patty pan. AAS winner. Numerous small golden yellow fruit, rounded with ribbed sides, for use as summer squash, pick when 7cm (3in).

**Table King:** 75 days. AAS winner. Bush acorn. Dark green fruit with sweet flesh. Good keeper.

**Triple Treat:** 110 days. Trailing pumpkin. Round orange fruits, 2.5-3.5kg (6-8lb) with excellent flavour. Hull-less seeds for cooking. Long keeping.

**Vegetable Spaghetti:** 100 days. Trailing winter squash. Stringy spaghetti-like flesh.

**Waltham Butternut:** 85 days. Trailing winter squash. AAS winner. Small cylindrical fruits, with few seeds, and bright orange, sweet nutty flavoured flesh. Keeps well.

## SOIL PREPARATION

All varieties are gross feeders and require a rich diet of manure. For each plant dig out a hole 30cm (1ft) deep and 45cm (18in) square. Break up the bottom with a fork to ensure good drainage, and then refill with a 50:50 mixture of soil and decayed manure. Lightly firm into place, leaving the surface raised in a low hill.

## SOWING AND PLANTING

Plants are sensitive to cold, wind and also high temperatures. Where summers are hot, give plants a little shade by growing them, for example, beneath sweet corn or where a fence or other plants cast shadows at midday. Elsewhere grow in a sunny but sheltered place. Do not plant out until after the last frosts, unless cloches are available for protection.

Seeds are viable until they are six to seven years old, and many gardeners find that older seeds produce a higher proportion of fruitful

female blooms. Start earliest crops two or three weeks before the last normal frosts, sowing three seeds on edge 2.5cm (1in) deep and 2.5-5cm (1-2in) apart in a group on the top of each mound, and cover with a cloche or large jar to hasten germination. When each seedling has made a pair of true leaves, thin to leave the strongest, or if there is room, leave all the seedlings of trailing varieties to grow.

Alternatively, sow groups of three seeds in the same way in peat pots filled with a gritty potting mixture, keeping them under glass in 12-15°C (55-60°F) until they emerge. Thin and gradually harden off for planting out after the last frost, or earlier if protected. Plant as deep as the lowest leaves and water immediately.

## CULTIVATION

Pinch out the growing tip of trailing varieties when 30-38cm (12-15in) tall, and spread the prostrate branches evenly across the ground, or on any support, tying them frequently to this as they grow. Courgette/zucchini plants tend to sprawl eventually and may develop mildew; discourage this by tying the stem when it is long enough to a vertical stake and removing any leaves below the lowest developing fruit; this helps air circulation and keeps plants tidy.

Water consistently (around, not over, the plants) in dry weather, at least twice weekly when fruits are swelling. Mulch after the first fruits have set, both to conserve moisture and to keep fruits clean. Male and female flowers are produced, the earliest ones tending to be male except on plants from old seed. Most varieties are self-fertilizing, but in cold weather marrows may need manual pollination in the same way as melons (see p. 40).

## HARVEST

Summer varieties taste better if gathered while still young, in the case of courgettes and summer squash when they are 7-10cm (3-4in) long. Frequent cutting encourages further fruits

and prolongs the season. Marrows, winter squash and pumpkins for store should be left on the plants until completely mature, or even until the vine dies, provided they are not frosted. Cut sound, ripe specimens with their stalks intact; cure for a week or two in the warm (up to 27°C/80°F), and then store in a dry, airy frost-free place, spreading them singly on the floor or suspending them in squares of netting to allow a good air circulation.

---

## ONIONS (*Allium cepa*)

| | |
|---|---|
| **Seeds:** | 250/g, 7-8,000/oz |
| **Germination:** | 2-3 weeks; 70% |
| **Height:** | 45-60cm (18-24in) |
| **Space:** | 5-10cm (2-4in) apart in rows 23-30cm (9-12in) apart, or 15-30cm (6-12in) sq |
| **Sow/plant:** | early spring to early summer, also late summer in mild regions |
| **Harvest:** | spring to autumn |
| **Yield:** | 450g (1lb) per 30cm (1ft) row |
| Annual crop | |

Second only to runner beans, bulbing onions are the most important vegetable crop for many gardeners, some of whom still observe the old custom of making their first sowings under glass on Boxing Day each year. These will produce large bulbs, for exhibition or bravado, but for cooking smaller onions are usually preferred. These are started in spring, from seed or miniature bulbs ('sets'), or in late summer using special winter-hardy varieties.

Onions are an ancient crop from the near East, from which the original species spread and diversified into the many different types available today. Most of these can be grown from seed to produce bulbs that rarely bolt and, in the case of spring-sown varieties, will keep until well into the following year. Many gardeners, however, prefer the simplicity of raising onions from sets, specially grown miniature bulbs that have already accumulated many weeks' growth and need only to be planted out to continue to maturity. They are easier to handle, but the number of available varieties is very limited; they also have a greater tendency to go to seed, and do not store so well. Shallots are always grown from sets.

All kinds of onions will grow well amongst other vegetables and flowers, provided they have plenty of sun, but the leaves of maincrop varieties turn brown and die down in late summer as the bulbs ripen. Perennial kinds, such as tree and bunching onions, are best for mingling with flowering plants, while the bulbing onions, shallots and garlic can be grown in blocks or rows with other vegetables and soft fruit, or beside paths.

## VARIETIES

Choosing the proper varieties for your region is critical to a successful crop. Onions begin forming bulbs according to day length. Long-day onions must be grown in northern latitudes and short-day onions must be grown in the south. In the south, long-day varieties may never begin bulbing whereas in the north, short-day onions will begin bulbing immediately while still small before they are strong enough to make large onions.

### Bulbing onions

**Buffalo:** 88 days. Long-day type. Very early from direct seeding in spring. Also suitable for autumn seeding. Large, yellow skinned. Keeps only until the new year.

**Burpee Yellow Globe Hybrid:** 102 days. Long-day type. Good keeper. Yellow onions 7-10cm (3-4in) in diameter.

**Burpee Sweet Spanish:** 110 days. Long-day

*Several less common onion species are well suited for inclusion within a flower border. One of the most unusual is the Egyptian or tree onion (left), a hardy perennial that reproduces itself by developing clusters of edible bulbs at the tips of tall stems. These eventually collapse, the young onions rooting wherever they touch the soil, but with support the tiny bulbs will themselves grow and produce their own offspring as a second tier of aerial bulblets. Like all onions, ordinary maincrop varieties (above) have slim, deep green leaves that contrast with the broader foliage of most other vegetables, such as the ornamental kale growing at the back of the border. These onions are widely spaced; in a restricted area they would grow at higher density with equal success. The tops are bent over to hasten ripening, but this is only necessary in a short or dull season.*

type. Mild-flavoured large onion, stores quite well. Crops well from direct seeding.

**Fiesta:** 110 days. Long-day type. Sweet Spanish hybrid. Yellow skinned with white, mild-flavoured flesh. Keeps quite well.

**Granex Yellow Hybrid:** 170 days. Short-day. Yellow mild skin, white flesh. Moderate storage capability. Best autumn-sown in the south.

**Sweet Sandwich:** 105 days. Long-day type. Brown skinned with pale yellow flesh. Good keeper – flavour gets milder and sweeter.

**Sweet Winter:** 95 days. Hardy enough to be sown in autumn. Will survive –28°C(–20°F). Large, light yellow mild-flavoured bulbs.

**Walla Walla Sweet:** 300 days, 125 if sown in spring. Long-day type. Sweet onion from the Pacific north-west where it grows best. Sow in autumn or early spring. Yellow, does not keep.

---

**Salad (spring) onions/scallions**
**Evergreen Hardy White and White Lisbon:** 120 and 60 days respectively. Fast growing with mild flavour. Will crop from March to October. Can overwinter, as they recover quickly if winters are not too severe. Japanese bunching onion varieties, such as Ishikura (65 days) and He-Shi-Ko (60 days), can be used like salad onions.

---

**Pickling onions**
**Barletta and Crystal Wax Pickling:** 60-70 days. Similar varieties with silvery-white skins, sown thickly to produce very small cocktail onions.

---

**Shallots**
These are bought as bulbs, each of which will grow and divide into a cluster of about six to ten bulbs. Varieties are either red or yellow skinned, and listed as Dutch, Giant or Long Keeping. There is little difference between them, with the exception of Hative de Niort and Sante, brown and yellow varieties respectively, usually grown for exhibition and producing only three to four very uniform bulbs each.

## SOIL PREPARATION
Preliminary cultivation need not be the elaborate ritual often suggested. Onions for store need an open site, exposed to full sun; other kinds will tolerate light shade. Fork over the ground thoroughly several weeks before planting or sowing, working in compost or decayed leaves, but not rich manure. Firm the soil and then loosen the top 2.5-5cm (1-2in), raking it level just before sowing. Lime if the soil is acid.

## GROWING ONIONS AND SHALLOTS FROM SETS
If the weather is not suitable for planting, spread the bulbs out in trays in a light cool place. Sort onion sets, choosing those of medium size: very small ones often do not grow, while the largest (over 2cm/¾in across) usually bolt. The best shallot sets are round and uniform in shape.

Plant onions when danger of heavy frost is past – overwintered varieties in September – 10cm (4in) apart in rows 23cm (9in) apart, or if grown in blocks, 15cm (6in) apart each way. Plant shallots 15cm (6in) apart in rows 23cm (9in) apart (or 15cm/6in square), as soon as possible in early spring; in mild areas the bulbs can be planted from late December to give the longest growing season before midsummer.

Always plant with a trowel, burying the sets so that the tips just show; pushing the bulbs into the ground can damage them, while those planted on the surface are often pulled out by birds. Cultivate and harvest onions in the same way as bulbs from seeds. Shallots are dug up

---

## OTHER ONIONS
Bunching onions – in Asia the main onion crop has always been *Allium fistulosum,* known in Europe and the USA variously as Welsh or Japanese bunching onions. These are perennial and can be grown in clumps amongst flowers and herbs in the same way as chives, or sown in rows like salad onions. For permanent clumps, sow pinches of seed in spring 23cm (9in) apart and leave unthinned. Use the leaf tips for flavouring, or pull a few plants from clumps for salad use. Divide clumps every three to four years in spring or autumn, replanting small groups of the outer bulbs.

Tree onions – sometimes known as the top or Egyptian onion (*Allium cepa* var. *viviparum),* these unusual and decorative plants produce tall stems 45-60cm (18-24in) tall. At the stem tips small bulbs form and start to shoot; the stems may continue growing and develop a second tier of bulbs above the first. The stems are normally tied to canes for support, otherwise they collapse and the aerial bulbs root to start fresh clumps. The plant is propagated from these little bulbs, burying them like onion sets 45cm (18in) apart in spring, but they can also be chopped up and used for flavouring.

---

when the foliage turns yellow in late summer, and the clusters are left to dry on the surface. Only when fully dried are the bulbs separated for storing the largest and saving smaller, even-shaped bulbs to plant the next crop.

## GROWING ONIONS FROM SEED
Sow salad and pickling varieties 1cm (½in) deep very thinly in rows 10-15cm (4-6in) apart, or broadcast in patches or wide strips, raking in

the seed; sow in late summer for spring use, and at monthly intervals beginning two to three months before the last frost date until midsummer for summer to autumn harvest. Water whenever necessary to keep them growing fast, and do not thin the plants.

Maincrop bulbing onions can be sown as soon as soil can be worked in spring, either two to three seeds at stations 15cm (6in) apart, or continuously in drills 23cm (9in) apart, thinning the seedlings to one every 10-15cm (4-6in) depending on the final size required. Alternatively, sow in soil blocks or cell trays under glass from January onwards, five to six seeds to each block or division; do not thin the seedlings, but harden them off and plant the clusters 30cm (1ft) apart each way in late March. The plants will jostle each other for room, and because of the restricted space mature to form groups of medium-sized bulbs.

Onions for overwintering in warm gardens are sown outdoors in late summer, in rows in the same way as maincrop onions and left unthinned until the worst of the winter weather is past. In spring they are thinned to leave single plants at 10cm (4in) spacings; those that are removed can be used as salad onions.

## CULTIVATION
Weed carefully while the seedlings are small, but do not hoe as this may damage surface roots. Water regularly until leaf tips start to turn yellow. Mulch with grass clippings, but pull away when the foliage yellows to admit as much sunlight as possible. Any flower stems that appear should be pinched off at an early stage. Do not bend over the yellow leaves as often advised, but leave to collapse naturally.

## HARVEST
Pull salad and pickling onions when large enough. Lift any misshapen or marked bulbing onions, and any that tried to flower, as soon as they are fully grown – do not attempt to store

them. Overwintered onions should be used immediately as they will only keep for about two months. Bulbs from sets ripen earlier than spring-sown crops, and do not keep so long.

When the tops of bulbing onions are brown, lift the bulbs with a fork and leave on the surface, or spread them on wire netting raised off the ground, to finish ripening. If the season is wet, dry the bulbs in trays or on a shed floor indoors. When fully dried, rub off the loose scales and dry roots, and store on shelves or in net bags, or hang up in a cool, dry place.

### GARLIC *(Allium sativum)*
This popular bulb for flavouring is very easily grown, as adventurous gardeners are increasingly discovering. Although textbooks usually recommend spring planting, commercial growers start in autumn, burying the cloves 23-30cm (9-12in) apart and 10-15cm (4-6in) deep in rich soil, so that the plants are about 15cm (6in) high at the beginning of winter. Garlic is very hardy and will start growing again in early spring like shallots, maturing about the same time, a few weeks after midsummer. Like shallots, however, it is best to delay planting until late winter in very cold areas. When the leaves turn yellow and start to die down, dig up the plants carefully and hang in the sun to dry. The main stem can then be discarded, and the bulb stored, either for use, or for separating into the individual cloves for replanting.

Great-headed garlic (elephant or jumbo garlic) is really *Allium ampeloprasum*, a bulbous close relative of the leek. Its bulbs weigh up to 450g (1lb) or more each and can be used as a mild substitute for true garlic. Make sure when buying any garlic for planting that it is from virus-free stock.

## PARSNIP *(Pastinaca sativa)*

| | |
|---|---|
| **Seeds:** | 300/g, 7-8,000/oz |
| **Germination:** | 1-4 weeks |
| **Height:** | 45cm (18in) |
| **Space:** | 30x15cm (12x6in) large roots, down to 20x10cm (8x4in) |
| **Sow:** | late February to May |
| **Harvest:** | October to April |
| **Yield:** | 450g (1lb) per 30cm (1ft) row |
| Annual crop | |

Parsnips were popular with the ancient Greeks, and also with North American Indians after the crop was introduced there in the early seventeenth century. Until the discovery of sugar-beet processing, the sweetly-flavoured parsnip roots were a recognized source of sugar. Anyone who finds them too sweet should sow the crop in May – the roots are usually smaller than those sown earlier, but the flavour will be milder. Frost, too, increases the

*Fast-growing radishes identify rows of seedling parsnips which often germinate slowly, while there is enough room between the drills for a quick catch crop of lettuces.*

151

sugar content, which is why parsnips unused after a winter in the ground make such an excellent wine.

Roots sown early and left outdoors over winter can occupy the ground for a whole year. Although the leaves are attractively cut and sweetly aromatic, they die down after the first frosts, leaving the bed bare. For this reason, parsnips are not easy to place in the garden, especially as in good soil they can grow quite long and will need digging up with a fork or spade. Amongst other plants it is often best to grow shorter roots fairly close together so that several can be harvested at once without too much disturbance. These can often be roasted whole, when they will have the best flavour.

## VARIETIES

**Avonresister:** 110 days. Small sweet roots, clean-skinned with cream flesh. High resistance to canker.

**Gladiator:** 100-105 days. F1 hybrid. Medium-sized, early and consistent. Smooth white skin and good flavour. Good resistance to canker.

**Harris Model:** 120 days. Slender roots, longer than Hollow Crown.

**Hollow Crown Improved:** 100 days. Long, broad-shouldered roots. Superior quality and fine flavour, but needs good soil.

**Tender and True:** 102 days. Long, tapering roots. Outstanding exhibition and flavour variety. Good resistance to canker.

## SOIL PREPARATION

Fork the ground as deeply as possible, adding lime if it is sour. Parsnips will crop well even on impoverished soils, but adding a little compost or decayed leaves improves the yield. Long varieties need very deep friable soil without any large stones or clods, and they should only be grown where it is possible to dig thoroughly to at least two spades' depth.

## SOWING

Seeds are sown in situ, spacing largest varieties and earliest sowings every 15cm (6in) in rows 30cm (1ft) apart; crops for smaller roots can stand as close as 10cm (4in) apart, with 20cm (8in) between rows, or 12-15cm (5-6in) square in blocks.

Choose a still day for sowing because the seeds are light, and use a fresh supply each year; even then germination levels can be low, and it is best to sow several seeds at each station, later thinning to the strongest. Crops can be sown as early as late February, but germination is slow at soil temperatures below 7°C (45°F) and the seeds may rot. Seedlings emerge fastest when the temperature is about 15°C (60°F); since sowing in April also seems to confer some freedom from canker, there are good reasons to delay sowing until mid- to late spring. If the soil is dry at this time, water the drill before sowing and cover the seeds, 1cm (½in) deep, with moist peat or sand.

## CULTIVATION

Seeds sown early are best mixed with radish as a marker, or lettuce seedlings can be planted between the sowing stations; otherwise, it will be difficult to keep weeds under control until the seedlings are distinguishable. Later sowings will not be a problem. If hoeing weeds, take extra care not to damage the shoulders of the roots as this can possibly introduce canker. Water plants every two to three weeks in very dry weather.

## HARVEST

Lift with a fork after the leaves have started to die. Roots can be left in the ground all winter, or they can be dug up and stored in boxes of sand in a frost-free shed or indoors. Parsnips left outdoors over winter should be used by April at the latest; growth resumes then and the roots can become woody and rather unpalatable.

## PEA (*Pisum sativum*)

**Seeds:** 1,500/pint, 6,000/kilo

**Germination:** 1-2 weeks; 80%

**Height:** 30-180cm (1-6ft)

**Space:** 5-10cm (2-4in), in broad rows same distance apart as plants' height

**Sow:** October to November under cloches in mild areas only, February to late June outdoors

**Harvest:** May to frosts

**Yield:** 450g-1kg (1-2lb) per 30cm (1ft) row

Annual crop

Many people are only familiar with peas as a frozen convenience food, whose flavour bears little comparison with the fresh product. There is little point in sowing large quantities of peas at home for freezing; commercial growers can do this much more cheaply, and with greater skill at timing and preserving the crop in peak condition. Fresh peas, on the other hand, are like sweet corn: they lose flavour quickly after picking, and so shop supplies can never match the quality of those gathered from the garden just before they are needed.

For the best flavour, especially raw, choose varieties with wrinkled seeds, which have a high sugar content. Most round-seeded peas, while not so sweet, are significantly hardier and are traditionally sown either in autumn or very early spring to give the first pickings of the season. Even in milder districts these sowings may need protecting with cloches, and many gardeners prefer to wait a few weeks longer for the first wrinkle-seeded crops with their superior quality.

The most popular varieties are dwarf or semi-dwarf. Although these undoubtedly benefit from the support of short sticks or netting, they

will often thrive without if grown fairly closely together with shelter from winds. Plants of semi-leafless varieties, many of whose leaves are transformed into additional tendrils, support each other and can be grown as an unusual productive hedge. Taller kinds give much heavier yields, but they need netting or twiggy sticks up which to climb – they grow particularly well on wire net fences and the sides of fruit cages. With their grey-green foliage and normally white flowers, tall plants are decorative in a flower border, sown in a ring around a vertical pole enclosed in garden netting, or trained up bamboo canes arranged in the same way as for runner beans, with netting or strings for additional support.

## VARIETIES

Peas fall into three categories. Garden peas are the long-cultivated standard varieties that must be shelled before being eaten. Snow peas, mangetouts and sugar peas are grown for their sweet edible pods which are harvested when the peas are still very small. Snap peas were introduced quite recently and have become very popular. They are very sweet with both edible pods and large peas.

Heights are average, and in good soils may be more – allow for this when providing support. Early varieties take about 55-65 days to mature, mid-season varieties 65-70 days, and late varieties 70-80 days.

**Alderman:**  68 days. Wrinkled, late garden pea. 150-180cm (5-6ft). Very long pods, each with 10-11 peas of outstanding flavour. Long season, and prolific.

**Alaska:**  55 days. Early garden pea 90cm (3ft) pale green 5cm (2in) pods, good for freezing, canning and drying as split peas.

*Tall peas are more productive than dwarf kinds and can be used to provide a vertical feature, or as here, to divide a bed into separate compartments.*

**Bikini/Novella:** 65 days. Semi-leafless, mid-season garden pea. Wrinkled, 45-60cm (18-24in). Self-supporting and uniform plants, pods in pairs. Sweet flavour. Best cleared en masse for freezing.

**Dwarf Grey Sugar:** 65 days. Mid-season snow pea. 60cm (2ft) tall. Heat and cold tolerant. Red flowers.

**Freezonian:** 63 days. Early garden pea. 60-75cm (24-30in) tall, especially recommended for freezing. Wilt resistant.

**Giroy:** 65 days. Petit pois, 90cm (3ft). Sow as mid-season. Used to produce the very sweet, tiny peas popular in France. Excellent fresh or frozen, harvest young. Resistant to Fusarium wilt and top yellows.

**Green Arrow:** 70 days. Mid-season garden pea. 60-70cm (24-28in) tall. 10cm (4in) pods are borne near top of plant for easy picking. Heavy producer.

**Lincoln:** 66 days. Mid-season garden pea. 75cm (30in). Pods 7cm (3in) long. Continues late into season.

**Little Marvel:** 59 days. Early garden pea, wrinkled. 38-45cm (15-18in). Neat plants and very fast growth. Excellent flavour.

**Maestro:** 61 days. Early garden pea. 60-75cm (24-30in) high with 10-12cm (4-5in) pods over a long season. Also good for autumn crop. Resistant to mildew.

**Oregon Sugar Pod:** 58 days. One of the earliest snow peas. 38-45cm (15-18in) tall with 7cm (3in) pods. Also good for autumn crops.

**Sugar Ann:** 56 days. Early snap pea. AAS winner. Two weeks earlier than Sugar Snap. Short 45cm (18in) plants need little support.

**Sugar Bon:** 56 days. Early snap pea. 60-75cm (24-30in) tall, needing little support. 5-7cm (2-3in) pods. Powdery mildew resistant.

**Sugar Daddy:** 74 days. Late snap pea. 60-75cm (24-30in) tall. Similar to Sugar Snap but stringless.

**Sugar Snap:** 70 days. AAS 'Gold Medal' winner. Mid-season snap pea. Thick fleshy pods, sweet with no fibre. May be used as a mangetout while young, or shelled when mature.

**Wando:** 68 days. Mid-season garden pea renowned for its heat tolerance. 70-80cm (28-32in) tall.

### SOIL PREPARATION
For the best crops, a deep, cool root run is necessary. Choose a position in full sun for early and late crops, in light shade for midsummer crops where possible. Work in liberal amounts of compost, leaves or decayed manure as deeply as possible a few weeks before sowing. Lime the soil if it is acid.

### SOWING
Peas prefer relatively cool conditions, and may not crop well at the height of summer; in hot areas, concentrate on producing early or late summer crops. Sow a (first) early round-seeded variety in a warm, sheltered part of the garden (in cold districts under cloches), either in late autumn or early spring, to crop in early summer. A fortnight later follow with an outdoor sowing of a (first) early wrinkled variety for peas in June and July.

In temperate regions small frequent sowings of a single variety ensure a succession of fresh pods. Alternatively, sow simultaneously two or three different peas that mature in sequence. Continue sowings until mid-July, when a mildew-resistant (first) early is used to produce the last crop of the season. Sowings of maincrop (late) varieties for bulk harvest are best made in late spring.

Always sow in broad bands or in patches, 5cm (2in) deep, and space seeds carefully. The plants dislike congestion, and it does not take much longer to distribute the seeds evenly, 7-10cm (3-4in) apart for tall varieties and 5-7cm (2-3in) for other kinds. Using a spade or hoe scoop out a flat-bottomed trench 5cm (2in) deep. This is usually the width of a spade and will take three parallel rows of peas, but with dwarf varieties larger dimensions can save space and give a thick productive hedge of plants: a bed 45cm (18in) wide, for example, can be sown with seven rows of seeds 7cm (3in) apart, and should yield 2.5-3.5kg per metre (6-8lb per yard).

### CULTIVATION
It is best to stake all varieties, except the very shortest and semi-leafless kinds; peas are much easier to manage if they are not trailing on the ground, yields are higher and the pods tend to be out of reach of slugs. Use twiggy sticks or netting, set in place before plants develop their first tendrils.

Keep the ground consistently moist, especially when plants are in flower, but in humid weather avoid wetting the foliage. Plants grown in blocks or hedges will tend to shade the ground and prevent evaporation; assist them by mulching down the sides of rows with grass clippings. Keep weeds under control, particularly during the early weeks of the plants' lives; weeds are difficult to remove once they are entangled in the pea tendrils.

### HARVEST
Gather pods, starting at the bottom of plants, when the peas are a good size but before the pods lose their freshness and bloom. Cut or pinch them off carefully to avoid injuring the plant stems, and check that all those ready have been gathered: pods left to fully ripen shorten the life of the crop. When all the pods are harvested, compost the stems, or cut into pieces and dig in – the roots in particular are very rich in nitrogen.

## ASPARAGUS PEA/GOA OR WINGED BEAN

This is a pretty vetch-like plant, about 30cm (1ft) high with conspicuous crimson flowers followed by small green pods, each with four raised longitudinal 'fins'. It is not a true pea or bean. Known botanically as either *Tetragonolobus purpureus* or *Lotus tetragonolobus,* it is sown after the last frosts to crop from late summer onwards. The sprawling plants are used primarily as very decorative ground cover or edging around larger subjects in pots and tubs, and can even be grown in hanging baskets. The edible pods are a bonus, picked while still crisp, 2.5-3.5cm (1-1½in) long, and cooked like mangetout peas.

# PEPPERS (*Capsicum* species)

| | |
|---|---|
| **Seeds:** | 150/g, 3,500/oz |
| **Germination:** | 2-3 weeks; 75% |
| **Height:** | 38-45cm (15-36in) |
| **Space:** | 45cm (18in) apart |
| **Sow:** | February for growing under glass; indoors 8-10 weeks before last frost date for planting outdoors |
| **Harvest:** | late July to October |
| **Yield:** | 5-10 fruits per plant |
| Annual crop | |

Peppers are native plants of central and south America, and have been cultivated there for several thousand years. Archaeological sites in

Mexico, dated earlier than 5000BC, have revealed seeds of wild capsicum species from which our familiar chillies, cayenne peppers, paprika and most recently the prolific modern race of sweet peppers have all been bred.

Peppers are essentially tropical or sub-tropical plants, requiring slightly higher temperatures than tomatoes to do well, and in most parts of Britain are best treated as a cool greenhouse or conservatory crop. Plants must not be set out until after all danger of frost is past and the soil has warmed up. Sweet peppers can be harvested while still green and mild, or left to ripen to red or yellow, when their sweet flavour develops more fully.

The plants have a lush and exotic appearance, freely branching into bushy shrubs with long broad leaves, dark green and glossy. Their white flowers are small and relatively

*In warmer gardens peppers grow successfully outdoors, especially if harvested green, although plants started early will ripen fully coloured fruits, given enough sunshine. Where summers are generally cool they are usually more reliable as greenhouse or conservatory plants. Here peppers in pots are ripening in a small garden greenhouse in early September, and make decorative companions for a prolific crop of cherry tomatoes. French marigolds, growing at the edge of the soil border, are said to deter greenhouse whitefly, a common pest of both tomatoes and peppers under glass.*

insignificant, but the bright conspicuous fruits that follow compensate for this, especially as they start to ripen, when a single plant might carry large green, yellow, orange and red fruits simultaneously; deep purple or striped peppers are also available. Some varieties will produce eight or ten large rectangular fruits that hang from the branches, while others, particularly the hot chillies, set numerous fruits that are held upright and stud the branches with colour.

Their shape and variety make peppers ideal plants for pots, whether indoors or on a patio. They can be grouped with aubergines/eggplants and tall or trailing tomatoes, or combined with bright flowering plants such as verbena, salvias, dwarf zinnias, tagetes (*T. signata pumila* cultivars) and African or French marigolds (the last are said to deter whitefly, which is very fond of peppers). In the open they are best grown in full sun but sheltered by taller plants such as peas, beans, fennel or soft fruit bushes.

## VARIETIES

**Bell Boy:** 72 days. F1 hybrid. AAS winner. Large deep green, thick-walled sweet peppers on vigorous plants. Tobacco mosaic resistant.

**Cherry Sweet:** 78 days. Small round 2.5-4cm (1-1½in) sweet peppers ripening to red.

**Golden Summer Hybrid:** 70 days. Large sweet thick-walled peppers ripen to golden yellow. Tobacco mosaic tolerant.

**Gypsy:** 65 days. F1 hybrid. AAS winner. Sweet pepper, with heavy crops of large thick-walled fruits. Prolific if sown under glass, ripening from yellowish-green. Tobacco mosaic tolerant.

**Mexi Bell Hybrid:** 75 days. AAS winner. Combines bell shape with mildly hot flavour. Three to four lobed peppers with medium to thick walls. Tobacco mosaic tolerant.

**New Ace:** 62 days. F1 hybrid. Early heavy yield of thin-walled sweet peppers. Good in northern regions or for forcing indoors.

**Purple Belle Hybrid:** 72 days. Large three to four lobed sweet peppers ripen from green to purple and finally to red.

**Super Chili Hybrid:** 75 days. AAS winner. Abundant crops of upright thin-walled chillies with pungent flavour. Pick green or red.

**Sweet Banana:** 65 days. Abundant pointed fruit, sweet. Yellow ripening to red.

## CULTIVATION

Peppers will survive outdoors only after the last frosts, but under glass can be planted in early spring provided the temperature is kept above 15°C (60°F). Sow in pots under glass six to eight weeks before planting, in a temperature of 18-21°C (65-70°F), sowing two seeds in each pot and thinning to the stronger one. Transplant first to 7cm (3in), then to 12cm (5in) pots, as the plants grow. Carefully harden off before planting outdoors 45cm (18in) apart in well-drained soil with plenty of added peat for humus and acidity.

Plants to stay indoors should be moved when about 15-20cm (6-8in) tall into 25cm (10in) pots of peat-based compost. At this height pinch out the growing tip to induce bushiness. Spray regularly with water, both to deter red spider mite and to help pollinate the flowers. Taller varieties may need support when carrying a full crop, and all plants will appreciate occasional liquid feeding when in fruit. At the end of the season, the strictly perennial plants can be overwintered if kept just moist in pots in a minimum temperature of 10°C (50°F), and will then fruit much earlier the following year.

## HARVEST

Cut fruits as required. If harvested green as sweet peppers, a much heavier overall crop will be borne by the plants. Green peppers that have reached full size take about three to four weeks more to change colour.

## POTATO (*Solanum tuberosum*)

**Seed:** 8-12/lb, 20-30/kg

**Height:** 45-90cm (18-36in)

**Space:** 1st early, 23x45cm (9x18in); 2nd early, 30x60cm (1x2ft); maincrop, 38x75cm (15x30in)

**Plant:** March to April (USA: April to June in the north, or January to March and August to September in the south)

**Harvest:** 1st early, June to July; 2nd early, July to August; maincrop, September to October

**Yield:** 1-1.3kg (2-3lb) per plant

Annual crop

It is not always easy to find room for potatoes in smaller gardens, nor are the plants particularly decorative. Maincrop (late season) varieties

*Although a valuable crop for breaking fresh ground or fitting into any vacant space in the garden, potatoes are equally profitable grown in large pots and containers.*

occupy the ground for most of the growing season, and although they help to break up new ground, they are best left to farmers as a field crop. A few plants of an early variety, on the other hand, will easily fit into quite a small space amongst fruit and flowering plants and give gardeners welcome 'new' potatoes while shop prices are still very high. Some varieties can be grown in pots with little effort for very early harvest or for use over Christmas (see panel).

Although usually grown in rows and earthed up to keep the tubers covered, crops can be raised by alternative methods, using polythene or organic mulches for example, but yields from these have rarely equalled plants grown conventionally. There is however no need to arrange plants in continuous rows – an advantage where only a few plants are grown. Each can be earthed up separately, raising individual hills to keep light from the tubers. They may be grown on the flat with very little cultivation, planting small tubers about 10cm (4in) deep amongst other plants, and using a thick mulch to keep weeds under control until the potato foliage is dense enough to smother competition.

## VARIETIES

Most suppliers retail only one or two varieties of potato seed tubers, usually the kind that have proved themselves on local soils. However there are numerous other kinds worth searching for: potatoes with coloured skins or flesh for example are available from specialist suppliers, and often have a distinctive flavour or texture. Although not always as pest and disease resistant or as vigorous as modern commercial kinds, they are worth growing as a delicacy or for variety, and in some cases tolerate a wider range of soils.

*Early varieties of potatoes grown in rows will be dug up and cleared for neighbouring plants such as celery (foreground) to continue growth unimpeded.*

**Katahdin:** late, white oval tubers. Plant closer because of lower yields per plant. Mosaic and blight resistant.

**Kennebec:** mid-season, high yielding variety with smooth, white skin with shallow eyes. Good flavour. Resistant to late blight and mosaic.

**Krantz:** early russet-skinned tubers good for baking, boiling or fries. Disease resistant.

**La Rouge:** red tubers. Keeps well.

**Norland:** early. Oblong tubers with smooth, red skin and shallow eyes. Best for small early crop. Moderately scab resistant.

**Premium Red:** a fine late red variety.

**Red Pontiac:** early to mid-season, oblong red skinned tubers with shallow eyes and white flesh. Good in heavy soils, heat tolerant, stores very successfully.

**Superior:** early white skinned oval tubers. Susceptible to drought. Scab resistant. Widely grown on the east coast.

## SEED POTATOES
Crops are raised from tubers ('seed' or 'sets'), the heaviest from small tubers planted at close spacings. Always buy seed certified as free from virus, and obtain it several weeks before planting. Discard any soft or diseased tubers, and spread the rest, with their recessed 'eyes' uppermost, in single layers in trays or boxes; keep them in a light frost-free place to 'chit' or produce fat green shoots from the eyes. This advances early varieties by two to three weeks and increases maincrop (late) yields.

## SOIL PREPARATION
This can be done at planting time. Choose a position in full sun, sheltered from cold winds for earliest plantings, and fork the ground deeply, working in plenty of compost or decayed leaves; do not use fresh manure nor

lime. Potatoes prefer an even crumbly soil structure, and any lumps should be broken up. On alkaline soils tubers can become disfigured with scab; prevent this by working in peat and plant the tubers on peat or grass clippings.

## PLANTING
It is best not to cut large tubers unless they have several sprouts, in which case divide them to leave three to four shoots on each piece. Plant 10-12cm (4-5in) deep when the soil is workable in spring (and again in autumn in southern USA). Make holes 23, 30 or 38cm (9, 12 or 15in) apart, in rows 45, 60 or 75cm (18, 24 or 30in) apart for 1st early, 2nd early and maincrop varieties respectively (alternatively plant 30, 38 or 45cm/12, 15 or 18in apart each way). Drop a tuber, shoots upwards, into each hole and cover with crumbly soil.

## CULTIVATION
Cover emerging shoots with a little soil if there is a threat of frost. When the shoots are 15-20cm (6-8in) high, mound soil around them so that just the tips are showing. Leave the tops of the mounds or ridges flat or slightly concave to catch rainfall. Keep weeds under control, and water well or the quality and size of tubers will be reduced.

## HARVEST
When the first flower buds appear, reveal one or two tubers. If large enough, plants can be dug up as required, using a fork and levering the whole root ball out of the soil. With maincrop varieties wait until the leaves have turned brown, but do not leave after the foliage has withered and collapsed as the tubers will be vulnerable to pests and diseases. Carefully dig up the whole crop, leaving the tubers to dry on the surface for a few hours. Discard damaged and green tubers, and store the rest in boxes or paper bags in a dry cool place, free from frost. Thoroughly compost or burn the foliage.

## POTATOES OUT OF SEASON
After harvesting first early varieties, keep a few small tubers in a warm light place; alternatively, save some tubers when planting in spring and keep them very cool (but in the light) until needed. In July, they can be planted in mild areas to produce a light but valuable crop in late autumn. Depending on the locality and available facilities, plant them like early varieties outdoors in a warm position for covering with cloches from early autumn onwards, or in the soil of a cold frame, which should be closed during periods of cold weather.

They may also be grown in pots and tubs, two or three small tubers in a 30cm (12in) pot (more in larger containers). Fill pots to half their depth with a good potting mixture, space out the tubers and cover with 5-7cm (2-3in) of the mix; as growth progresses, gradually fill the pot until the soil reaches 2.5cm (1in) from the rim. If there is still time for further growth, set a deep ring of metal, waterproof card or similar material inside the rim and continue to fill with potting mixture. Keep the plants evenly moist and support floppy growth with small twigs.

Using fresh sprouted seed or sound tubers saved from the previous season's harvest, earlier crops can be started in spring in the same way, growing them in a cold frame, or in pots in a greenhouse with a minimum temperature of 10-12°C (50-55°F). Tubers potted in January will often crop in April, and can continue for several weeks if the largest of the new potatoes are carefully removed from the mass of roots, leaving the smaller ones to continue growing.

# RADISH (*Raphanus sativus*)

**Seeds:** 100-150/g, 2,500-3,500/oz

**Germination:** 1 week; 70%

**Height:** 10-15cm (4-6in)

**Space:** 2.5x15cm (1x6in) or broadcast; winter kinds 10x30cm (4x12in) or 15cm (6in) sq

**Sow:** January to March in a greenhouse or frame, mid-March to late August outside; winter kinds July

**Harvest:** mid-March to end September; winter kinds late autumn

**Yield:** 225g (8oz) per 30cm (1ft) row; double for winter varieties

Annual crop

Radishes are a popular summer salad crop, less often grown for winter use. Small-rooted kinds prefer a cool season, which is why later sowings never match the quality of early spring ones. Ordinary varieties would have greater chance of success if given moist conditions and a little shade, together with timely thinning, since overcrowding is a common cause of bolting. On hot dry soils the mooli (Daikon), or Japanese radish, is a better choice for summer sowings.

Winter varieties are larger (although they can be pulled while young) and have a stronger flavour. They take 60-80 days to mature, compared to the 20-40 days for most summer varieties. Since they are not in the ground for long, it is usual to treat them as catch crops, sowing between or beside other plants, or even mixing summer varieties as a marker for slower-germinating plants, such as parsley or parsnips. Sow small amounts frequently and grow them wherever there is room temporarily for a few plants, but remember to keep them moist and in continuous growth for sweet tender roots.

*Less widely grown than summer varieties, winter radishes such as Black Spanish Round give reliable crops of large juicy roots with white, mildly-flavoured flesh.*

## VARIETIES
Radishes are normally described as globe-shaped (round, turnip), long, or half-long (intermediate, oval or olive).

**April Cross:** 65 days. F1 hybrid mooli. Long straight white pungent roots, 30-38cm (12-15in) long. Will not bolt from spring sowing.

**Cherry Belle:** 22 days. Globe, red. Rapid growth and good flavour, stands well. Ideal for succession and forcing.

**China Rose:** 52 days. Half-long, deep pink winter variety. White pungent flesh.

**Easter Egg:** 25 days. Globe. Mixed colours of red, pink, lavender, reddish purple and white. Tangy white flesh. Decorative in salads.

**French Breakfast:** 24 days. Half-long, red with white tip. Good flavour and popular for succession, but quickly becomes hollow.

**Long White/Icicle:** 28 days. Long, white. Fast-maturing crisp mild roots, fairly long-standing.

**Minowase Summer:** 48 days. F1 hybrid mooli. Heat resistant and best sown after July, to produce long white roots, crisp and mild, and up to 1.75-2kg (4-5lb).

**Rave d'Amiens:** 30 days. Long, red. Crisp and tender with mild flavour. Takes longer to mature but stands well.

**Black Spanish Round:** 55 days. Globe, black winter variety. Crisp white flesh, strong flavour. Long version available.

**Scarlet Globe:** 23 days. Globe, bright red. Popular old variety for successional sowings, uniform and fast maturing.

**White Globe:** 18 days. White variety that holds shape well.

## SOIL PREPARATION
Radishes appreciate a friable, moisture-retentive soil, especially summer sowings which on poorer ground may bolt before forming useable roots. Work in plenty of peat, leaves or garden compost when forking over the ground prior to sowing. Choose a sunny position for all except summer crops, which prefer a little shade.

## SOWING
Sow 1cm (½in) deep in broad strips or drills 15cm (6in) apart, and thin to 2.5cm (1in) apart as soon as seedlings can be handled. Start in late January in a cold frame or greenhouse (outdoors under cloches in mild gardens), and sow at three to four week intervals until mid-March, when seeds can normally be sown outdoors. From then until mid-June sow a little seed at ten to fourteen day intervals for continuity. Japanese varieties are best used for June and July sowings, thinning plants to 5-7cm (2-3in) apart. In July or August, sow winter radishes at stations 15cm (6in) apart, or in rows 30cm (1ft) apart, thinning the seedlings to 10cm (4in). In dry weather water drills before sowing.

## CULTIVATION

Grow all kinds fast, by keeping plants consistently moist from sowing onwards. Thin at an early stage, because crowded plants quickly bolt without their roots swelling.

## HARVEST

Pull the largest roots of summer varieties as soon as they are useable, and continue to gather regularly before plants bolt. Winter crops are best lifted in November, twisting off their tops and storing them in boxes of peat or sand; in mild areas, however, they can be left outdoors over winter, protected by a covering of leaves. Surplus plants may be left to flower, gathering the seed pods for cooking or salad use; any variety can be used for pods, although the best and largest are produced by winter varieties late the following spring.

# SALSIFY (*Tragopogon porrifolius*) and SCORZONERA (*Scorzonera hispanica*)

| | |
|---|---|
| **Seeds:** | 100/g, 2,500/oz |
| **Germination:** | 2 weeks |
| **Height:** | 30-45cm (12-18in) |
| **Space:** | 30x10cm (12x4in) in rows, or 15cm (6in) sq |
| **Sow:** | early spring outdoors |
| **Harvest:** | autumn to early spring |
| **Yield:** | 112-168g (4-6oz) per plant |
| Annual crop | |

Salsify ('vegetable oyster') and scorzonera are related hardy plants, well worth a little room for their delicately flavoured roots, the delicious young flowering shoots, and for their bright attractive flowers. Seldom seen in smaller

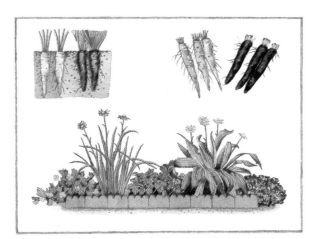

*Salsify* (left) *and scorzonera or black salsify* (right) *are similar in season, flavour and culture, but differ in leaf shape and the colour of their flowers.*

gardens until recent years, both crops are arousing interest now that well-grown roots are more common in shops. They are long-season crops, sown about the same time as parsnips or a little earlier, but occupy less room. They fit easily in groups amongst other vegetables, or in flower borders both for ornament and an occasional handful of flowering stems.

Salsify is a biennial with a fat pale tap root, 20-30cm (8-12in) long. Each plant produces a neat clump of leaves, blue-green and grassy, and 90-120cm (3-4ft) flowering stems with violet-purple daisies in early summer, followed by seedheads like thistles. There are yellow-flowered species (*T. pratensis* and *T. orientalis*), edible and grown in the same way, but their seeds are rarely offered.

Scorzonera has broader leaves, oval and pointed, its flowers yellow and daisy-shaped, borne on 90cm (3ft) stems in late summer. The straight roots are usually slimmer than salsify, and black-skinned, but their flavour and cultivation are very similar. Plants are perennial and may be grown for several years for their flowers and edible stems, although roots become woody after the second season.

## VARIETIES

### Salsify

Several named strains are widely available – Giant, Mammoth, Sandwich Island, or simply Salsify – but there is little to choose between them, and all are usually reliable.

### Scorzonera

Like salsify, a number of comparable varieties is offered. Black Russian, Giant (Rooted), Long Black, Long John and Russian Giant are all good. Habil has more uniform roots than most kinds, but is otherwise similar.

## SOIL PREPARATION

As with parsnips, the best roots are grown on deep friable soils, especially those of a sandy composition, but both crops tolerate low fertility. Thoroughly fork over a sunny site to a depth of at least 30cm (1ft), adding a little compost or decayed leaves to enrich poor soils (but not manure).

## SOWING

Since transplanting often results in deformed roots, both vegetables are normally sown where they are to crop, unless they are grown only for their flowers and edible stems. Sow 2.5cm (1in) deep in early spring as soon as the soil is workable, dropping three to four seeds at 10cm (4in) intervals along rows 30cm (1ft) apart, or 15cm (6in) apart each way. Reduce each group of seedlings to one plant when they are about 5cm (2in) tall – these may be transplanted elsewhere for flowering.

## CULTIVATION

Water occasionally if very dry, control weeds and mulch with grass clippings. Otherwise plants need little attention.

## HARVEST

Dig up roots carefully from early autumn onwards. The rest may be lifted as required over winter, but if the ground is likely to freeze solid, dig up several roots, twist off their tops and store in boxes of dry sand. Salsify roots should be used by the end of winter, but smaller scorzonera roots can be left to increase their size in the second year. Some of the young leaves can be picked in spring in the same way as spinach. The flowering stems of both species are a delicacy; cut the top 15cm (6in) of some of these and cook like sprouting broccoli.

## SEAKALE (*Crambe maritima*)

**Seeds:**  30/g, 750/oz

**Germination:**  3 weeks

**Height:**  45-75cm (18-30in)

**Space:**  60cm (2ft) apart

**Sow/plant:**  early spring outdoors

**Harvest:**  December to April

**Yield:**  225-450g (8-16oz) per plant

Perennial; zones 5-9

Seakale is a dramatic plant for a prominent situation in any sunny flower border, or near the edge of a bed. It is a native of English cliffs and shingly seashores, where for centuries the young shoots were blanched by local inhabitants and cut for market. From the wild it graduated to greenhouses where it was forced as a luxury crop from December onwards.

It should not be confused with seakale beet (see **Spinach** p.164), although the midribs from the latter's leaves are very similar in flavour and appearance to the blanched stalks of seakale. When the blanching season is over, the perennial plants develop very broad silvery blue leaves with crimped edges; a single plant several years old can spread 90-120cm (3-4ft) across. Between June and August, sturdy flower

*Formerly an important seasonal crop in traditional kitchen gardens, seakale is not grown as widely these days as it deserves, and many people have never tasted the tender, blanched stems in early spring (top left). Established plants can be dug up for forcing in a greenhouse in winter, after which the exhausted roots are usually thrown away: but they are more easily blanched in situ by covering them with a pot or upturned bucket to exclude all light. After the crisp white stems have been cut a centimetre or two above ground level, plants are then left uncovered to resume normal growth. Provided they are fed generously each year, the plants can be allowed to flower without harming their cropping potential. The magnificent heads of bloom (bottom left) are pollinated by small flies, each flower then maturing into a large spherical seed capsule. These seedheads may be cut when ripe and hung upside down to dry for indoor decoration.*

stems appear, opening into enormous flattened heads of small white scented flowers, each of which produces a solitary seed enclosed in a spherical white capsule. A complete head, perhaps 60cm (2ft) across, of ripe seed pods is a startling sight; it can be cut and hung up for seed, or used with dried flowers.

## VARIETIES
**Lily White:** the only kind normally available. Produces the whitest shoots after blanching, considered to have the best flavour. Young forced shoot tips outdoors may be damaged by severe frost.

**Ordinary/Common:** occasionally seakale is listed without any varietal name, and this usually is the unimproved ordinary kind. It is not to be despised – after blanching it is not inferior to Lily White, and in some gardens has proved hardier.

## SOIL PREPARATION
Light well-drained soil is best. Seakale is a close relative of the cabbage, and in some respects enjoys similar conditions: lime the ground if necessary, and work in garden compost or very decayed manure for moisture retention. As plants are naturally maritime, fertilizers and soil conditioners based on seaweed are particularly appreciated, but the traditional use of agricultural salt is discredited these days.

## SOWING
Seakale raised from seed needs an extra year before it can be cropped, and as seeds have short viability germination may not be good. However, it is often easier to obtain seeds than to locate suppliers of root cuttings ('thongs'). Sow sparingly in spring, 2.5cm (1in) deep in rows outdoors, and later thin to about 15cm (6in) apart. These will remain in the seed bed until ready to be planted out the following spring.

## PLANTING
Plant 60cm (2ft) apart in early spring, using one-year-old transplants or bought thongs. These are sections of root several centimetres long, usually trimmed square at the top and obliquely at the bottom. Bury these upright, covering their tops.

## CULTIVATION
Water whenever needed, and control weeds until the young plants are established. Prevent any attempt to bloom at this stage by snapping off flower heads before they open. In the autumn, clear away dead leaves and mulch with compost or decayed manure. Replace plants after five to six years (or earlier if exhausted).

## BLANCHING
Plants cannot be cropped until the spring after planting. During winter, invert a large box or

> ### PORTUGAL CABBAGE/COUVE TRONCHUDA (*Brassica oleracea* var. *costata*)
>
> A fascinating vegetable, rarely seen anywhere today, but still available from one or two seedsmen, and well worth growing for its broad cabbage-like heads of wavy, rich green leaves, decorated with a clear network of thick white ribs. The tender leaves are eaten like those of conventional cabbage, while the fleshy ribs with their own distinctive flavour are cooked like seakale (an older alternative name was 'Seakale Cabbage'). Although plants are as hardy as an early savoy cabbage, in colder areas it might be safer to sow in spring and grow in the same way as summer and early autumn cabbages. Grow them in rich soil with plenty of water to promote rapid growth and keep the main leaf ribs tender.

pot (its drainage holes covered by a stone) over the plant. Alternatively, wait until the first signs of growth in spring and then mound soil over the plants to a depth of about 10cm (4in); when the shoots are about to emerge, ridge up more soil to a total depth of 20cm (8in). Strong plants may also be dug up in November or December for forcing in a greenhouse (see p. 177).

## HARVEST
When the blanched leaf stalks are about 20-23cm (8-9in) long, or just appearing at the top of the soil ridge, snap them off at their base or cut them with a short section of root. After harvest, uncover outdoor plants, and leave to grow normally. Plants forced indoors will be useless afterwards (except perhaps for root cuttings) and should be thrown away.

# SPINACH (*Spinacea oleracea*)

**Seeds:** 100/g, 2,000/oz

**Germination:** 2-3 weeks; 75%

**Height:** 20-60cm (8-24in)

**Space:** 7cm (3in) sq broad bands; winter 15x30cm (6x12in) or 23cm (9in) sq

**Sow:** summer 4-6 weeks before last spring frost onwards; winter 4-6 weeks before first autumn frost

**Harvest:** summer May to October; winter October to May

**Yield:** 450g (1lb) per plant

Annual crop

True spinach is notorious, not only for its distinctive flavour but also because it is a cool season crop normally only reliable in spring and autumn. Plants are very sensitive to hot weather and long hours of daylight, but on the other hand even winter varieties are only dependable in mild areas. Rather than gamble with the fickle nature of true spinach, many gardeners understandably prefer to grow the very hardy spinach beet or drought-tolerant New Zealand spinach (see panel).

Two kinds of spinach are traditionally distinguished – smooth-seeded or half-hardy summer spinach, and the hardy, prickly-seeded winter type – but more recently introduced round-seeded varieties have been bred for all-year-round production in milder districts. True and New Zealand spinach have rich green foliage that looks well combined with lettuces, especially those with decorative leaves, or with the coloured forms of chard. For summer production, intercrop spinach between taller plants whose foliage will lightly shade the crop from hot sun.

## VARIETIES

**Bloomsdale Long-Standing:** 48 days. Deep green fleshy leaves. Slow to bolt.

**Fordhook Giant:** 55 days. White stalks and dark green savoyed leaves.

**Melody:** 42 days: F1 hybrid. AAS winner. Thick dark green leaves, good resistance to mildew and virus. Good for spring/autumn crops.

**New Zealand Spinach:** see panel.

**Rainbow Chard:** 60 days. A mixture of Swiss Chard colour variants. Red, white, yellow, orange or purple midribs.

**Rhubarb Chard:** 60 days. A very decorative form of Swiss Chard with bright scarlet midribs.

**Sigmaleaf:** 50 days. Long-standing and high quality plants for all year round production. Sow spring and autumn.

**Spinach Beet/Silver Beet/Perpetual Spinach:** see panel.

**Swiss Chard/Seakale Beet:** see panel.

**Tyee:** 39 days. Vigorous with large dark green savoy leaves. Mildew tolerant. Spring or autumn crops.

**Wolter:** 50 days. Dutch hybrid with mild flavour and resistance to mildew.

*Orach or red mountain spinach is one of the more spectacular forms of this leaf crop, often grown as an ornamental foliage plant and usually seeding itself freely thereafter.*

## MOUNTAIN SPINACH/ORACH(E)
### (*Atriplex hortensis*)

Frequently grown as a decorative cottage garden foliage plant, orach is also a useful spinach substitute. Green, red and pale yellow ('white') forms are available, all reaching 90-150cm (3-5ft) tall. They are handsome hardy annuals, with large, edible leaves, triangular and slightly ruffled; eventually spires of tightly clustered flowers, the same colour as the foliage, appear – these flowers are very attractive when dried. Flowering can be delayed by occasionally pinching out growing tips and by adding plenty of humus to the soil before sowing (although orach will tolerate dry soils, plants flower quickly and leaf quality suffers).

Grow orach where its colour and stature can be seen above neighbouring plants, in full sun or light shade, the latter preferable for summer sowings. Sow groups of seed 2.5cm (1in) deep and 38-45cm (15-18in) apart each way, any time from early spring to late summer (every five to six weeks on light soils if continuity is required). Water freely in dry weather. Pick leaves here and there before they are too large and coarse. Leave a few plants to flower and sow themselves, which they will do liberally.

## SOIL PREPARATION

Spinach prefers plenty of moisture-retentive humus in the soil for fast lush growth. Where this cannot be provided, grow New Zealand spinach (see panel); elsewhere, work in as much compost or decayed leaf as possible while breaking up the soil 15-30cm (6-12in) deep prior to sowing. Add lime on acid soils. Choose a sunny site for spring and autumn bearing; summer crops, however, benefit from light shade.

## SOWING

Seeds are normally sown in situ. In a cold spring, sow indoors in soil blocks or peat pots, three seeds to each, and plant out unthinned as soon as the weather improves. Outdoors, sow summer spinach four to five weeks before the last frost and repeat every four to six weeks for succession if hot summers are liable to cause early bolting. Sow a winter variety or one of the hardier summer kinds in early autumn four to six weeks before the first frost, for overwintering outdoors (cloche in cold weather) or in a cold frame to provide early spring crops. Sow 1cm (½in) deep and keep moist until seedlings emerge. Sow summer types in broad bands or blocks and thin seedlings to 7cm (3in) apart each way; space rows 15-30cm (6-12in) apart and thin to 7cm (3in). Winter kinds are sown in the same way, thinning larger prickly- seeded varieties to 10-15cm (4-6in) apart.

*When grown well with plenty of moisture, most kinds of spinach have a rich, succulent appearance that makes a dramatic contrast with crops such as beetroot (foreground).*

### SPINACH SUBSTITUTES
### New Zealand Spinach (*Tetragonia expansa*)

A prostrate tender annual, with good mild spinach flavour and remarkable tolerance of hot dry conditions. Plants flower continuously, but this does not affect the yield. Grow them as ground cover amongst taller plants, or as a lush sprawling edge to patios (branches can reach 60-90cm (2-3ft) long if not regularly picked). Sow two to three seeds per station outdoors in April (in cold areas under glass for planting out after the last frosts) after soaking them overnight. Space plants 90cm (3ft) apart, and pinch out the growing tip once when 12-15cm (5-6in) high. For heaviest crops water regularly. Gather whole trailing stems, leaving 7-10cm (3-4in) for regrowth, and strip off the leaves and tips for use. Plants crop until the first frosts, but usually seed themselves, the seedlings often emerging earlier than those sown deliberately.

### Spinach Beet/Silver Beet/Perpetual Spinach

This is a hardy kind of beet, bred for leaf rather than root production. The leaves are larger and more succulent than those of true spinach, upright and light to mid-green in colour; their flavour is a little sweeter and milder. Plants need similar conditions to true spinach, but will thrive in drier soils. Sow in spring, two to three seeds at stations 30cm (1ft) apart each way, to give crops from summer onwards. Except in cold districts, plants usually survive the winter to give useful pickings in spring and summer as long as any flower stems are promptly removed. On hot or dry soils, second-year plants may start to bolt early in a mild spring; mulch and crop the plants regularly, while making an early sowing for replacement, if necessary starting the seeds under glass.

Where winters are severe, sow in autumn and overwinter seedlings under cloches or in a cold frame. Plants can also be grown at high density for cutting in the same way as summer spinach.

### Swiss Chard/Seakale Beet

This is another form of beet, resembling a cross between seakale and spinach beet. Leaves have thick crisp stalks and midribs, which may be white or coloured, and these are usually cut out and cooked like blanched seakale. The leaf blades are smaller than those of spinach beet, especially on the coloured kinds, and are sometimes attractively crinkled; after removing the midrib this part is treated like spinach. They are highly decorative hardy plants, useful for providing colour amongst green vegetables and contrasting foliage with flowering plants. Most soils are suitable, especially heavier kinds. Grow in the same way as spinach beet.

## CULTIVATION
Keep weeds under control and water frequently in dry weather to maintain consistent growth. Mulch generously to reduce evaporation.

## HARVEST
Plants grown at close spacing should never be allowed to get too large. Gather when four to five leaves are formed, cutting the whole plant down to just above the base of the leaves – do not cut the main stem itself, or regrowth may be delayed. New leaves should appear fairly quickly for further cutting. Plants at wider spacing may be harvested traditionally, by picking a few outer leaves from each, provided they are not too old.

# RUTABAGA see TURNIP & SWEDE

# SQUASH see MARROW

# SWEET CORN/MAIZE (*Zea mays*)

| | |
|---|---|
| **Seeds:** | 5-6/g, 125-150/oz |
| **Germination:** | 1-2 weeks |
| **Height:** | 120-180cm (4-6ft) |
| **Space:** | 45cm (18in)sq, very dwarf 30cm (1ft); if underplanted, 60cm (2ft) |
| **Sow:** | 5-6 weeks before last frost indoors or after frost outdoors |
| **Harvest:** | late summer to early autumn |
| **Yield:** | 1-2 cobs per plant |
| Annual crop | |

Sweet corn is a summer vegetable that thrives in hot weather. The flavour of modern 'supersweet' varieties tends to remain stable for longer than the original sugary varieties (SU). 'Shrunken Two' (Sh2) varieties are sweeter than average and remain so for seven to ten days in a refrigerator; 'Sugar Enhancer' (SE) or 'Everlasting Heritage' (EH) varieties are also very sweet but generally more tender and hold their sweetness for four to five days. Cross-pollination between groups adversely affects quality, and ideally different supersweet groups should be grown at least 75m (250ft) apart. Varieties from the same group, however, may be grown together, as can ordinary varieties.

In some regions sweet corn is traditionally underplanted with other crops, and also used to support twining plants such as climbing French beans or Dwarf French beans, trailing marrows or pumpkins will all flourish amongst corn stems grown at 60cm (2ft) spacings. Corn plants are best grouped in squares to ensure efficient pollen distribution by wind.

*There should be no problem fitting a block of dwarf sweet corn (maize) into a garden border, amongst leafy summer vegetables or, as here, surrounded by alpine strawberries.*

## VARIETIES

**Early Xtra Sweet:** 71 days. Sh2. AAS winner. Early yellow variety. Two weeks before Illini Xtra Sweet.

**Early Sunglow:** 68 days. SU. The first yellow sweet corn to be harvested.

**Golden Cross Bantam:** 75 days. SU. Standard yellow variety. Sweet and tender.

**Honey 'N Pearl:** 78 days. Sh2. AAS winner. A super sweet bicolour with tender white and yellow kernels filling 23cm (9in) cobs.

**How Sweet It Is:** 78 days. Sh2. AAS winner.

One of the sweetest varieties. White.

**Illini Xtra Sweet:** 83 days. Sh2. Very sweet yellow corn with 45% sugar content.

**Kandy Korn:** 89 days. EH. Sweet yellow variety with purplish husks and stalks.

**Platinum Lady:** 70 days. EH. Very sweet white kernels in green and purple husks.

**Silver Queen:** 94 days. SU. Popular late white.

## SOIL PREPARATION

Full sun is important, together with a little shelter from cold winds. Most soils are suitable provided they are free draining, but not liable to dry too fast. Fork over the soil, adding compost or peat (a slightly acid soil is preferable), or grow to follow a heavily manured crop.

## SOWING AND PLANTING

For successful germination and growth, soil temperatures must be above 10-15°C (50-60°F). Seeds may be sown outdoors when all danger of frost is past, sowing two seeds 2.5cm (1in) deep at stations 30, 45 or 60cm (12, 18 or 24in) square for dwarf, conventional or underplanted crops respectively. At wider spacings both seedlings may be left; otherwise remove the weaker one.

For earlier crops, start plants under glass five to six weeks before the last frosts, or a little earlier if transplants can be covered with cloches. Sweet corn dislikes root disturbance and is best sown in peat pots or soil blocks, two seeds to each after being soaked overnight. Keep in a minimum temperature of 10°C (50°F), and transplant single seedlings when large enough. (Alternatively, sow four to five seeds in each, and plant out the groups – unthinned and hardened off – 90cm/3ft apart each way.)

Harden off protected sowings before planting out. It is unwise to hold plants back because of inclement weather; they should be planted out on time, protected with cloches or wind breaks.

## CULTIVATION

Plants require little more than routine care. In exposed gardens, stake or support tall plants and mound soil around the base of the stems. Do not remove any side shoots that appear, nor is there any need to water plants in a normal season until they start to flower. After that, water regularly to improve the quality and size of cobs.

## HARVEST

When the tassel at the end of a cob is dry and dark brown, test one or two of the kernels by pressing with the thumb nail – if ready the contents will still be liquid, but with the consistency of cream. Delay picking ripe cobs until immediately before use. Pull up used stems, and compost or bury where runner beans are to grow.

# TOMATO (*Lycopersicon esculentum*)

| | |
|---|---|
| **Seeds:** | 300/g, 7-8,000/oz |
| **Germination:** | 1-2 weeks; 75% |
| **Height:** | 15-180cm (6in-6ft) |
| **Space:** | 30-90cm (1-3ft) apart; bush varieties 45cm (18in) sq for high early yields |
| **Sow:** | January to March under glass; late summer outdoors (USA: deep south) |
| **Harvest:** | June to first frosts |
| **Yield:** | 2.5-4.5kg (6-10lb) per plant |
| Annual crop | |

It is difficult to believe that the tomato, today an indispensable garden vegetable and lucrative commercial crop, was regarded with suspicion by British gardeners only 200 years ago. Love-apples, as they were then called, were considered exotic and probably aphrodisiac; certainly they were thought to be too difficult for most people to grow.

They are a warm season crop, more difficult to grow in regions with cool summers, where early or short season varieties are required, or the added heat of a greenhouse as is needed in many parts of Britain. In southern USA, prolonged hot weather causes blossom drop, but light shade or spring and autumn crops avoid the highest temperatures.

In Britain and northern USA gardeners with a greenhouse can grow a summer crop of cordon (single stem) tomatoes, using very little artificial heat. Numerous highly productive techniques have been devised – ring culture on sterile aggregate, hydroponics and growing on straw bales, for example – but these require closer attention than growing them in pots, still the simplest method under glass. In mild districts an outdoor tomato crop can be the least demanding of all. Although the plants are not hardy and must usually be started indoors to give a long fruiting season, in most seasons good crops can be gathered either from modern bush varieties or plants grown as cordons in full sun. Many people prefer the more pronounced flavour of outdoor tomatoes, particularly the bush varieties.

Tomatoes have widely varying shapes, sizes and colours, all with some decorative value. The brightly coloured fruits may be red, pink, yellow and even striped. Shapes vary from long Italian plum varieties to tiny cherry tomatoes; these contain sucrose and are very sweet, but they lack the savour and bouquet of normal varieties. At the other extreme are beefsteak or oxheart tomatoes, fleshy and unattractive in appearance but often outstanding for flavour. Plants may be grown in rows or as specimens, smaller bushes as edging or in pots and even hanging baskets, taller varieties trained against walls, trellises and fences as single stems, multiple cordons and espaliers. Grow them with basil and other leafy herbs, peppers, parsley and bright French marigolds for colourful groups in sunny corners or in tubs.

## VARIETIES

---

**DISEASE RESISTANCE KEY**

A – Alternaria alternata crown rot

F – Fusarium

L – Septoria leafspot

N – Nematodes

T – Tobacco mosaic virus

V – Verticillium

---

Tomatoes have either an indeterminate growth habit where they keep on growing and bearing or a determinate growth habit where they produce a certain number of trusses and then stop growing.

*It is essential to stake greenhouse tomatoes grown in pots securely, and to remove all surplus side shoots to admit as much light as possible.*

**Celebrity:** 70 days. AAS winner. VFNT. Very disease resistant variety even resistant to both Fusarium I and II strains. Heavy bearer. Red crack-resistant fruits of medium size. Good flavour. Determinate.

**Early Girl:** 62 days. V. Medium size fruits ripen very early. Red with good flavour. Continues well. Indeterminate.

**Gardener's Delight/Sugar Lump:** 65 days. Sweet cherry tomato with lots of tomato flavour. Similar to Sweet 100. Bred in Germany. Determinate.

**Greenhouse VFNT 130:** 70 days. Best for greenhouses and tolerant of lower light. Indeterminate vines keep growing and bearing.

**Jubilee:** 72 days. AAS winner. Golden orange round fruit with mild flavour. Heavy bearing.

**Lemon Boy:** 72 days. VFN. Small to medium size. Lemon yellow fruit. Prolific. Very good flavour. Indeterminate.

**Long Keeper:** 78 days. Light golden orange when ripe. Stores six to twelve weeks or more into winter with good quality. Indeterminate.

**Pixie Hybrid II:** 52 days. VFT. Very fast ripening compact plant bred for pots on patios, greenhouses, and even windowsills. Small fruit with good flavour. Determinate.

**Roma VF:** 76 days. Red plum-shaped fruit superb for sauces, paste and Catsup and canning. Determinate.

**Super Beefsteak:** 80 days. VFN. Very large red fruit with good flavour on prolific vines. Indeterminate.

**Supersteak Hybrid:** 80 days. VFN. Very large, 450-900g (1-2lb) fruit with firm meaty flesh and good flavour.

**Sweet 100:** 65 days. Long trusses of very sweet cherry tomatoes on indeterminate plants.

**VF Hybrid:** 72 days. Medium-size crack resistant red fruit. Meaty. Also good in greenhouse. One of the best. Indeterminate.

## SOIL PREPARATION

Tomatoes need a sunny, sheltered position on fertile, well-drained soil. Fork in plenty of compost, leaves or peat at least 30cm (1ft) deep, well before planting, and leave the soil to settle thoroughly.

## SOWING AND PLANTING

Tomatoes are very sensitive to cold and must not be grown outdoors until after the last frosts. Start seeds indoors ten to twelve weeks before planting out. For indoor crops sow from January onwards in pans and transfer seedlings to 7cm (3in) pots when two true leaves are formed, or sow two to three seeds per pot and thin. Germinate in about 21°C (70°F).

Grow plants on in full light to keep them sturdy. When the pots are full of roots, transfer to 12cm (5in) pots; set the plants low in the pots, removing the lowest pair of true leaves from each and burying the stem up to the next pair to encourage extra rooting. Harden plants off thoroughly before planting outdoors.

The best time to plant is when the first flowers just begin to open, setting small bush varieties 30cm (1ft) square, larger bushes 45cm (18in) square, and tall kinds 45cm (18in) apart for single cordons, 90cm (3ft) for multiples, and up to 180cm (6ft) for espaliers. Plant the moist root ball 2.5-5cm (1-2in) below the soil surface and firm into place. Any plants that have become drawn and 'leggy' are still worth using – plant them at an angle and bury the lower portion of stem, but not too deeply as the soil may not yet be warmed.

## CULTIVATION

Irregular watering can cause physiological disorders. Give about 2.5cm (1in) of water per week (5cm/2in per week in very hot areas), and avoid overfeeding with nitrogenous fertilizers which will cause excessive growth and few flowers. If flavour is very important, reduce the watering slightly (provided plants do not visibly suffer) and give high-potash feeds at three-weekly intervals from the time first fruits set; smaller but richly flavoured fruits will then be produced. Mulch under each plant, to protect the fruit from soil splashes.

Bush varieties need no pruning, but heavily laden branches may benefit from support. Stake single cordons, removing side shoots as they form, and pinching out the growing top two leaves above the fourth truss of flowers. If side shoots are left until 7-10cm (3-4in) long, they can be snapped off at their base and rooted in pots to provide later fruiting plants.

For multiple cordons, allow two side shoots to develop low down and train these at 45° on each side of the main stem, pinching out all other side shoots. On low fences and walls, either train a single cordon at an angle, or pinch out the main stem two leaves above the first truss, allow two new stems to develop and train these at 45° in a 'V' shape. Several stems from each plant may be espaliered on walls and trelliswork, but care must be taken to provide strong supports for the heavy plants.

For pot cultivation on patios or in a greenhouse, transfer taller varieties to 23-25cm (9-10in) pots of good soil-based potting mixture, inserting a strong cane for each plant. Tie at frequent intervals, and remove any side shoots that form at the base of leaves. Water regularly and ventilate when temperatures rise above 21°C (70°F), or stand plants outdoors in prolonged warm weather. Tap flowering plants to disperse the pollen, pinch out the growing tips at the tops of the canes (leaving two leaves beyond the top flower truss) and cleanly remove all the leaves below the lowest truss, repeating this as each truss of fruit is cleared. Bush varieties can be grown in 10-15cm (4-6in) pots according to size and need no staking.

## HARVEST

Pick fruits when almost fully coloured – they will finish ripening indoors, while others are encouraged to mature on the plant. There is no need to thin any healthy leaves unless these heavily shade fruit. At the end of the season, cover smaller plants outdoors with cloches to complete ripening, or pull up plants altogether. They may be hung upside down in an airy shed for a week or two, or the tomatoes can be laid in a box lined with newspaper (include one or two fruits already changing colour as these produce ethylene and help the others to ripen).

# TURNIP (*Brassica campestris* ssp. *rapifera*), and **SWEDE/RUTABAGA** (*Brassica napus*)

**Seeds:** 400/g, 10,000/oz

**Germination:** 1-2 weeks; 80%

**Height:** 30-45cm (12-18in)

**Space:** turnips – summer 15cm (6in) sq; winter 23cm (9in) sq; 7cm (3in) for tops; swedes 20-25cm (8-10in) sq

**Sow:** turnips – February in a cold frame; outdoors – summer March to June; winter July to August; tops August to September; swedes May to June

**Harvest:** turnips – summer May to September; winter October to March; tops March to April; swedes August to March

**Yield:** 450g-1.3kg (1-3lb) per 30 cm (1ft) row

Annual crop

To many people turnips are a rather uninteresting winter root vegetable. Yet an early variety, grown fast and pulled while young, will produce crisp tender roots with good flavour cooked or raw. Both white- and yellow-fleshed varieties are available, the latter often keeping sound for longer in store. The best turnips are grown in late spring and early summer, and again in late autumn and winter. It is a cool season crop, rarely succeeding in hot summers or on dry soils; on the other hand, the seeds are sensitive to cold temperatures and plants sown too early will run to flower without developing useful roots.

Compared with turnips, swedes are a recent introduction, coming to Britain only about 200 years ago from Sweden. At first they were called Swedish turnips, turnip-rooted cabbages, or rutabagas (as they are known in the USA), and grown mainly as a forage crop. Garden

*Swedes (rutabaga) are safely stored in a cool shed* (top right). *Do not discard misshapen or surplus roots, but force them instead in the same way as chicory.*

varieties, however, are always worth cultivating, especially where winters are generally too severe for turnips; swedes are much hardier, and given sufficient water during growth, will crop more heavily than turnips and also store better. Dormant roots can be forced into growth, either in heat or by mounding soil over them outdoors, to produce very succulent and tasty young leaves.

Fast turnip varieties take about 60 days to mature, and plants can be grown as catch crops between other slower vegetables. Swedes take about a month longer to reach useable size, and are best given a small area to themselves, perhaps around soft fruit bushes where they will appreciate the high fertility and make attractive leafy ground cover.

## VARIETIES
### Turnip
**American Purple Top:** 90 days. Large round yellow roots with purple shoulder.

**DeNancy:** 42 days. Crisp, mild-flavoured round turnips, purple on top.

**Gilfeather Turnip:** 75 days. Old American

## HAMBURG/TURNIP-ROOTED PARSLEY (*Petroselinum crispum* var. *tuberosum*)

Although seeds are regularly offered in most catalogues, this dual-purpose crop is not yet as popular with British or American gardeners as it is throughout the rest of Europe. The root resembles a parsnip more than a turnip; it grows about 15-25cm (6-10in) long, tapering from 5-7cm (2-3in) across at the top, and tastes rather like parsley when used raw, or celeriac when cooked. The very decorative foliage resembles plain-leaved parsley in appearance and taste, and can be picked for flavouring any time during its long season of growth. Plants succeed in any good friable soil, in full sun or light shade. Grow them in the same way as parsnips, and use the roots from late autumn onwards; surplus roots can be lifted and stored, or will survive an average winter if left in the ground until they are needed.

*In addition to more conventional cultivation for their roots, turnips have always been appreciated as a spring leaf crop, which can be earthed up and blanched.*

variety developed in Vermont. Sweet white egg-shaped variety. Good for greens, too.

**Just Right:**  60 days. AAS winner. White roots with flat shape. Also good for greens.

**Purple Top White Globe:**  57 days. Round white roots, purple on top. Stores well.

**Royal Crown:**  52 days. Vigorous fast variety with round white roots and purple shoulders. Holds well. Thick deep green leaves.

**Tokyo Cross:**  35 days. AAS winner. Very early variety that can be harvested when 5cm (2in) in diameter until it reaches 15cm (6in), without getting woody.

**White Lady Hybrid:**  40 days. Crisp, sweet white flesh even when large. Tender greens.

### Rutabaga
**American Purple Top:**  90 days. Large yellow roots with purple shoulders.

**Laurentian:**  95 days. Purple-topped roots with pale yellow flesh.

**Pike:**  100 days. Large tops provide better protection from frost so roots can be dug later in autumn. Popular in Maine.

### SOIL PREPARATION
If tough woody roots are to be avoided, soils must include moisture-retentive humus. Fork over the soil before sowing, mixing in plenty of compost or rotted leaves, and a dressing of lime if the ground is acid. Extra potash improves the flavour and firmness of swedes.

### SOWING
Both crops are sown where they are to grow. For earliest turnips, sow a forcing variety under cloches or in a cold frame during March, thinning seedlings to 15cm (6in) apart each way. Sow a summer variety outdoors every three to four weeks thereafter for succession. In hot gardens, however, summer sowings are a waste of time, and it is best to sow in March and April, and then again in July.

For winter crops, sow a hardy variety in July or August, thinning seedlings to 23cm (9in) apart each way. Plants intended for spring 'greens' are sown in late August or early September, in rows 23cm (9in) apart and thinned to leave seedlings every 7cm (3in).

Make a single sowing of swedes (rutabagas) in May in the north, midsummer in the south, thin seedlings to 20-25cm (8-10in) each way.

### CULTIVATION
Both crops need consistently moist soils. Water before the ground dries out, and mulch plants with grass clippings; beware of watering too often, however, as this increases the weight of the roots at the expense of flavour.

### HARVEST
Pull early varieties as soon as they are a useable size, and clear before they become large and woody. Winter crops can be dug as required, or the roots can be lifted in late autumn before the soil freezes and stored in the same way as beet.

Plants grown for 'greens' are left in the ground over winter. Cut their leaves in spring when they are about 15cm (6in) high, and repeat whenever re-growth reaches this height.

Start to use swedes (rutabagas) when they are still medium-sized; at this stage they are at their best – crisp, tender and juicy. The rest of the crop can be left in the ground in warm regions for digging over winter, or roots may be lifted and stored as for turnips. Do not discard misshapen or overgrown roots, as these are useful for producing swede (rutabaga) tops.

To force swede (rutabaga) tops, pack a box with a single layer of roots, upright and touching, and fill the gaps with soil; cover and force in the same way as chicory. Roots buried outdoors can be covered with about 15cm (6in) of soil to blanch their new growth in spring, again like chicory (see page 136).

# GREENFINGERS TOOLS

**SELECTION** (for **Pruning Tools**, see p. 64)
Good tools are expensive, but can last a lifetime. Although cheaper models are adequate for occasional light work, their prolonged use can sometimes cause discomfort and tiredness, and in clay soils poor-quality tools are liable to bend or even break. Test a tool's weight and balance before buying; there is usually a choice of lighter or heavier models and different styles of handle. Many gardeners find traditional wooden handles more shock-absorbent than metal or plastic ones, and therefore less tiring to use; they are also more easily repaired.

## GARDEN FORKS AND SPADES
Buy one of each, in the size that feels most comfortable to use. A fork is the less dispensable of the two, equally useful for digging and raking, superficial cultivation and spreading mulches or manure. With both tools there is usually a choice of D-or T-shaped grips; occasionally they can be fitted with long, straight handles, which some people prefer for their increased leverage. Stainless steel models are very expensive, but durable and easier to keep clean and rust-free. On sticky ground other kinds need frequent cleaning while in use: an old paint scraper is valuable for this, although it sometimes helps during use to dip the blades regularly in a bucket of water to prevent soil from accumulating. When digging, always keep a spade or fork upright and insert it to its full depth – if it is hard work at first, do a little at a time rather than allow the quality of the work to deteriorate.

## HOES
Numerous kinds of hoe are available with specialized heads for weeding or tilling, but the most versatile are still the two main traditional kinds. The Dutch or scuffle hoe has a blade set at a slight angle to its handle, and is pushed forwards to loosen the soil and slice off the tops of weeds. The blade of the draw or common garden hoe, on the other hand, is attached to a curved neck and used to chop out weeds, mark drills for sowing, and to earth up plants. Both have long handles, and are easy to use if kept clean and sharp.

## RAKES
A metal-toothed garden rake has many roles apart from preparing a level tilth. Many gardeners use only a rake when sowing seeds outdoors, using the back or the flat of the head for opening, refilling and tamping the drills. Seedlings can be thinned by drawing a rake across the rows, while an old one with broken teeth can be adapted for marking out parallel seed drills or loosening the soil between close rows of seedlings. For levelling large areas, a wide wooden rake is quicker and more accurate; the wooden peg teeth sometimes break, but replacements can either be bought or whittled with a knife.

## SMALL HAND TOOLS
For close work between plants a short-handled fork is invaluable, especially a sturdy model with prongs turned at right angles to the blade, as these do not easily bend. A similar size fork with a long handle is useful for reaching the back of beds. A hand trowel, preferably with a cranked neck, will be needed for planting. Test it for comfort when held like a dagger; this is the easiest way to make a hole in the soil, and a plant can be firmed in with the end of the handle without changing one's grip. Forks and trowels are both available in stainless steel; and brightly coloured handles help to prevent tools being lost outside. Various other small tools, such as an onion hoe or short-handled cultivator for stirring the soil in confined places between plants, can be acquired as needed.

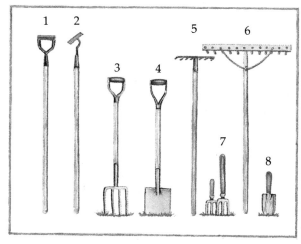

*A basic collection of essential gardening tools. Most valuable of all is the digging fork (3) or its smaller version the border fork, both adaptable for cultivating the soil surface and raking it roughly level. The digging spade (4) should be as large as is manageable. Dutch (1) and draw hoes (2) are used for weed control and sowing. For preparing a fine soil tilth, use the standard metal rake (5), but for levelling large areas the old-fashioned wooden rake (6) is best. A variety of smaller tools will be needed, especially hand-forks (7) and trowels (8).*

## CLEANING AND MAINTENANCE
Scrape off accumulated soil from all tools before putting them away, ideally hung up clear of the ground. If they are not likely to be used for a week or two, clean off any dried soil with a wire or scrubbing brush (pay particular attention to the handles because dried lumps of soil can cause blisters). Brush or wipe bare metal with old sump oil to keep it free from rust, and once a year paint wooden handles with linseed oil to prevent cracking. Occasionally sharpen the blades of Dutch (scuffle) hoes to keep them efficient. Pruners need re-grinding each season and can then be kept keen with a small oilstone. Sharpen pruning saws with a triangular file and reset the teeth to the correct angle. Bow-saw blades with hardened teeth cannot be sharpened, but resetting may prolong their life.

# SOILS

Plants in a garden can only be as good as the soil in which they grow. Few gardeners have perfect soil which produces reliable crops in almost any season with little or no effort, and even the best ground needs annual replenishment to maintain its fertility. No soil is hopeless, and all kinds will benefit from a continuous programme of soil husbandry. Permanent change takes time, especially on exhausted, neglected or very inhospitable ground, but within a season or two of starting to feed and cultivate the soil rather than the plants, an improvement will be noticeable.

## IMPROVING SOILS

All ground that is to grow crops has to be friable and free-draining to encourage healthy root development. This is hardest to achieve on clay soil, often very fertile but sticky or greasy, and frequently refusing to crumble even with annual deep digging. The fine clay particles bind tightly together to exclude air and impede drainage; cultivation consists of opening the texture by working in coarse materials such as strawy manure, partly decayed leaves or grit.

Hasten this physical improvement by adding annual dressings of a clay-soil conditioner. These are often expensive, but a cheap and effective substitute can be made at home by mixing 80 per cent gypsum (calcium sulphate) with 20 per cent dolomite (magnesium limestone). Spread 125g per sq m (4oz per sq yd) in autumn and again in spring, hoeing it in where possible or leaving for rain to wash it into the ground. Repeat annually until the soil is acceptably crumbly, when 60-125g per sq m (2-4oz per sq yd) in the autumn should be sufficient each year if the soil is also mulched.

*Vigorous growth and consistently heavy yields depend primarily on high soil fertility, which can be maintained with cultivation and the regular addition of humus.*

Check the drainage if clay stays persistently wet – local patches can often be cured by a surface drain to a soakaway, or by using extra soil to raise the level of the cultivated bed. Clay naturally retains water, often a virtue in summer, but it can delay sowing and planting in spring.

Sandy soils are much easier to cultivate, warm up faster, and drain freely, but they do not hold moisture long in summer, and nutrients soon disappear, especially in a wet season. They need to be packed with organic matter to increase their absorbency, and benefit from mulching to prevent a hard crust forming after heavy rain (see also **Feeding** p.174).

## ACID AND ALKALINE SOILS

Most soils need lime to help make nutrients available to plants. In alkaline or 'chalky' soils excess lime locks up elements needed for healthy growth. A more common problem is soil acidity, which reduces the activities of essential micro-organisms and can cause toxic accumulations of normally beneficial elements.

Inexpensive test kits can be bought for checking soil samples taken from several evenly-spaced sites around the garden. The result will be given as a 'pH' value, usually between 4.5 (very acid) and 7.5 (moderately alkaline). Although some crops such as potatoes like moderately acid soil, and brassicas prefer alkaline conditions, most plants grow best within the range 6.5-7.0.

Cultivated ground tends to become more acid, a tendency corrected by the addition of lime (as ground limestone or dolomite) or calcified seaweed. Application rates vary considerably according to the type of soil (see 'pH', **Glossary** p.184), but precision is rarely critical, and it is usually enough to give a dressing of lime before cultivating the ground for lime-loving crops. Alkaline soils can be made more acid with sulphur, peat, leaf mould or garden compost made without supplementary lime.

# SOWING & PLANTING

Seeds need warmth, moisture and air to germinate, which is why seedlings emerge slowly, if at all, in cold, dry or compacted soils. To grow into healthy plants, seeds must germinate quickly. In spring it is often better to delay outdoor sowing for a week or two until temperatures rise; very early sowings are a waste of time if the ground has not warmed up, as many seeds will rot before they can germinate. If an early start is to be made, first warm the soil with cloches for a fortnight, or sow in a cold frame or greenhouse (see **Glass** pp.176-177).

Where seeds are to be sown in situ, choose a suitable aspect for the time of year – a warm, sunny position for spring and autumn lettuces, for example, but a lightly shaded one for summer crops. Alternatively, sow in a seed bed and transplant to the appropriate position. This is often the easiest method if vegetables are to be fitted amongst other plants.

A surface that is very firm or that has developed a crust after heavy rains must be broken up to produce a crumbly tilth; on the other hand, ground that has recently been deeply cultivated will be too loose and soft for sowing, and should either be consolidated by light treading or left for a week or two to settle. Prepare a tilth for sowing by stirring the surface with a hoe, fork or, on a larger scale, with a rotary tiller. Rake as level as possible, skimming off any stones and clods of soil to leave a fine seed bed.

## SINGLE ROWS

Rows are easier to keep cultivated if they are straight. To mark out longer rows, stretch a line between a peg at each end; lay a board on the ground with the edge as a guide for short ones. Using a stick, or the corner of a hoe or rake (teeth turned upwards), draw out an even shallow furrow or 'drill'; for short rows lay the hoe or rake handle on the ground and lightly step on it. Do not make the drill too deep, a common mistake that often results in seedlings failing to emerge. If the soil is dry, flood the drill with water and leave to drain before sowing.

Large seeds can be spaced at regular distances. Always sow smaller seeds sparingly to reduce later thinning and root disturbance. Tip a quantity from the packet into the palm of one hand, and with finger and thumb of the other sprinkle a pinch at a time along the drill. With the back of the rake draw the displaced soil into the drill to cover the seeds, and label the end of the row. On very light ground, gently tamp down the refilled soil with the head of the rake held upright.

## WIDE ROWS

Single rows widely spaced are easy to cultivate but waste space, and heavier yields can be raised by sowing broad rows, the width of a spade or rake. For larger seeds, scoop out a wide furrow with a spade piling the excavated soil to one side, space seeds in three or more equidistant parallel rows, and then cover with the displaced soil.

Alternatively, prepare a seed bed the width of the rake, and any length from a small patch to a full row. Sprinkle seeds thinly and evenly over the loose surface and gently firm them into the soil with the head of the rake. Cover the seeds with a little soil raked from one side of the strip and tamped into place. Wide rows are best watered after sowing, using a sprinkler or a watering-can with a rose (spray) fitted.

## CIRCLES AND STATIONS

In small gardens there may not be room for a special seed bed. Although short rows of seeds often fit neatly beside paths or amongst other plants, an alternative way to save space is to mark out small circles, each of which need be no more than 12-15cm (5-6in) in diameter. Loosen the surface to make a tilth for sowing, and press

*Where there is insufficient room for conventional straight rows, small quantities of seed may be sown in circles wherever there is a suitable space. Cuttings too can be rooted in the same economical way.*

the rim of a medium-sized pot into the soil, turning it gently until the circular furrow reaches the correct depth. Sow in the normal way, water the area after sowing, and insert a label in the centre of the circle. Transplant seedlings as soon as they are large enough.

Transplanting, and most thinning, will be unnecessary if seeds are sown where they are to grow, and at their final spacings. This can be done in drills instead of continuous sowing, or in individual holes made with a finger or stick to the right depth. Seeds must be large enough to separate easily into small groups – parsnips, beet, lettuce or spinach are ideal – or pelleted seed can be used. These are individually coated with a degradable substance such as clay, to make them larger and more easily sown with precision (they must be kept moist after sowing to ensure the coating breaks down). Sow normally, dropping three or four seeds into each hole or at roughly equal distances along a drill. As soon as the seedlings are large enough to handle, water them and then pull up all but the strongest at each station, firming this back

into the soil. Alternatively, ease up the seedlings with a fork, replace one and transplant the others (this does not apply to root crops, which should not be transplanted).

## TRANSPLANTING

The younger a seedling is transplanted, the quicker it recovers. Obviously it must be large enough to handle – generally the best time is when one or two true leaves have appeared, or when it is three to six weeks old. The soil must be moist; either transplant on a showery day, or water seedlings before they are dug up and again after planting. In very dry weather plants benefit from being 'puddled in': position them in their planting holes and fill these with water, which is allowed to drain away before the roots are covered with soil and firmed into place.

There is no point trimming roots or foliage in the hope of reducing the shock of transplanting, but in summer transplants can be helped to recover quickly by inverting pots over them for two or three days, and removing them each night. Early in the season, make sure that transplants from a cold frame or greenhouse have been fully hardened off (see **Glass** pp. 176-177), and cover them with cloches or newspaper in a sudden cold snap.

Although it is the leafy portion of a plant that is visible, its roots are equally important, if not more so: a plant will often survive a broken stem to grow again from below the injury, whereas serious root damage may be fatal. As well as transplanting in moist conditions, always try to avoid tearing roots.

Leave some soil adhering to the roots (with larger transplants, preserve a complete root ball), and transfer to a hole generous enough to contain them comfortably. Always plant securely, firming the soil by hand or with the end of a trowel; soil around brassicas and large plants is trodden firm. Leave the surface level and loose, and then where appropriate, mulch after watering.

## THE LIFE OF SEEDS

Home-saved seeds should be thoroughly ripened on the plant if possible, and stored in dry conditions. Many bought seeds are sealed in foil or plastic envelopes to keep them in peak condition; if these are stored unopened, the seeds will remain usable for several years. Once seeds are exposed to the air, however, they start to age normally until eventually they are too old to germinate. Stored dry and cool – perhaps in screw-top jars with a sachet of silica gel to absorb moisture – many opened packets will be worth keeping until the following season, or longer, as shown in the table, although seedling vigour can decline with age.

| SEEDS | KEEPING TIME |
|---|---|
| parsnips, scorzonera | use when opened |
| salsify, swede (rutabaga), turnip | until following year |
| beans, sweet corn (maize), peas, spinach | 2 years |
| beet (root) and leaf beets, broccoli, Brussels sprouts, cabbage, carrot, cauliflower, chicory, endive, kale, kohl rabi, leeks, lettuce | 3 years |
| aubergine (eggplant), celeriac, celery, cucumbers, marrows and other squashes, melons, onion, peppers, radish, tomato | 4 years or more |

# FEEDING & WATERING

Although some gardeners argue endlessly about the respective merits of chemical and organic (or 'natural') fertilizers, most people use a combination of both. While there is no particular virtue in using either kind exclusively, it is unfortunately true that chemical fertilizers are easier to buy and distribute around plants, with the result that in some gardens the quality of the soil deteriorates through lack of humus (partly decayed organic matter, derived usually from animal manures and plant refuse).

An essential ingredient of all cultivated soil, humus helps to break up sticky clay, binds dusty or sandy soils into a more crumbly texture, and stabilizes the drainage and water retention of both. No amount of inorganic fertilizer will compensate for its absence, because the chemicals are purely fertilizers and contribute nothing to soil texture and structure. Like them, however, humus disappears from the soil, although at a slower rate, and more must be added each year, especially where cultivation is intensive. The best way to do this is by mulching (see p.175).

While the primary use of humus is as a physical soil conditioner, many animal and plant residues also have varying amounts of nutritional value and release plant foods as they decay. Peat is an excellent conditioner and will help to increase soil acidity, but it has no food value whatsoever. Rotted leaves have a little, but the best sources are animal manures and well-made garden compost (see **Weeds** p.178), initially dug or forked into the soil, and then added as a mulch in subsequent seasons. Fresh manure is too strong for most crops; let it mature in a stack until dark and crumbly, or add it to the compost heap for blending with plant refuse. Dry concentrated manure bought in bags is an excellent and convenient substitute used in moderation as a fertilizer.

## FERTILIZERS

Regular dressings of manure or garden compost will often supply the food required by most garden crops. Their nutrients tend to be released slowly, however, and a concentrated source of immediately available food is sometimes needed when, say, plants are cropping heavily, or in spring to start over-wintered crops into growth. In these situations fertilizers, either chemical or organic, and minerals are valuable, but they seldom need to be used often or in great quantity.

Fertilizers add no bulk to the soil, nor do they improve its character. There are too many kinds to list here, but all supply nitrogen, potassium or phosphorus, either exclusively or in varying ratios, together, in some cases, with essential trace elements. Dry powders or granules are applied to the soil, while liquid concentrates and soluble powders are used to make liquid fertilizers to feed plants directly outdoors or in pots. For general use, a balanced mixture is best; fertilizers with a high proportion of nitrogen will encourage leaf and stem growth, while those rich in potash improve the quality of flowers and crops.

## WATERING

Most gardeners will be familiar with the basic need for watering in dry weather. The frequency of this can be reduced by growing plants close together so that their foliage shades the ground in between. Soils rich in humus are much slower to dry, and mulching further reduces evaporation.

When watering plants soak them thoroughly; in the case of fruit trees leave a hose trickling for several hours at the base. Merely to dampen the surface encourages vulnerable surface roots which suffer as the soil quickly dries out again. But do not water so heavily that the surplus runs away to waste. If the soil is hard or crusted, break up the surface with a fork or hoe to allow the water to soak in.

Certain crops benefit most when watered at particular stages in their development, usually from flowering onwards, or when fruits are starting to swell; leafy vegetables, on the other hand, need regular watering to ensure rapid growth. Specific requirements are noted in the individual plant entries, but it is safe to assume that all crops will grow best when the soil is kept uniformly moist.

In the absence of rain moisture is continually being lost from the soil, both by evaporation and as a result of uptake by the plants themselves. A considerable volume of water is stored in the ground, but to delay watering until obvious signs of distress appear is to wait too long, since much of the available reservoir will by then be depleted, and large amounts of water will need to be applied before an adequate moisture content is restored.

Aim then to delay water loss by adding moisture-retentive humus and by mulching. Plants growing at high density increase the demands on the reservoir, and it is better to water an integrated garden early in a drought, rather than wait until the need is obvious.

*After standing on the soil to tend plants or harvest crops, loosen the compacted surface with a hoe or fork, especially before watering; this helps the soil absorb water that otherwise would lie in puddles.*

# PROTECTION

There are a number of ways to protect plants from the weather; few of us are lucky enough to garden in ideal conditions, and most crops have to contend with the vagaries of frost, wind and drought (see **Glass** pp.176-177 for advice on frost protection).

Although, as a general rule, most crops prefer an open, sunny position, a number will tolerate light shade, especially at the height of summer when some leafy plants can scorch or run quickly to flower. Tender plants such as tomatoes, aubergines (eggplants) and the marrow or squash family appreciate full sun, as do early spring sowings of lettuce, radish, peas and carrots; the best place for these is in warm soil in front of a wall or fence facing south or south-west. Later in the season salads will be happier grown in the shade of taller plants.

Too much shade, however, can be harmful and it is no use growing the majority of crops close to large overhanging trees or tall hedges; as well as heavily shading the plants, their roots will compete for water and nutrients. Smaller shrubs, bush fruit and rows of raspberries or tall peas provide valuable shade for summer salads, cauliflowers and leafy crops.

Wind, too, can be a problem in exposed gardens. Persistent wind rapidly dries ground and checks growth, while many pollinating insects cannot work in windy conditions. Where strong winds are prevalent, it is wise to concentrate on dwarf varieties of vegetables and shorter forms of trained trees.

A wind-break may be useful, and can often shelter a distance up to ten times its height. Solid structures such as walls and close-boarded fences sometimes create turbulence, and an open fence or hedge that filters the wind is usually more effective. Wind-breaks can be used to support trained fruit or climbing vegetables, mixed perhaps with flowering plants such as roses and clematis.

*Trained on a simple framework of two or three horizontal wires, blackberries (left) make an efficient and profitable wind-break to keep cold winds away from plants such as tender varieties of globe artichokes or winter cauliflower.*

Though unattractive, a fence of wire netting is resilient and valuable as a framework for coverage by plants. In a few years it can be transformed into a hedge by planting various kinds of ivy along its base, and training these up a fence until they disguise the wire. At intervals along its length, plant rambling roses, blackberries and loganberries together with one or two small fruit trees. The ivy is clipped back to form a neat slim hedge when the roses or brambles are pruned at the end of the season.

Sometimes only temporary wind-breaks are needed. In exposed gardens, it may be advisable to erect a shelter made from one or two thicknesses of sacking supported on short stakes, to protect newly planted fruit bushes or evergreen shrubs from cold seasonal winds until they are established. Where a semi-permanent arrangement is necessary, to shelter a young bay tree during its early years for example, woven hurdles are a more attractive and durable substitute. Rows of Jerusalem artichokes or raspberries will also serve as efficient wind-breaks, but they will need support of some kind.

## MULCHING

Most plants benefit considerably from mulching; covering the soil protects against extreme weather conditions, prevents rapid evaporation of moisture, and in many cases provides a steady supply of nutrients. While it is not a substitute for thorough cultivation, mulching ground that has been prepared and cleared of weeds will greatly reduce the need for further cultivation.

A mulch of organic material will preserve the cultivated structure of both heavy and light soils, and encourage worms, whose activity gradually improves the soil texture. Mulching also keeps soil temperatures more constant in hot or cold weather, and suppresses annual weed growth.

Many kinds of material make useful mulches; animal manures can be spread around greedy plants such as brassicas or blackcurrants, and garden compost is suitable for most plants if it is well made and free from weed seeds. Grass clippings are excellent, provided lawns have not recently been treated with weedkillers; if spread thickly, clippings tend to get very hot at first, and it is better to lay two or three 5cm (2in) layers at fortnightly intervals. Mixing grass clippings with autumn leaves will hasten their decomposition and produce a coarse, fibrous blend for mulching.

Mulches delay changes to the soil and tend to maintain those conditions prevailing at the time of application. Always apply a mulch, therefore, when the soil is moist, but not soaking wet. In areas with very cold winters, spread a thick mulch in autumn before the first frosts to protect plants from alternate freezing and thawing. Where winters are normally mild, mulch in spring after the soil has started to warm up. Do not pack the material too closely around stems, as this can encourage disease. Replace mulches annually after first lightly turning in residues from the previous layer when cultivating in spring or autumn.

# GLASS

(see also **Fruit in the Greenhouse** pp. 72-73)
Greenhouses, cold frames and cloches are all valuable for extending the cropping season, and for protecting plants in climates colder than those to which they are naturally adapted. A small greenhouse, whether made of glass or plastic, can be used for overwintering tender plants or housing early flowering fruit in pots. If it has a soil border, winter salads and even one or two fruit trees will grow happily in frost-free temperatures, while in cooler districts summer crops such as tomatoes, cucumbers and aubergines (eggplants) all fruit more reliably under glass. Perhaps its most popular use, however, is for protecting early sowings.

## SOWING UNDER GLASS
Seeds can be sown in shallow pots or pans, the seedlings then transferred when large enough to grow on in trays (flats). This transplanting (or 'pricking out') can be avoided by using special trays, sometimes called cell trays or modules, each divided into a number of separate cells. In these, seeds are sown individually or in clusters and grow undisturbed until planted out; seedlings may also be pricked out into these trays to reduce root damage at planting time. Trays can be bought with cells of various sizes, and are usually supplied with a special board for firming the compost prior to sowing.

When using ordinary seed trays, cover the bottom with a thin layer of peat, and then fill with the sowing mixture; firm around the edges with your fingers, and level. Soil-based mixtures should be pressed down with a block of wood, but trays filled with peat mixtures are just tapped sharply to settle the contents. The final level should be about 1cm (½in) below the rim. Water the compost and sow the seeds thinly with finger and thumb, and cover with a sprinkling of finely sieved compost (the easiest way to spread this is to half fill a plastic pot that

has small drainage holes, and shake it over the tray to dredge the surface evenly). Cover the tray with a pane of glass and then a sheet of newspaper (or enclose the tray in an opaque plastic bag), which are removed as soon as seedlings emerge.

## PRICKING OUT
Most seedlings in trays or pots need to be pricked out to other trays, filled with a potting mixture. As soon as seedlings can be handled, loosen a few from the soil with a table fork or the point of a pencil, and transfer them one at a time to holes made with the pencil about 5cm (2in) apart each way. Always hold a seedling by

*Large cloches give plants room to develop and improve the circulation of air, which discourages mildew. This model has sliding panels for easy access and ventilation.*

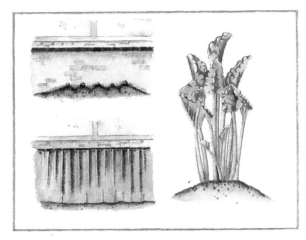

*Empty space beneath greenhouse staging is an ideal place to force early supplies of seakale, chicory or rhubarb (above). Crowns must be surrounded by thick material to exclude all light, but extra heat is not necessary unless very early crops are required.*

one leaf, because the stem is very fragile at this stage and easily crushed. Lightly firm in each seedling, tap the tray at each end to level the soil, and water with a fine spray. Keep out of direct sunlight for a few days until the seedlings are actively growing.

## POTTING
Seedlings such as tomatoes and aubergines (eggplants) can be pricked out individually into small pots filled with potting mixture and tapped to settle the contents. As soon as the roots begin to grow uniformly around the inside, the plant is ready to be moved on into the next size pot, or planted in a growing bag or (after hardening off) outdoors. When potting on, either tap the plant out of its container and transfer directly to the new pot, filling the space around the root ball with fresh potting mixture; or first make a mould by packing compost around the empty pot, and then fit the plant's root ball into this, tapping it gently into place and watering.

## FORCING

Do not throw away used sowing and potting soil after pricking out or repotting as it can be emptied into a cold frame for direct sowings, or used for mixing into heavy soil where root crops are to be grown. It is also valuable for packing around roots that are being forced in the greenhouse, because these will contain enough food to support their forced growth and therefore do not need fresh soil. A crop such as Witloof chicory is forced in pots (see p.136), whereas rhubarb or seakale crowns are usually packed together on the floor of a greenhouse, preferably under staging where they can be enclosed with a curtain of sacking to exclude light. Surround the roots with used compost and keep this consistently moist until the forced crop is finished. The roots are then discarded, and the potting mixture spread outdoors or in a cold frame.

## COLD FRAMES

Although a cold frame, unless heated, is not a totally safe place in which to overwinter tender plants, most kinds will protect their contents from a few degrees of frost, especially if covered on very cold nights with several layers of sacking or old carpets. Whether fixed or portable, a frame with a soil base is the best investment and is likely to be in use all year round. It is very useful for sowing seeds early or rooting cuttings directly into the soil, for growing winter crops such as lettuce or other salads, and later in the season can be planted with melons, bush tomatoes or self-blanching celery. A cold frame is also important when hardening off plants; gradually increase the amount of ventilation given, first by day and then at night, until plants are fully adjusted to outdoor conditions.

## CLOCHES

One of the simplest ways to protect early or late crops from cold weather is to use cloches, made from glass or polythene in a wide variety of designs. On a large scale cloches are usually laid end to end to cover long rows, but in an integrated garden the most useful kinds are short units complete with ends, or separate four-sided hand lights (these can be improvised from large plastic containers with their bottoms removed, or even clear plastic bags over wire hoops). They can be placed over small sowings or individual plants, or may be used for covering patches of ground for a week or two in early spring to warm and dry the soil in preparation for sowing. In sunny weather temperatures beneath cloches can rise dramatically; ventilate either by raising one side of the cloche on a stone or block, or by temporarily removing it altogether. This should also be done to admit pollinating insects to plants in flower, and occasionally during a warm shower or for watering in dry weather.

*Unlike modern cloches, which are strictly functional, traditional versions such as the bell-jar (left) and the lantern frame (right) are decorative but no less efficient.*

## POTTING AND SOWING MIXTURES

Good soil- and peat-based mixtures are readily available for all sowing and potting requirements. However, many people prefer to blend their own. Chemical supplements can be bought for adding, in varying proportions, to peat or a peat/sand mixture, and these are usually adequate, although incorporated fertilizers (unless specifically slow-release) tend to be exhausted after six to eight weeks.

High-quality mixtures based on fibrous loam (soil rich in plant remains) are more stable and long-lasting, especially for potted trees. Bought soil-based mixtures are usually made to the John Innes formulae and classed as JI seed compost, and JI potting compost No. 1, 2 or 3 according to the level of included fertilizers. For general purposes the JI formulae can be adapted, using either very good garden soil or loam specially prepared from turf (see p.179).

Seed mix: mix together two parts (by volume) loam, two parts sphagnum moss peat and one part coarse sand. To every 9-litre (2 gal) bucketful add 28g (1oz) lime.

Potting mix: mix seven parts loam, three parts peat and two parts coarse sand. To each bucketful add 28g (1oz) lime and 112g (4oz) seaweed meal (or balanced chemical fertilizer according to maker's recommendations). This mixture is adequate for young plants; for later potting on and for trees in pots, double the lime and fertilizer rates. For acid-loving plants such as blueberries, omit the lime.

Use within a few weeks of mixing because long storage can cause deterioration in quality; warm the mixture overnight in a greenhouse before use.

# WEEDS

By the broadest definition, a weed is any plant in the wrong place. Self-sown lupins in the middle of a sage bush or unwanted forget-me-nots amongst mats of thyme are as much weeds as couch grass growing inaccessibly beneath gooseberry bushes and convolvulus climbing up raspberry canes. In any kind of garden weeds will be sure to appear, from seeds brought to the surface during cultivation, scattered by plants that have not been dead-headed, or carried in on the wind or by birds. Whether they become a problem depends on the methods that can be adopted to control them.

Where vegetables and fruit are grown in widely spaced rows, frequent surface cultivation is used to prevent weed growth. These days commercial growers use a variety of herbicides formulated to kill specific weeds without harming adjacent crops, but these are rarely available to amateurs, who usually have to make do with broad spectrum weedkillers applied carefully amongst other plants. In an integrated garden, however, close planting leaves little room for extensive hoeing, while herbicides are difficult to apply except for spot treatment of individual weeds.

Alternative approaches will reduce the incidence of weeds. Where possible start with clean ground, either by thoroughly forking out all fragments of perennial weed roots, or by clearing the ground before planting with a short-lived total weedkiller such as glyphosate or ammonium sulphamate. Most perennial weeds have easily identifiable roots that can be removed with patience from friable soil; usually any piece left behind will grow, and it is worth taking time to fork out as many pieces as possible, since these will be harder to eradicate once plants are in place.

It is sometimes suggested that the cottage garden tradition of close planting prevents

*With the exception of vigorous perennial species, the growth of most weeds is suppressed by a deep mulch. Gravel is one suitable material, both spread around woody plants or, as here, used for permanently surfacing areas between beds.*

weeds from growing, but this is not strictly true: plants that touch each other shade the soil and depress a lot of weed growth, but some always manage to grow. In properly tended soil, hand-weeding need not be a chore, and is advisable where valuable self-sown seedlings may be mixed with the weeds. Feeding and protecting plants with a mulch discourages many annual weeds from germinating, partly by smothering them and also by avoiding soil disturbance which would otherwise bring buried seeds to the surface.

In dry weather, watering individual plants rather than soaking a whole area concentrates the water where it is needed, but also denies it to weed seeds lying dormant in bare ground amongst plants. Always pull up weeds before they set seed (for safety, before they flower), and do not leave bundles of removed weeds lying on the ground as seeds will continue to ripen and fall where the plants lie. Unless seedlings are wanted for transplanting elsewhere, dead-head all flowering plants before they can disperse their seeds; this saves much work later and by conserving a plant's energy will often extend its life.

If prevented from seeding, otherwise invasive plants such as dandelions, both attractive and edible, can be left to grow. Remember weeds only grow in congenial surroundings and are therefore useful indicators of soil type and condition. Mosses and dock, for example, grow best in sour (acid), wet soil that usually needs liming and draining for other plants to grow well. Chicory, goosegrass, sun spurge (wartweed) and coltsfoot, on the other hand, should encourage gardeners as they usually indicate a balanced, fertile soil.

## DISPOSING OF WEEDS
Even the most pernicious weeds release plant nutrients as they decay, and where possible they should be put to use. A surface covering of annual weeds can be dug or rotavated in as a green manure. Doing this with perennial weeds, however, merely propagates them and encourages their spread; pull or fork them up and disperse them in a compost heap if enough heat can be generated to kill them. Altern-atively, first lay them in the sun on a hard surface until thoroughly dried, and then compost them; couch grass and convolvulus roots treated in this way are rich sources of minerals and can be composted safely. Otherwise, perennial weeds, together with all diseased plants, are best burnt, saving the resulting ash to spread on the garden as a free supply of potash.

## COMPOST HEAPS
Most gardeners try to construct a compost heap, but few succeed in making good-quality garden compost free from weed seeds or viable roots. Much has been written and discussed about the art of efficient composting, which depends ultimately on generating enough heat to kill all unwelcome seeds and organisms. Many kinds

of compost container are available, or a home-made version can be constructed by erecting a square pen of wire netting, lined on the inside with sheets of cardboard. Any vegetable matter that will decompose can be included in the heap, except diseased plants, which are best burnt, as are twigs and other woody materials unless first passed through a shredder. Always spread the materials in thin layers to avoid soggy concentrations, and add a sprinkling of lime and/or a compost activator every few centimetres as the heap is built. When the bin is full, cover with a piece of old carpet and leave for several months. Turning the heap once or twice to mix the contents will accelerate the process. The finished compost can be spread as a mulch or dug into the soil if not thoroughly decomposed.

## USING LEAVES
Never burn autumn leaves as these are a valuable free source of humus and small amounts of nutrients. If space is available, stack the gathered leaves like a compost heap and leave to decay. They will rot quicker if first shredded by passing a rotary mower over them once or twice, or if mixed with grass clippings and then stacked. After six to twelve months' decay the coarse leaf mould can be used for mulching or forking into the soil; if left for a further year, the material will be fine enough to use as a substitute for peat in potting mixtures. Autumn leaves can be spread fresh on the ground and forked or rotavated in, and are also useful for heaping over dormant tender plants in winter.

## TURF
Surplus turf is another useful waste product, the top centimetre or two being full of roots which, when decayed, will supply coarse humus. Where lawns encroach on to paths, or turf is cut when making or extending a bed, save the lifted pieces and build them into a

stack, laying them upside down on top of each other. After a year all the grass except that on the outside of the stack will be dead. The fibrous roots can then be torn apart for adding to compost mixtures when potting fruit or filling larger tubs. When well decayed it can be used as part or all of the loam content of soil-based potting mixtures. Where turf cannot be stacked, bury it upside down at the bottom of planting holes for fruit, or in trenches when digging open ground. Small pieces of decayed turf were once sown with peas and other early crops under glass, in the same way as peat blocks are used today, while whole turves have sometimes been used to construct the sides of improvised cold frames.

*Wood-chip or shredded-bark mulches are ideal for protecting prostrate crops such as marrows/squash* (above) *and for covering old mats or newspapers laid as access paths.*

# FIRST AID

Gardens in which many different kinds of plants are freely mixed seldom experience the widespread incidence of pests and diseases that commonly affect large areas of single crops; there are not enough of any particular host plant to sustain a large pest population or epidemic of disease. However, many insects and disorders have alternative hosts, and this adaptability on their part, combined with successional plantings of susceptible plants, usually makes total pest eradication impossible. Gardeners therefore have to accept the permanent presence, albeit at a low level, of insect pests and disorders.

In most gardens where fertile soil supports healthy, vigorous plants, disorders are few and rarely serious. A balanced community of insect prey and predators normally exists if the equilibrium is not disrupted by the over-zealous use of chemical insecticides, and diseases are usually kept under control if emphasis is laid on the health and vitality of the plants. If the plants are encouraged to grow well, a few simple precautionary measures will save a lot of urgent attention later.

Rotation (see p.13) is a valuable means of preventing any disorder from becoming endemic. Although some serious pests and diseases can survive for many years in the soil, they can often be prevented from occurring in the first place by waiting two or three years before again growing a crop in the same piece of ground. For a similar reason, never plant a tree or shrub in soil where a member of the same family previously grew; a debilitating condition known as specific replant disease is likely to prevent the new plant from thriving.

Where possible, and certainly in areas where problems are known to be endemic, choose varieties that are resistant to a pest or disease. Plant breeding is concentrating on the development of genetic resistance as the most

promising method of preventing disorders, and in soils known to be infected with eelworm or canker, for example, it would be sensible to choose resistant varieties of potato and parsnip. Fungal disorders such as mildew are often more prevalent in early autumn, and peas sown to crop at this time are liable to infection unless mildew resistant.

Where health certification exists, plant only approved stocks; this applies particularly to potatoes and fruit, which are normally inspected for freedom from virus infection. Many kinds of virus exist, and most gradually reduce the vigour and yield of affected plants. Some fruit varieties are virus tolerant, which means the plants may carry the infection for years without developing symptoms, but the disease can be passed on by insect pests to any susceptible variety planted nearby.

As well as buying only virus-free plants, learn to recognize early symptoms of disease. Yellow, spotted, crinkled or unusually small leaves are all possible signs of virus infection. Previous generations of gardeners did not try to cure plant diseases, but ruthlessly dug up and destroyed any unthrifty plant to protect the rest. This policy is sound, and should become part of routine garden hygiene. Never leave diseased material lying around, even on a compost heap, and this includes dead leaves and prunings, all of which are potential hosts for fungal disorders that depend on neglect to gain a foothold.

Encourage natural predators which often keep insect pest populations under control. Ladybird, lacewing and hover-fly larvae are all voracious predators of aphids, and can be attracted into the garden by many species of flowers, especially members of the Aster family, such as chrysanthemums, cosmos and tagetes (marigolds). Most black beetles feed on soil pests and should be regarded as allies; they tend to live beneath stones and prostrate plants, and welcome the protection of mulches. Larger

predators such as frogs and birds are all worth encouraging into the garden.

By a combination of promoting the positive health of the garden and avoiding situations that invite trouble, it should be possible to treat any disorders with the simplest remedies. There is rarely any need to apply broad-spectrum chemicals, the frequent and liberal use of which is liable to kill beneficial insects and predators, as well as fostering resistant strains of the pest or disease they are intended to control.

Where possible, only non-chemical or specific remedies non-toxic to beneficial species are recommended here, and only the commonest pests and diseases likely to occur in a mixed garden are listed; for fuller details or information about rarer ailments, consult a handbook of pests and diseases.

## MAJOR PLANT PESTS

**Aphids:** a large group of small soft-bodied insects that feed on plant juices. The commonest kinds are green, black, or woolly grey (these may occur above or below ground). Large colonies can develop and usually exude sticky honeydew, which turns black as it becomes infected with sooty mould. Heavy infestations of aphids weaken plants and often spread virus diseases from one plant to another. Watch out for invasion by winged aphids, which tend to migrate en masse on certain warm summer days. These settle and produce wingless generations that rapidly colonize soft shoots, buds and the undersides of leaves. They are a popular food for many predators and this may prevent a population explosion. Spray at an early stage with insecticidal soap (or a solution of two tablespoons dish-washing liquid in 4.5 litres/1 gal of water), or with derris (rotenone), pyrethrum or malathion.

**Caterpillars and other larvae:** these can be serious pests, especially on brassicas and fruit, where the larvae of several moths will turn leaves into skeletons, or bore into stems and fruit and render it inedible. Those that feed on leaves quickly betray their presence and can be picked off and destroyed. Where there are too many for this simple treatment, spray with salt solution (60g per 4.5 litre/2oz per gal of water), derris (rotenone), quassia or *Bacillus thuringiensis,* a specific fungal preparation that kills most moth and butterfly caterpillars. The only control for larvae that have bored into stems is to prune back to unaffected wood or insert a length of wire into the tunnel to kill the larvae. Tying a greaseband around tree trunks in autumn will trap many wingless moths as they crawl up to lay their eggs. The codling moth, whose larva is the familiar maggot in apples, can be controlled by suspending pheromone traps in the trees. Soil caterpillars such as cutworms and leatherjackets can be treated with *Bacillus thuringiensis,* but frequent forking and cultivation will usually expose most to natural predators such as birds and beetles.

**Red spider mite:** minute sucking insects whose presence is usually betrayed by a yellow spotting and bronze sheen on leaves; with serious infestations, fine webs appear draped between leaves and stems. These pests are encouraged by warm dry conditions, both outdoors and under glass. Insecticidal soap and derris are useful against heavy infestations, but it is better to deter the mites, which dislike damp conditions, by forcefully spraying foliage with a hose whenever watering. Under glass, dampen paths and staging daily in hot weather and spray the undersides of leaves early in the day to allow time to dry by nightfall.

**Scale insects:** small sap-feeding insects that normally live beneath hard or waxy shells stuck to stems and the undersides of leaves. Honeydew is produced and sooty mould usually follows. A serious infestation can be debilitating, but treatment is difficult. Check new stock for signs of scales, and sponge them

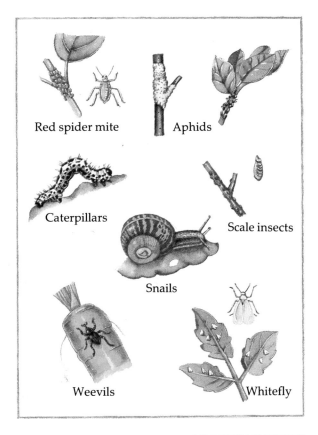

Red spider mite  Aphids

Caterpillars

Scale insects

Snails

Weevils  Whitefly

off with soapy water. Unprotected juveniles migrate around plants in late spring and can be controlled by spraying with pyrethrum. Carbaryl or winter wash may be effective against older scales, although these treatments should be used with care.

**Slugs and snails:** these can be serious pests, especially in damp gardens or where plant debris is left lying about. Since they usually feed at night or after rain, this is the time to inspect plants and collect any that are to be found: drop them in a jam jar filled with brine. Rings of dry ashes or fresh soot around plants help to deter them, but if all else fails the most effective remedies are metaldehyde slug pellets, or, if there is a risk of pets and birds eating these,

aluminium sulphate granules, liquid or tape – this affects only slugs and snails by destroying their ability to produce slime.

**Weevils:** these are like beetles with absurdly long snouts, and can be serious pests on fruits, nuts and leaves. Fortunately, they are rarely seen in quantity. Destroy any that are found, and control larger numbers with derris (rotenone), or, if this fails, with nicotine (take care, as this is extremely poisonous to humans, although harmless to most beneficial insects). Weevils can be effectively collected at night by carefully spreading a piece of newspaper under the affected plants and giving them a sharp tap.

**Whitefly:** small white delta-shaped flies that live and feed on the undersides of leaves, and fly up in clouds when disturbed. Different species infest greenhouse and outdoor plants. Their young are visible as tiny scales on the leaf surface; these are readily parasitized by encarsia wasps, which can be bought from mail order suppliers to control greenhouse infestations (in warmer climates they occur naturally and are reliable against outdoor populations). Outdoor whitefly in Britain is best treated by spraying the undersides of leaves with pyrethrum or insecticidal soap.

## MAJOR PLANT DISEASES

**Cankers:** these are lesions or clearly defined patches of decay on stems or trunks of woody plants. Frequently they are limited and do not spread, but other disease organisms are liable to enter and take hold. The affected wood is best cut out, back to clean tissue, and burnt; paint the wound with pruning compound. Cankers of vegetables such as parsnips are really a kind of rot and they are best prevented by growing resistant varieties.

**Club root:** a serious fungal disease of brassicas, which causes thickening and stunting of the roots, and general poor growth. It is typical of acid, poorly drained soils and can persist for many years. Regular liming usually prevents its occurrence. Either avoid growing brassicas on soil known to be infected, or add lime to affected areas to raise the pH to between 7.2 and 7.5, a method that has had some success in curing infection. Always raise brassica seedlings in the garden, rather than buy plants grown on unknown ground.

**Fire blight:** a bacterial infection of members of the rose family (for example, apples, pears and quinces). Infected flowers, leaves and twigs die back to leave an appearance of having been scorched by fire. It is more prevalent in warm, humid summers, and is often spread by heavy rainfall, which scatters the bacteria on to unaffected tissues. Prune back infected stems to clean wood, dipping tools frequently in strong disinfectant, and burn the prunings. Seriously affected plants may have to be dug up and burnt. In areas where the disease is endemic, choose resistant varieties of fruit. In parts of the UK the disease is notifiable, and suspected outbreaks must be reported to the Ministry of Agriculture before any treatment is attempted.

**Honey fungus/Bootlace fungus/Armillaria:** this fungus usually spreads by means of long dark threads like bootlaces, starting from dead tree stumps and going on to infect living trees and shrubs, sometimes killing young specimens and often weakening older trees so that other diseases take hold. The fruiting bodies are honey-coloured toadstools, which appear in autumn low down on infected trunks and stems. Home treatment is difficult, and professional advice should be sought. Some species and varieties seem to be more resistant than others.

**Mildews:** these are parasitic fungi that usually appear in humid weather or late in the season when nights are damp. Dusty or slimy white deposits appear on stems and leaves of many

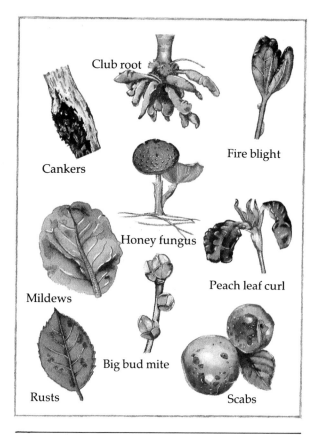

Club root

Cankers

Fire blight

Honey fungus

Peach leaf curl

Mildews

Big bud mite

Rusts

Scabs

plants, gradually weakening them if left untreated. Pick off badly affected leaves and spray plants with synthetic urea, or urine diluted with four times the quantity of water; alternatively, spray with benomyl. Do not overcrowd closely planted crops to the point where air circulation is impaired, as this encourages mildew.

**Peach leaf curl:** a fungal disease that causes the leaves of peaches, nectarines and almonds to twist and curl soon after they appear. Red blisters develop and eventually the leaves fall prematurely. A new crop of leaves follows, which also becomes infected. A fungicide such as Bordeaux mixture is usually recommended, but trees growing under glass are rarely

affected, and where practicable protecting outdoor trees from air-borne spores seems to be a more reliable method of control. Fan-trained trees can be covered with a curtain of polythene from early autumn until the flowers are set.

**Reversion:** this disease affects blackcurrants, causing them to lose their cultivated characteristics and revert to leafy unprofitable bushes. The leaves become narrow, almost like those of nettles, hence its alternative name of 'nettlehead'. There is no cure and affected bushes must be grubbed and burnt. The disease is spread by the big bud mite which penetrates dormant buds and causes them to swell during winter and early spring. Pick off any unnaturally large buds during winter and burn them.

**Rusts:** a large group of fungi that produce yellow spots on the tops of leaves and bright orange or brown spore-bearing pustules underneath. Most are merely disfiguring but some can seriously weaken plants. Pick off affected leaves and burn, and spray the plant with a copper fungicide. Clear away fallen leaves to prevent a carry-over of the disease.

**Scabs:** fungal and bacterial diseases that can disfigure fruit and vegetable tubers, especially in hot, dry seasons and on light soils. Dark blotches, blisters and cracks appear on leaves, twigs and apple, pear and root crops. Soil infections can be prevented by growing resistant varieties, adding humus to light soil and avoiding over-liming, and by watering crops regularly. Control of fruit scabs depends on prevention, unless resistant apple varieties are planted. Clear fallen leaves and burn if affected; spray the trees at fortnightly intervals from bud burst until the petals drop, although if scab is present generally, spraying should continue until the autumn, using synthetic urea, urine mixed with four times its volume of water, benomyl or captan. Prune all affected twigs at the end of the season.

# GLOSSARY

**Annual:** a plant which completes its life cycle in a single season. Many vegetables, strictly *biennial* or *perennial*, are normally harvested the same year they are sown, and these are known as annual crops.

**Biennial:** a plant that grows from seed during one season, but does not flower and set seed until the following year, after which it dies.

**Blanch:** to *earth up* or otherwise exclude light from a crop's stems and leaves, to make them pale, tender and more palatable.

**Bolt:** vegetables are said to bolt when they abruptly flower and go to seed, often as the result of extreme heat, drought or some cultural check to growth.

**Brassica:** a botanical group of plants with similar flowers that includes cabbages, cauliflowers, kale, Brussels sprouts, turnips, swedes and radishes.

**Cordon:** a form of trained fruit tree, confined by pruning to one or more straight stems, upright or oblique, each furnished with fruiting *spurs* but no other *side shoots*.

**Crown:** used by gardeners to describe the large, fleshy rootstock of plants such as rhubarb, asparagus or seakale.

**Cultivar:** (abbr. of 'cultivated variety'). The correct name for a distinct plant form that has arisen accidentally or by design in cultivation. In everyday usage, loosely synonymous with *variety*.

**Earth up:** to raise a mound of soil around plants to *blanch* or *force* them. Also known as 'mound up', 'mould up' or 'hill up'.

**Espalier:** a form of tree that has been trained on an 'espalier' framework so that it has a vertical trunk with parallel and evenly spaced branches extending horizontally.

**Force:** to encourage a plant into unnaturally early growth, by bringing it into a warm environment or by covering it outdoors where it is growing.

**Grow hard:** to withold fertilizer and other inducements to rapid lush growth, so that a plant becomes relatively tough and able to withstand cold weather.

**Half-ripe cuttings:** cuttings taken from shoots that have grown during the same season and are beginning to harden at their base. Also known as 'semi-ripe' or 'semi-hardwood' cuttings.

**Harden off:** to gradually acclimatize plants initially grown under glass to outdoor conditions by progressively exposing them to fresh air, often in a cold frame.

**Humus:** partly decayed vegetable matter, an essential ingredient of all good cultivated soil.

**Hybrid:** a plant resulting from cross-fertilization between two distinct species or cultivars. F1 hybrids are the immediate and uniform progeny of a deliberate cross, and are usually designed to combine the best qualities of both parents. Seeds saved from F1 hybrids do not normally produce good plants.

**Maincrop:** varieties that grow or fruit during the normal season, usually giving the heaviest yields compared with 'early' varieties with lighter, but faster-maturing crops.

**Perennial:** a plant with a life span of at least three years and usually many more.

**pH:** (abbr. for the level of hydrogen ion concentration in a substance). Gardeners measure the acidity or alkalinity of soils by a simple chemical test, the results of which are given as a number on the pH scale. Low pH numbers indicate acid (sour) soil; pH 7.0 is neutral, and higher figures record increasingly alkaline (chalky or limy) conditions. Most plants prefer a soil pH between 6.5 and 7.0. Acid soils are made more alkaline by the addition of lime, while the pH of chalky soils can be reduced by incorporating peat, leaf mould or sulphur – loamy soils need twice as heavy a dressing as light soils, and clay soils three times as much.

**Pot on:** to transfer a well-rooted pot plant to a larger sized pot.

**Prick out:** to remove seedlings individually or in small groups from the seed tray or drill in which they have germinated, replanting them in trays or the open ground with more room to develop.

**Root ball:** the intact mass of roots and soil on a plant lifted from the ground or knocked out of its pot.

**Rootstock:** normally, the lower rooted portion of a grafted or budded plant, but also used to describe a *crown* or *stool*.

**Side shoot:** also known as a 'lateral'. A shoot produced from the side of a plant's main stem or branches.

**Single:** to reduce a cluster of several fruits or seedlings to leave just one survivor.

**Spur:** a short, fruiting *side shoot* formed naturally or by pruning.

**Standard:** a tree or shrub with a clear single stem, up to about 180cm (6 ft) tall on fruit trees, but only about 90cm (3 ft) for soft fruit and 'half-standard' top fruit.

**Stool:** the permanent base of a woody plant to which the top growth is cut back at the end of each year, often for propagation – eg apple rootstocks, p.69.

**Stop:** to pinch out or cut off the end of a stem to prevent further extension, sometimes to encourage side shoots or the development of fruit.

**Subsoil:** ground below the layer of cultivated topsoil, often less fertile and workable unless improved by deep digging and trenching.

**Tamp:** to settle loose soil into place, using a wooden block to firm the freshly filled contents of a seed tray, for example, or a rake-head to compress the soil after sowing outdoors.

**Thong:** an alternative name for a root cutting, traditionally applied to such plants as seakale and horseradish.

**Tilth:** cultivated *topsoil* that has been finely broken up in preparation for sowing.

**Topsoil:** the surface layer of soil, generally the most fertile and extending to the depth of normal cultivation.

**Transplant:** to transfer a plant from one growing position to another. Plants during or after removal are sometimes called 'transplants'.

**Truss:** a bunch, cluster or string of fruit or flowers carried on a single main stem.

**Variety:** strictly, a separate and named natural variation of a plant, but the term is widely used by gardeners as a synonym for *cultivar*.

# BIBLIOGRAPHY

There is a lack of comprehensive guides to growing fruit, vegetables and herbs as part of the integrated garden, but tantalizing hints of past practice can be found in two classic books:

J. Harvey, *Medieval Gardens*; Batsford, London, 1981. (Out of print.)
A well-illustrated, scholarly account, including the monastic style.

E. Hyams and E. Smith, *English Cottage Gardens*; Penguin, London, 1986.

### Books on specific subjects

Diane E. Bilderbeck and Dorothy Hinshaw Patent, *Backyard Fruits and Berries*; Rodale Press, Pennsylvania, 1984.

J. K. A. Bleasdale, P. J. Salter and others, *Know and Grow Vegetables*;
O.U.P., Oxford, vol. 1 1979, vol. 2 1982.
Very readable account of the scientific background, prepared by staff at one of the leading research stations. Essential for understanding successful vegetable culture.

*The Complete Guide to Growing America's Favorite Fruits and Vegetables*; The National Gardening Association, 1986.

Raymond Dick, *Joy of Gardening*; Garden Way, Inc., 1983.
About vegetables.

L. D. Hills, *A Month-by-Month Guide to Organic Gardening*; Thorsons, Wellingborough, 1983.
Clearly arranged manual packed with tips and wrinkles for growing fruit and vegetables, valuable to gardeners of all persuasions.

The H. P. Book Series covers fruit, vegetable, herb and flower subjects;
H. P. Books, Tucson, Arizona.

C. Loewenfeld, *Herb Gardening*; Faber, London, 1970.
Does not cover all the herbs mentioned in this book, but contains very detailed and practical entries on most common species.

*Organic Gardener's Complete Guide to Vegetables and Herbs*; Rodale Press, Pennsylvania, 1987.

*Rodale's Illustrated Encyclopedia of Herbs*; Rodale Press, Pennsylvania, 1987.

S. Stickland, *Planning the Organic Herb Garden*; Thorsons, Wellingborough, 1986.
Intelligent and comprehensive approach to planning and growing herbs organically in a number of environments.

Vilmorin-Andrieux, *The Vegetable Garden* (1885); reprinted by John Murray, London, 1977 and Ten Speed Press, California, 1983.
The varieties and some of the methods have changed; otherwise this has never been excelled as a practical encyclopedia of vegetables.

S. B. Whitehead, *Fruit from Trained Trees*, J. M. Dent, London, 1954
California, 1954.
Clear and sound; needs revision in some places, but still cherished by professional gardeners in the absence of anything more up-to-date.

# SUPPLIERS INDEX

## UK SUPPLIERS

### Seeds

*J. W. Boyce*, Bush Pasture, Lower Carter St, Fordham, Ely, Cambs.
Comprehensive list of traditional vegetable varieties, together with flowers and herbs, supplied as packets or in a range of larger quantities.

*Henry Doubleday Research Association*, Ryton Gardens, Ryton-on-Dunsmore, Coventry CV8 3LG.
Vegetable and herb seeds, many of them classic varieties from home and abroad, all selected for good flavour and reliability.

The *HDRA* issues a comprehensive catalogue that in addition to plants and seeds also lists fertilizers, minerals and many of the safer substances for controlling pests and diseases.

*S. E. Marshall & Co. Ltd*, Wisbech, Cambs PE13 2RF.
Renowned specialist vegetable seedsman, with a wide selection of varieties, many originally their own introduction.

*Suffolk Herbs*, Sawyers Farm, Little Cornard, Sudbury, Suffolk CO10 0NY.
A rich collection of herb, vegetable and wild flower seeds.

*Thompson and Morgan Ltd*, London Road, Ipswich, Suffolk.
Very large list of vegetable and herb seeds, especially unusual kinds and interesting novelties.

### Fruit plants

*Chris Bowers & Sons*, Whispering Trees Nursery, Wimbotsham, Norfolk PE34 8QB.
All kinds of hardy fruit, with a particularly large soft fruit collection including Medana varieties and many new introductions.

*Deacons Nursery*, Moor View House, Godshill, Isle of Wight PO38 3HW.
Owned by a compulsive propagator offering enormous range of hardy fruit, especially family trees and espaliers, each budded with several different varieties.

*Highfield Nurseries*, Whitminster, Gloucester GL2 7PL.
General nursery with a good basic range of hardy fruit, including single dwarf espaliers ('step-over trees').

*Read's Nursery*, Hales Hall, Loddon, Norfolk.
Specialist nursery with an extensive and growing list of fig, grape and citrus varieties.

*Scotts Nurseries Ltd*, Marriott, Somerset TA16 5PL.
Long-established nursery, renowned for top fruit, especially the enormous collection of apples, pears and plums. They will propagate unlisted varieties to order.

### Herb plants

Most culinary herbs and many other decorative kinds are widely available from garden centres.

*Culpeper Ltd*, Hadstock Road, Linton, Cambridge CB1 6NJ.
A large collection of traditional and unusual herb plants, all grown organically and available by post.

### Vegetable plants

*D. Maclean*, Dornoch Farm, Crieff, Perthshire.
Potato specialist with large collection of all kinds, many historical. Send SAE for list.

*A. R. Paske*, Regal Lodge, Newmarket, Suffolk.
Asparagus, globe artichokes and seakale plants or cuttings.

## US AND CANADIAN SUPPLIERS

### Seeds

*W. Atlee Burpee Co.*, 300 Park Ave., Warminster, PA 18991.
Vegetable and flower seeds, bulbs, perennials, trees, shrubs. Full line of garden products.

*Harris Seeds*, Moreton Farm, 3670 Buffalo Rd, Rochester, NY 14624.
Vegetable seeds.

*Park Seed Co. Inc.*, Highway 254 North, Greenwood, SC29647-0001.
Vegetable, flower and herb seeds.

*Stokes Seeds Inc.*, Box 548, Buffalo, N.Y. 14240 and Stokes Seeds Ltd, 39 James St, Box 10, St Catherines, Ontario L2R 6R6.
Vegetable and flower seeds, gardening supplies.

*Thompson & Morgan Inc.*, Farraday and Gramme Avenues, P.O. Box 1308, Jackson, NJ 08527.
Vegetable and flower seeds.

### Berry and small-fruit specialities

*Brittingham Plant Farms*, P.O. Box 2538, Salisbury, MD 21801.
Strawberry, blueberry, raspberry and thornless blackberry plants.

*Edible Landscaping*, Route 2 Box 343A, Afton, VA 22920.
Hardy kiwis, blueberries, currants, gooseberries, mulberries, wineberries, figs, persimmons, grapes.

### Fruit and nut tree nurseries

*Bear Creek Nursery*, P.O. Box 411, Northport, WA 99157.
Huge variety of antique apple trees; rare nut tree varieties.

*Henry Leuthardt Nurseries*, Montauk Highway, P.O. Box 666-0, East Moriches, NY 11940.
Dwarf and semi-dwarf fruit trees, espaliered fruit trees, hybrid grapes, berry plants.

### Unusual and rare fruit varieties

*Stark Bro's Nurseries & Orchards*, Box 2281F, Louisiana, MO 63353-0010.
Specializes in dwarf, semi-dwarf and standard fruit trees.

### Herb seeds and plants

*Richters*, Goodwood, Ontario LOC 1AO.

*Taylor's Herb Gardens Inc.*, 1535 Lone Oak Rd, Vista, CA 92083.

### Vegetable specialities

*Becker's Seed Potatoes*, RR1, Trout Creek, Ontario POH 2LO.
Unusual potato varieties.

*The Cook's Garden*, Box 65, Londonderry, VT 05148.
Wide selection of salads, gourmet greens and Italian vegetables.

*Johnny's Selected Seeds*, Box 310, Albion, ME 04910.
Hardy early varieties of vegetable seeds for the north.

*Shepherd's Garden Seeds*, 7389 W. Zayante Rd, Felton, CA 95018.
Individual varieties and special collections of French, Italian, Oriental and Mexican vegetables, also herb and salad garden collections, baby vegetables and edible flowers.

# ACKNOWLEDGEMENTS

My special thanks to Ted Humphris for his recollections of Aynho; and to Mrs P. Mitchell for letting me neglect the weeds while writing the book.
**A.M. Clevely**

The author and publishers are very grateful to the following people for allowing their gardens to be photographed:

Mr and Mrs A. J. Buchanan, Hillbarn House, Great Bedwyn, Marlborough, Wilts.

Sue Stickland and the Henry Doubleday Research Association, Ryton Gardens, Ryton-on-Dunsmore, Coventry CV8 3LG.

Mrs Mary Hart Dyke, North Gatehouse, Lullingstone Castle, Eynsford, Kent.

King's Farm, Ford End, Essex.

The Reverend and Mrs L. Marsh, The Rectory, Fen Ditton, Cambs.

Mrs Samuel, Orchard Cottage, Cookham, Maidenhead, Berks.

Mrs Rosemary Verey, Barnsley House, Barnsley, Nr Cirencester, Glos.

**Photo credits**
All photographs are by Jerry Harpur except for those listed below:

Heather Angel/Biofotos: 28
Michael Boys Syndication: 119
Pat Brindley: 50
Eric Crichton: 8, 38 (top), 79 (right), 81, 96, 101, 102 (right), 119, 121, 157, 161 (bottom)
Sharon Hutton: 11, 24, 51, 54, 55, 58, 83, 156
Lorraine Johnson: 63, 79 (left), 97
Louisa McDonnell: 9, 117, 147 (right), 178
Photos Horticultural: 22, 26 (bottom), 39, 41, 52 (left), 80, 110 (left), 112, 114, 126, 127, 159, 161 (top)
Scottish Crop Research Institute: 26 (top)
The Harry Smith Horticultural Photographic Collection: 110 (left), 112, 128, 139, 159

# INDEX

grafting fruit, 69
grapes, 35-7
  cultivation, 35-7
  harvesting and storage, 36
  ornamental value, 35
  propagation, 69
  training unusual forms, 37
  under glass, 73
  varieties, 35
greater celandine, 100
greenfly, 180
greenhouses, 176
  cucumbers, 138
  French beans in, 117
  fruit in, 72-3
  grapes, 73

*H*amburg parsley, 169
  varieties, 169
hardiness zones, 14
haricot beans, 118
hazelnuts, 41-3
  cultivation, 42-3
  harvesting and storage, 43
  ornamental value, 42
  propagation, 69
  varieties, 41-2
heartsease, 100
heather, 100
hedges, 9, 11
  herbs, 76-7
*Helianthus tuberosus*, 111-12
herbicides, 178
herbs, 11, 75-105
  aspect, 103
  bees and, 79
  carpeting, 77-8
  drying, 105
  as edgings, 8, 77
  gathering and preserving, 104-5
  as hedges, 76-7
  maintenance, 103
  in pots, 9, 79, 104
  seats, 78-9
  shelter, 103

*herbs, cont.*
  soil, 103
  storage, 105
  winter care, 104
hoes, 170
hollyhocks, 100
honey fungus, 182
hops, 86-7
horseradish, 87
houseleek, 102
*Humulus lupulus*, 86-7
humus, 174
hydrangeas, 100
hyssop, 87-8
*Hyssopus officinalis*, 87-8

*I*beris, 101
*Inula helenium*, 76

*J*apanese bunching onions, 150
Jerusalem artichokes, 111-12
  cultivation, 112
  harvesting, 112
  varieties, 111-12
jostaberries, 25

*K*ale, 138-40
  cultivation, 139-40
  harvesting, 140
  varieties, 139
Kidlington, 22
kohl rabi, 140-1
  cultivation, 140-1
  harvesting, 141
  varieties, 140
kumquat, 29

*L*actuca sativa, 143-5
lady's mantle, 100-1
lamb's lettuce, 145
land cress, 145

larvae, 180-1
*Laurus nobilis*, 81
lavender, 101
lawns, chamomile, 77, 83-4
layers, fruit, 67-8
leaf lettuce, 145
leaves, composting, 179
leeks, 141-2
  cultivation, 141-2
  harvesting, 142
  varieties, 141
legumes, rotation, 14
lemon balm, 88
lemon verbena, 97-8
lemons, 29
lettuce, 143-5
  cultivation, 144
  harvesting, 144
  succession sowing, 143
  varieties, 143-5
*Levisticum officinale*, 88-9
lily of the valley, 101
*Lippia citriodora*, 97-8
loganberries, 23
loppers, 64
*Lotus tetragonolobus*, 155
lovage, 88-9
*Lycopersicon esculentum*, 166-8

*M*âche, 145
maize, 165-6
  cultivation, 165-6
  harvesting, 166
  varieties, 165
mangetout, 153
marjoram, 89-90
marrows, 147-8
  cultivation, 148
  harvesting, 148
  varieties, 147-8
*Matricaria recutita*, 83
medlars, 37-8
  cultivation, 38
  harvesting and storage, 38
  ornamental value, 37

*medlars, cont.*
  propagation, 70
  varieties, 37
*Melissa officinalis*, 88
melons, 39-40
  cultivation, 39-40
  harvesting and storage, 40
  ornamental value, 39
  propagation, 70
  training, 40
  varieties, 39
*Mentha*, 90-1
  *M. requienii*, 77
mercury, 113
mignonette, 101
mildews, 182
mini-cauliflowers, 132
mint, 90
*Monarda didyma*, 81
mountain spinach, 163
mugwort, 76
mulberries, 40-1
  cultivation, 41
  harvesting and storage, 41
  ornamental value, 40
  propagation, 70
  varieties, 40
mulching, 11, 175
  fruit, 62
mullein, 100
myrobalan plums, 10, 50
*Myrrhis odorata*, 95

*N*ectarines, 44, 70
New Zealand spinach, 164
nuts, 41-3, 69

*O*cimum, 80-1
onions, 148-51
  cultivation, 150-1
  harvesting, 151
  varieties, 149-50
orach, 163
oranges, 29